純米
Maker's Mark
I.W. HARPER
12

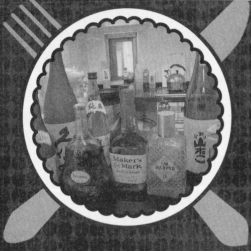

My favorite drinks made an appearance in the manga! It was easier to look at the real things than to scrounge for reference photos. (My current weight...71 kg!! Hrmm... I can't let up! I have to get active!)

–Mitsutoshi Shimabukuro, 2012

Mitsutoshi Shimabukuro made his debut in **Weekly Shonen Jump** in 1996. He is best known for **Seikimatsu Leader Den Takeshi!** for which he won the 46th Shogakukan Manga Award for children's manga in 2001. His current series, **Toriko**, began serialization in Japan in 2008.

TORIKO VOL. 18
SHONEN JUMP Manga Edition

STORY AND ART BY **MITSUTOSHI SHIMABUKURO**

Translation/Christine Dashiell
Touch-Up Art & Lettering/Maui Girl
Design/Matt Hinrichs
Editor/Hope Donovan

Printed in Canada

Published by VIZ Media, LLC
P.O. Box 77010
San Francisco, CA 94107

10 9 8 7 6 5 4 3 2 1
First printing, October 2013

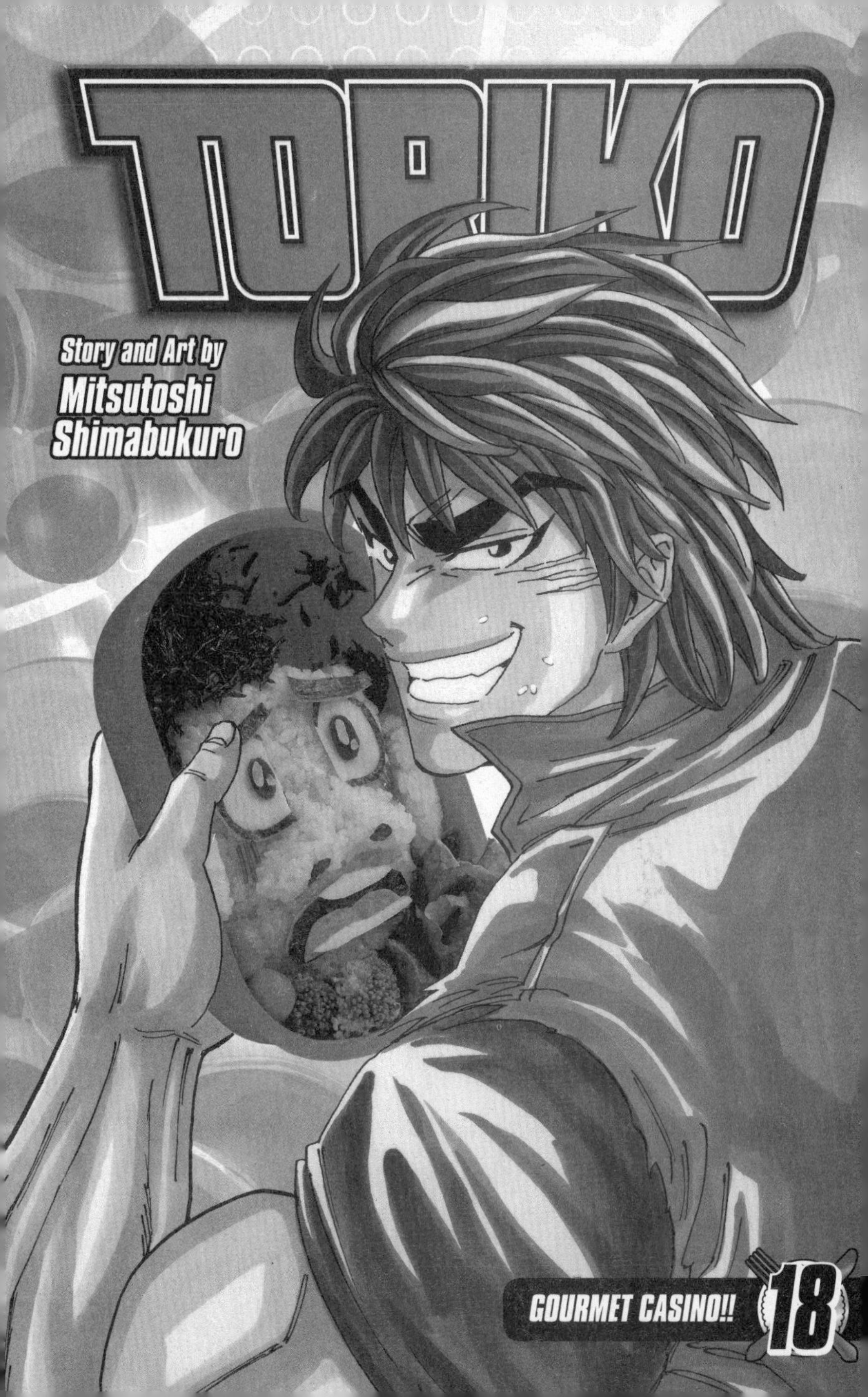
TORIKO
Story and Art by
Mitsutoshi
Shimabukuro
GOURMET CASINO!!
18

TORIKO

THE ULTIMATE GOURMET HUNTER WHO'S ON A NEVER-ENDING QUEST TO FIND AND SCARF UP THE RAREST FOODS ON EARTH! HE FIGHTS WITH A KNIFE (HIS FIST), A FORK (HIS FIST), AND SPIKED PUNCH (ALSO HIS FISTS).

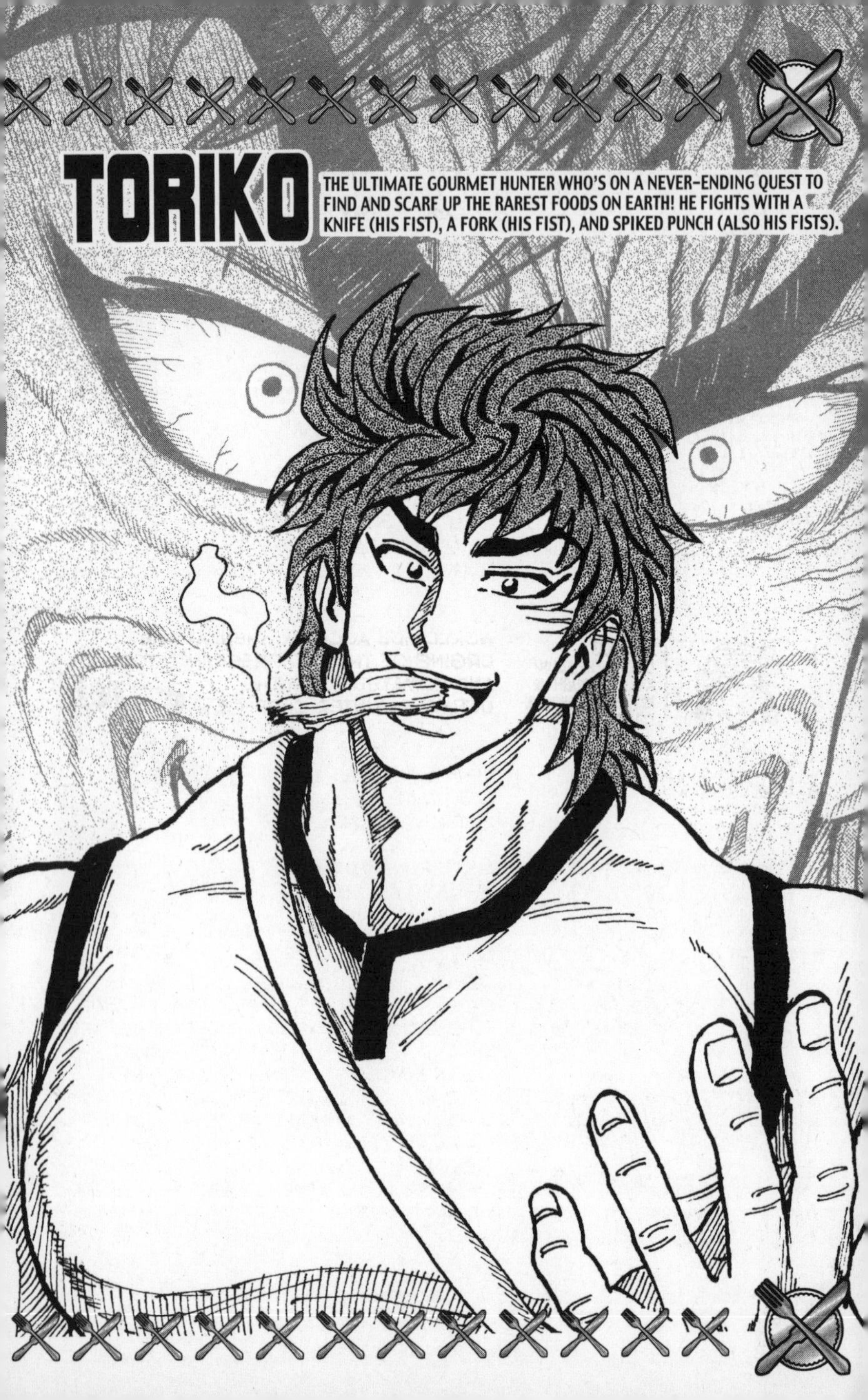

WHAT'S FOR DINNER

IT'S THE AGE OF GOURMET! KOMATSU, THE HEAD CHEF AT THE HOTEL OWNED BY THE IGO (INTERNATIONAL GOURMET ORGANIZATION), BECAME FAST FRIENDS WITH THE LEGENDARY GOURMET HUNTER TORIKO WHILE GATOR HUNTING. NOW KOMATSU ACCOMPANIES TORIKO ON HIS LIFELONG QUEST TO CREATE THE PERFECT FULL-COURSE MEAL.

ALTHOUGH THEY OFTEN FIND THEMSELVES PITTED AGAINST GOURMET CORP.'S NEFARIOUS AGENTS, THERE'S NOTHING THAT CAN STOP THEIR ADVENTURES! TORIKO AND KOMATSU COME AWAY FROM THEIR QUEST FOR CENTURY SOUP EMPTY-HANDED, BUT KOMATSU RE-CREATES THE SOUP TO WORLDWIDE ACCLAIM. THEN, AT THE URGING OF THE IGO PRESIDENT, TORIKO AND KOMATSU FORM THE ULTIMATE HUNTER-CHEF PARTNERSHIP!

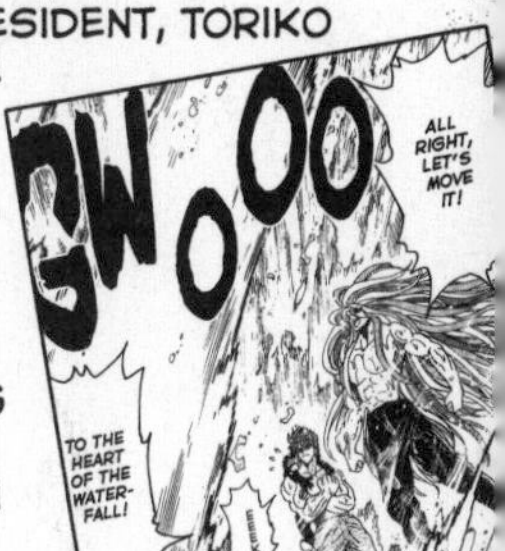
GWOOO
ALL RIGHT, LET'S MOVE IT!
TO THE HEART OF THE WATER-FALL!

TO PREPARE THEM FOR ENTRY INTO THE GOURMET WORLD, THEY SET ABOUT GATHERING FOODS FROM A TRAINING LIST PROVIDED BY THE PRESIDENT. THE FOURTH ITEM IS THE SHINING GOURAMI, A FISH THAT LIVES IN THE EXECUTION FALLS, DEATH FALLS! TORIKO ENLISTS THE HELP OF SUNNY, WHO HAS LEVELED UP THANKS TO COACHING FROM GOURMET GANG LEADER GUEMON. SUNNY'S PET SNAKE QUINN BRINGS THE TRIO TO A WATERFALL BEYOND IMAGINATION. HOWEVER, BY COMBINING SUNNY'S SUPER SPATULA AND TORIKO'S TWIN SPIKED PUNCH, THEY FINALLY TURN THE TABLES ON THE WATERFALL AND REVEAL THE CAVERNS BEHIND.

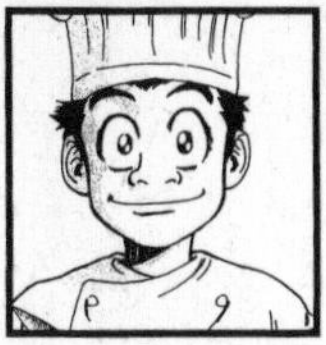

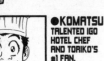

●KOMATSU
TALENTED IGO HOTEL CHEF AND TORIKO'S #1 FAN.

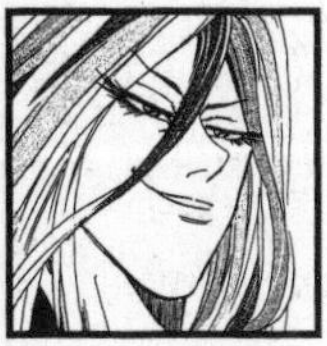

●SUNNY
A GOURMET HUNTER AND ONE OF THE FOUR KINGS. SENSORS IN HIS LONG HAIR ENABLE HIM TO "TASTE" THE WORLD. OBSESSED WITH ALL THAT IS BEAUTIFUL.

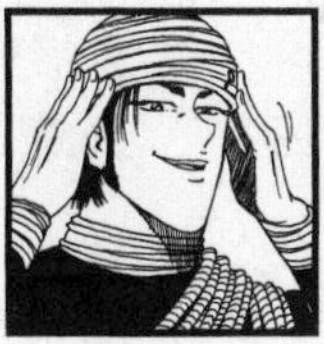

●COCO
ONE OF THE FOUR KINGS, THOUGH HE IS ALSO A FORTUNE-TELLER. SPECIAL ABILITY: POISON FLOWS IN HIS VEINS.

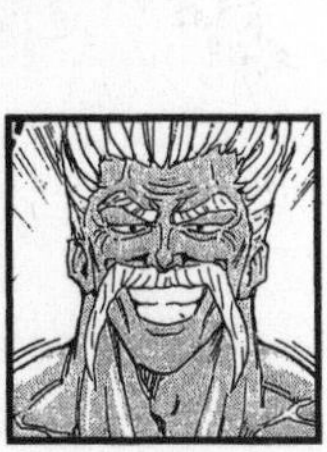

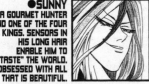

●ICHIRYU
HARDY IGO PRESIDENT AND DISCIPLE OF THE LATE GOURMET GOD ACACIA.

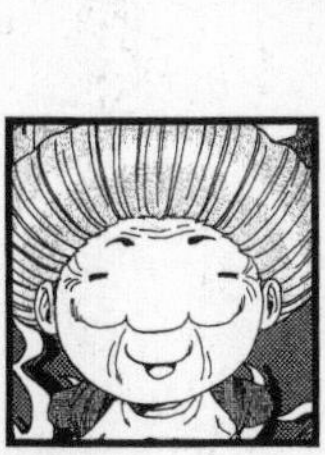

●SETSUNO
AKA GRANNY SETSU. FAMOUS CHEF AND GOURMET LIVING LEGEND.

Contents

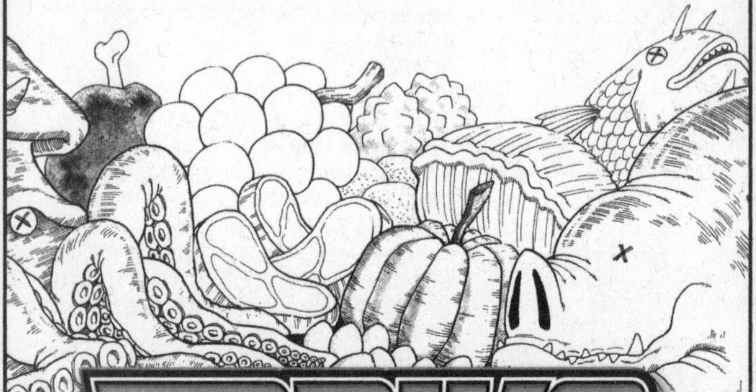

TORIKO

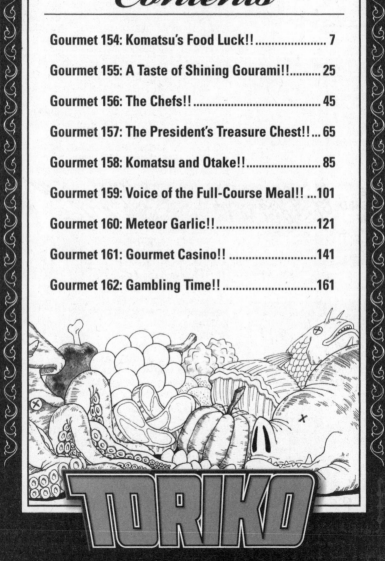

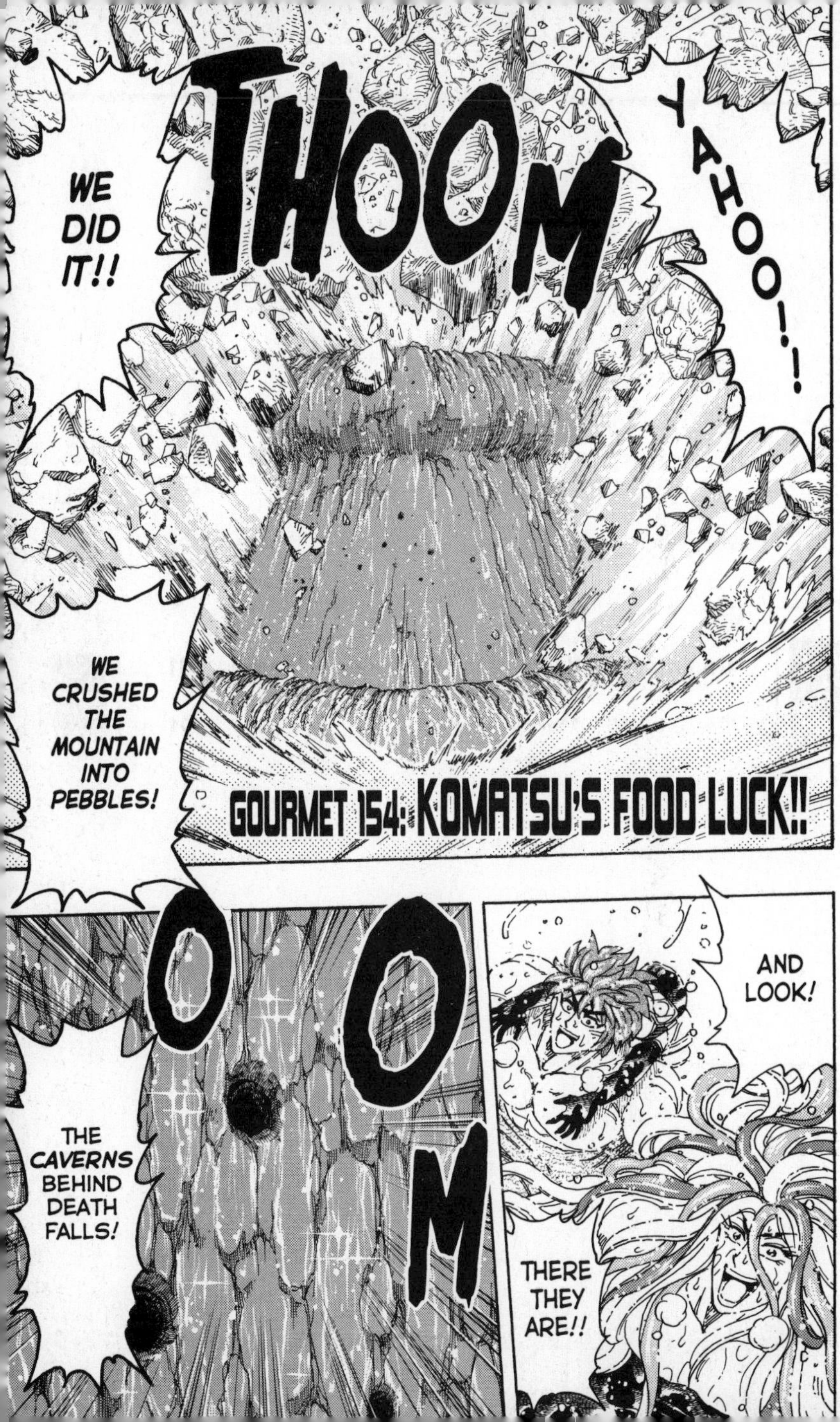
YAHOO!!!
THOOM
WE DID IT!!
WE CRUSHED THE MOUNTAIN INTO PEBBLES!
GOURMET 154: KOMATSU'S FOOD LUCK!!
AND LOOK!
THERE THEY ARE!!
OOOM
THE CAVERNS BEHIND DEATH FALLS!

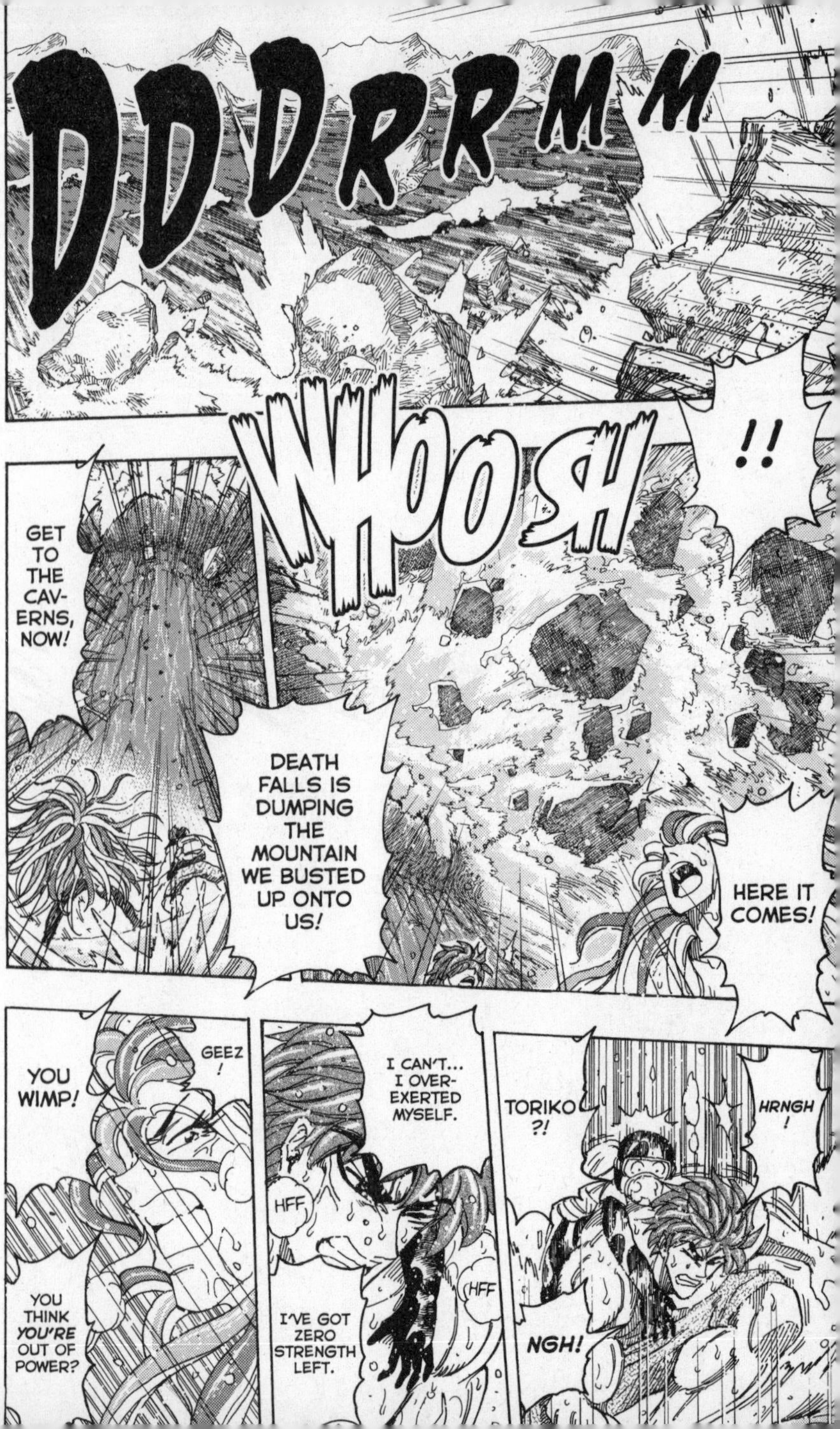
DDDRRMM
WHOOSH!!
HERE IT COMES!
DEATH FALLS IS DUMPING THE MOUNTAIN WE BUSTED UP ONTO US!
GET TO THE CAVERNS, NOW!
HRNGH!
TORIKO?!
NGH!
I CAN'T... I OVER-EXERTED MYSELF.
HFF
HFF
I'VE GOT ZERO STRENGTH LEFT.
GEEZ!
YOU WIMP!
YOU THINK *YOU'RE* OUT OF POWER?

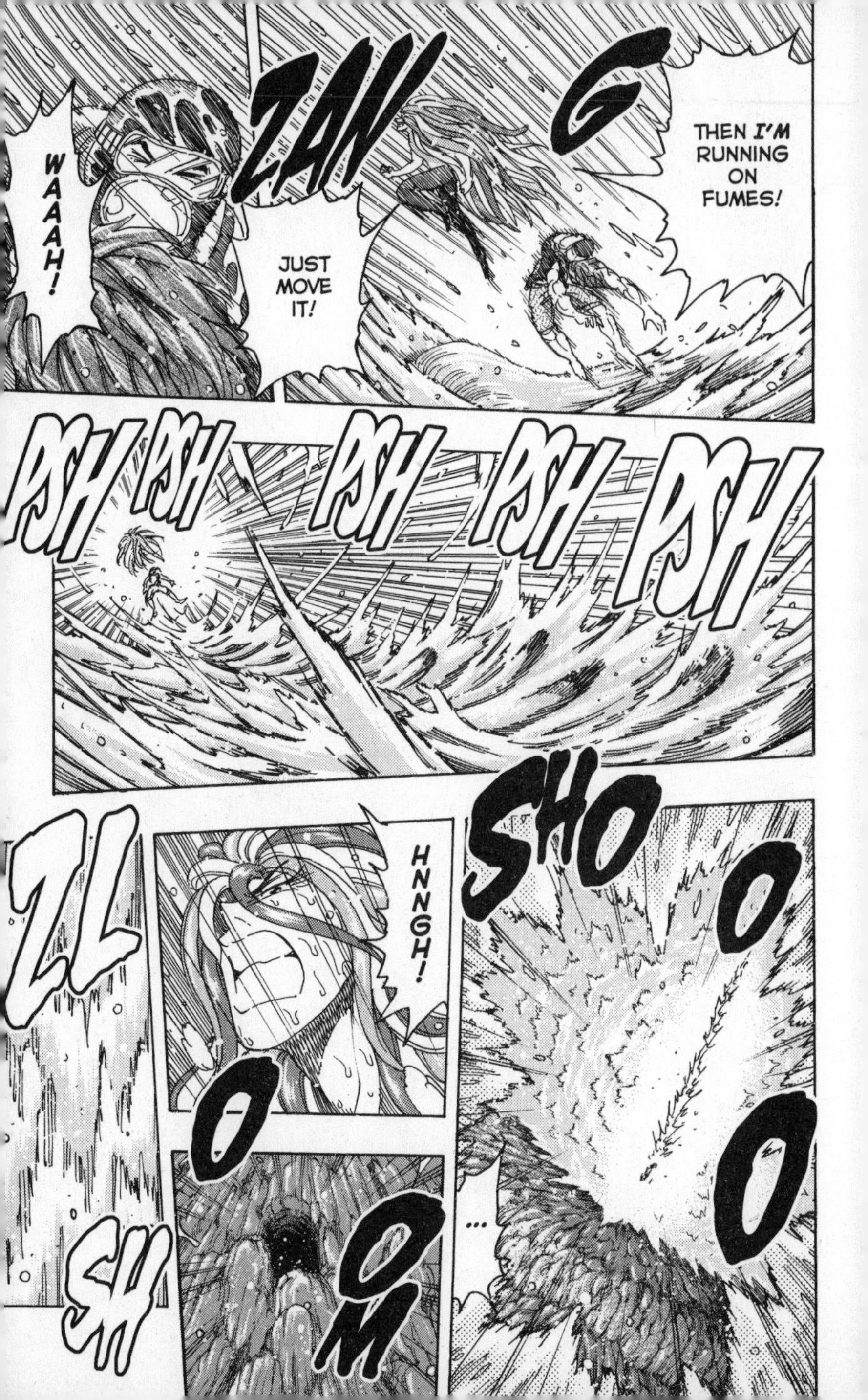
THEN I'M RUNNING ON FUMES!
ZANG
JUST MOVE IT!
WAAAAH!
PSH PSH PSH PSH PSH
SHOOOO
...
HNNGH!
OOM
ZLSH

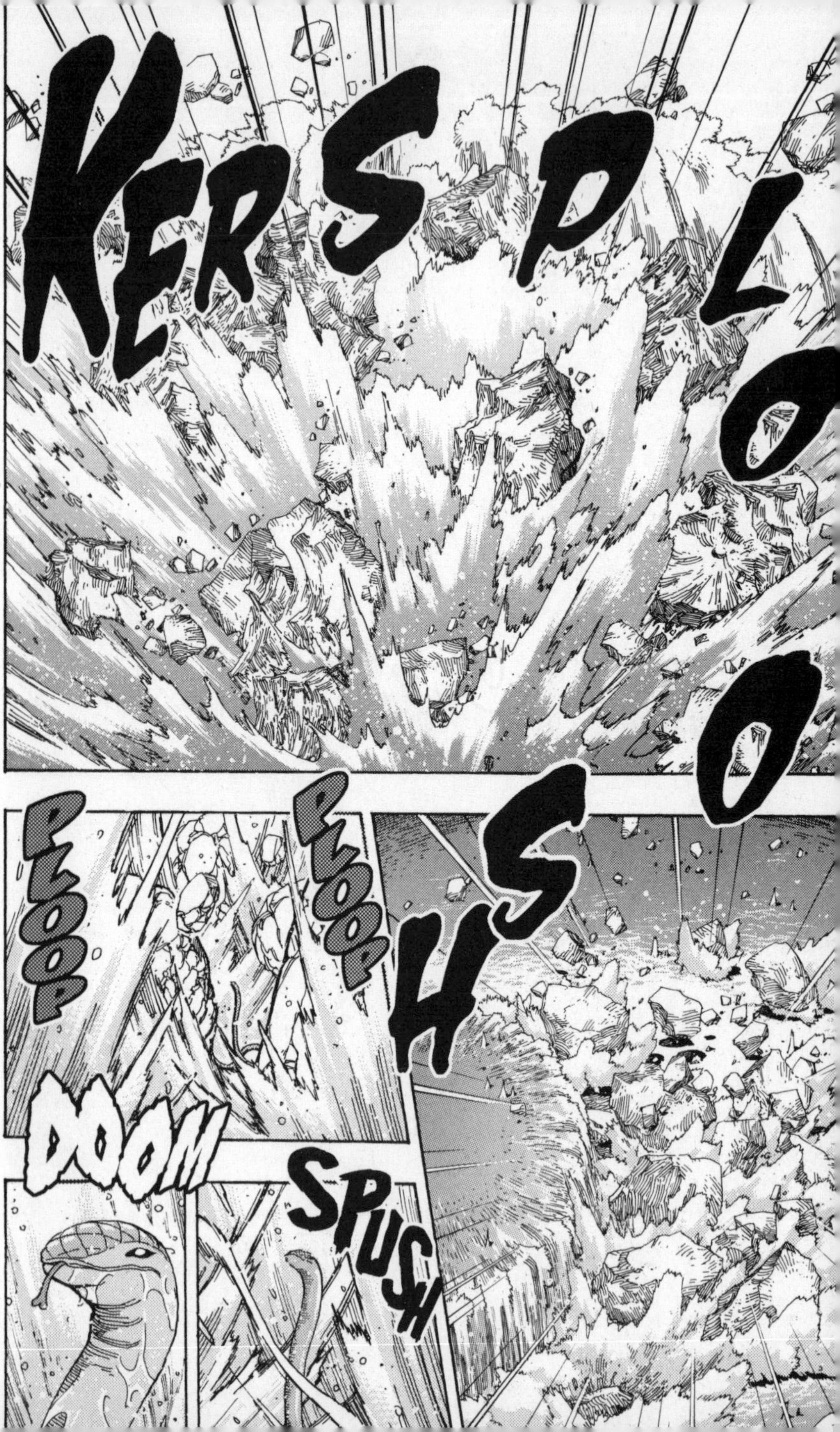
KERSPLOOOSH
PLOOOP
PLOOOP
DOOM
SPUSH

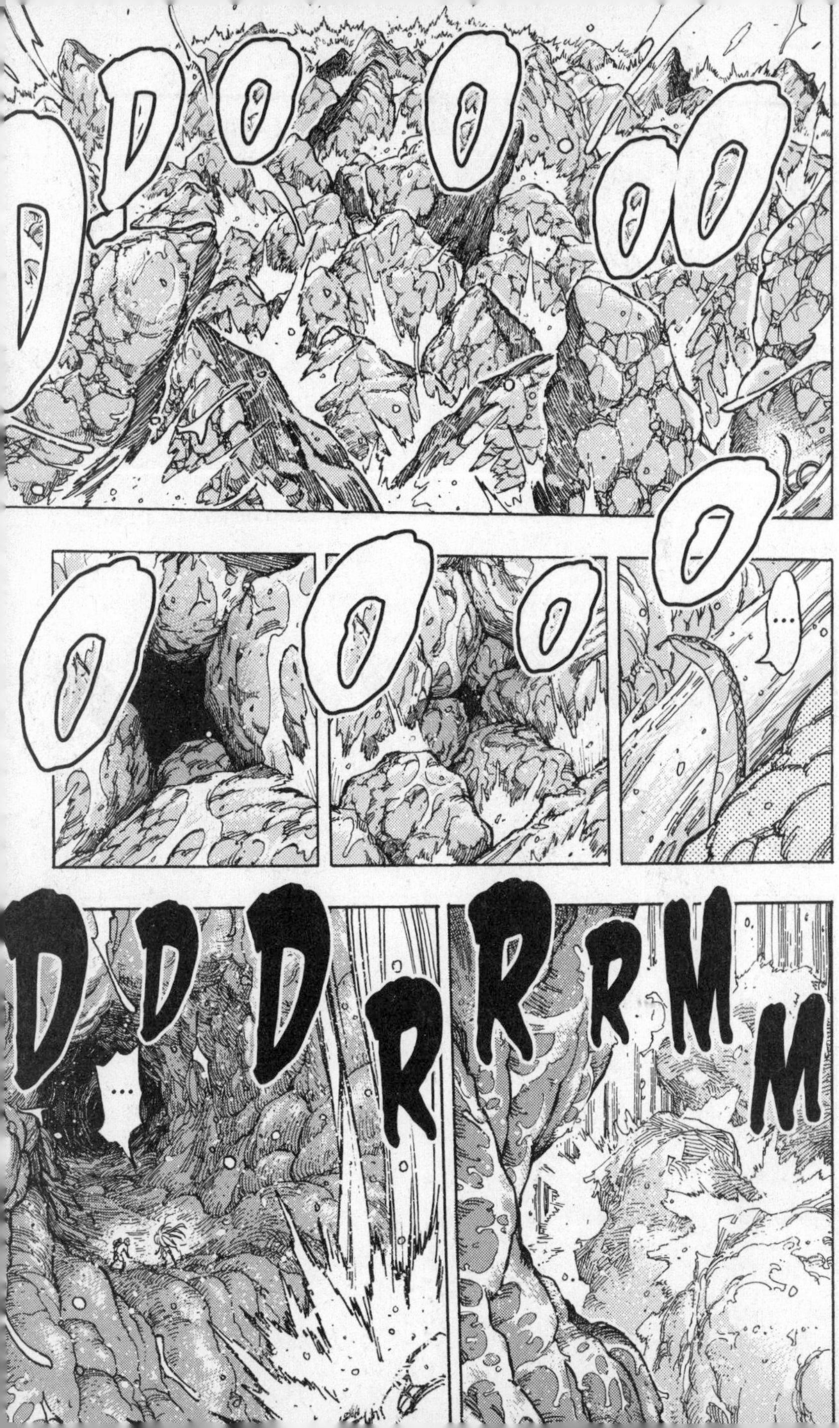

DDOOOOOO
OOOO
...
DDDRRRRMM
...

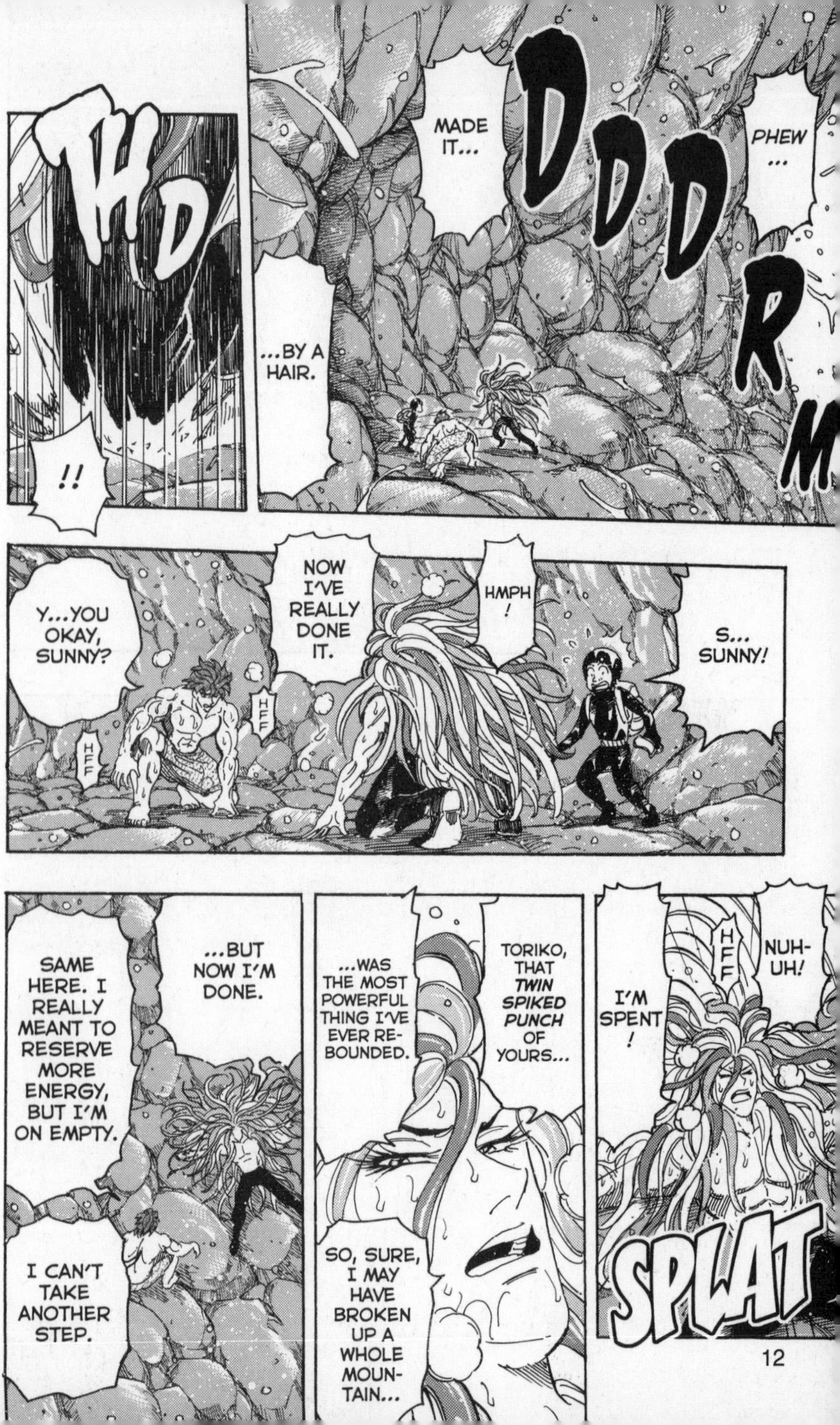
PHEW ...
DDDDRM
MADE IT...
...BY A HAIR.
THD
!!
S... SUNNY!
HMPH!
NOW I'VE REALLY DONE IT.
HFF
HFF
Y...YOU OKAY, SUNNY?
NUH-UH!
HFF
I'M SPENT!
SPLAT
TORIKO, THAT *TWIN SPIKED PUNCH* OF YOURS...
...WAS THE MOST POWERFUL THING I'VE EVER REBOUNDED.
SO, SURE, I MAY HAVE BROKEN UP A WHOLE MOUNTAIN...
...BUT NOW I'M DONE.
SAME HERE. I REALLY MEANT TO RESERVE MORE ENERGY, BUT I'M ON EMPTY.
I CAN'T TAKE ANOTHER STEP.

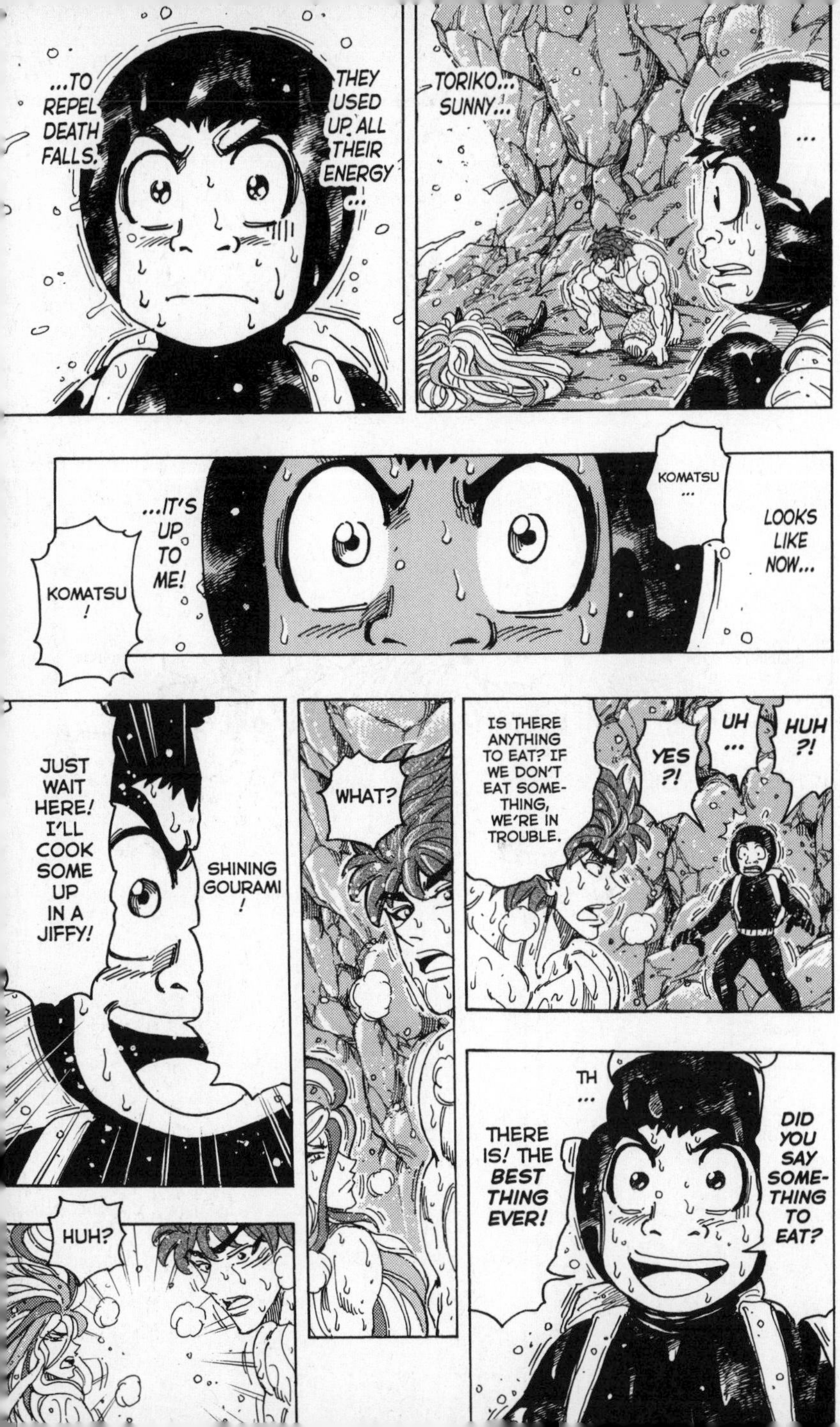

TORIKO... SUNNY...
...
THEY USED UP ALL THEIR ENERGY...
...TO REPEL DEATH FALLS.
KOMATSU...
LOOKS LIKE NOW...
...IT'S UP TO ME!
KOMATSU!
HUH?!
UH...
YES?!
IS THERE ANYTHING TO EAT? IF WE DON'T EAT SOMETHING, WE'RE IN TROUBLE.
DID YOU SAY SOMETHING TO EAT?
TH...
THERE IS! THE BEST THING EVER!
WHAT?
SHINING GOURAMI!
JUST WAIT HERE! I'LL COOK SOME UP IN A JIFFY!
HUH?

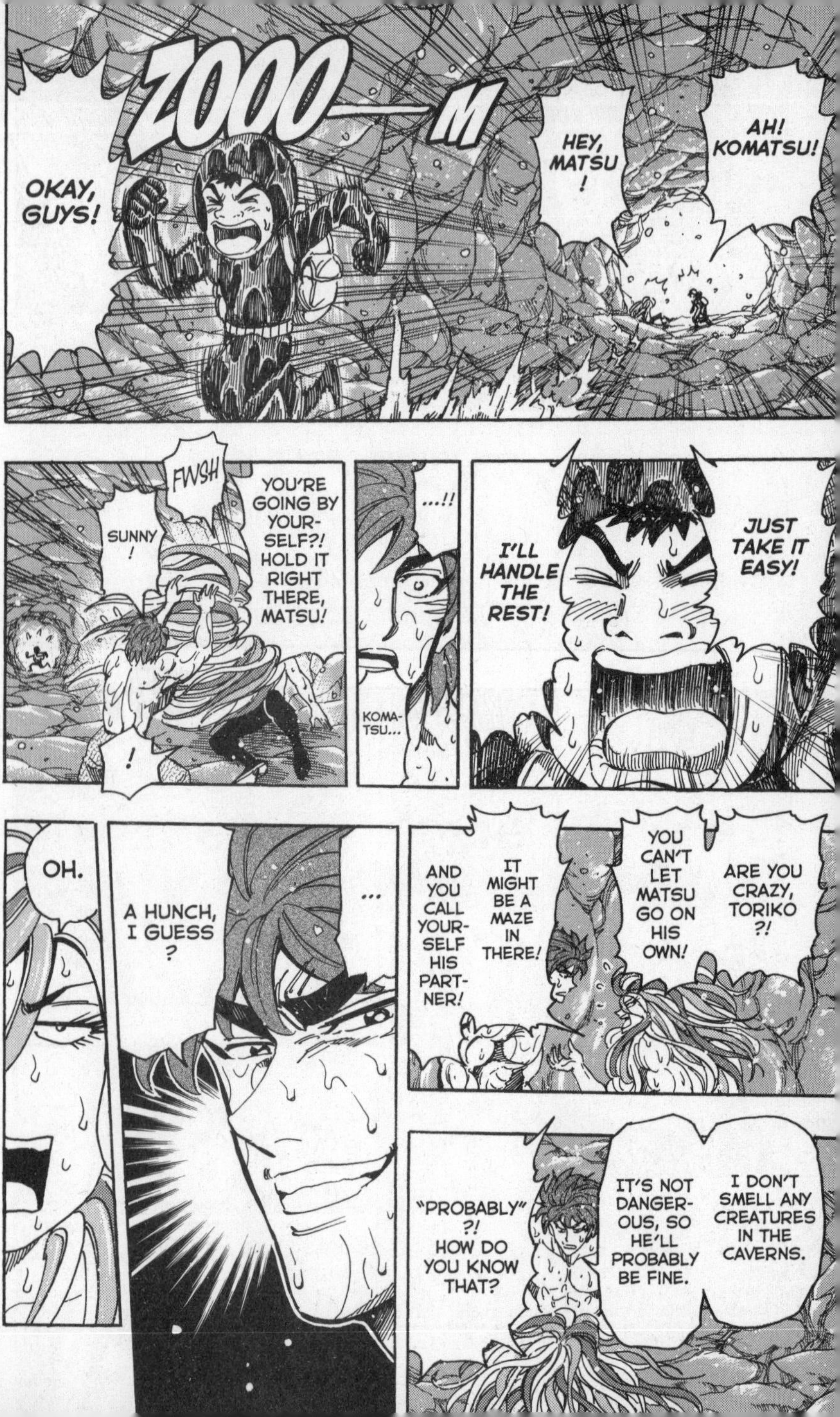
AH! KOMATSU!
HEY, MATSU!
ZOOO—M
OKAY, GUYS!
JUST TAKE IT EASY!
I'LL HANDLE THE REST!
...!!
KOMATSU...
YOU'RE GOING BY YOURSELF?! HOLD IT RIGHT THERE, MATSU!
FWSH
SUNNY!
!
ARE YOU CRAZY, TORIKO?!
YOU CAN'T LET MATSU GO ON HIS OWN!
IT MIGHT BE A MAZE IN THERE!
AND YOU CALL YOURSELF HIS PARTNER!
I DON'T SMELL ANY CREATURES IN THE CAVERNS.
IT'S NOT DANGEROUS, SO HE'LL PROBABLY BE FINE.
"PROBABLY"?! HOW DO YOU KNOW THAT?
...
A HUNCH, I GUESS?
OH.

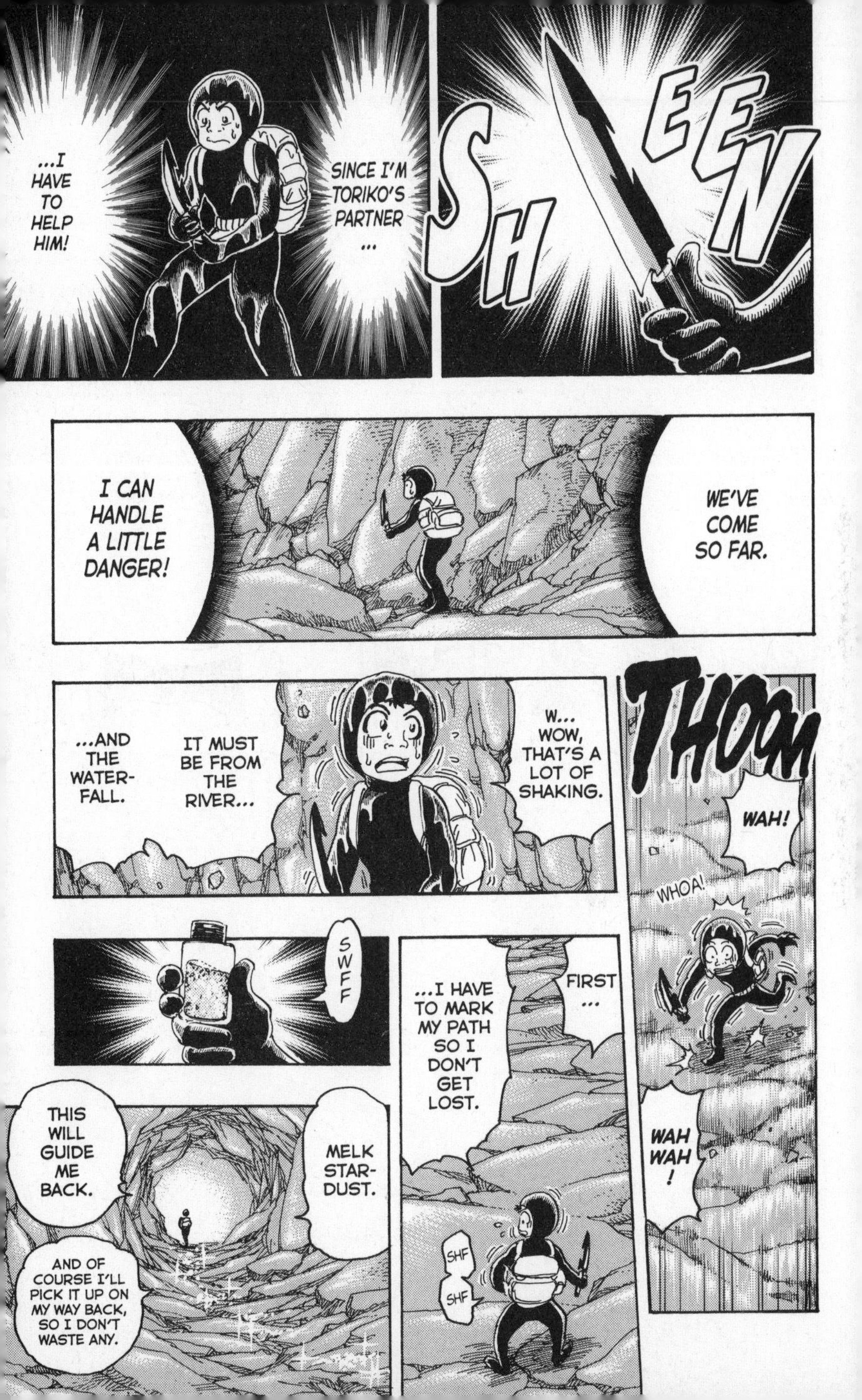
SHEEN
SINCE I'M TORIKO'S PARTNER...
...I HAVE TO HELP HIM!
WE'VE COME SO FAR.
I CAN HANDLE A LITTLE DANGER!
THOOM
WAH!
WHOA!
WAH WAH!
W... WOW, THAT'S A LOT OF SHAKING.
IT MUST BE FROM THE RIVER...
...AND THE WATER-FALL.
FIRST...
...I HAVE TO MARK MY PATH SO I DON'T GET LOST.
SHF
SHF
SWFF
MELK STAR-DUST.
THIS WILL GUIDE ME BACK.
AND OF COURSE I'LL PICK IT UP ON MY WAY BACK, SO I DON'T WASTE ANY.

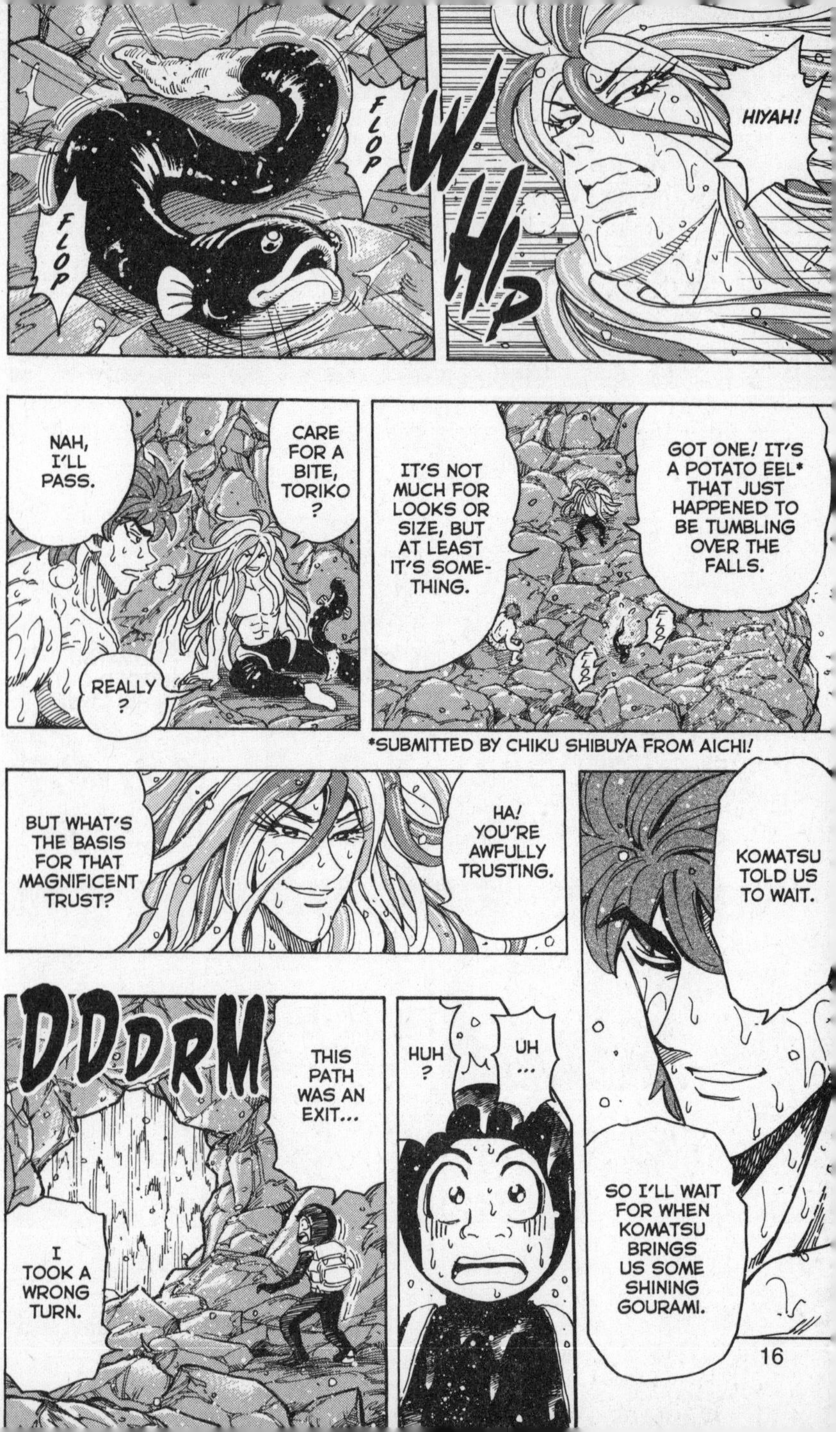
HIYAH!
WHIP
FLOP
FLOP
GOT ONE! IT'S A POTATO EEL* THAT JUST HAPPENED TO BE TUMBLING OVER THE FALLS.
IT'S NOT MUCH FOR LOOKS OR SIZE, BUT AT LEAST IT'S SOME-THING.
FLOP
FLOP
CARE FOR A BITE, TORIKO?
NAH, I'LL PASS.
REALLY?
*SUBMITTED BY CHIKU SHIBUYA FROM AICHI!
KOMATSU TOLD US TO WAIT.
SO I'LL WAIT FOR WHEN KOMATSU BRINGS US SOME SHINING GOURAMI.
HA! YOU'RE AWFULLY TRUSTING.
BUT WHAT'S THE BASIS FOR THAT MAGNIFICENT TRUST?
UH...
HUH?
THIS PATH WAS AN EXIT...
I TOOK A WRONG TURN.
DDDRM

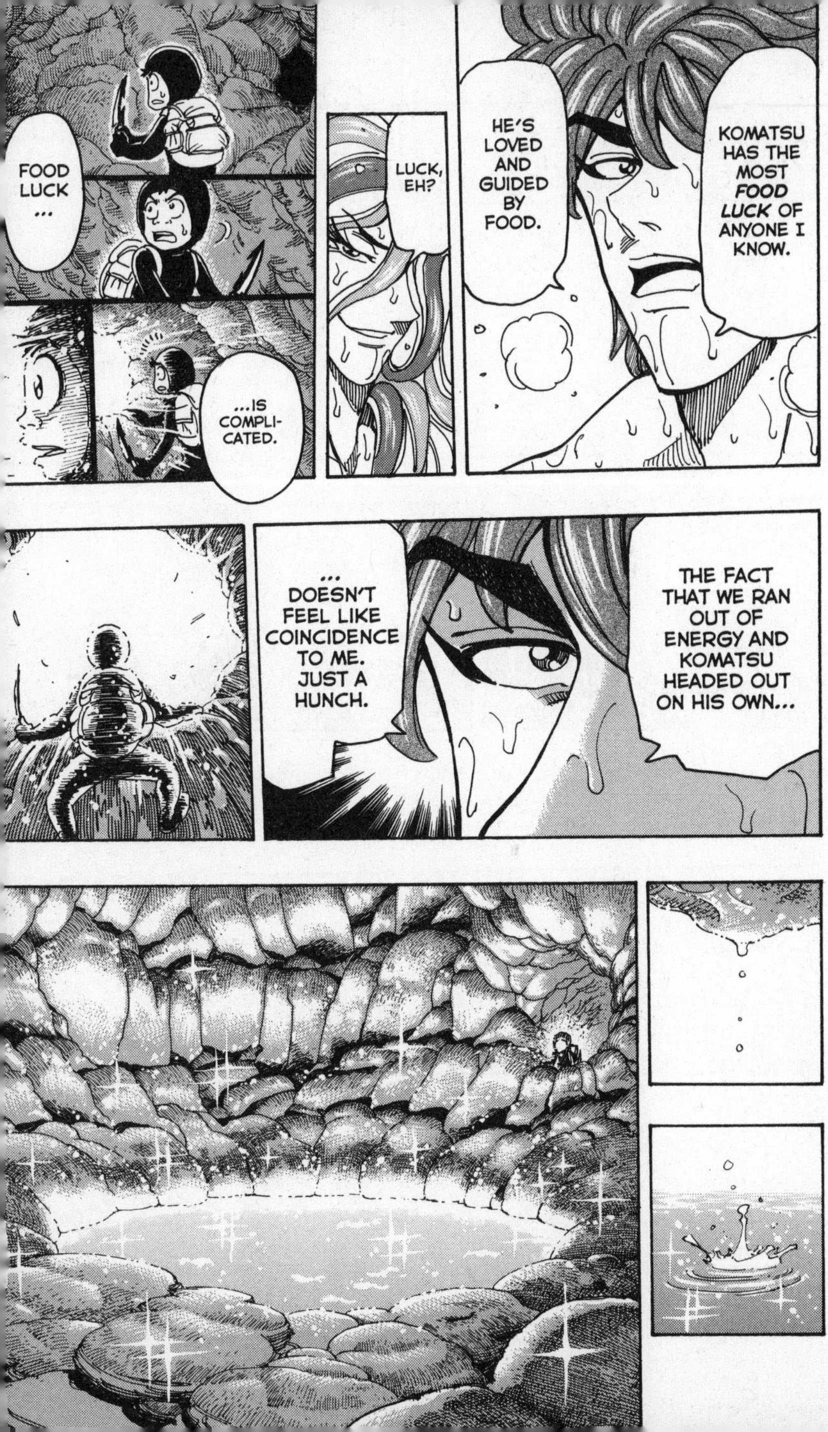
KOMATSU HAS THE MOST *FOOD LUCK* OF ANYONE I KNOW.
HE'S LOVED AND GUIDED BY FOOD.
LUCK, EH?
FOOD LUCK ...
...IS COMPLICATED.
THE FACT THAT WE RAN OUT OF ENERGY AND KOMATSU HEADED OUT ON HIS OWN...
... DOESN'T FEEL LIKE COINCIDENCE TO ME. JUST A HUNCH.

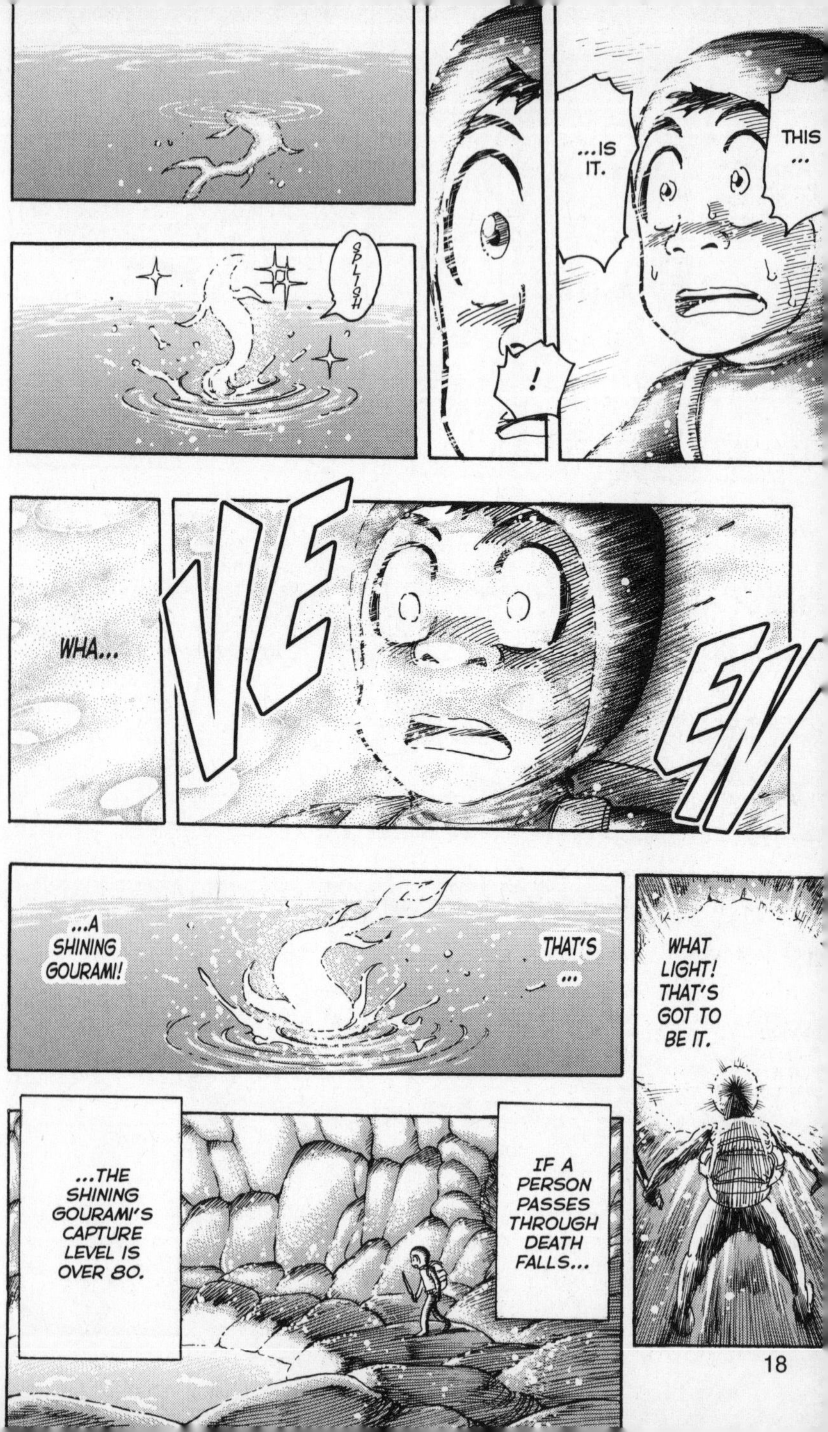
THIS ...
...IS IT.
!
SPLISH
VE
EN
WHA...
WHAT LIGHT! THAT'S GOT TO BE IT.
THAT'S ...
...A SHINING GOURAMI!
IF A PERSON PASSES THROUGH DEATH FALLS...
...THE SHINING GOURAMI'S CAPTURE LEVEL IS OVER 80.

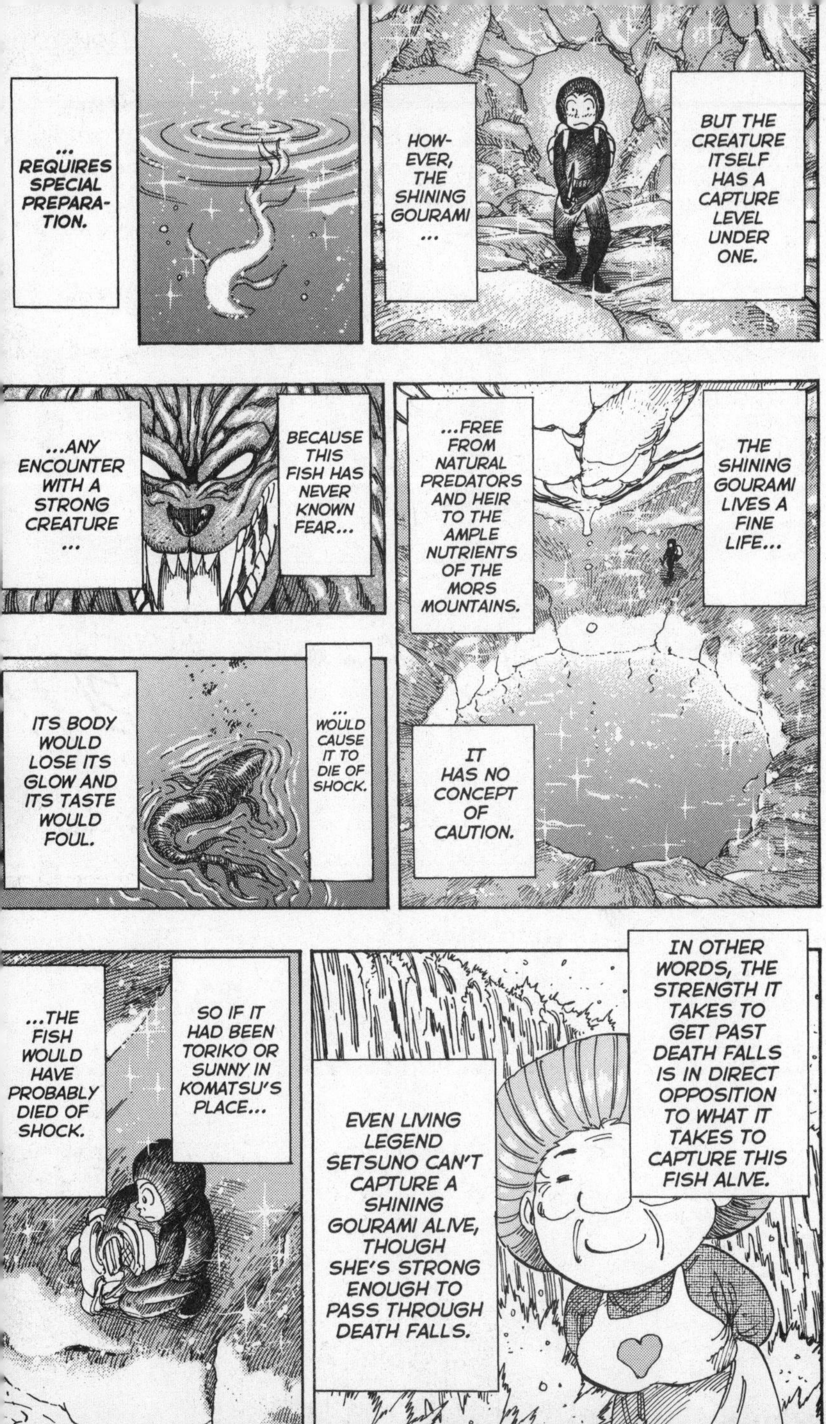
BUT THE CREATURE ITSELF HAS A CAPTURE LEVEL UNDER ONE.
HOW-EVER, THE SHINING GOURAMI ...
... REQUIRES SPECIAL PREPARA-TION.
THE SHINING GOURAMI LIVES A FINE LIFE...
...FREE FROM NATURAL PREDATORS AND HEIR TO THE AMPLE NUTRIENTS OF THE MORS MOUNTAINS.
IT HAS NO CONCEPT OF CAUTION.
BECAUSE THIS FISH HAS NEVER KNOWN FEAR...
...ANY ENCOUNTER WITH A STRONG CREATURE ...
... WOULD CAUSE IT TO DIE OF SHOCK.
ITS BODY WOULD LOSE ITS GLOW AND ITS TASTE WOULD FOUL.
IN OTHER WORDS, THE STRENGTH IT TAKES TO GET PAST DEATH FALLS IS IN DIRECT OPPOSITION TO WHAT IT TAKES TO CAPTURE THIS FISH ALIVE.
EVEN LIVING LEGEND SETSUNO CAN'T CAPTURE A SHINING GOURAMI ALIVE, THOUGH SHE'S STRONG ENOUGH TO PASS THROUGH DEATH FALLS.
SO IF IT HAD BEEN TORIKO OR SUNNY IN KOMATSU'S PLACE...
...THE FISH WOULD HAVE PROBABLY DIED OF SHOCK.

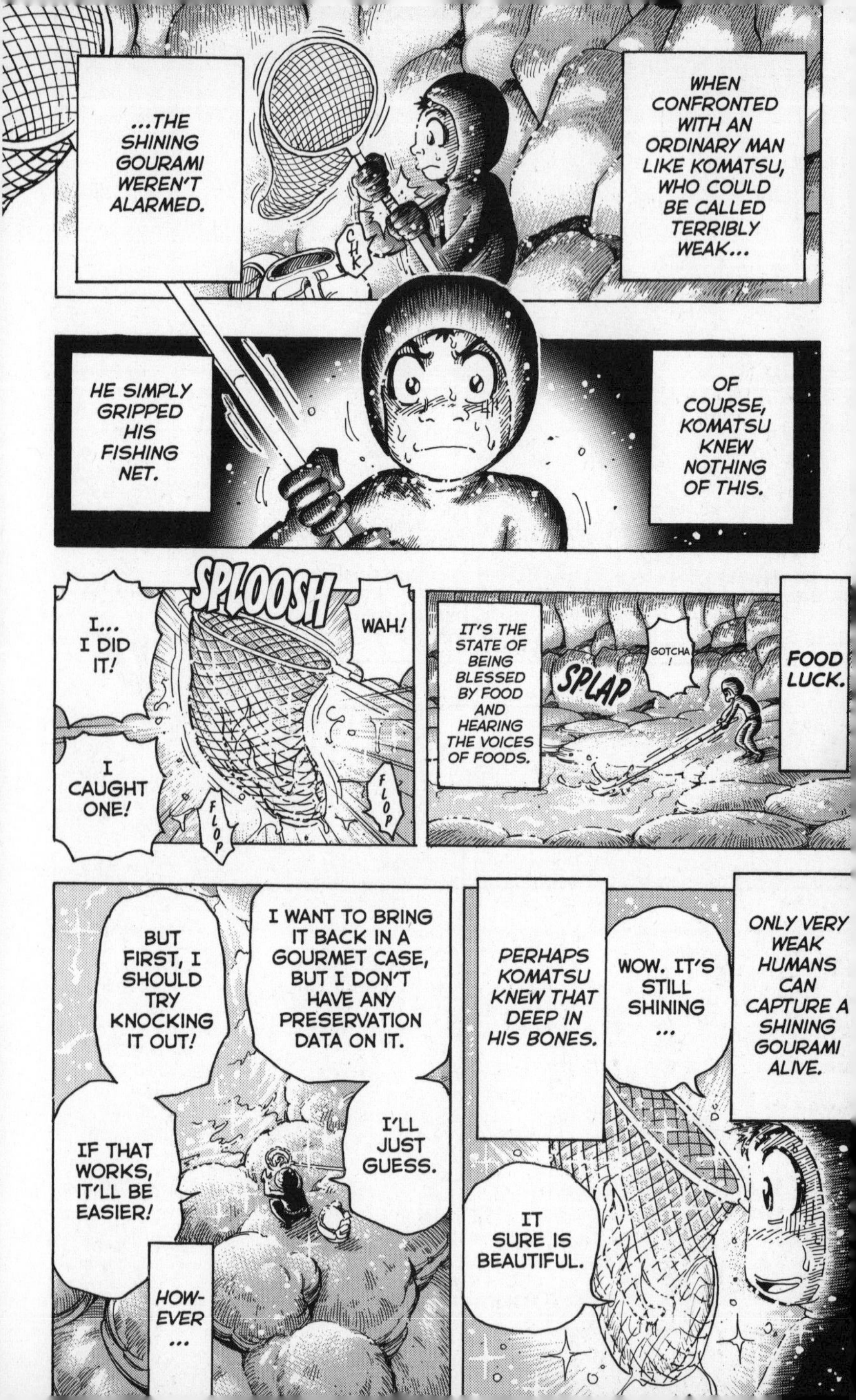
WHEN CONFRONTED WITH AN ORDINARY MAN LIKE KOMATSU, WHO COULD BE CALLED TERRIBLY WEAK...
...THE SHINING GOURAMI WEREN'T ALARMED.
CHK
OF COURSE, KOMATSU KNEW NOTHING OF THIS.
HE SIMPLY GRIPPED HIS FISHING NET.
FOOD LUCK.
IT'S THE STATE OF BEING BLESSED BY FOOD AND HEARING THE VOICES OF FOODS.
GOTCHA!
SPLAP
SPLOOSH
WAH!
I... I DID IT!
I CAUGHT ONE!
FLOP
FLOP
ONLY VERY WEAK HUMANS CAN CAPTURE A SHINING GOURAMI ALIVE.
WOW. IT'S STILL SHINING...
PERHAPS KOMATSU KNEW THAT DEEP IN HIS BONES.
IT SURE IS BEAUTIFUL.
I WANT TO BRING IT BACK IN A GOURMET CASE, BUT I DON'T HAVE ANY PRESERVATION DATA ON IT.
BUT FIRST, I SHOULD TRY KNOCKING IT OUT!
I'LL JUST GUESS.
IF THAT WORKS, IT'LL BE EASIER!
HOW-EVER...

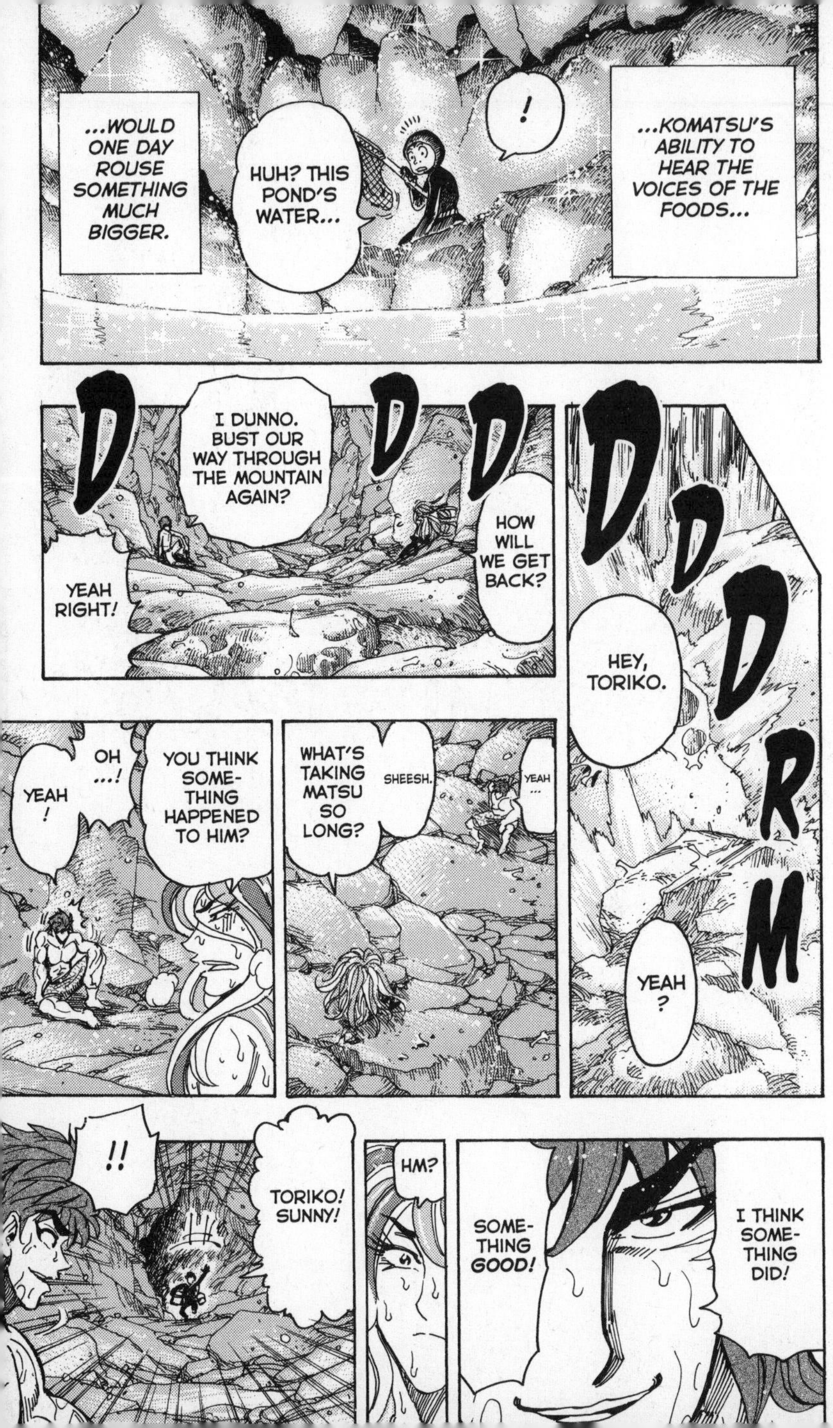

...KOMATSU'S ABILITY TO HEAR THE VOICES OF THE FOODS...
!
HUH? THIS POND'S WATER...
...WOULD ONE DAY ROUSE SOMETHING MUCH BIGGER.
DDDDDDDRM
HEY, TORIKO.
YEAH?
HOW WILL WE GET BACK?
I DUNNO. BUST OUR WAY THROUGH THE MOUNTAIN AGAIN?
YEAH RIGHT!
YEAH...
SHEESH.
WHAT'S TAKING MATSU SO LONG?
YOU THINK SOME-THING HAPPENED TO HIM?
OH...!
YEAH!
I THINK SOME-THING DID!
HM?
SOME-THING GOOD!
TORIKO! SUNNY!
!!

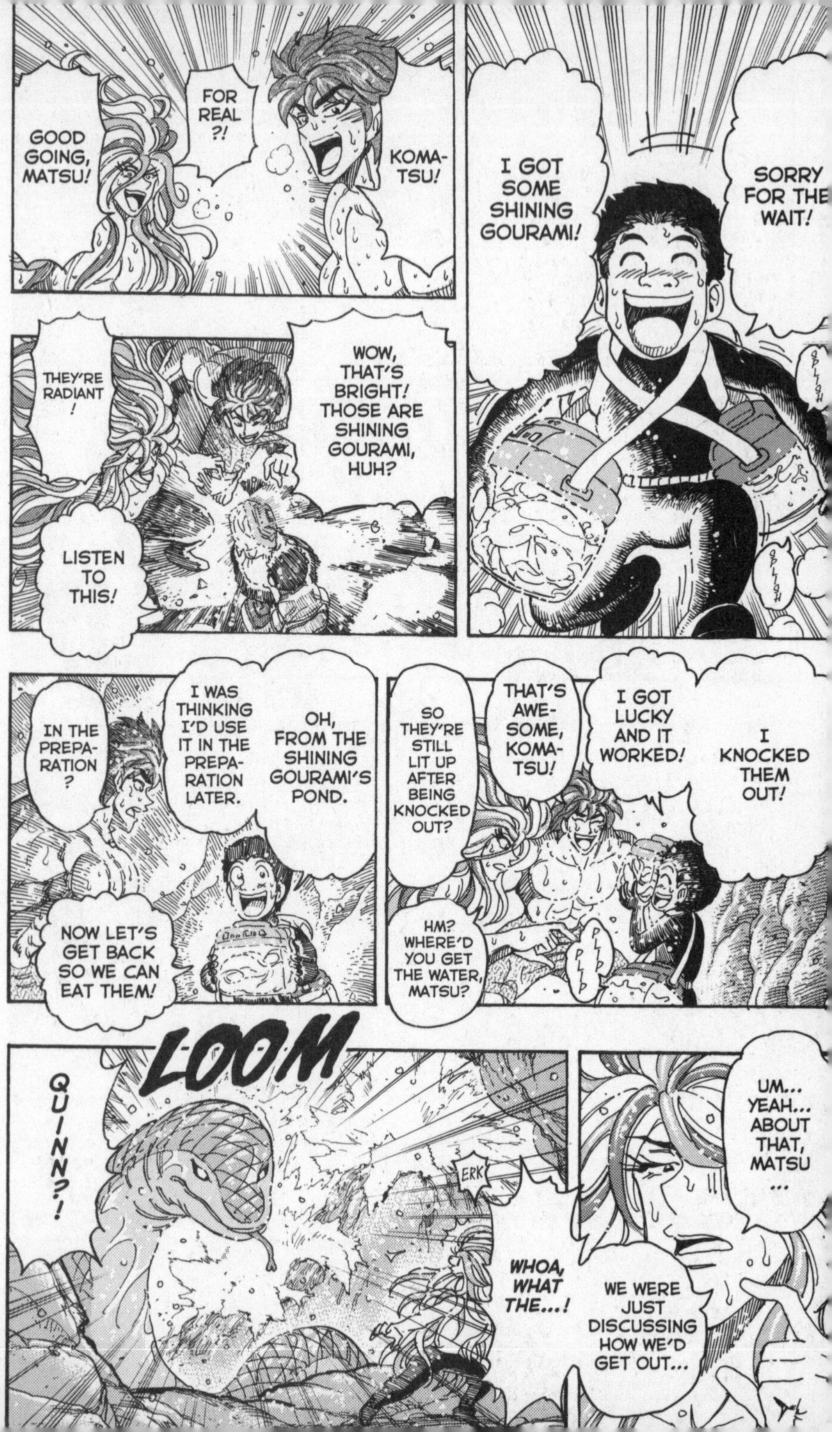
SORRY FOR THE WAIT!
I GOT SOME SHINING GOURAMI!
SPLISH
SPLISH
KOMA-TSU!
FOR REAL?!
GOOD GOING, MATSU!
WOW, THAT'S BRIGHT! THOSE ARE SHINING GOURAMI, HUH?
THEY'RE RADIANT!
LISTEN TO THIS!
I KNOCKED THEM OUT!
I GOT LUCKY AND IT WORKED!
THAT'S AWE-SOME, KOMA-TSU!
SO THEY'RE STILL LIT UP AFTER BEING KNOCKED OUT?
PLIP PLIP
HM? WHERE'D YOU GET THE WATER, MATSU?
OH, FROM THE SHINING GOURAMI'S POND.
I WAS THINKING I'D USE IT IN THE PREPA-RATION LATER.
IN THE PREPA-RATION?
NOW LET'S GET BACK SO WE CAN EAT THEM!
UM... YEAH... ABOUT THAT, MATSU...
WE WERE JUST DISCUSSING HOW WE'D GET OUT...
LOOM
ERK
QUINN?!
WHOA, WHAT THE...!

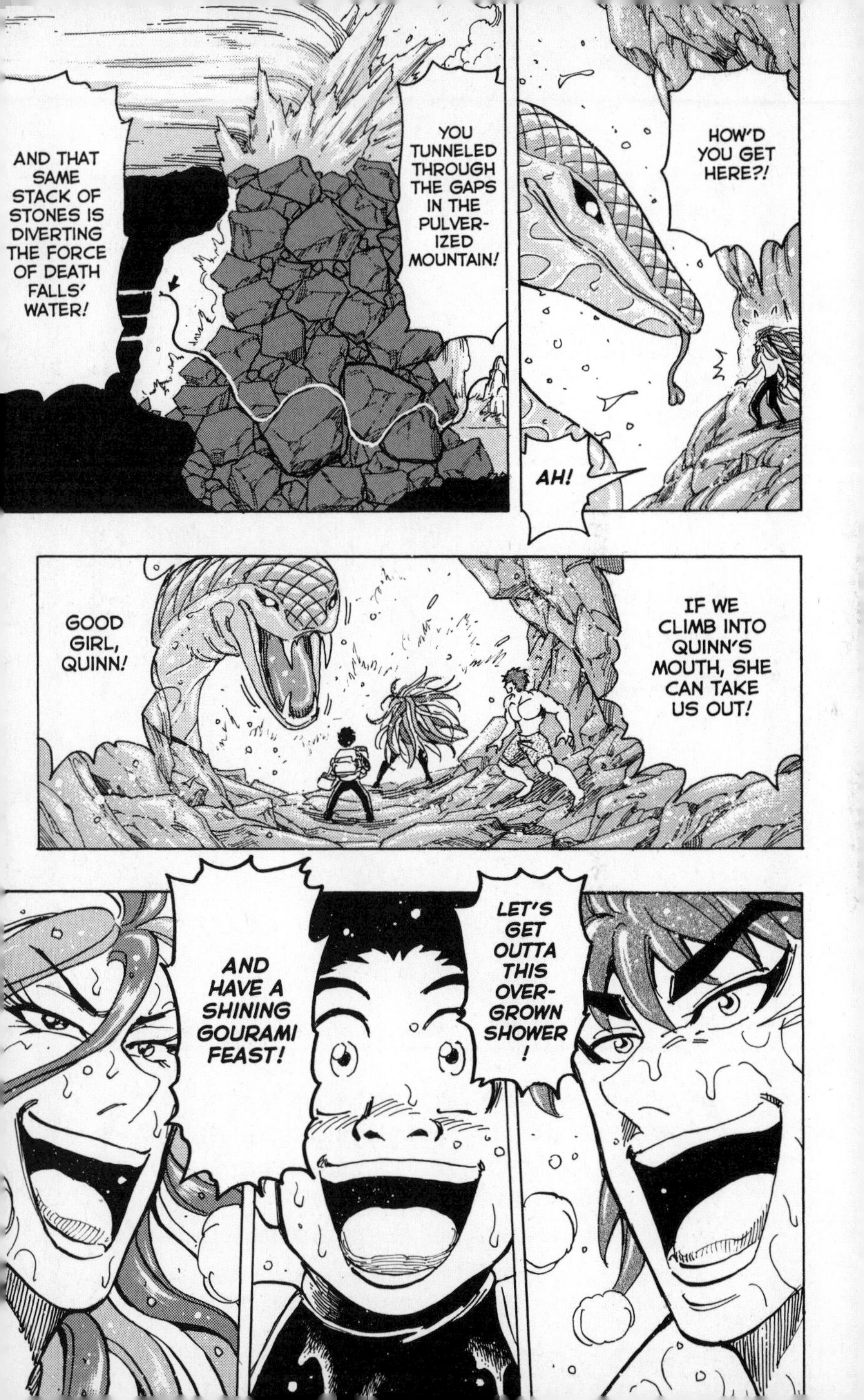
HOW'D YOU GET HERE?!
AH!
YOU TUNNELED THROUGH THE GAPS IN THE PULVER-IZED MOUNTAIN!
AND THAT SAME STACK OF STONES IS DIVERTING THE FORCE OF DEATH FALLS' WATER!
IF WE CLIMB INTO QUINN'S MOUTH, SHE CAN TAKE US OUT!
GOOD GIRL, QUINN!
LET'S GET OUTTA THIS OVER-GROWN SHOWER!
AND HAVE A SHINING GOURAMI FEAST!

TORIKO

GOURMET CHECKLIST

Vol. 185

GROWSAURUS

(MAMMAL)

CAPTURE LEVEL: 57

HABITAT: NO SPECIFIC HABITAT

LENGTH: 750 METERS

HEIGHT: 430 METERS

WEIGHT: 500,000 TONS

PRICE: 100 G / 1,200 YEN

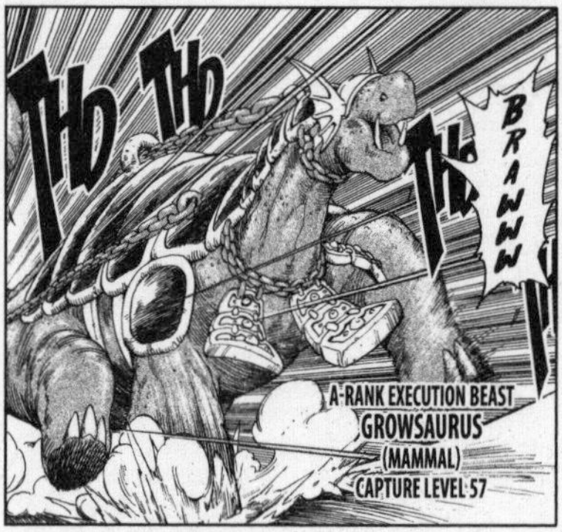
THD
THD
THD
BRAWWW
A-RANK EXECUTION BEAST
GROWSAURUS
(MAMMAL)
CAPTURE LEVEL 57

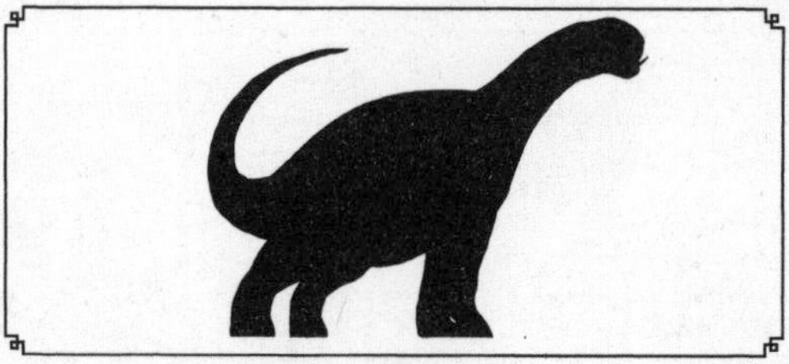

SCALE

ONE OF HONEY PRISON'S A-RANK EXECUTION BEASTS. UNDER THE INFLUENCE OF WARDEN LOVE'S PHEROMONES, THE GROWSAURUS OBEDIENTLY CARRIES OUT ITS EXECUTION DUTIES. HOWEVER, IN THE WILD THEY ARE SO FEROCIOUS AND AGGRESSIVE THEY WILL TRAMPLE ENTIRE CITIES IN HALF A DAY. SWIFT MILITARY ACTION IS GENERALLY LEVIED AGAINST ANY GROWSAURUS THAT ENTERS A CITY, BUT IT TAKES A SKILLED GOURMET HUNTER TO DOWN ONE OF THESE BIG BRUISERS.

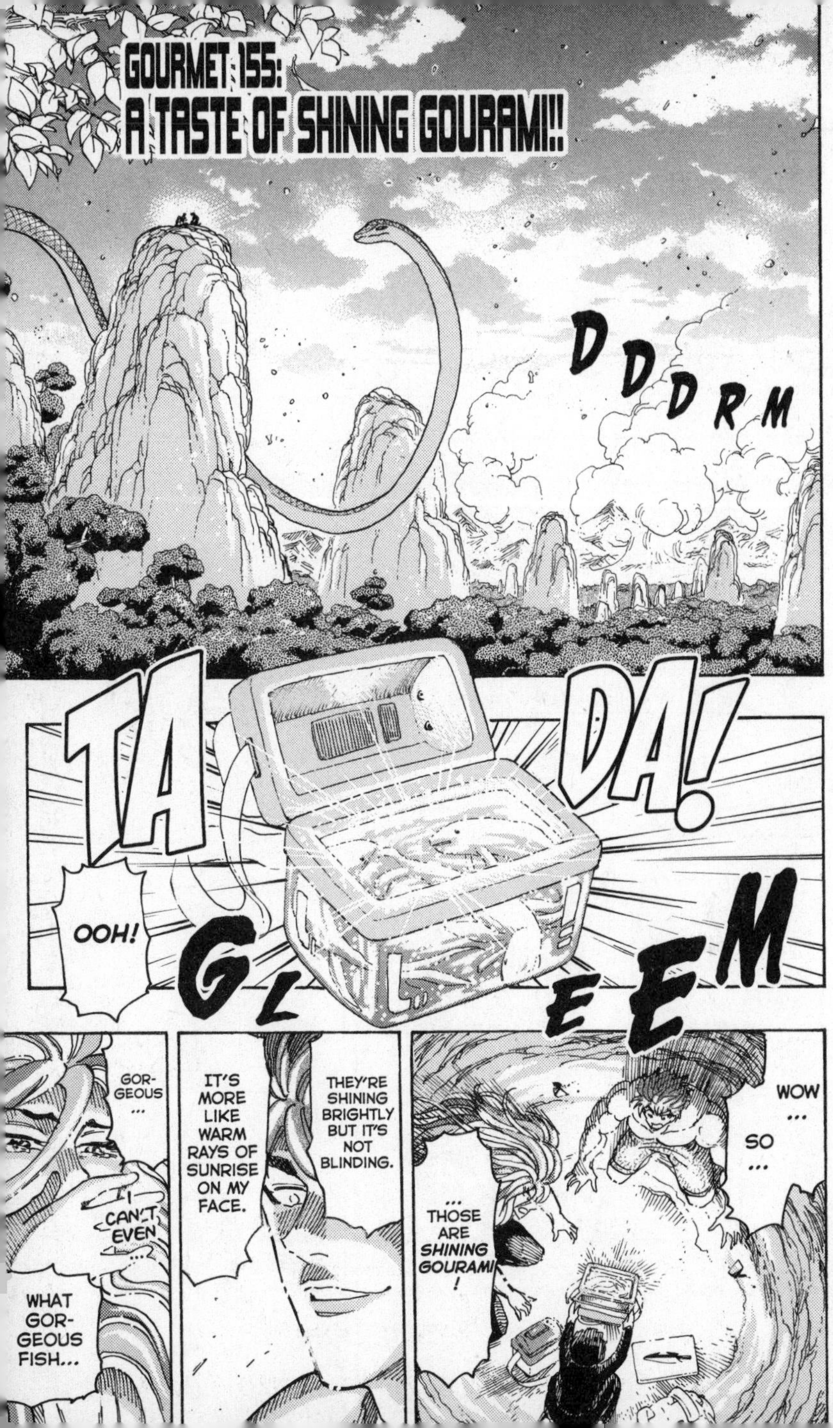
GOURMET 155:
A TASTE OF SHINING GOURAMI!!
DDDRM
TA DA!
OOH!
GLEEEM
WOW... SO...
...THOSE ARE SHINING GOURAMI!
THEY'RE SHINING BRIGHTLY BUT IT'S NOT BLINDING.
IT'S MORE LIKE WARM RAYS OF SUNRISE ON MY FACE.
GOR-GEOUS...
I CAN'T EVEN...
WHAT GOR-GEOUS FISH...

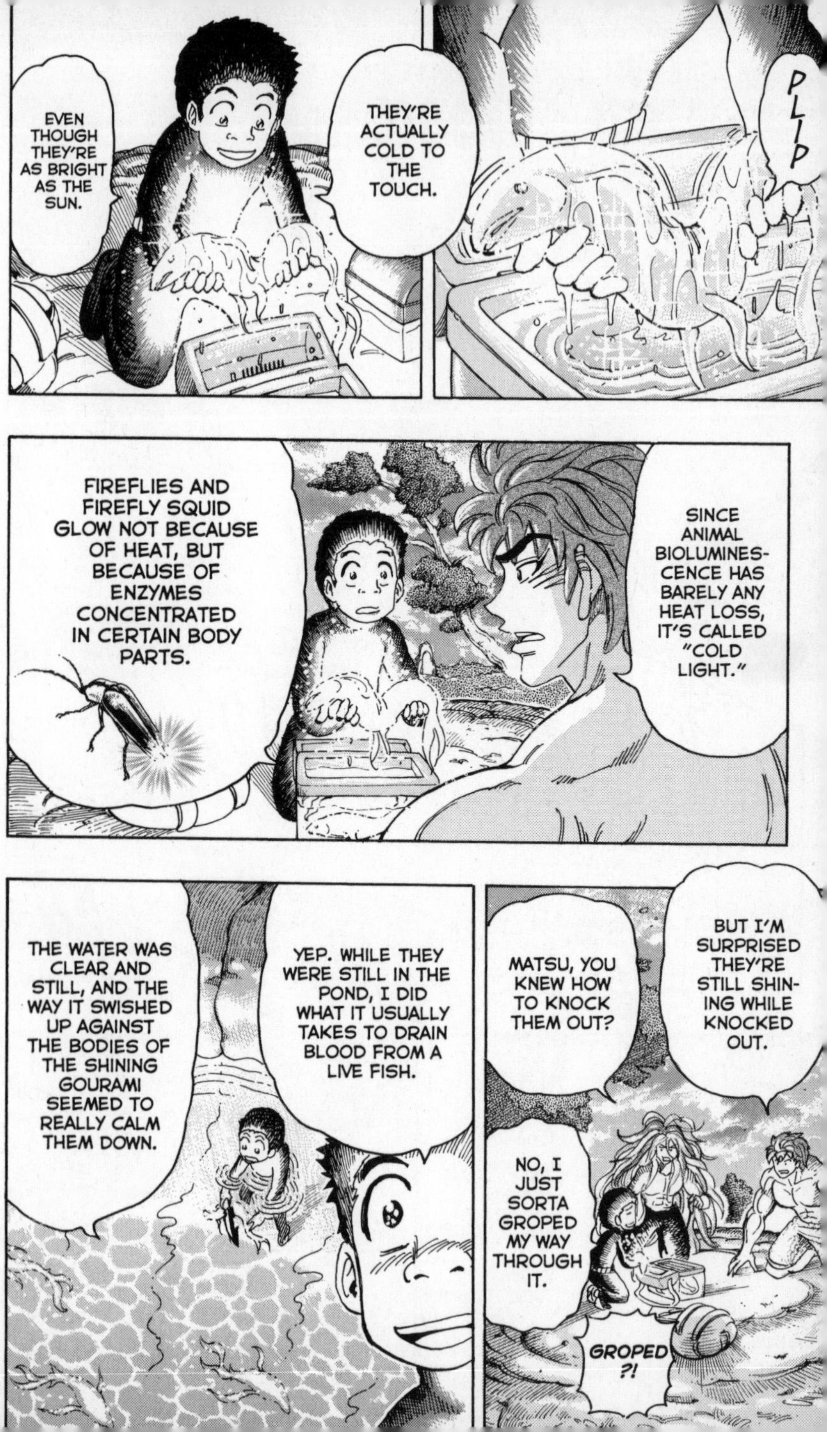
PLIP
THEY'RE ACTUALLY COLD TO THE TOUCH.
EVEN THOUGH THEY'RE AS BRIGHT AS THE SUN.
SINCE ANIMAL BIOLUMINES-CENCE HAS BARELY ANY HEAT LOSS, IT'S CALLED "COLD LIGHT."
FIREFLIES AND FIREFLY SQUID GLOW NOT BECAUSE OF HEAT, BUT BECAUSE OF ENZYMES CONCENTRATED IN CERTAIN BODY PARTS.
BUT I'M SURPRISED THEY'RE STILL SHIN-ING WHILE KNOCKED OUT.
MATSU, YOU KNEW HOW TO KNOCK THEM OUT?
NO, I JUST SORTA GROPED MY WAY THROUGH IT.
GROPED ?!
YEP. WHILE THEY WERE STILL IN THE POND, I DID WHAT IT USUALLY TAKES TO DRAIN BLOOD FROM A LIVE FISH.
THE WATER WAS CLEAR AND STILL, AND THE WAY IT SWISHED UP AGAINST THE BODIES OF THE SHINING GOURAMI SEEMED TO REALLY CALM THEM DOWN.

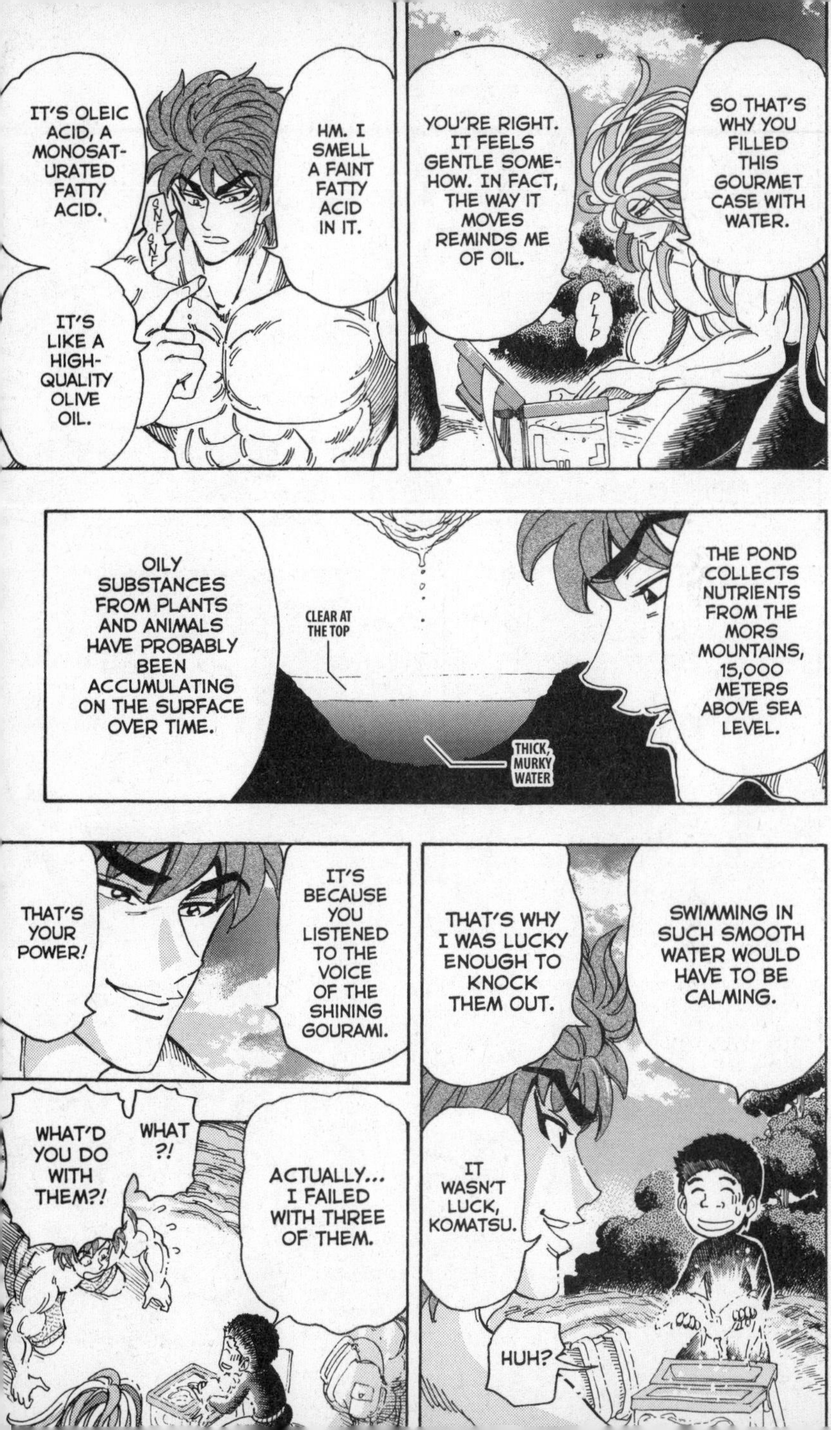
SO THAT'S WHY YOU FILLED THIS GOURMET CASE WITH WATER.
YOU'RE RIGHT. IT FEELS GENTLE SOME-HOW. IN FACT, THE WAY IT MOVES REMINDS ME OF OIL.
PLP
HM. I SMELL A FAINT FATTY ACID IN IT.
SNF SNF
IT'S OLEIC ACID, A MONOSAT-URATED FATTY ACID.
IT'S LIKE A HIGH-QUALITY OLIVE OIL.
THE POND COLLECTS NUTRIENTS FROM THE MORS MOUNTAINS, 15,000 METERS ABOVE SEA LEVEL.
OILY SUBSTANCES FROM PLANTS AND ANIMALS HAVE PROBABLY BEEN ACCUMULATING ON THE SURFACE OVER TIME.
CLEAR AT THE TOP
THICK, MURKY WATER
SWIMMING IN SUCH SMOOTH WATER WOULD HAVE TO BE CALMING.
THAT'S WHY I WAS LUCKY ENOUGH TO KNOCK THEM OUT.
IT WASN'T LUCK, KOMATSU.
HUH?
IT'S BECAUSE YOU LISTENED TO THE VOICE OF THE SHINING GOURAMI.
THAT'S YOUR POWER!
ACTUALLY... I FAILED WITH THREE OF THEM.
WHAT ?!
WHAT'D YOU DO WITH THEM?!

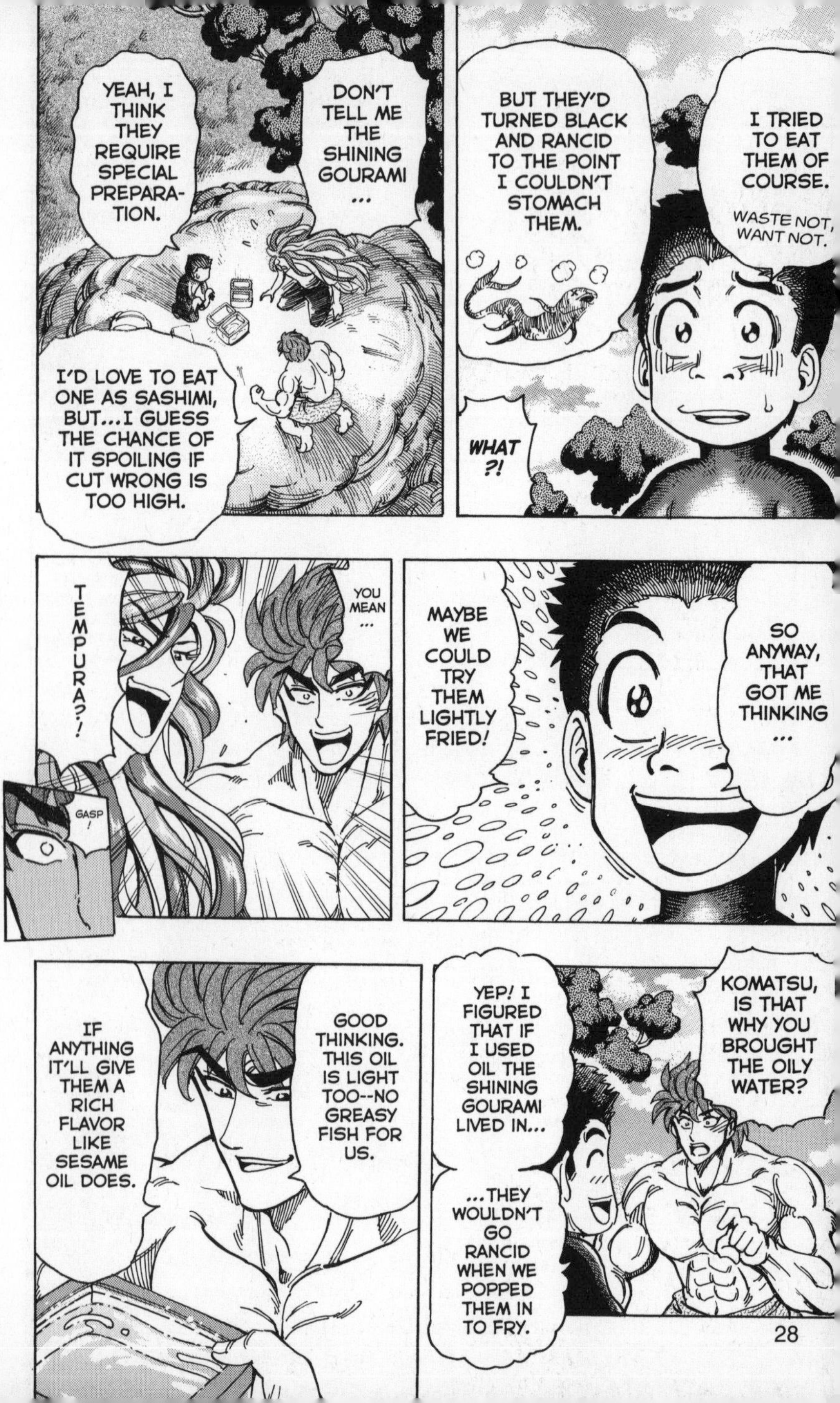
I TRIED TO EAT THEM OF COURSE.
WASTE NOT, WANT NOT.
BUT THEY'D TURNED BLACK AND RANCID TO THE POINT I COULDN'T STOMACH THEM.
WHAT?!
DON'T TELL ME THE SHINING GOURAMI...
YEAH, I THINK THEY REQUIRE SPECIAL PREPARATION.
I'D LOVE TO EAT ONE AS SASHIMI, BUT...I GUESS THE CHANCE OF IT SPOILING IF CUT WRONG IS TOO HIGH.
SO ANYWAY, THAT GOT ME THINKING...
MAYBE WE COULD TRY THEM LIGHTLY FRIED!
YOU MEAN...
TEMPURA?!
GASP!
KOMATSU, IS THAT WHY YOU BROUGHT THE OILY WATER?
YEP! I FIGURED THAT IF I USED OIL THE SHINING GOURAMI LIVED IN...
...THEY WOULDN'T GO RANCID WHEN WE POPPED THEM IN TO FRY.
GOOD THINKING. THIS OIL IS LIGHT TOO--NO GREASY FISH FOR US.
IF ANYTHING IT'LL GIVE THEM A RICH FLAVOR LIKE SESAME OIL DOES.

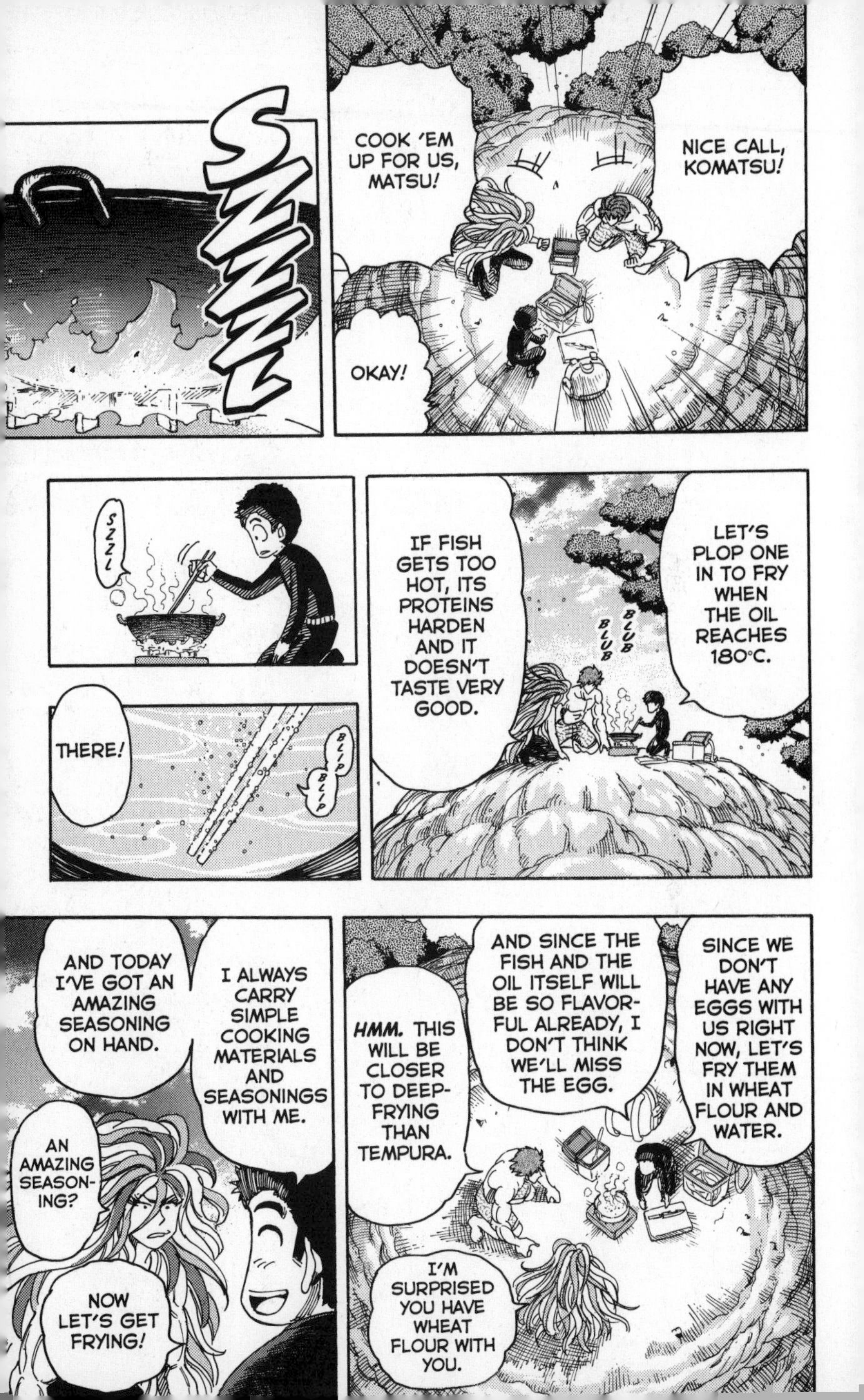
NICE CALL, KOMATSU!
COOK 'EM UP FOR US, MATSU!
OKAY!
LET'S PLOP ONE IN TO FRY WHEN THE OIL REACHES 180°C.
BLUB BLUB
IF FISH GETS TOO HOT, ITS PROTEINS HARDEN AND IT DOESN'T TASTE VERY GOOD.
SZZL
BLIP BLIP
THERE!
SINCE WE DON'T HAVE ANY EGGS WITH US RIGHT NOW, LET'S FRY THEM IN WHEAT FLOUR AND WATER.
AND SINCE THE FISH AND THE OIL ITSELF WILL BE SO FLAVOR-FUL ALREADY, I DON'T THINK WE'LL MISS THE EGG.
HMM. THIS WILL BE CLOSER TO DEEP-FRYING THAN TEMPURA.
I'M SURPRISED YOU HAVE WHEAT FLOUR WITH YOU.
I ALWAYS CARRY SIMPLE COOKING MATERIALS AND SEASONINGS WITH ME.
AND TODAY I'VE GOT AN AMAZING SEASONING ON HAND.
AN AMAZING SEASON-ING?
NOW LET'S GET FRYING!

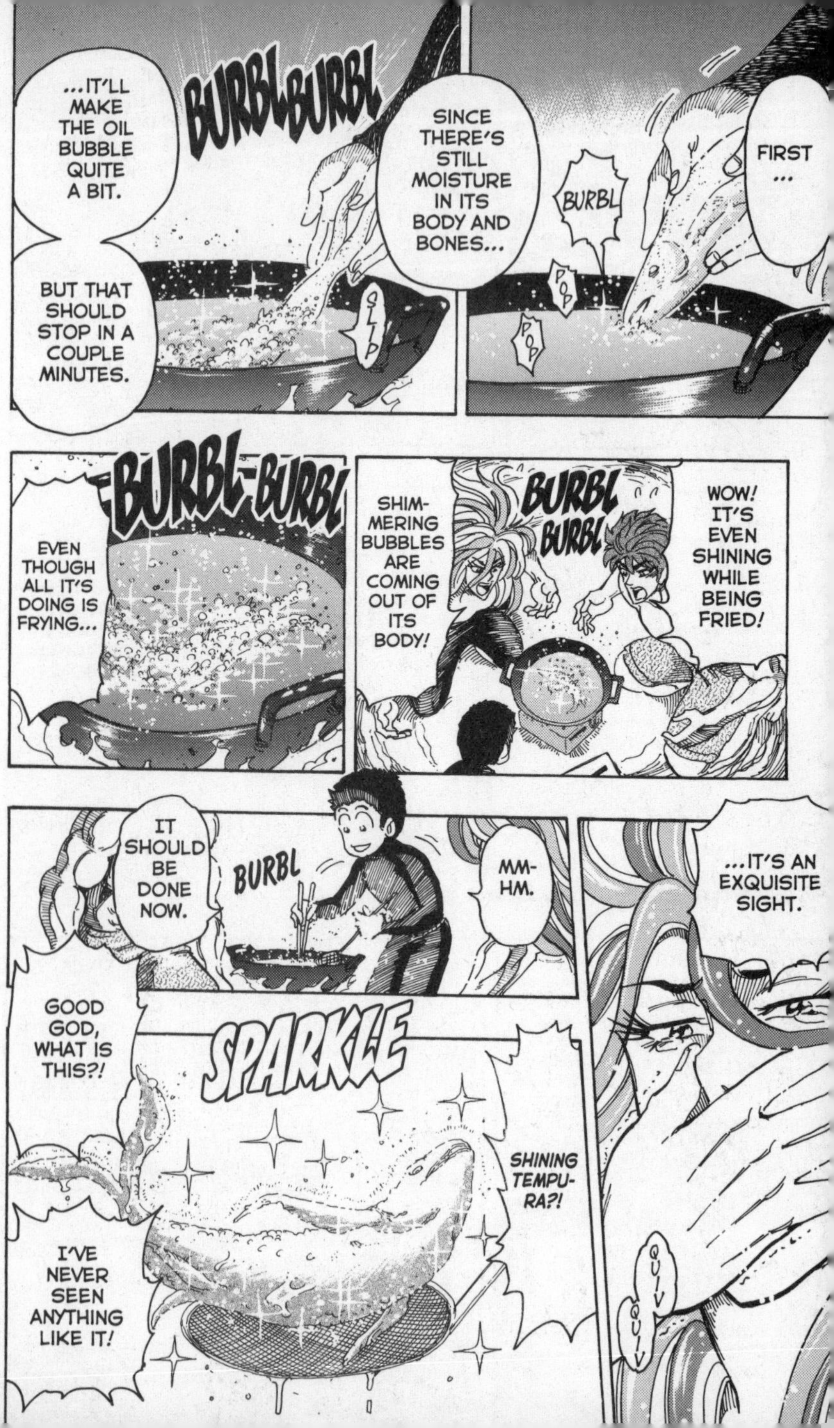
FIRST ...
BURBL
POP
POP
SINCE THERE'S STILL MOISTURE IN ITS BODY AND BONES...
BURBLBURBL
...IT'LL MAKE THE OIL BUBBLE QUITE A BIT.
BUT THAT SHOULD STOP IN A COUPLE MINUTES.
SLIP
WOW! IT'S EVEN SHINING WHILE BEING FRIED!
BURBL BURBL
SHIMMERING BUBBLES ARE COMING OUT OF ITS BODY!
BURBL-BURBL
EVEN THOUGH ALL IT'S DOING IS FRYING...
...IT'S AN EXQUISITE SIGHT.
QUIV QUIV
MM-HM.
BURBL
IT SHOULD BE DONE NOW.
SHINING TEMPURA?!
SPARKLE
GOOD GOD, WHAT IS THIS?!
I'VE NEVER SEEN ANYTHING LIKE IT!

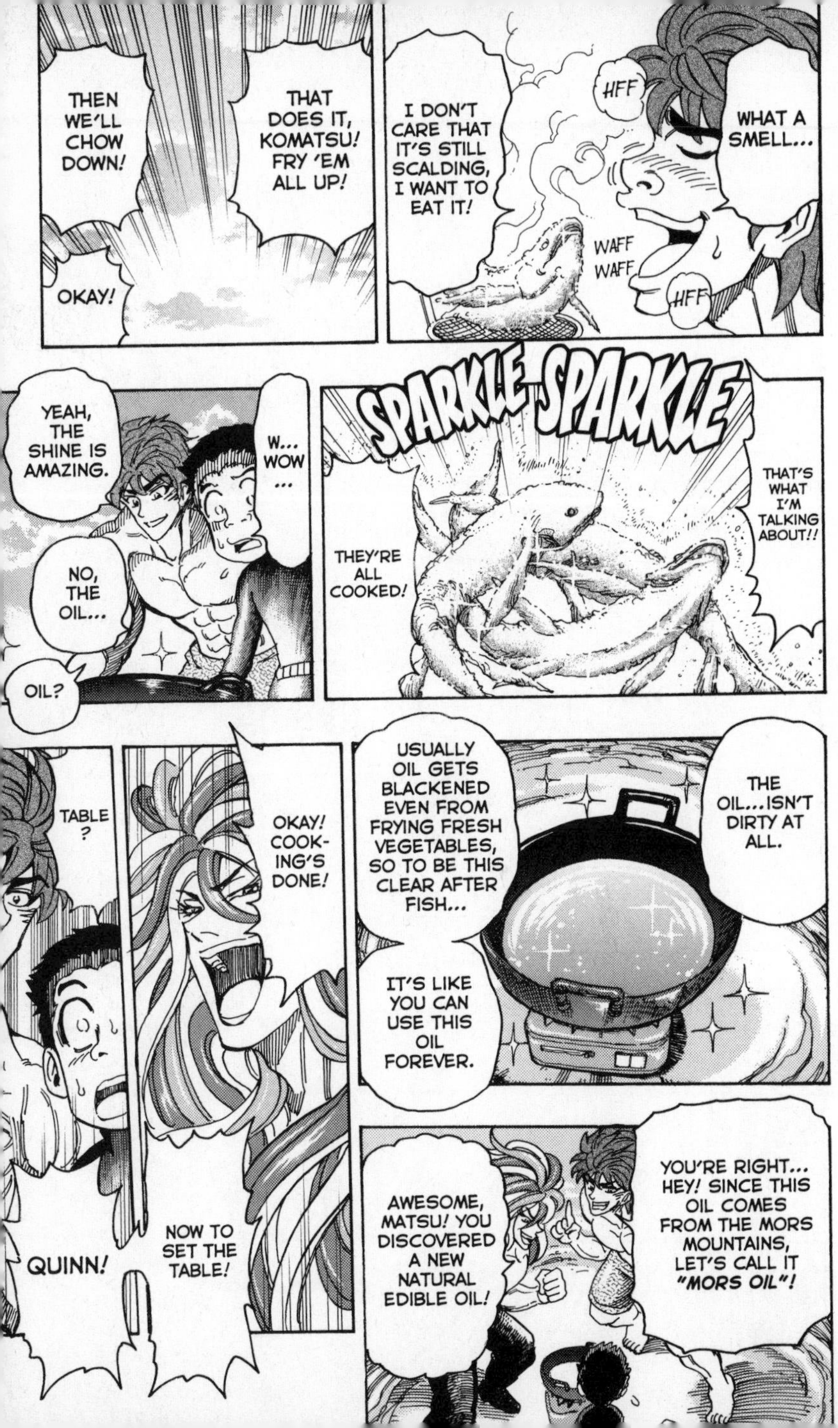
WHAT A SMELL...
HFF
I DON'T CARE THAT IT'S STILL SCALDING, I WANT TO EAT IT!
WAFF WAFF
HFF
THAT DOES IT, KOMATSU! FRY 'EM ALL UP!
THEN WE'LL CHOW DOWN!
OKAY!
SPARKLE SPARKLE
THAT'S WHAT I'M TALKING ABOUT!!
THEY'RE ALL COOKED!
W... WOW...
YEAH, THE SHINE IS AMAZING.
NO, THE OIL...
OIL?
THE OIL...ISN'T DIRTY AT ALL.
USUALLY OIL GETS BLACKENED EVEN FROM FRYING FRESH VEGETABLES, SO TO BE THIS CLEAR AFTER FISH...
IT'S LIKE YOU CAN USE THIS OIL FOREVER.
YOU'RE RIGHT... HEY! SINCE THIS OIL COMES FROM THE MORS MOUNTAINS, LET'S CALL IT "MORS OIL"!
AWESOME, MATSU! YOU DISCOVERED A NEW NATURAL EDIBLE OIL!
OKAY! COOKING'S DONE!
NOW TO SET THE TABLE!
QUINN!
TABLE?

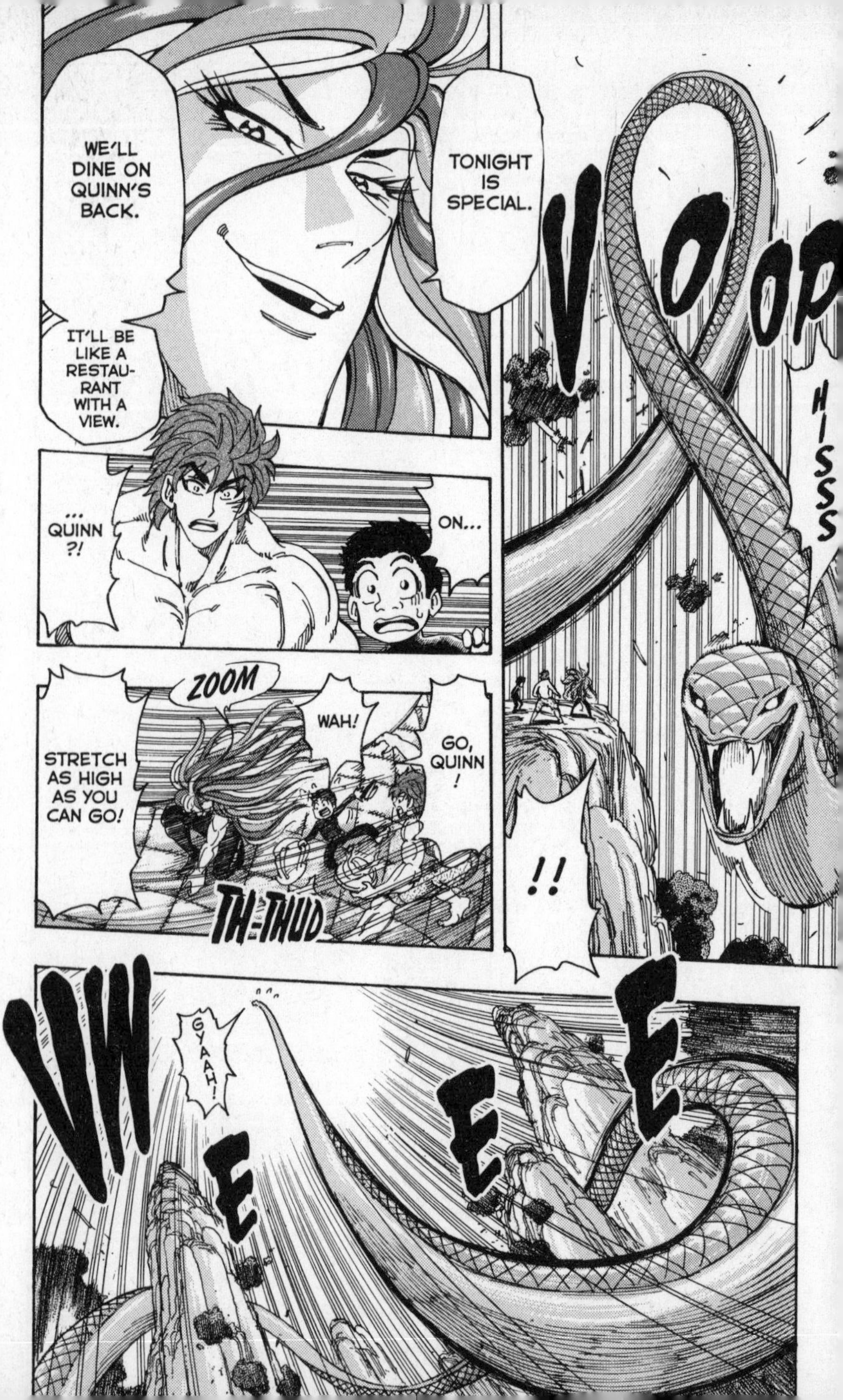
VOOOP
HISSS
!!
TONIGHT IS SPECIAL.
WE'LL DINE ON QUINN'S BACK.
IT'LL BE LIKE A RESTAU-RANT WITH A VIEW.
ON...
...QUINN?!
GO, QUINN!
WAH!
ZOOM
STRETCH AS HIGH AS YOU CAN GO!
TH-THUD
VWEEE
GYAAH!

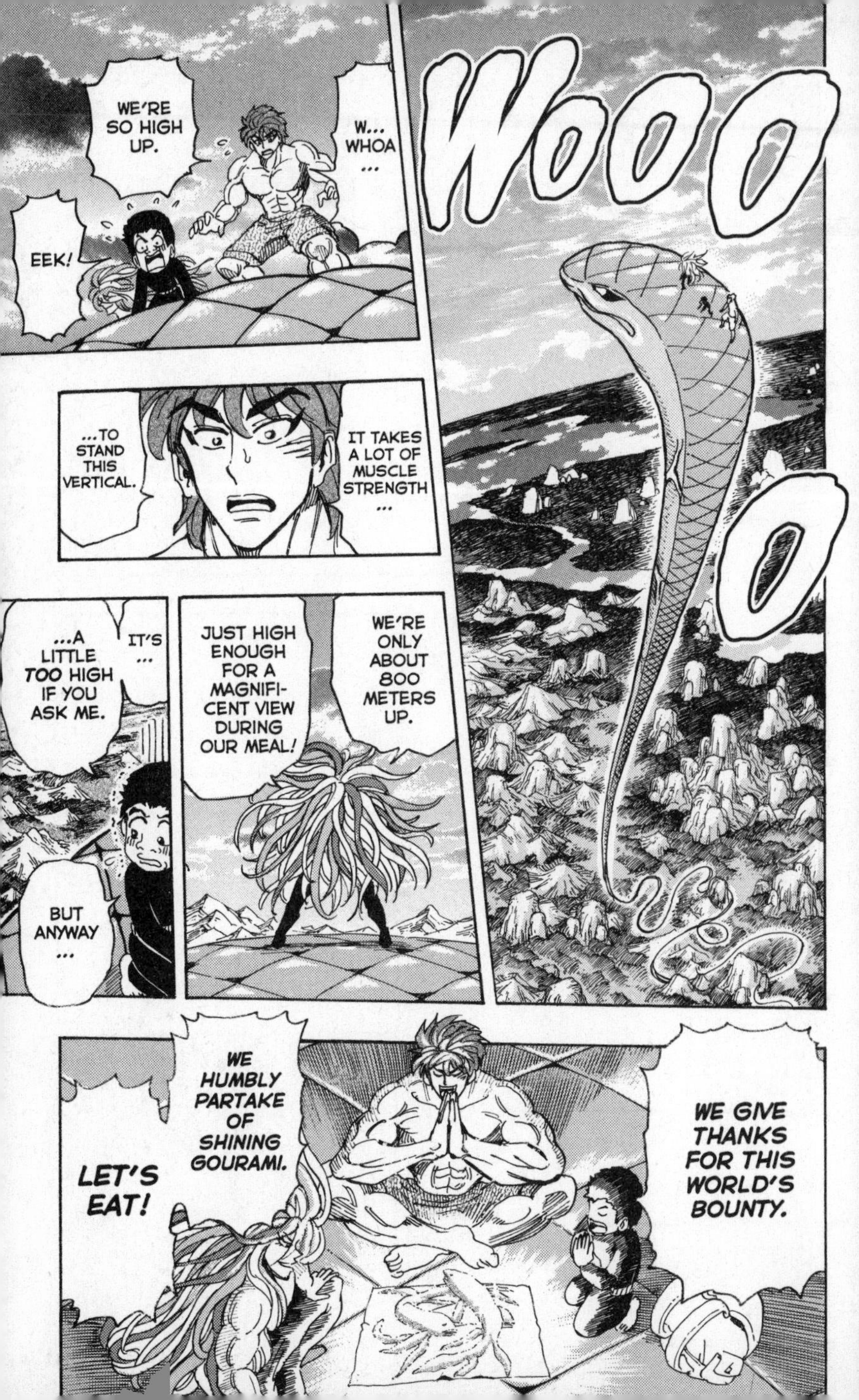
WOOOO
O
W... WHOA ...
WE'RE SO HIGH UP.
EEK!
IT TAKES A LOT OF MUSCLE STRENGTH ...
...TO STAND THIS VERTICAL.
WE'RE ONLY ABOUT 800 METERS UP.
JUST HIGH ENOUGH FOR A MAGNIFI-CENT VIEW DURING OUR MEAL!
IT'S ...
...A LITTLE *TOO* HIGH IF YOU ASK ME.
BUT ANYWAY ...
WE GIVE THANKS FOR THIS WORLD'S BOUNTY.
WE HUMBLY PARTAKE OF SHINING GOURAMI.
LET'S EAT!

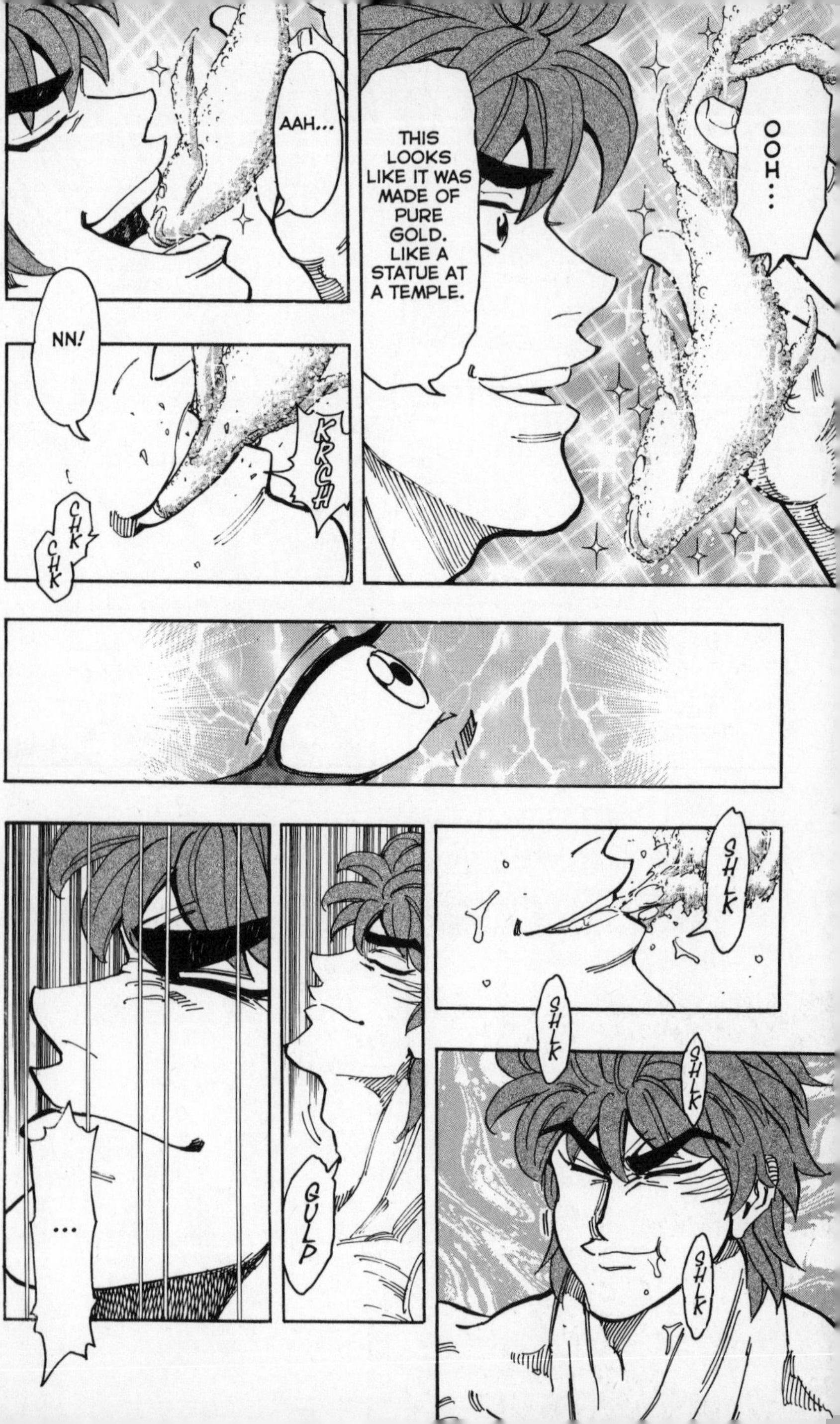
OOH...
THIS LOOKS LIKE IT WAS MADE OF PURE GOLD. LIKE A STATUE AT A TEMPLE.
AAH...
NN!
KRCH
CHK CHK
SHLK
SHLK
SHLK
SHLK
GULP
...

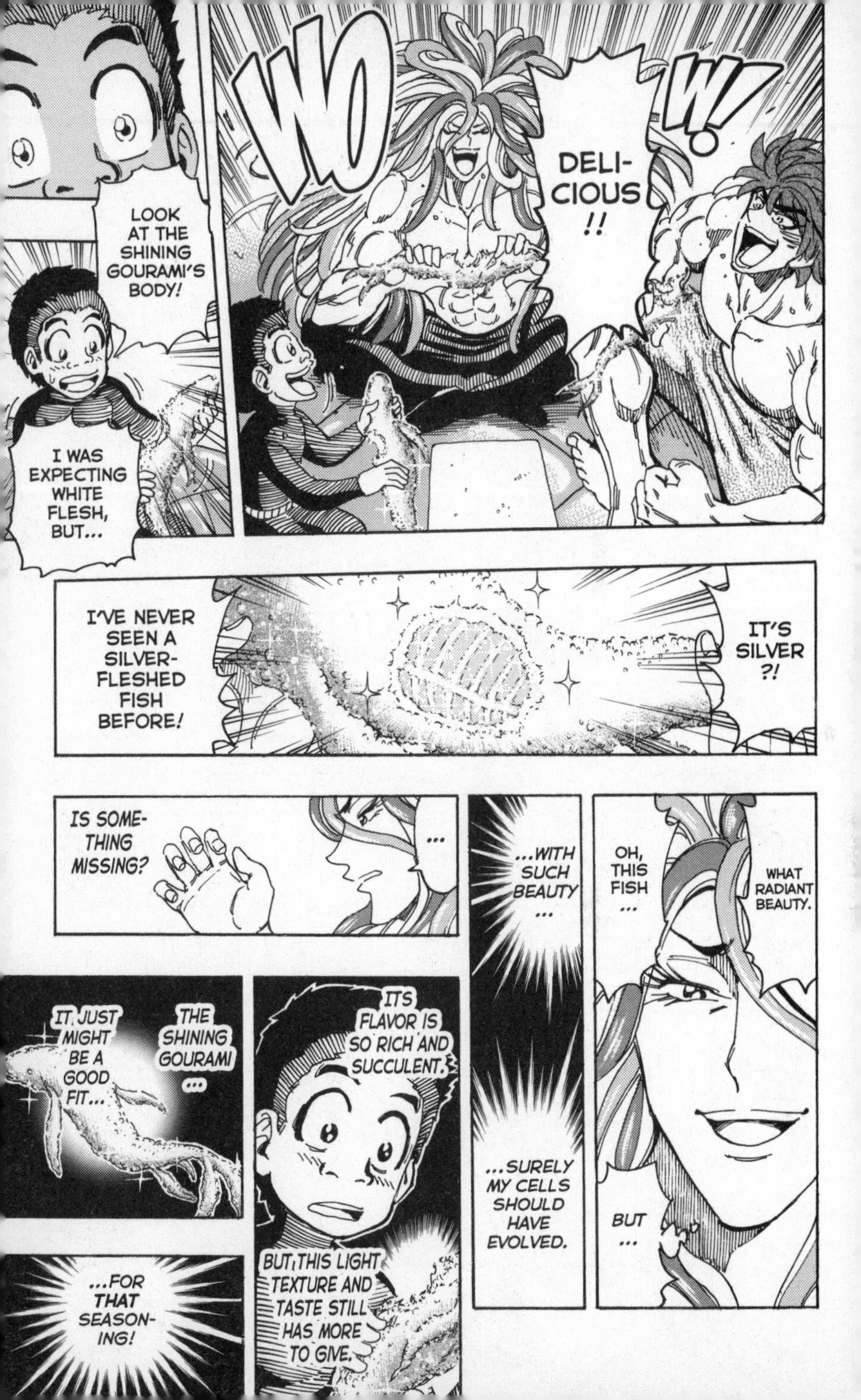
WOO W!
DELI-CIOUS !!
LOOK AT THE SHINING GOURAMI'S BODY!
I WAS EXPECTING WHITE FLESH, BUT...
IT'S SILVER ?!
I'VE NEVER SEEN A SILVER-FLESHED FISH BEFORE!
WHAT RADIANT BEAUTY.
OH, THIS FISH ...
BUT ...
...WITH SUCH BEAUTY ...
...SURELY MY CELLS SHOULD HAVE EVOLVED.
...
IS SOME-THING MISSING?
ITS FLAVOR IS SO RICH AND SUCCULENT.
BUT THIS LIGHT TEXTURE AND TASTE STILL HAS MORE TO GIVE.
THE SHINING GOURAMI ...
IT JUST MIGHT BE A GOOD FIT...
...FOR THAT SEASON-ING!

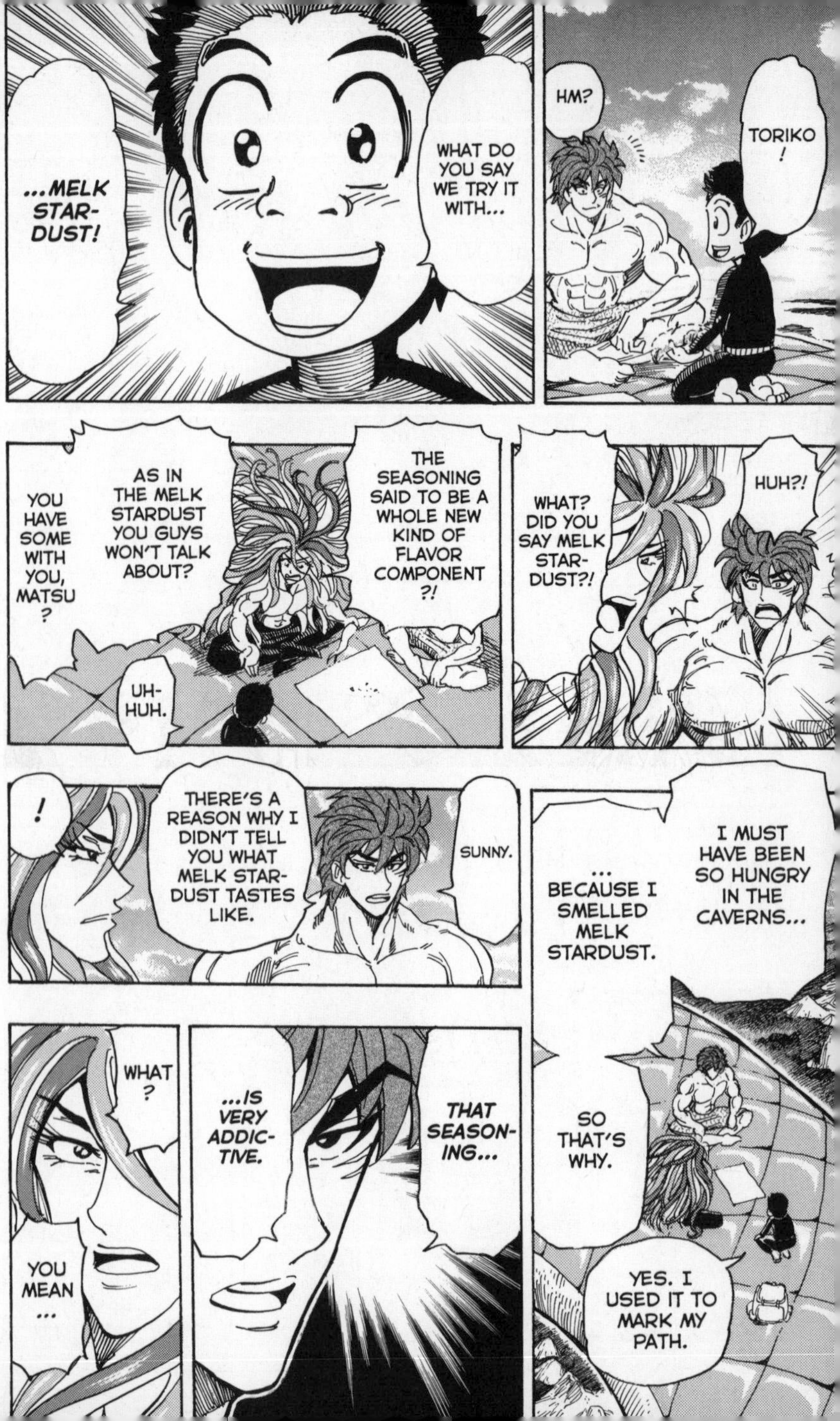
TORIKO!
HM?
WHAT DO YOU SAY WE TRY IT WITH...
...MELK STAR-DUST!
HUH?!
WHAT? DID YOU SAY MELK STAR-DUST?!
THE SEASONING SAID TO BE A WHOLE NEW KIND OF FLAVOR COMPONENT?!
AS IN THE MELK STARDUST YOU GUYS WON'T TALK ABOUT?
YOU HAVE SOME WITH YOU, MATSU?
UH-HUH.
I MUST HAVE BEEN SO HUNGRY IN THE CAVERNS...
...BECAUSE I SMELLED MELK STARDUST.
SO THAT'S WHY.
YES. I USED IT TO MARK MY PATH.
SUNNY.
THERE'S A REASON WHY I DIDN'T TELL YOU WHAT MELK STAR-DUST TASTES LIKE.
!
THAT SEASON-ING...
...IS VERY ADDIC-TIVE.
WHAT?
YOU MEAN...

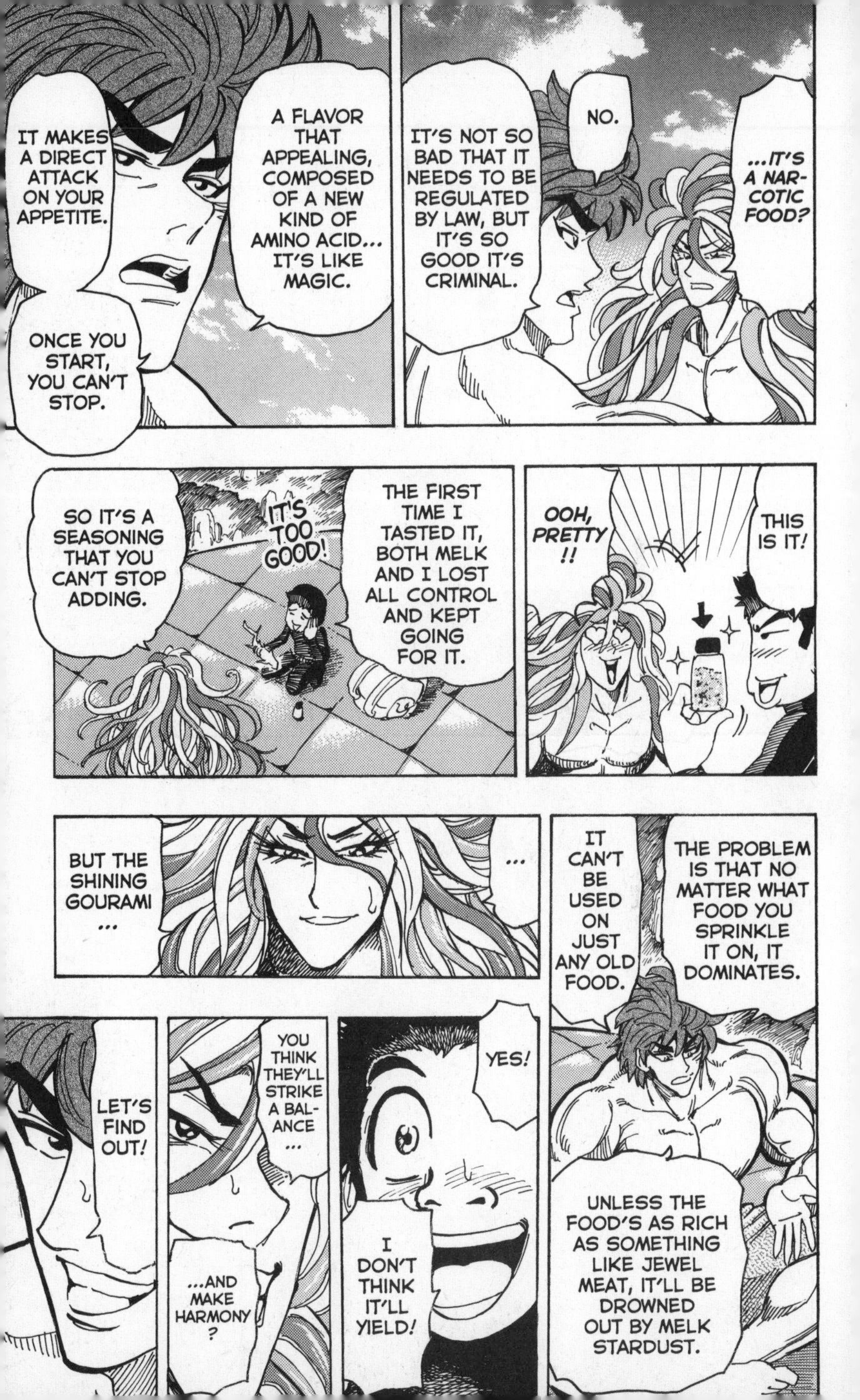
...IT'S A NARCOTIC FOOD?
NO.
IT'S NOT SO BAD THAT IT NEEDS TO BE REGULATED BY LAW, BUT IT'S SO GOOD IT'S CRIMINAL.
A FLAVOR THAT APPEALING, COMPOSED OF A NEW KIND OF AMINO ACID... IT'S LIKE MAGIC.
IT MAKES A DIRECT ATTACK ON YOUR APPETITE.
ONCE YOU START, YOU CAN'T STOP.
THIS IS IT!
OOH, PRETTY!!
THE FIRST TIME I TASTED IT, BOTH MELK AND I LOST ALL CONTROL AND KEPT GOING FOR IT.
IT'S TOO GOOD!
SO IT'S A SEASONING THAT YOU CAN'T STOP ADDING.
THE PROBLEM IS THAT NO MATTER WHAT FOOD YOU SPRINKLE IT ON, IT DOMINATES.
IT CAN'T BE USED ON JUST ANY OLD FOOD.
...
BUT THE SHINING GOURAMI ...
UNLESS THE FOOD'S AS RICH AS SOMETHING LIKE JEWEL MEAT, IT'LL BE DROWNED OUT BY MELK STARDUST.
YES!
I DON'T THINK IT'LL YIELD!
YOU THINK THEY'LL STRIKE A BALANCE ...
...AND MAKE HARMONY?
LET'S FIND OUT!

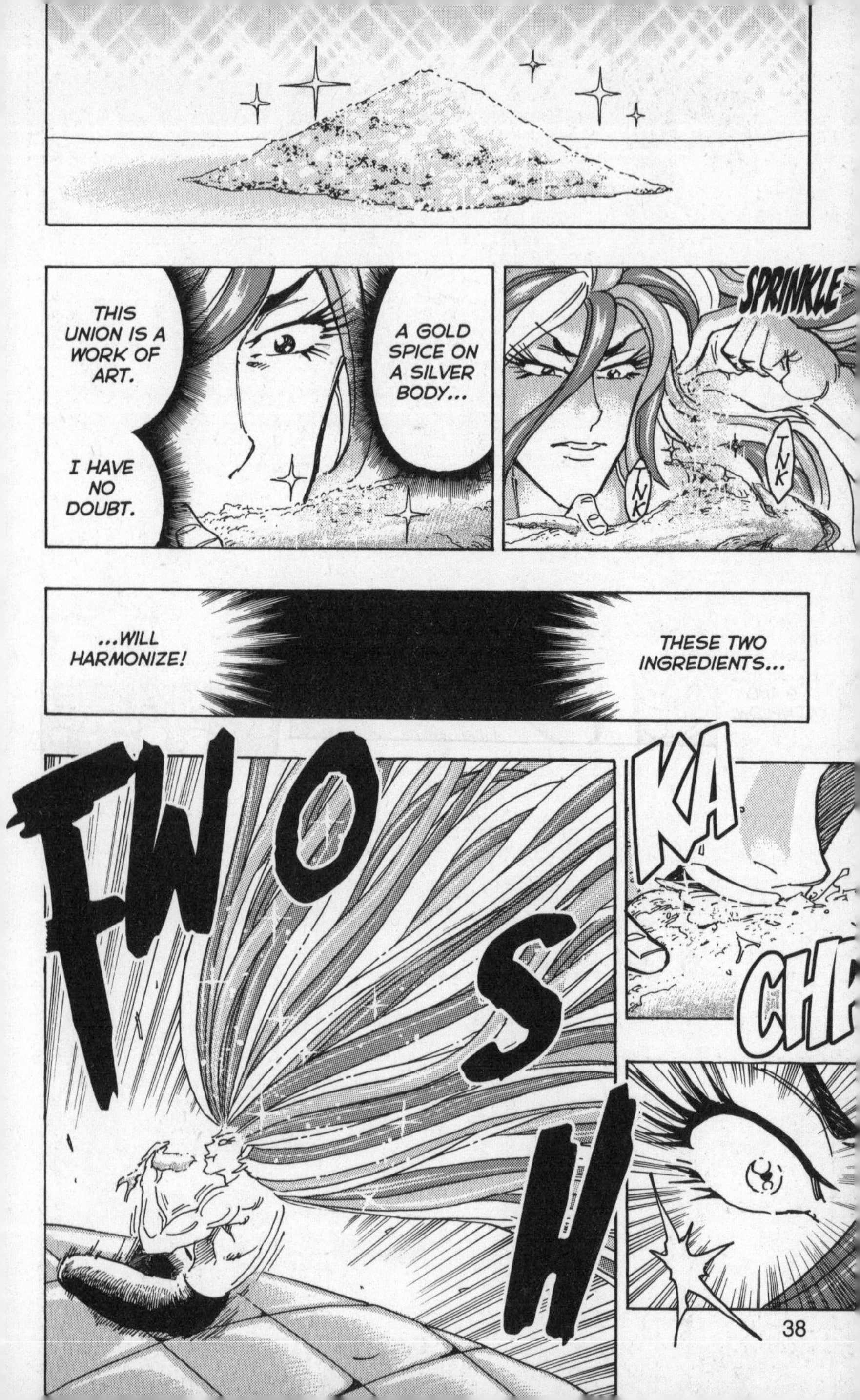
SPRINKLE
TNK
TNK
A GOLD SPICE ON A SILVER BODY...
THIS UNION IS A WORK OF ART.
I HAVE NO DOUBT.
THESE TWO INGREDIENTS...
...WILL HARMONIZE!
KA
CH
FWOSH

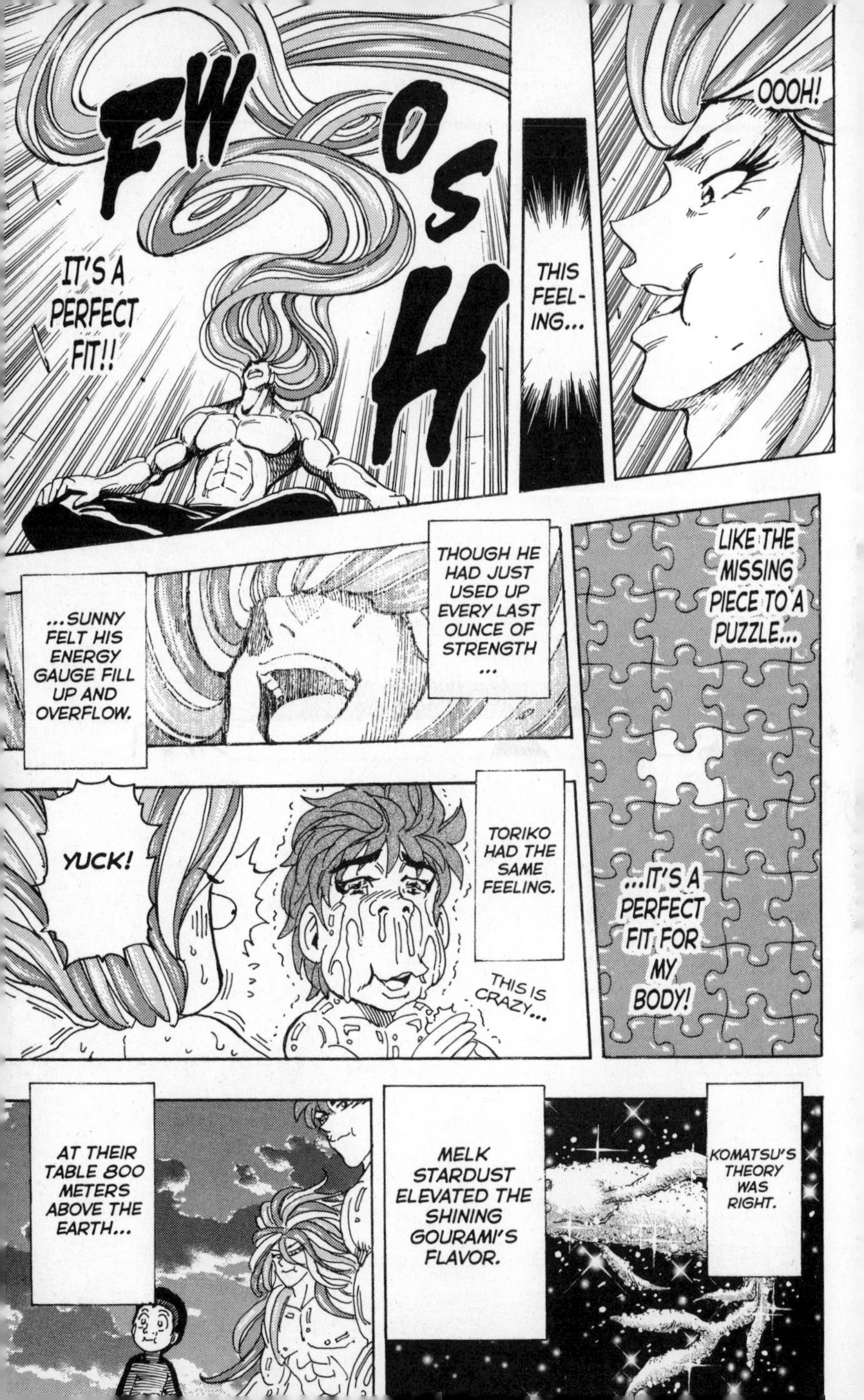
OOOH!
THIS FEEL-ING...
FWOOSH
IT'S A PERFECT FIT!!
LIKE THE MISSING PIECE TO A PUZZLE...
...IT'S A PERFECT FIT FOR MY BODY!
THOUGH HE HAD JUST USED UP EVERY LAST OUNCE OF STRENGTH...
...SUNNY FELT HIS ENERGY GAUGE FILL UP AND OVERFLOW.
TORIKO HAD THE SAME FEELING.
THIS IS CRAZY...
YUCK!
KOMATSU'S THEORY WAS RIGHT.
MELK STARDUST ELEVATED THE SHINING GOURAMI'S FLAVOR.
AT THEIR TABLE 800 METERS ABOVE THE EARTH...

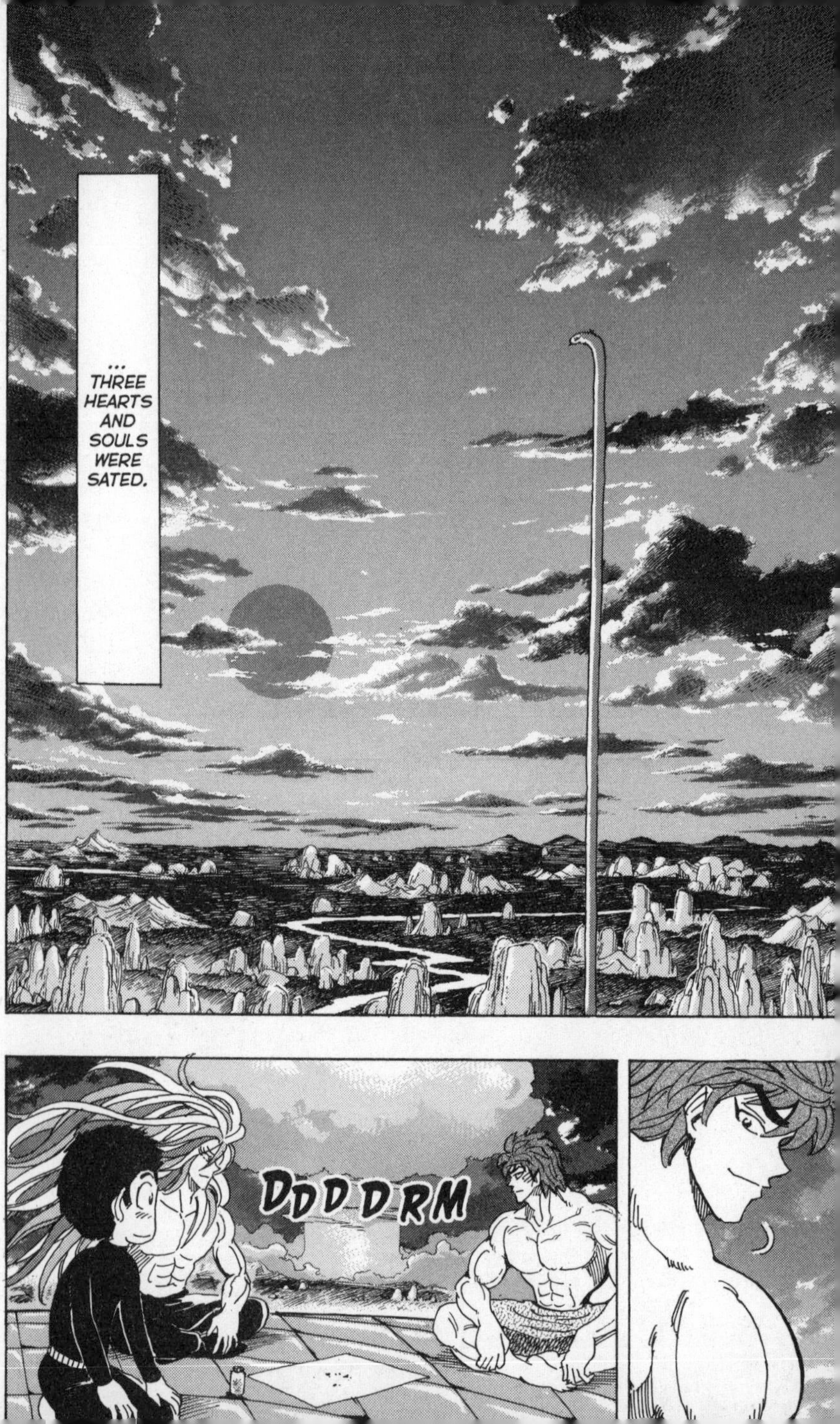

... THREE HEARTS AND SOULS WERE SATED.
DDDDRM

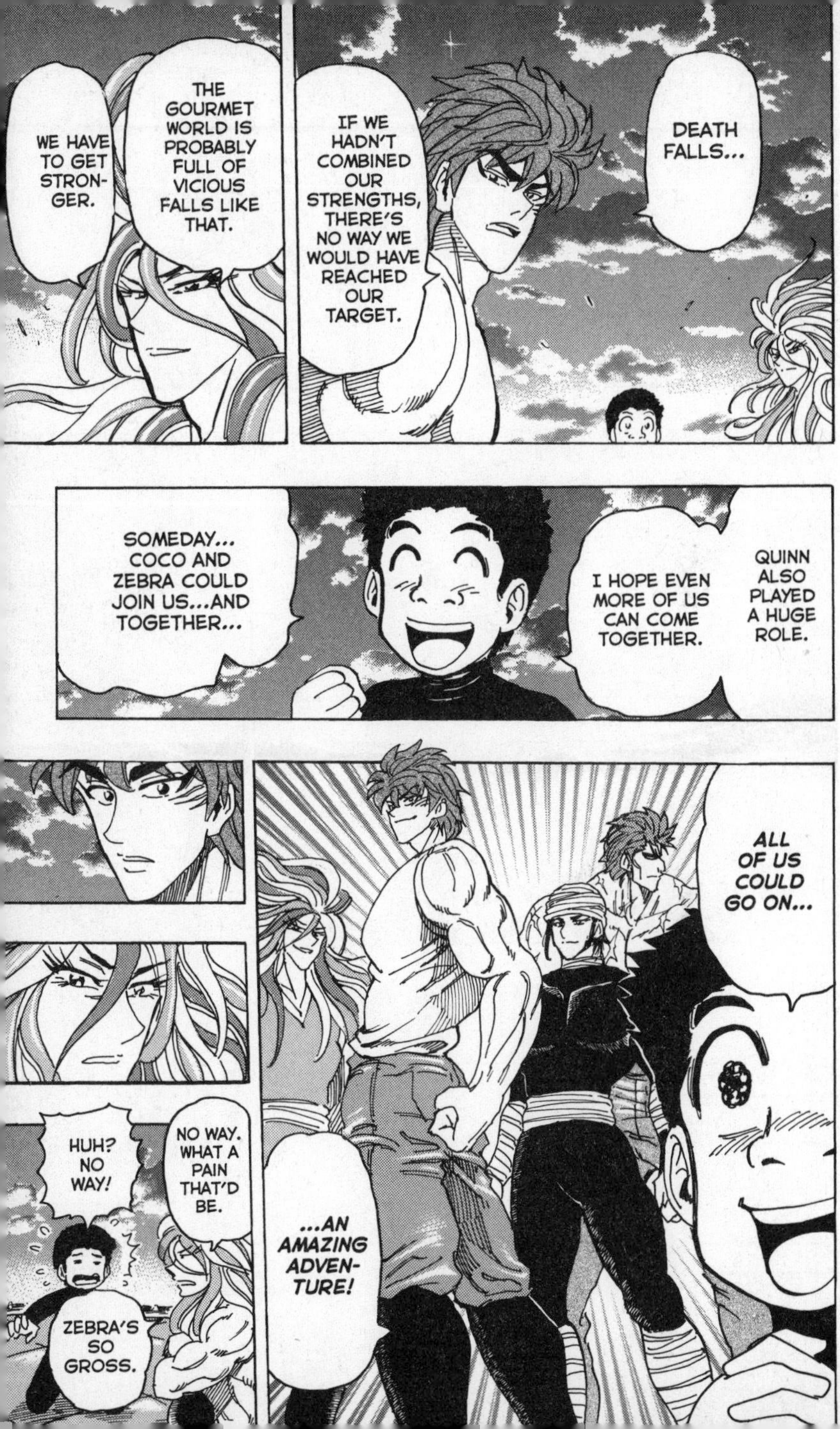
DEATH FALLS...
IF WE HADN'T COMBINED OUR STRENGTHS, THERE'S NO WAY WE WOULD HAVE REACHED OUR TARGET.
THE GOURMET WORLD IS PROBABLY FULL OF VICIOUS FALLS LIKE THAT.
WE HAVE TO GET STRONGER.
QUINN ALSO PLAYED A HUGE ROLE.
I HOPE EVEN MORE OF US CAN COME TOGETHER.
SOMEDAY... COCO AND ZEBRA COULD JOIN US...AND TOGETHER...
ALL OF US COULD GO ON...
...AN AMAZING ADVENTURE!
NO WAY. WHAT A PAIN THAT'D BE.
HUH? NO WAY!
ZEBRA'S SO GROSS.

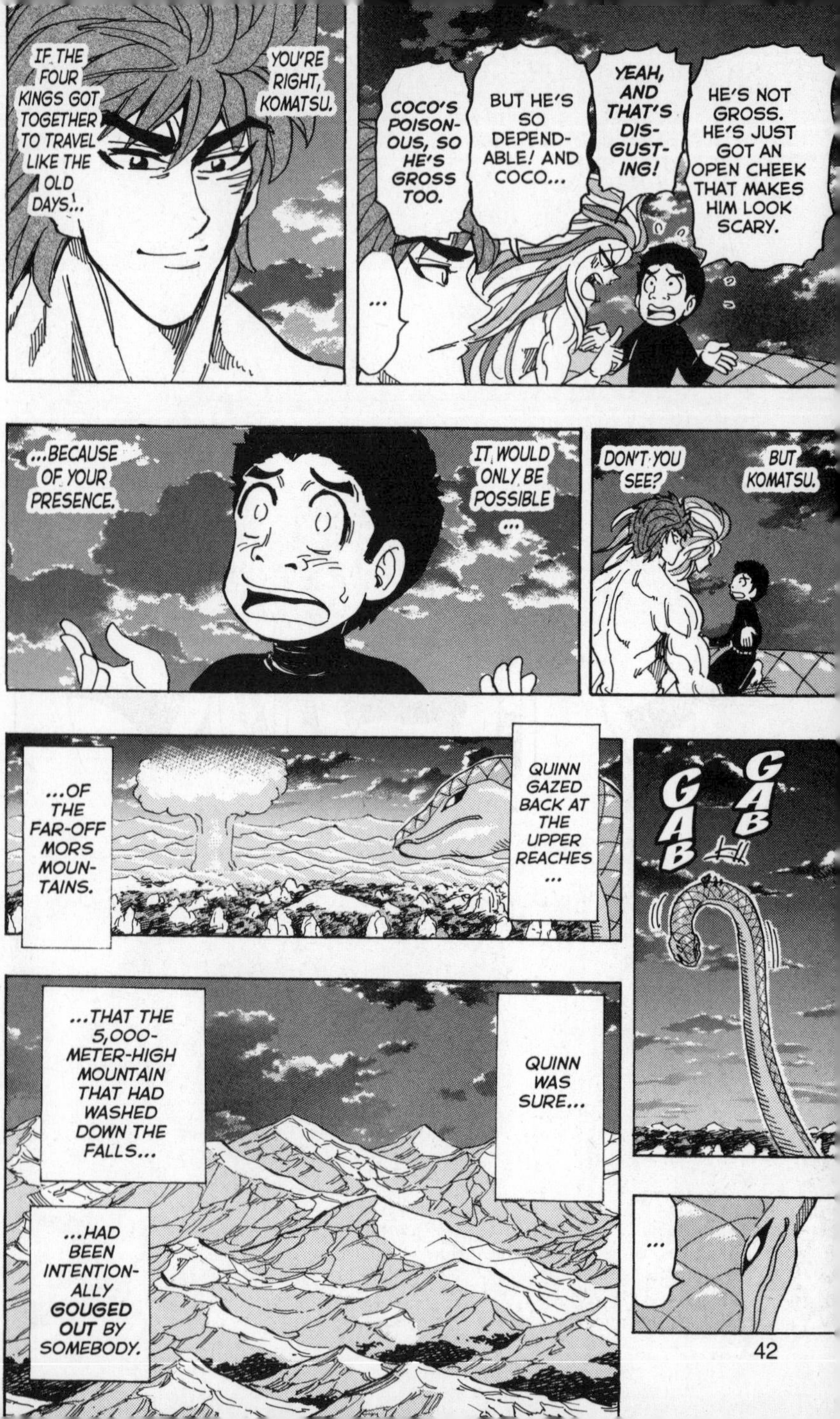
HE'S NOT GROSS. HE'S JUST GOT AN OPEN CHEEK THAT MAKES HIM LOOK SCARY.
YEAH, AND THAT'S DIS-GUST-ING!
BUT HE'S SO DEPEND-ABLE! AND COCO...
COCO'S POISON-OUS, SO HE'S GROSS TOO.
...
YOU'RE RIGHT, KOMATSU.
IF THE FOUR KINGS GOT TOGETHER TO TRAVEL LIKE THE OLD DAYS...
BUT KOMATSU.
DON'T YOU SEE?
IT WOULD ONLY BE POSSIBLE...
...BECAUSE OF YOUR PRESENCE.
GAB GAB
QUINN GAZED BACK AT THE UPPER REACHES...
...OF THE FAR-OFF MORS MOUN-TAINS.
...
QUINN WAS SURE...
...THAT THE 5,000-METER-HIGH MOUNTAIN THAT HAD WASHED DOWN THE FALLS...
...HAD BEEN INTENTION-ALLY GOUGED OUT BY SOMEBODY.

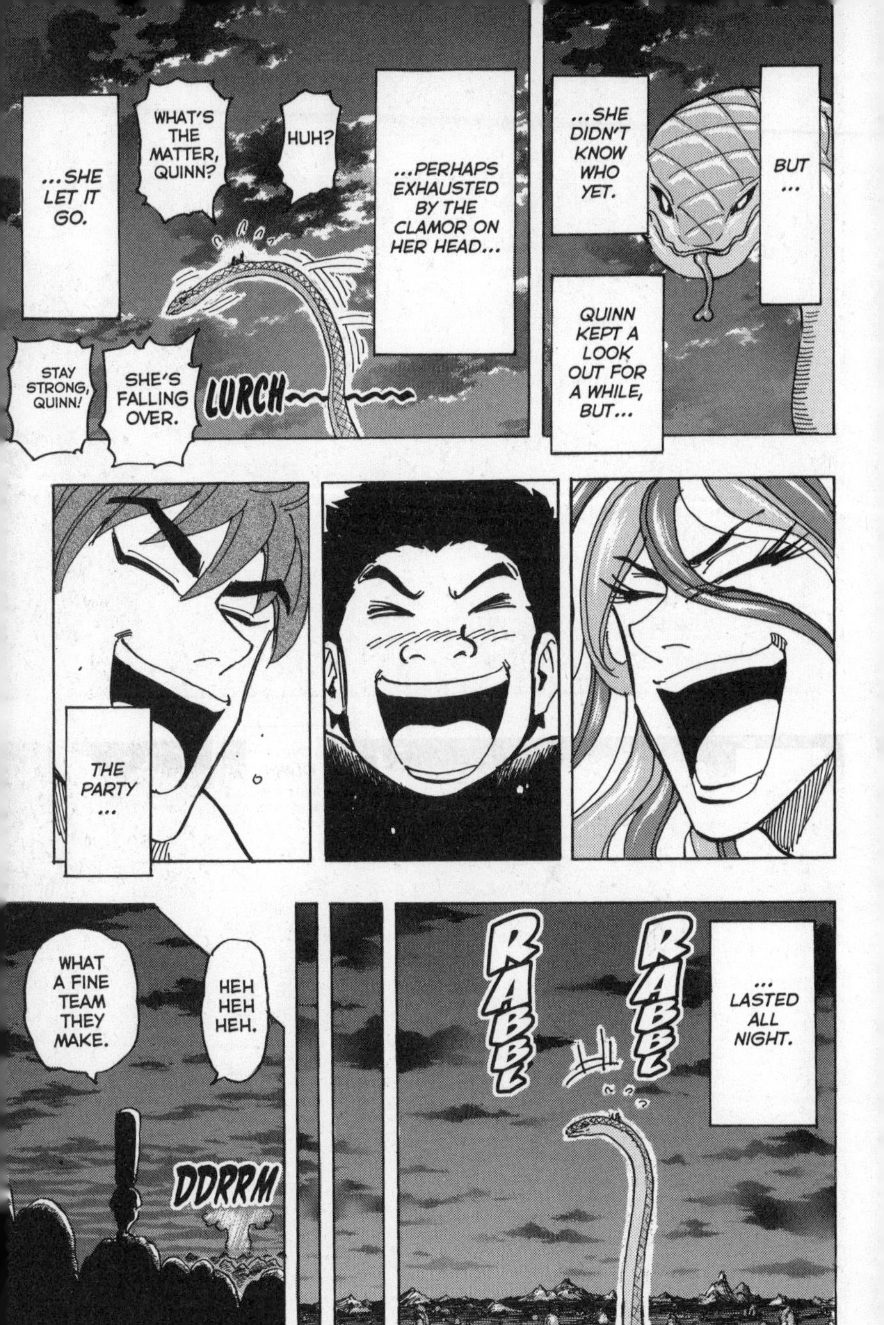
BUT...
...SHE DIDN'T KNOW WHO YET.
QUINN KEPT A LOOK OUT FOR A WHILE, BUT...
...PERHAPS EXHAUSTED BY THE CLAMOR ON HER HEAD...
HUH?
WHAT'S THE MATTER, QUINN?
...SHE LET IT GO.
LURCH
SHE'S FALLING OVER.
STAY STRONG, QUINN!
THE PARTY...
...LASTED ALL NIGHT.
RABBL
RABBL
HEH HEH HEH.
WHAT A FINE TEAM THEY MAKE.
DDRRM

TORIKO

GOURMET CHECKLIST

Vol. 186

MAGMA TORTOISE

CAPTURE LEVEL: 70

HABITAT: DEATH SEASONS FOREST

LENGTH: 1,700 METERS

HEIGHT: ---

WEIGHT: 65 MILLION TONS (ESTIMATE)

PRICE: 100 G / 30,000 YEN; 1 LITER OF
MAGMA / 150,000 YEN

"FOREST GOBLIN"
MAGMA TORTOISE*
CAPTURE LEVEL 70

SCALE

NICKNAMED THE "FOREST GOBLIN," THIS GIANT TORTOISE REIGNS OVER THE
MILLIONS OF FEROCIOUS CREATURES AWAKENED IN THE DEATH SEASONS FOREST'S
MONSTER SEASON. IT'S THE STRONGEST AMONG A COHORT OF MONSTERS WHOSE
AVERAGE CAPTURE LEVEL IS 60. ITS MAGMA IS A DELICIOUS AND UNRIVALED
RESTORATIVE WHEN PREPARED CORRECTLY, BUT PROCURING THE RAW INGREDIENT
IS, SHALL WE SAY, QUITE DIFFICULT. EVERY YEAR, GOURMET HUNTERS ENTER THE
DEATH SEASONS FOREST DURING MONSTER SEASON TO CLAIM THE MAGMA
TORTOISE'S MAGMA, BUT MOST OF THEM ARE NEVER HEARD FROM AGAIN.

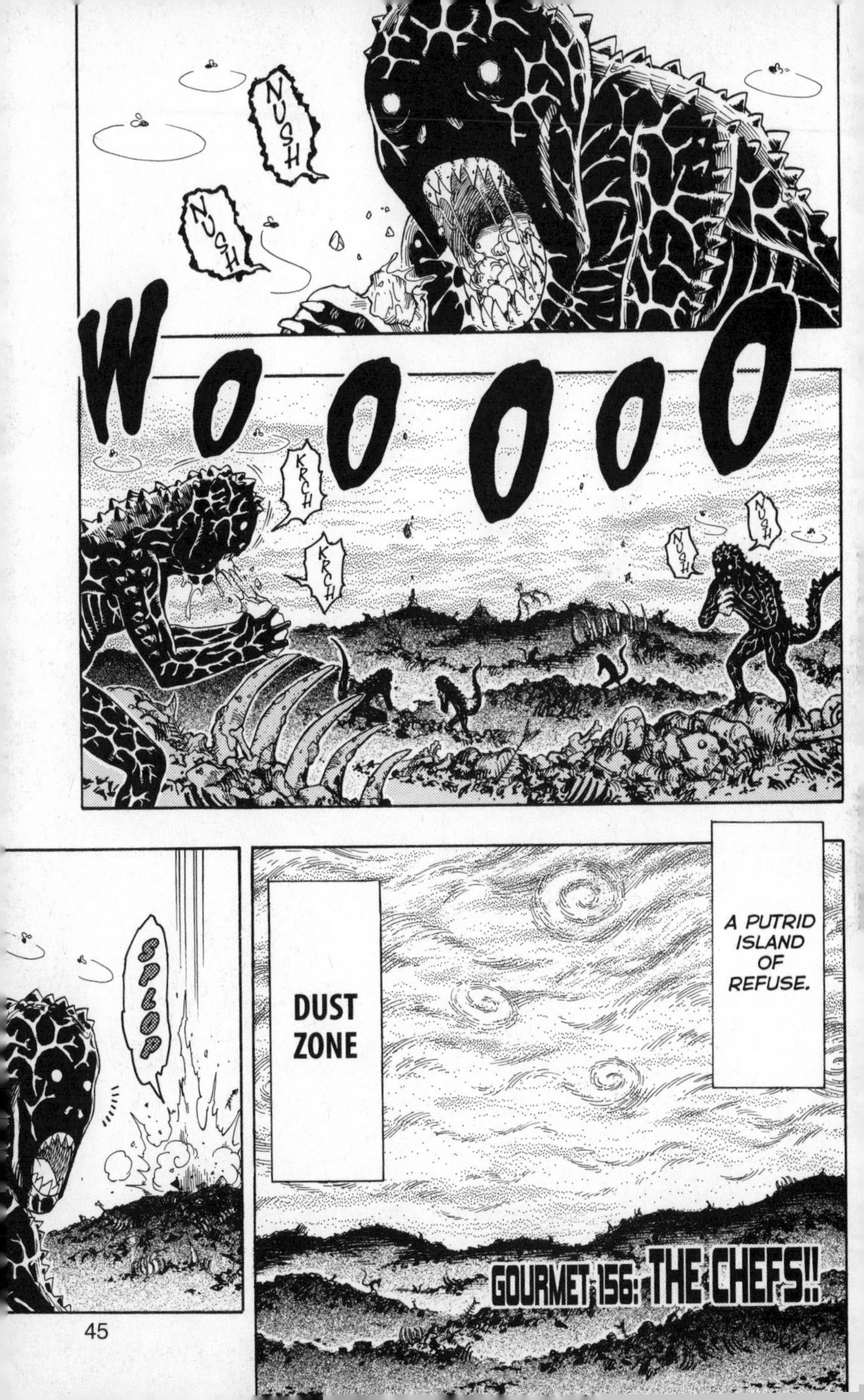
NUSH
NUSH
WOOOOOO
NUSH
NUSH
KRCH
KRCH
A PUTRID ISLAND OF REFUSE.
DUST ZONE
GOURMET 156: THE CHEFS!!
SPLOP

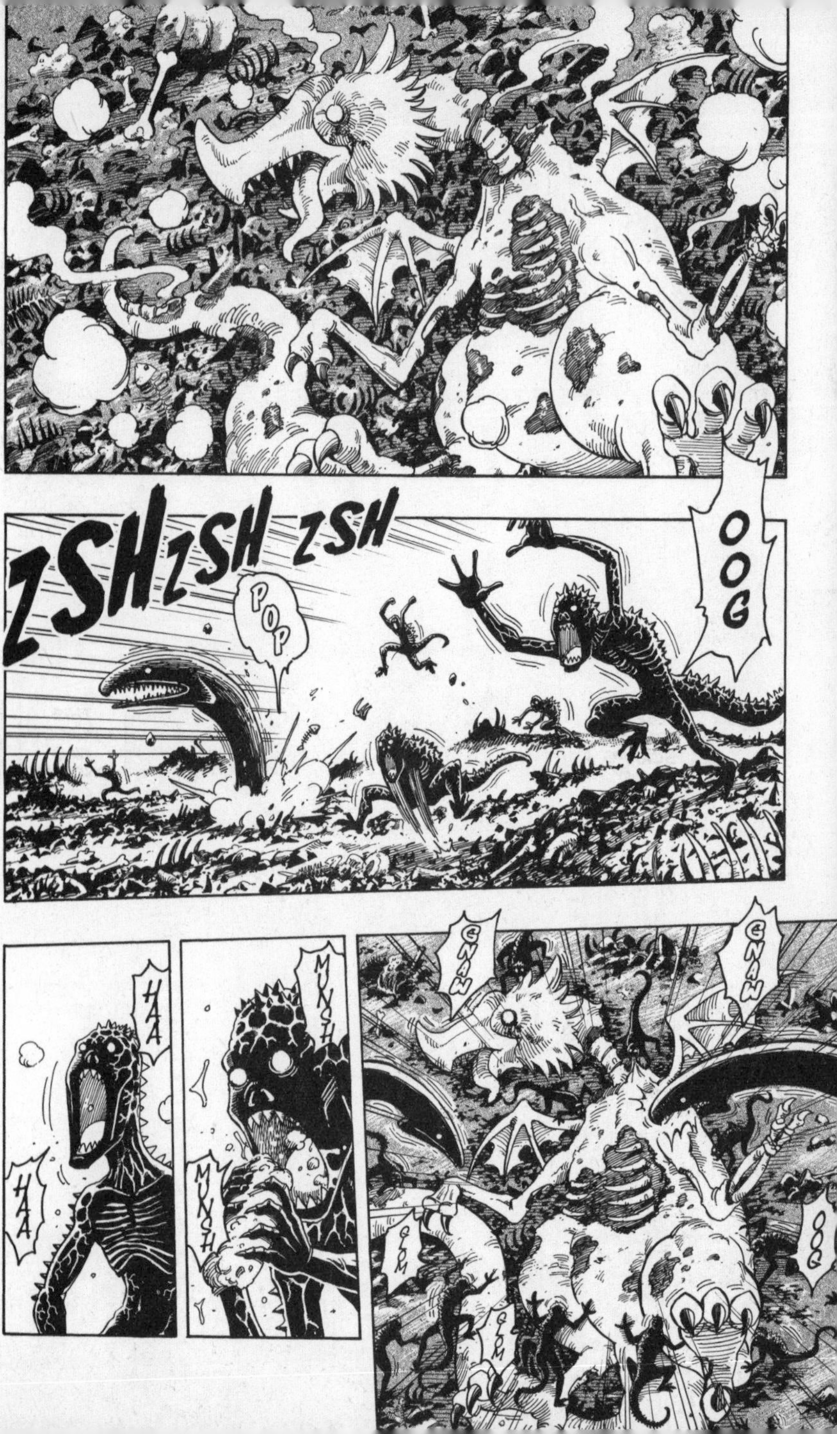
OOG
ZSH ZSH ZSH
POP
GNAW
GNAW
OOG
GLOM
GLOM
MUNCH
MUNCH
HAA
HAA

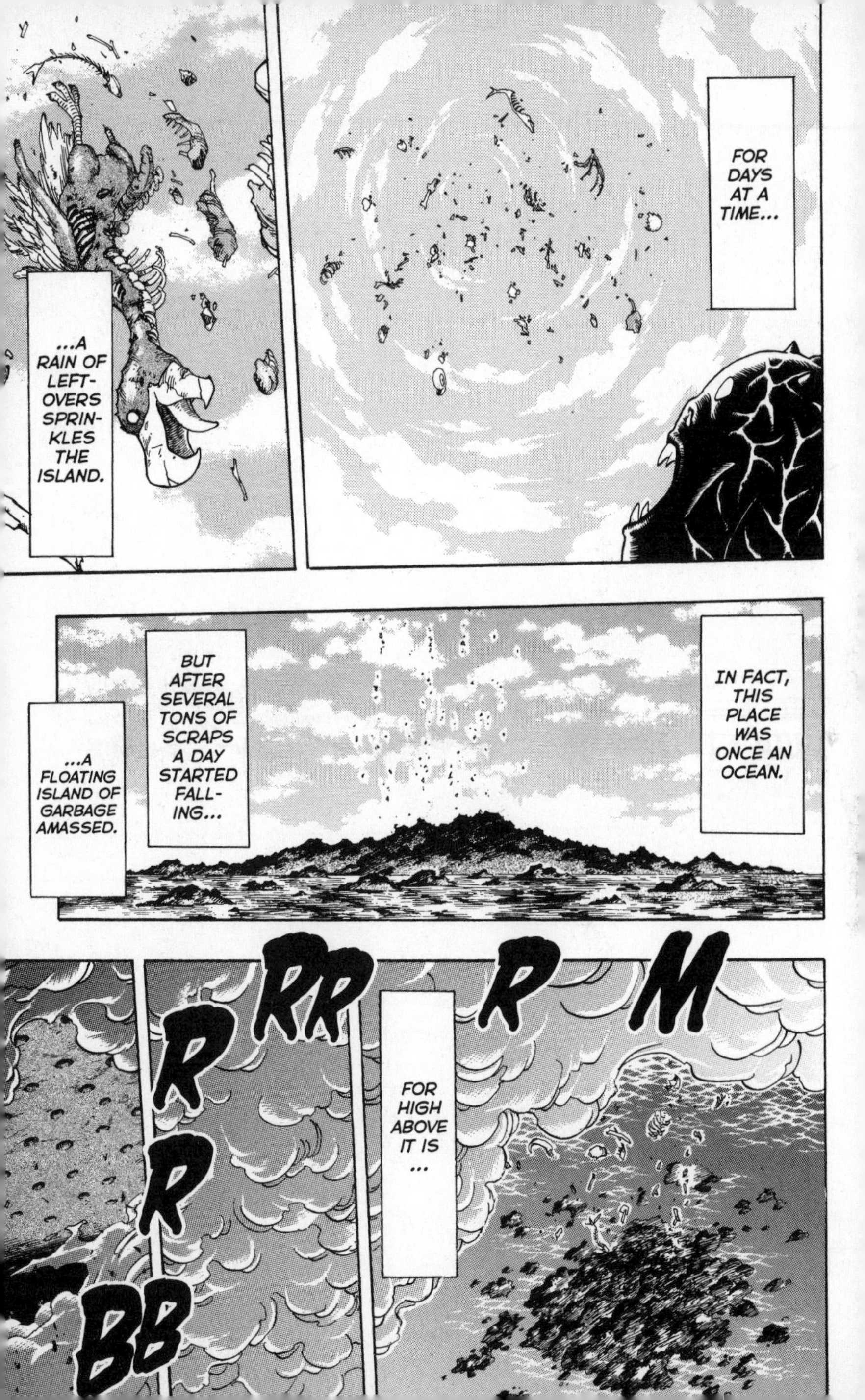
FOR DAYS AT A TIME...
...A RAIN OF LEFT-OVERS SPRIN-KLES THE ISLAND.
IN FACT, THIS PLACE WAS ONCE AN OCEAN.
BUT AFTER SEVERAL TONS OF SCRAPS A DAY STARTED FALL-ING...
...A FLOATING ISLAND OF GARBAGE AMASSED.
RR R M
R R BB
FOR HIGH ABOVE IT IS ...

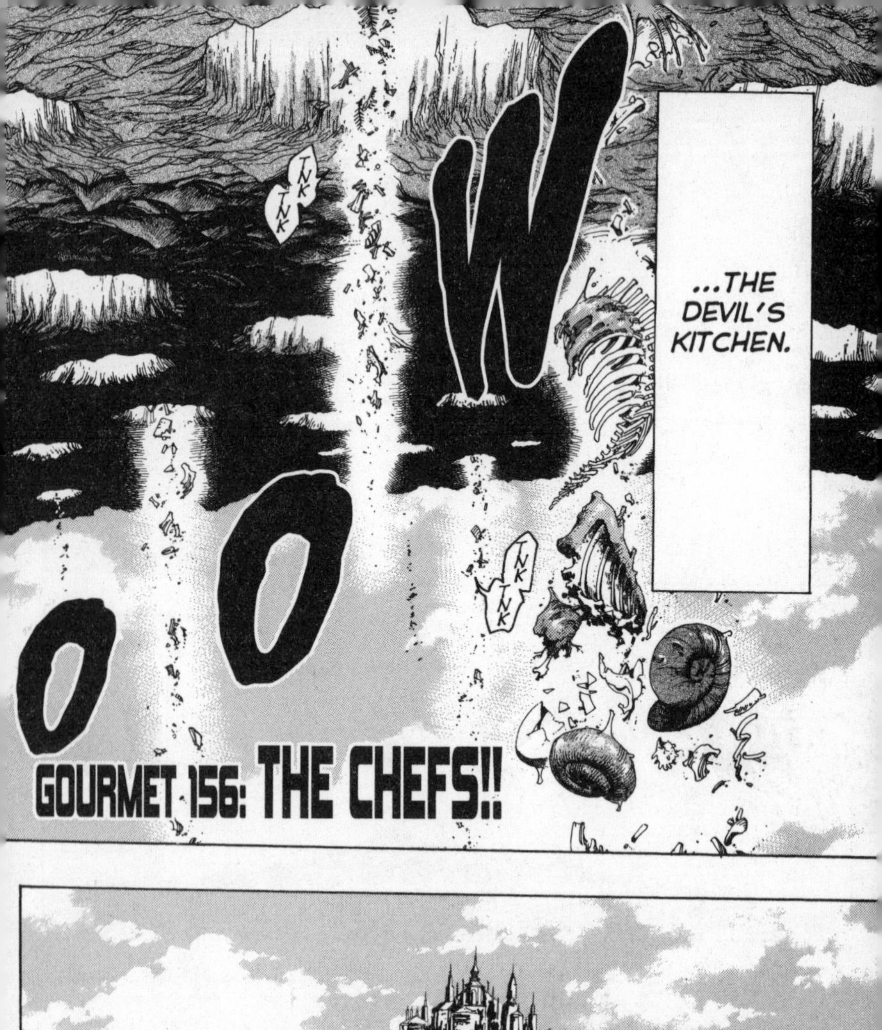
...THE DEVIL'S KITCHEN.
WOO
TNK TNK
TNK TNK

GOURMET 156: THE CHEFS!!

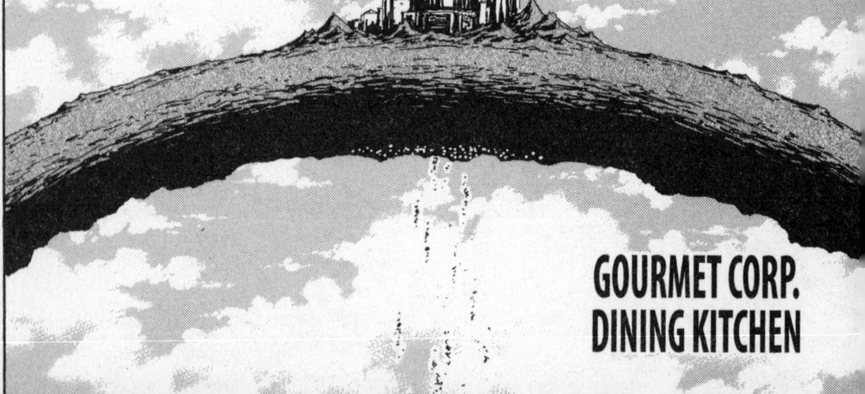
GOURMET CORP.
DINING KITCHEN

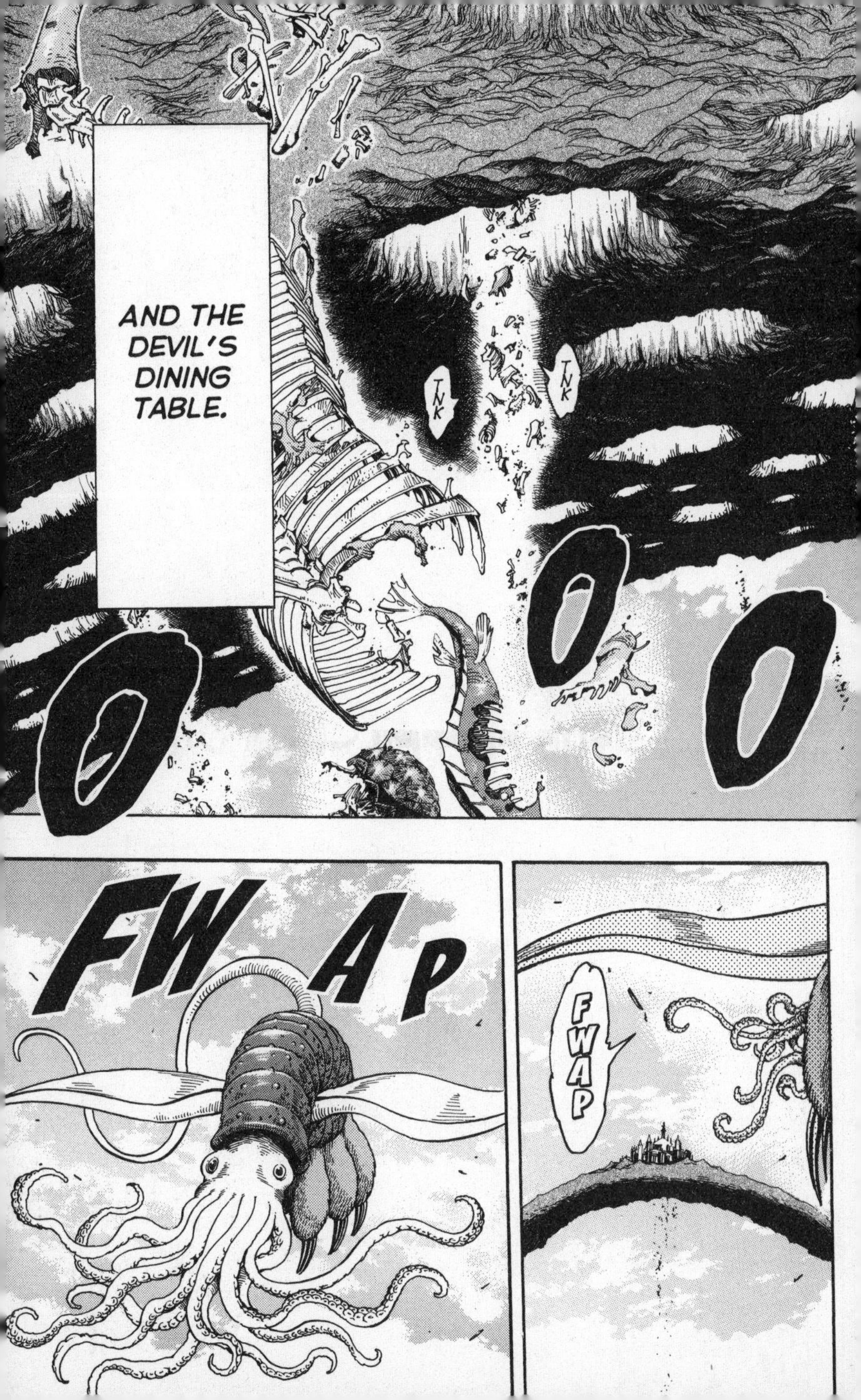
AND THE DEVIL'S DINING TABLE.
TNK
TNK
FWAP
FWAP

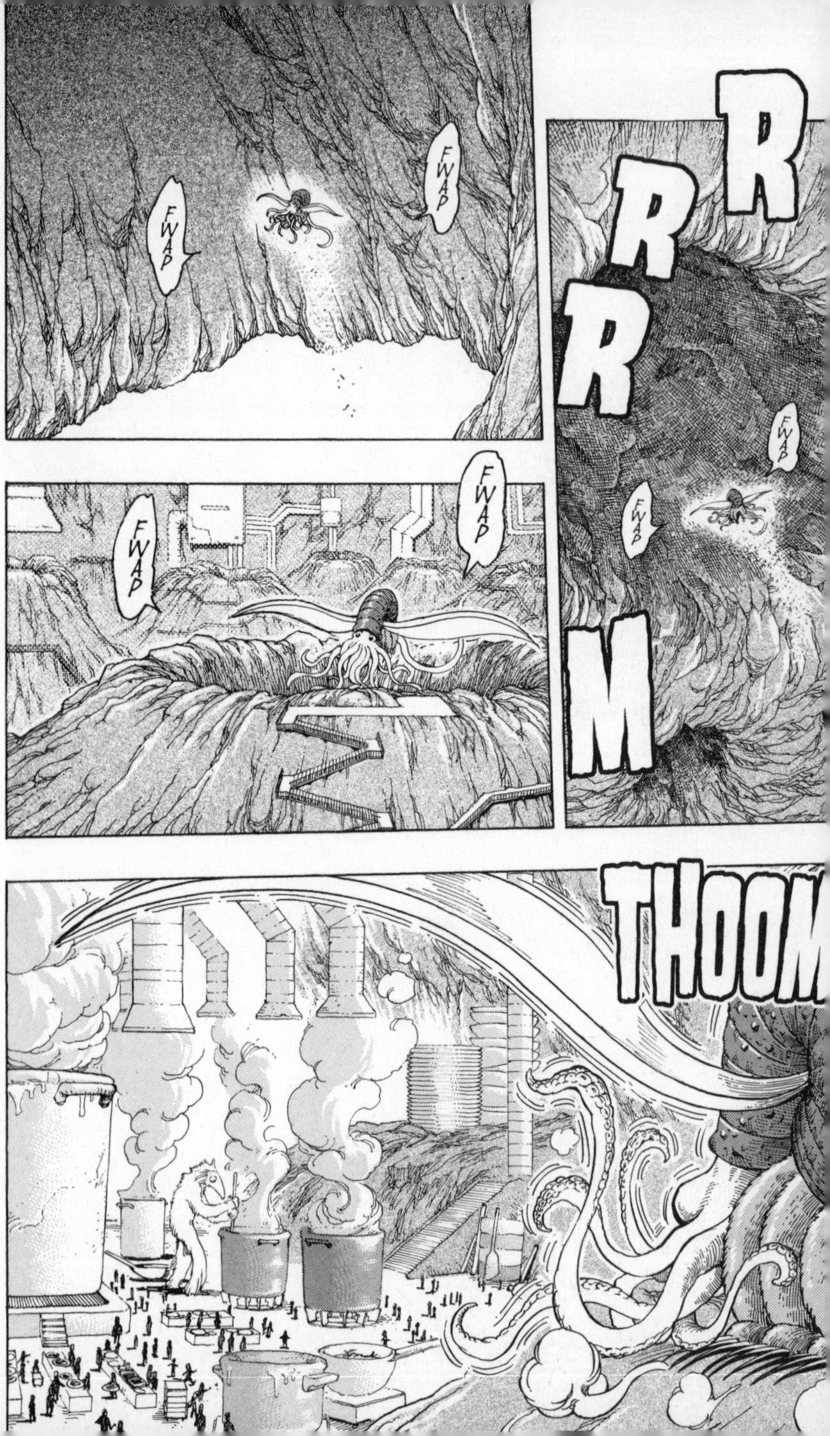
RRRM
FWAP
FWAP
FWAP
FWAP
FWAP
FWAP
THOOM

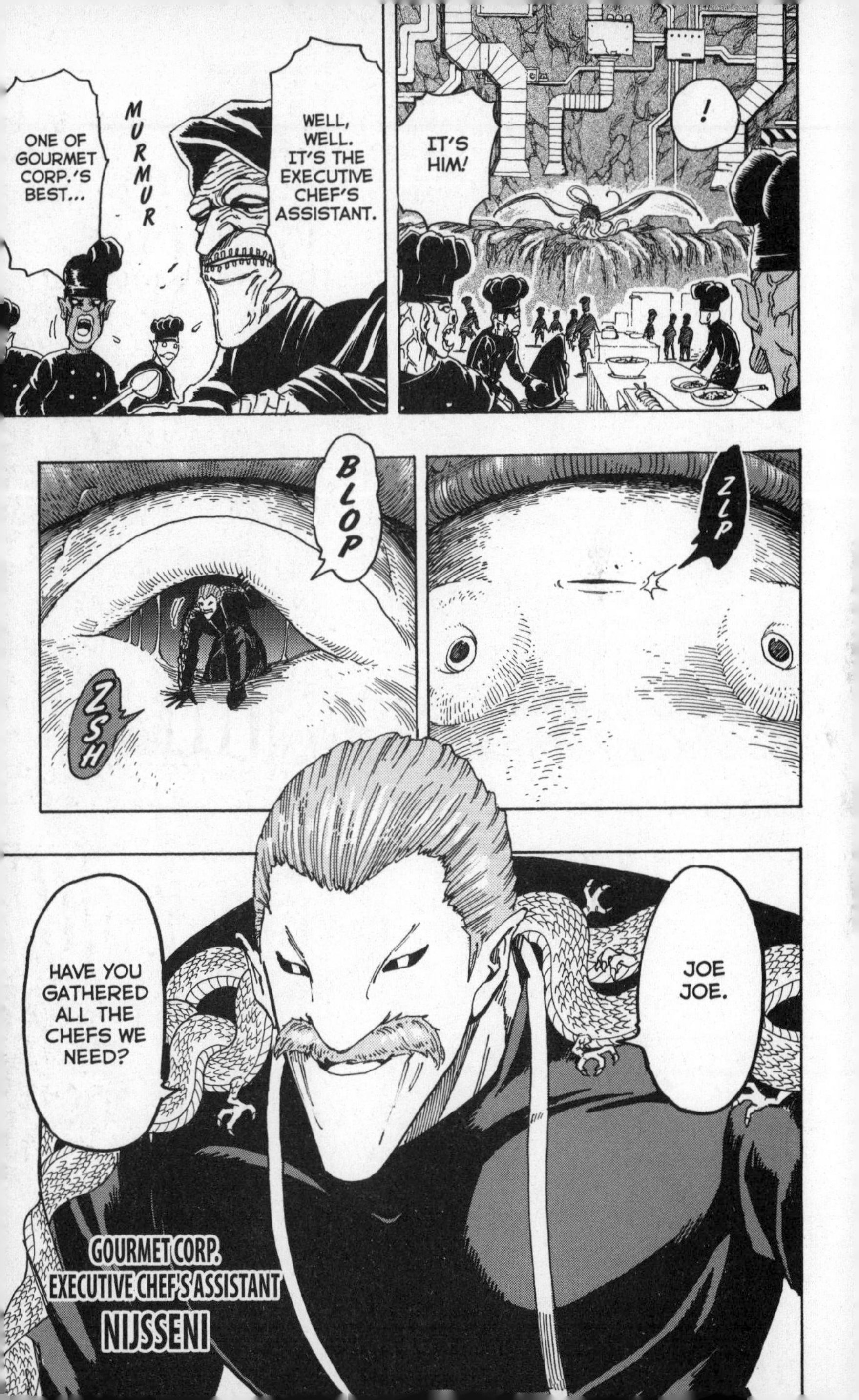
!
IT'S HIM!
WELL, WELL. IT'S THE EXECUTIVE CHEF'S ASSISTANT.
MURMUR
ONE OF GOURMET CORP.'S BEST...
ZLP
BLOP
ZSH
JOE JOE.
HAVE YOU GATHERED ALL THE CHEFS WE NEED?
GOURMET CORP. EXECUTIVE CHEF'S ASSISTANT NIJSSENI

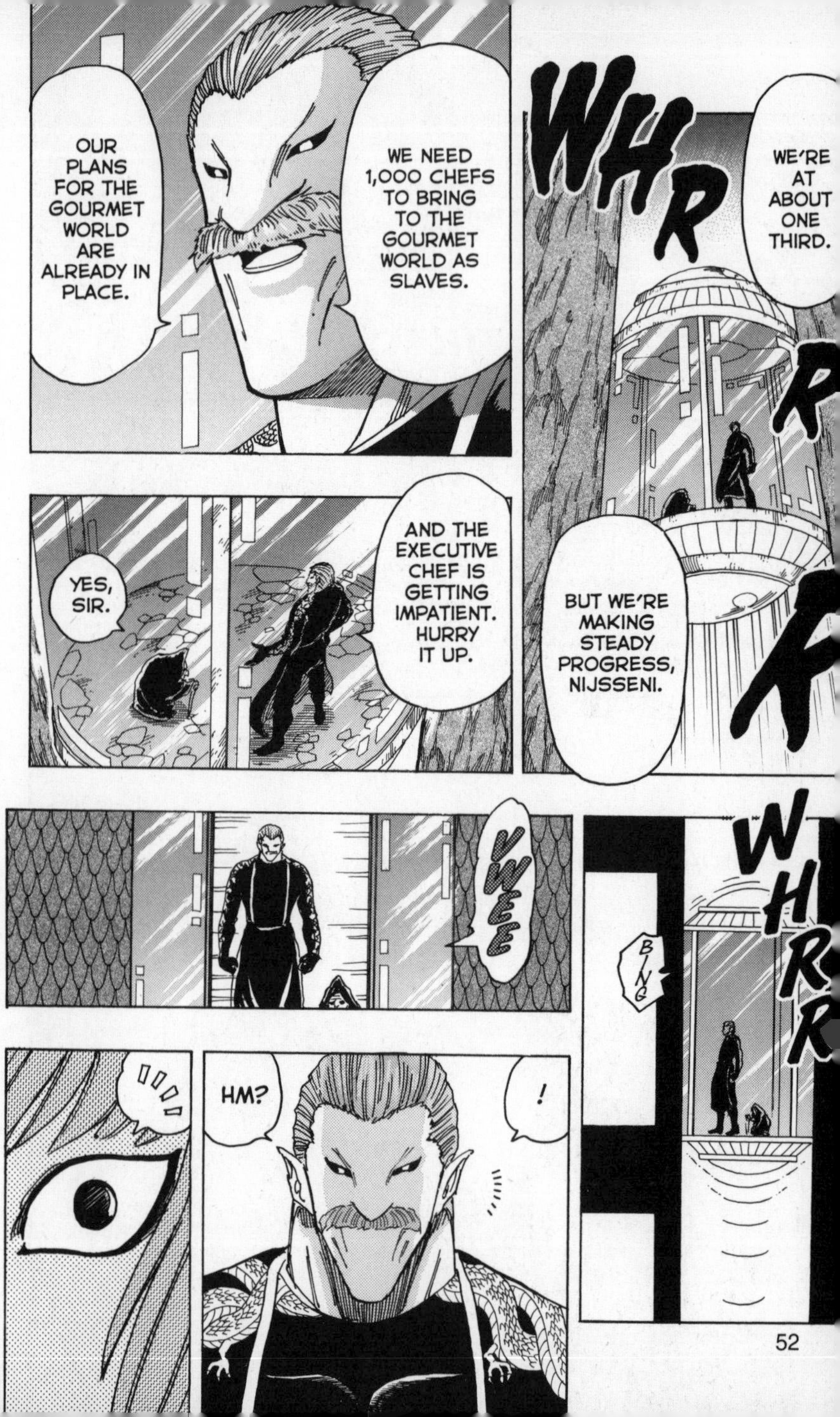

WHRRRR
WE'RE AT ABOUT ONE THIRD.
BUT WE'RE MAKING STEADY PROGRESS, NIJSSENI.
OUR PLANS FOR THE GOURMET WORLD ARE ALREADY IN PLACE.
WE NEED 1,000 CHEFS TO BRING TO THE GOURMET WORLD AS SLAVES.
AND THE EXECUTIVE CHEF IS GETTING IMPATIENT. HURRY IT UP.
YES, SIR.
WHRRR
BING
VWEE
!
HM?

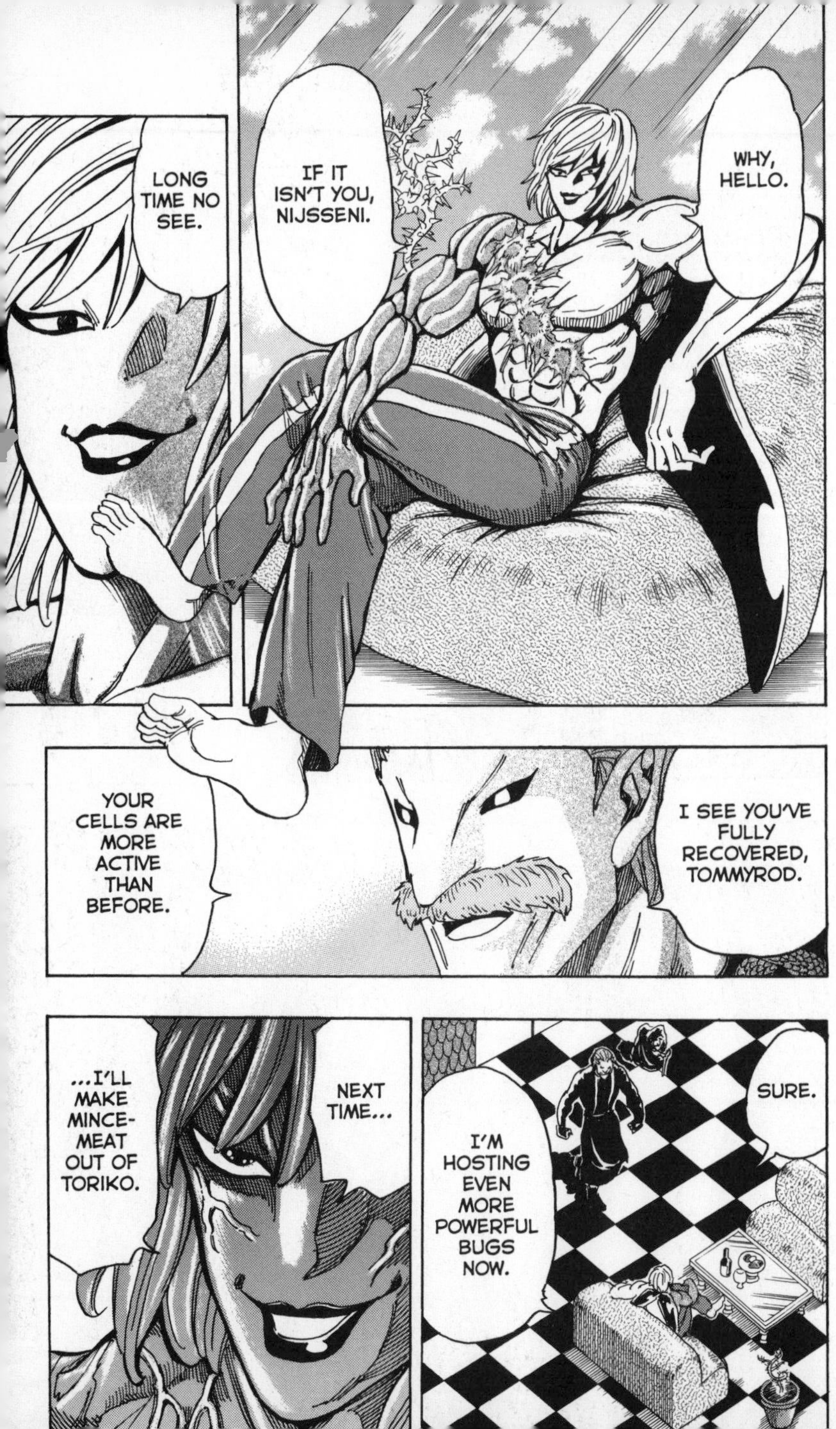
WHY, HELLO.
IF IT ISN'T YOU, NIJSSENI.
LONG TIME NO SEE.
I SEE YOU'VE FULLY RECOVERED, TOMMYROD.
YOUR CELLS ARE MORE ACTIVE THAN BEFORE.
SURE.
I'M HOSTING EVEN MORE POWERFUL BUGS NOW.
NEXT TIME...
...I'LL MAKE MINCE-MEAT OUT OF TORIKO.

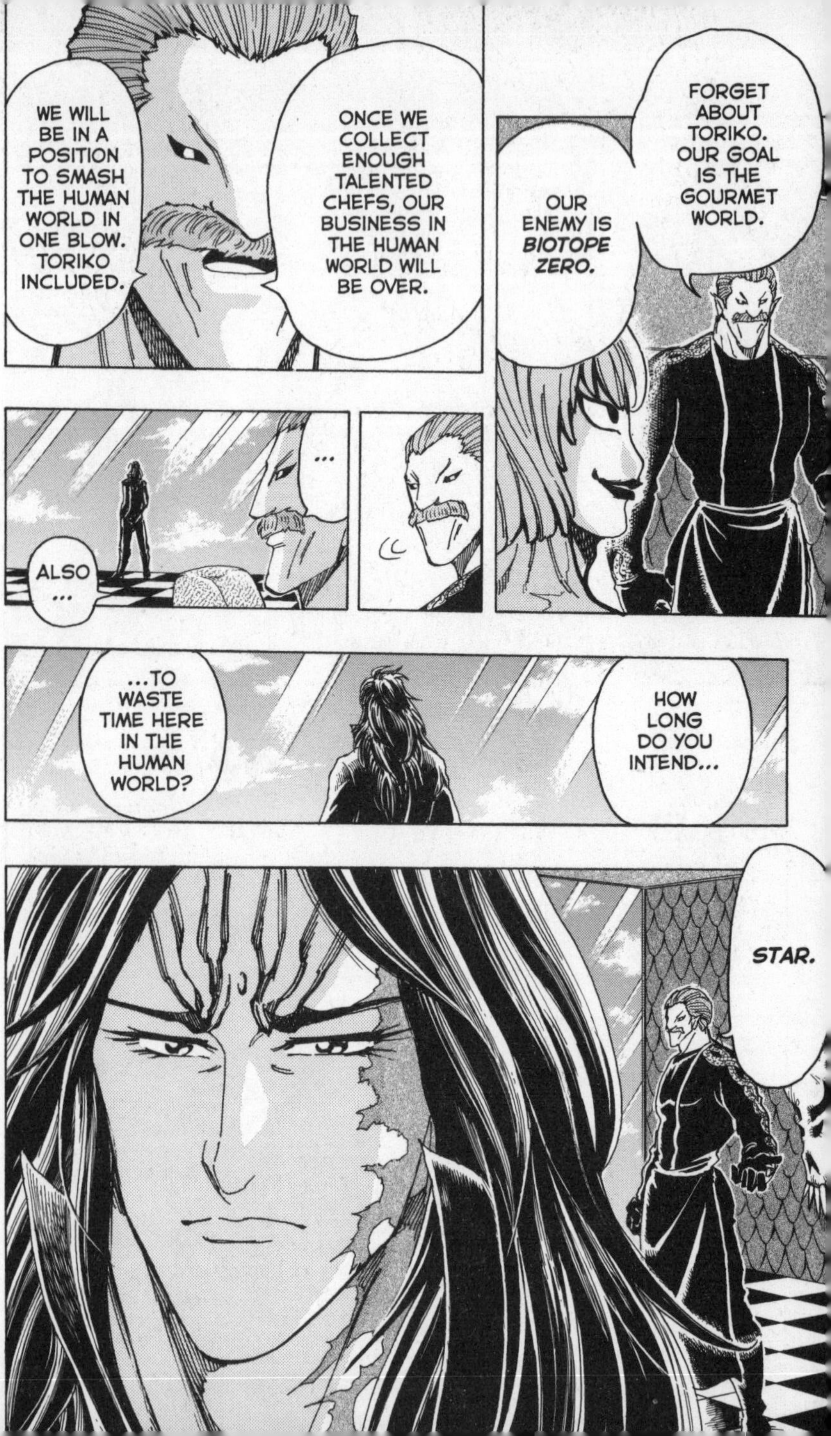
FORGET ABOUT TORIKO. OUR GOAL IS THE GOURMET WORLD.
OUR ENEMY IS *BIOTOPE ZERO.*
ONCE WE COLLECT ENOUGH TALENTED CHEFS, OUR BUSINESS IN THE HUMAN WORLD WILL BE OVER.
WE WILL BE IN A POSITION TO SMASH THE HUMAN WORLD IN ONE BLOW. TORIKO INCLUDED.
...
ALSO ...
HOW LONG DO YOU INTEND...
...TO WASTE TIME HERE IN THE HUMAN WORLD?
STAR.

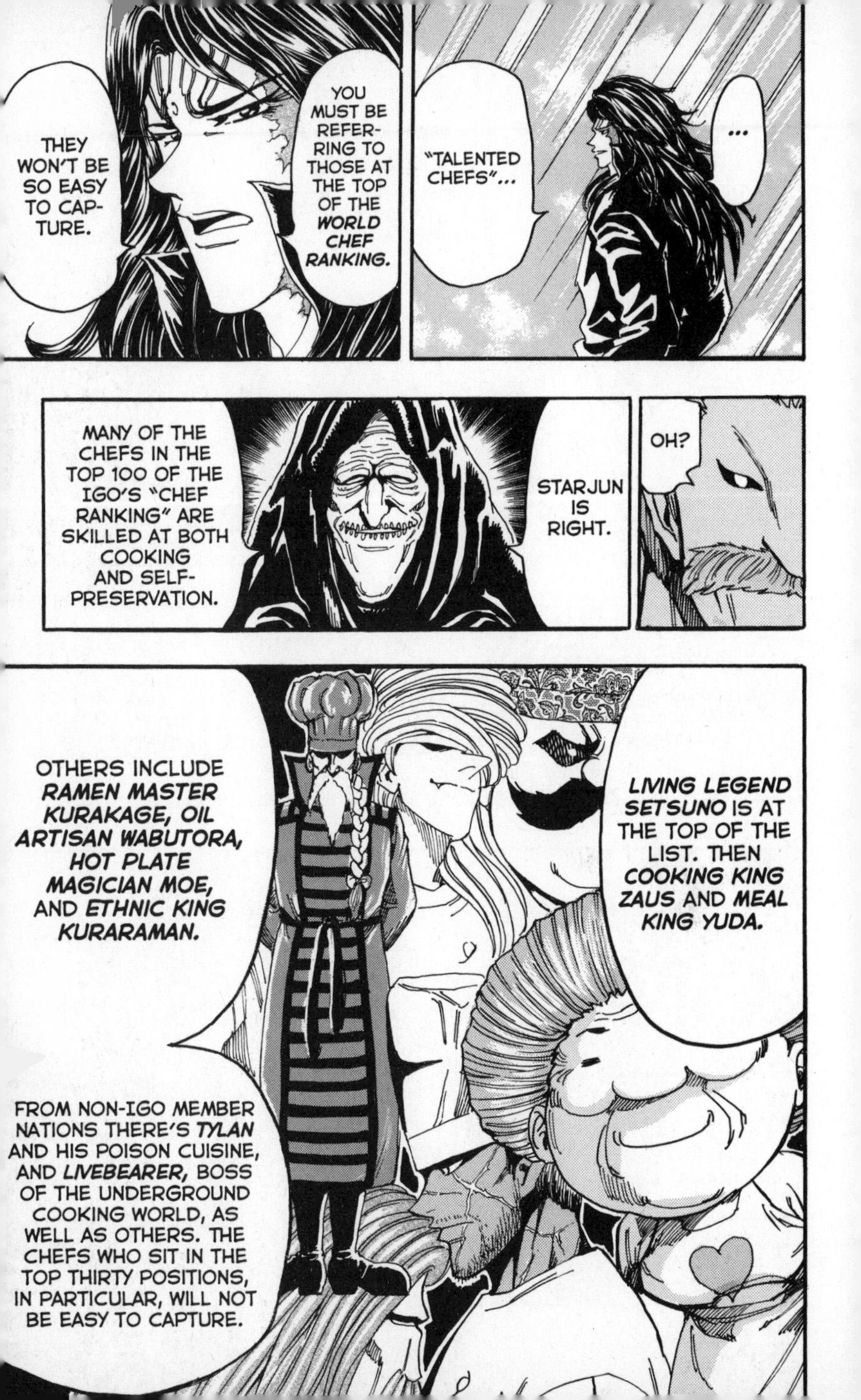
...
"TALENTED CHEFS"...
YOU MUST BE REFERRING TO THOSE AT THE TOP OF THE *WORLD CHEF RANKING.*
THEY WON'T BE SO EASY TO CAPTURE.
OH?
STARJUN IS RIGHT.
MANY OF THE CHEFS IN THE TOP 100 OF THE IGO'S "CHEF RANKING" ARE SKILLED AT BOTH COOKING AND SELF-PRESERVATION.
LIVING LEGEND SETSUNO IS AT THE TOP OF THE LIST. THEN *COOKING KING ZAUS* AND *MEAL KING YUDA.*
OTHERS INCLUDE *RAMEN MASTER KURAKAGE, OIL ARTISAN WABUTORA, HOT PLATE MAGICIAN MOE,* AND *ETHNIC KING KURARAMAN.*
FROM NON-IGO MEMBER NATIONS THERE'S *TYLAN* AND HIS POISON CUISINE, AND *LIVEBEARER,* BOSS OF THE UNDERGROUND COOKING WORLD, AS WELL AS OTHERS. THE CHEFS WHO SIT IN THE TOP THIRTY POSITIONS, IN PARTICULAR, WILL NOT BE EASY TO CAPTURE.

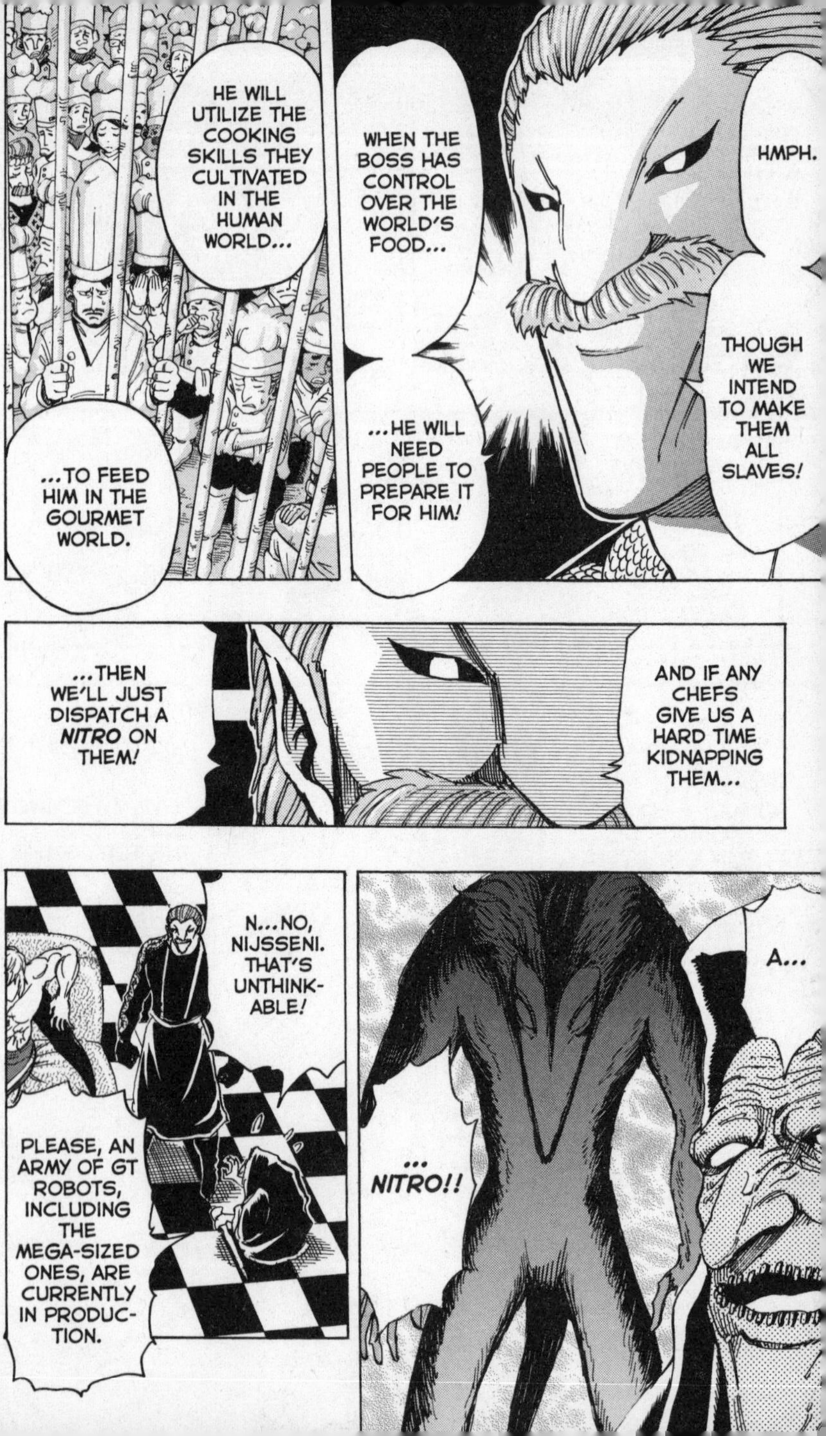
HMPH.
THOUGH WE INTEND TO MAKE THEM ALL SLAVES!
WHEN THE BOSS HAS CONTROL OVER THE WORLD'S FOOD...
...HE WILL NEED PEOPLE TO PREPARE IT FOR HIM!
HE WILL UTILIZE THE COOKING SKILLS THEY CULTIVATED IN THE HUMAN WORLD...
...TO FEED HIM IN THE GOURMET WORLD.
AND IF ANY CHEFS GIVE US A HARD TIME KIDNAPPING THEM...
...THEN WE'LL JUST DISPATCH A *NITRO* ON THEM!
A...
... *NITRO!!*
N...NO, NIJSSENI. THAT'S UNTHINK-ABLE!
PLEASE, AN ARMY OF GT ROBOTS, INCLUDING THE MEGA-SIZED ONES, ARE CURRENTLY IN PRODUC-TION.

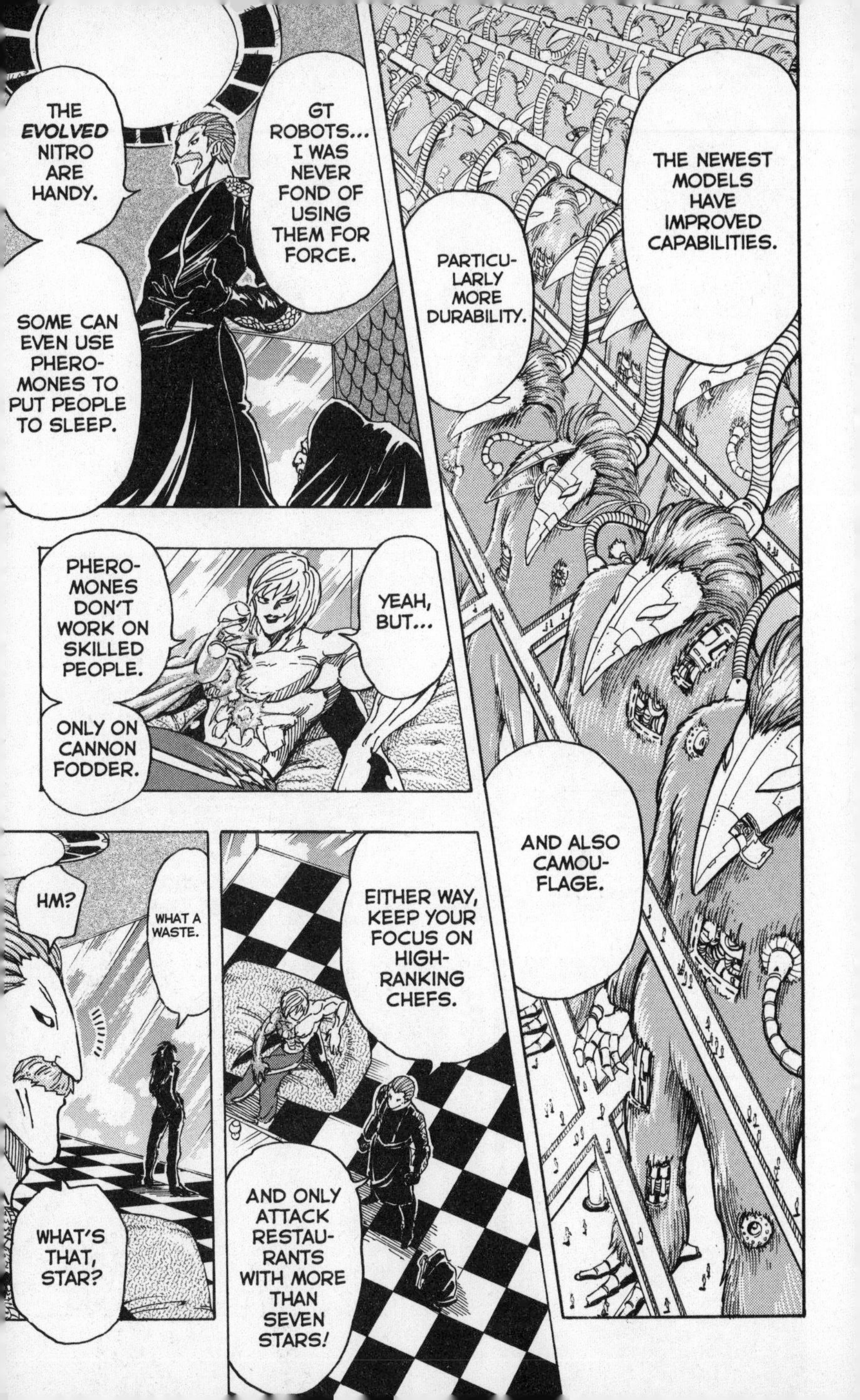
THE NEWEST MODELS HAVE IMPROVED CAPABILITIES.
PARTICULARLY MORE DURABILITY.
AND ALSO CAMOUFLAGE.
GT ROBOTS... I WAS NEVER FOND OF USING THEM FOR FORCE.
THE *EVOLVED* NITRO ARE HANDY.
SOME CAN EVEN USE PHEROMONES TO PUT PEOPLE TO SLEEP.
YEAH, BUT...
PHEROMONES DON'T WORK ON SKILLED PEOPLE.
ONLY ON CANNON FODDER.
EITHER WAY, KEEP YOUR FOCUS ON HIGH-RANKING CHEFS.
AND ONLY ATTACK RESTAURANTS WITH MORE THAN SEVEN STARS!
WHAT A WASTE.
HM?
WHAT'S THAT, STAR?

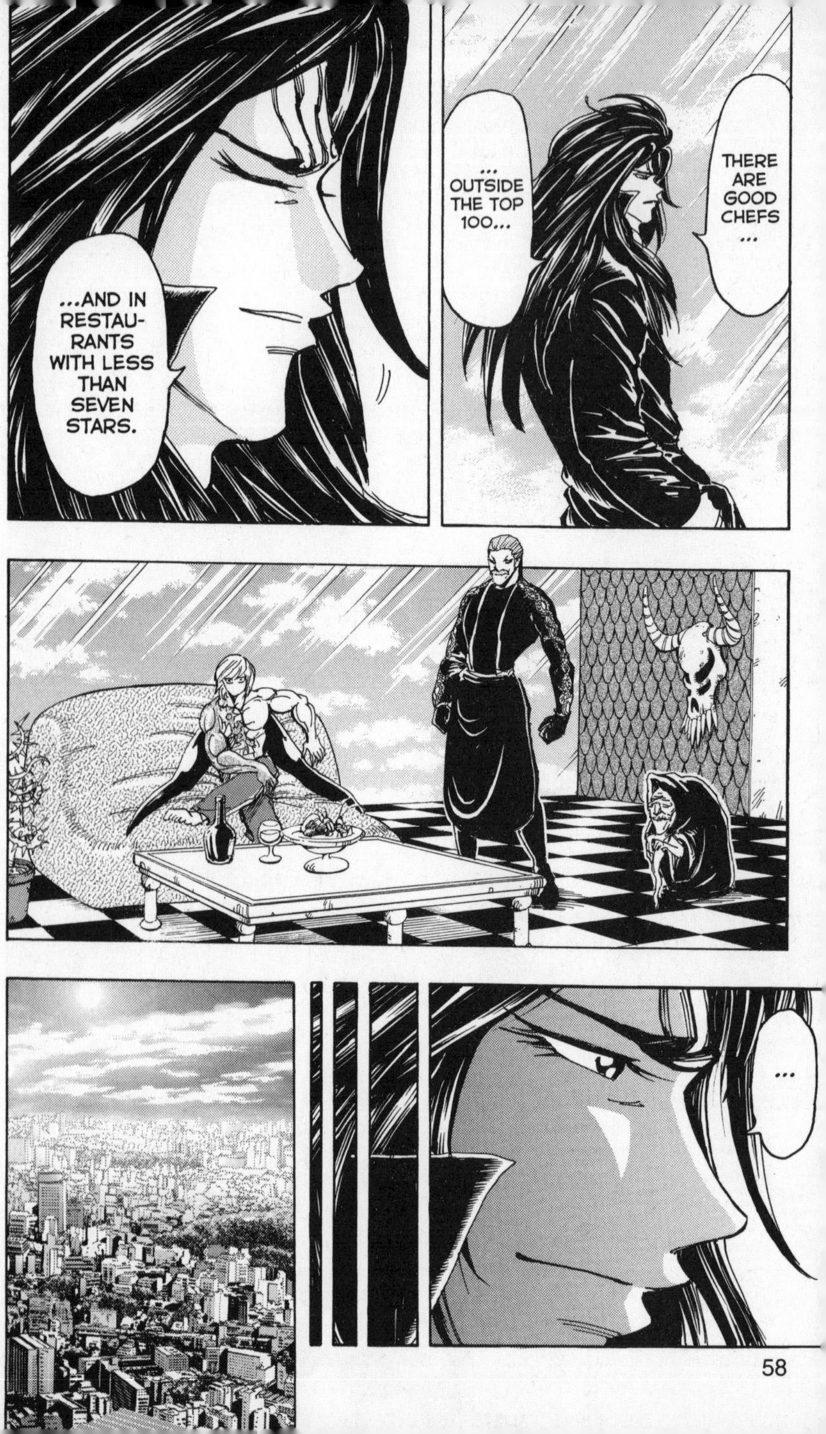
THERE ARE GOOD CHEFS ...
... OUTSIDE THE TOP 100...
...AND IN RESTAU-RANTS WITH LESS THAN SEVEN STARS.
...

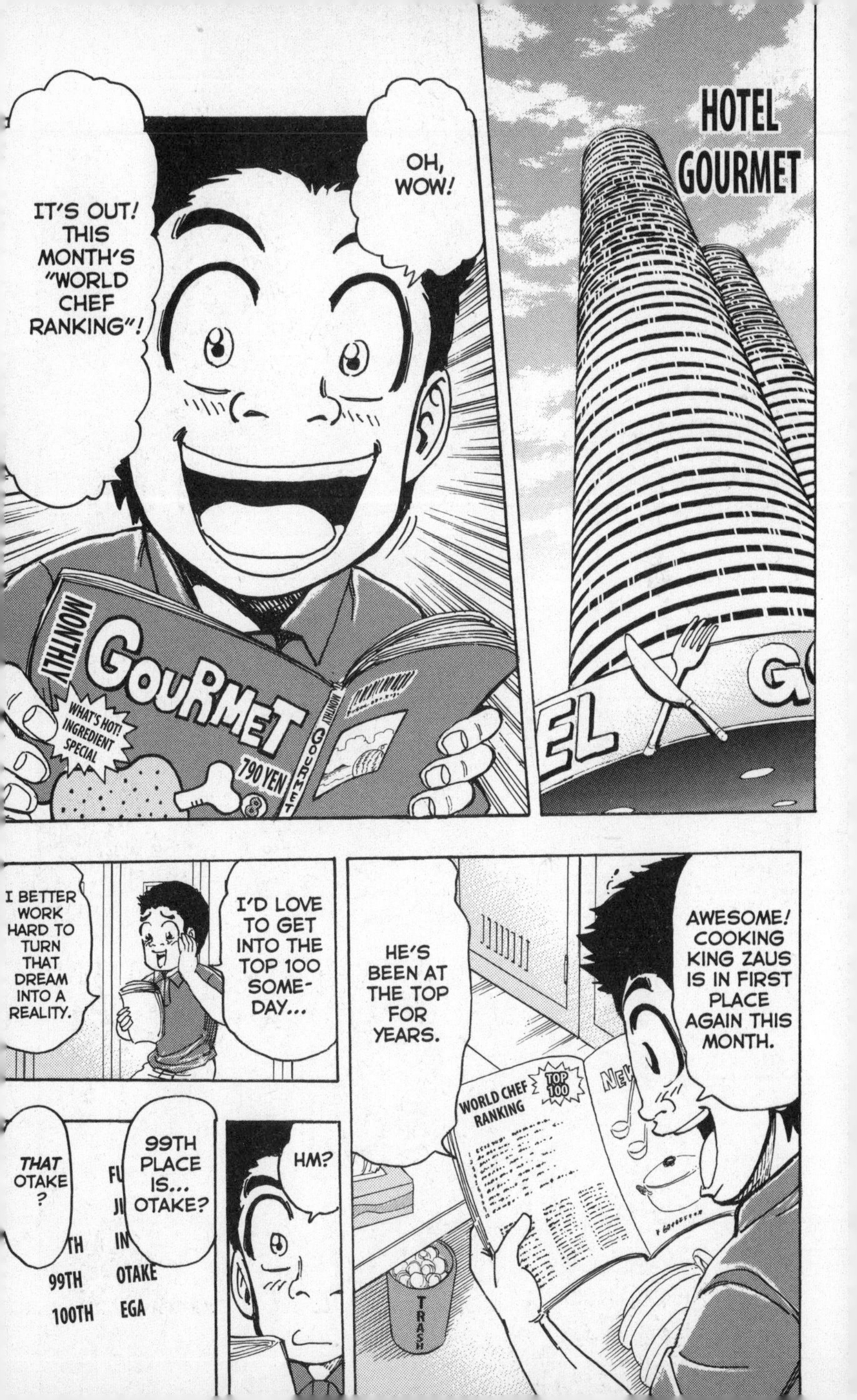
HOTEL GOURMET
OH, WOW!
IT'S OUT! THIS MONTH'S "WORLD CHEF RANKING"!
MONTHLY GOURMET
WHAT'S HOT! INGREDIENT SPECIAL
790 YEN
AWESOME! COOKING KING ZAUS IS IN FIRST PLACE AGAIN THIS MONTH.
HE'S BEEN AT THE TOP FOR YEARS.
WORLD CHEF RANKING
TOP 100
TRASH
I'D LOVE TO GET INTO THE TOP 100 SOME-DAY...
I BETTER WORK HARD TO TURN THAT DREAM INTO A REALITY.
HM?
99TH PLACE IS... OTAKE?
THAT OTAKE?
99TH OTAKE
100TH EGA

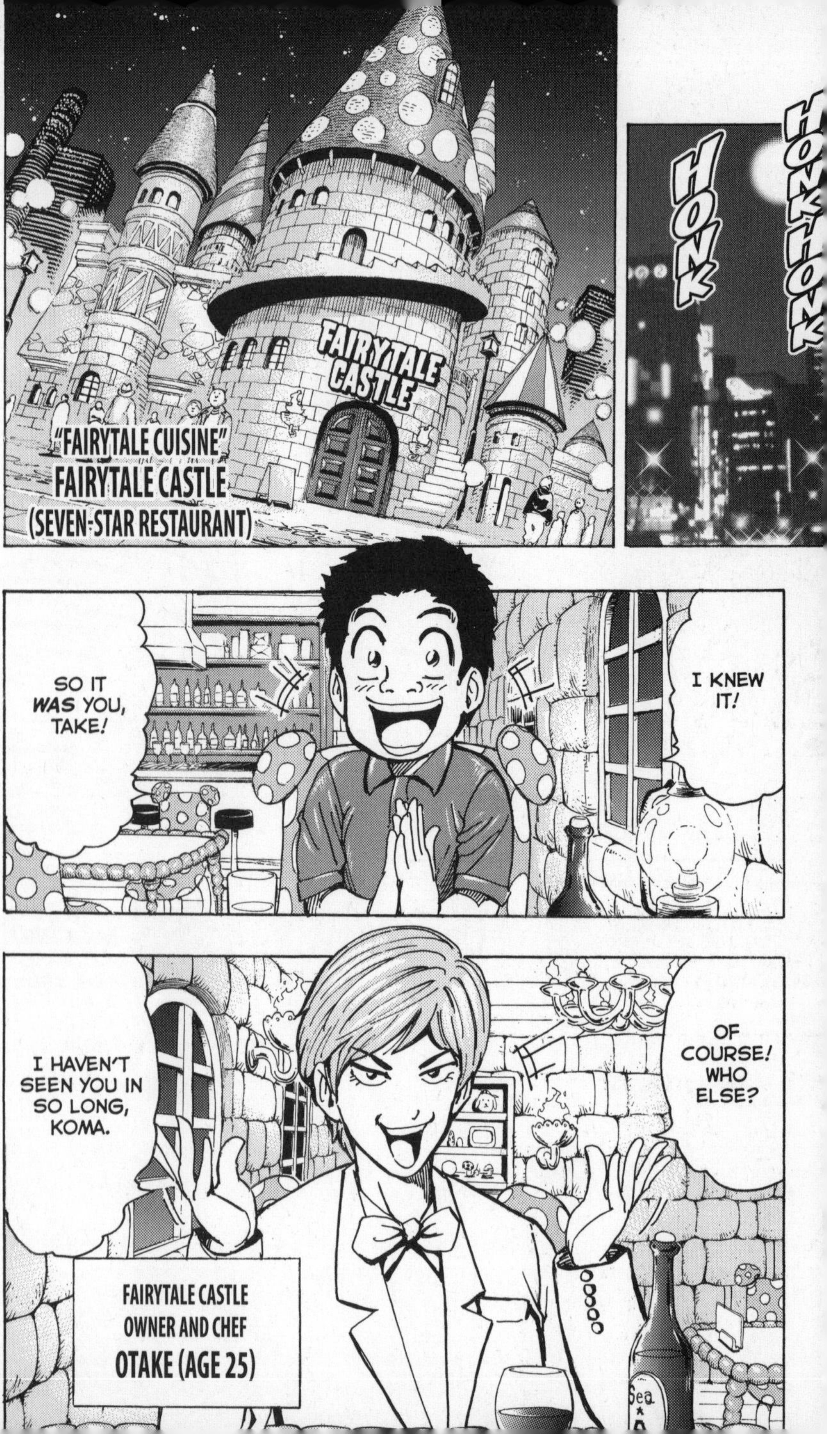
HONK HONK
HONK
FAIRYTALE CASTLE
"FAIRYTALE CUISINE" FAIRYTALE CASTLE (SEVEN-STAR RESTAURANT)
I KNEW IT!
SO IT *WAS* YOU, TAKE!
OF COURSE! WHO ELSE?
I HAVEN'T SEEN YOU IN SO LONG, KOMA.
FAIRYTALE CASTLE OWNER AND CHEF OTAKE (AGE 25)

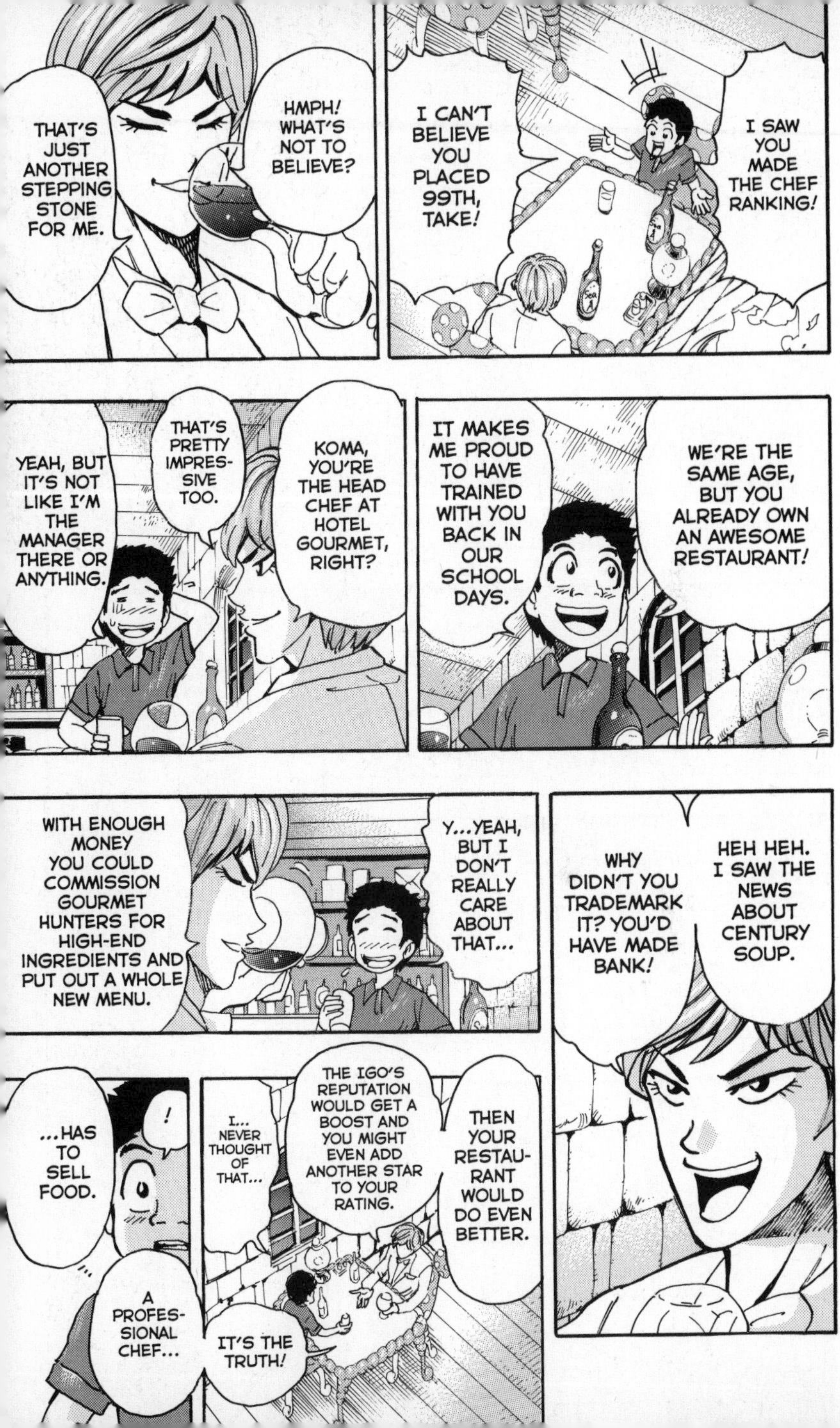
I SAW YOU MADE THE CHEF RANKING!
I CAN'T BELIEVE YOU PLACED 99TH, TAKE!
HMPH! WHAT'S NOT TO BELIEVE?
THAT'S JUST ANOTHER STEPPING STONE FOR ME.
WE'RE THE SAME AGE, BUT YOU ALREADY OWN AN AWESOME RESTAURANT!
IT MAKES ME PROUD TO HAVE TRAINED WITH YOU BACK IN OUR SCHOOL DAYS.
KOMA, YOU'RE THE HEAD CHEF AT HOTEL GOURMET, RIGHT?
THAT'S PRETTY IMPRES-SIVE TOO.
YEAH, BUT IT'S NOT LIKE I'M THE MANAGER THERE OR ANYTHING.
HEH HEH. I SAW THE NEWS ABOUT CENTURY SOUP.
WHY DIDN'T YOU TRADEMARK IT? YOU'D HAVE MADE BANK!
Y...YEAH, BUT I DON'T REALLY CARE ABOUT THAT...
WITH ENOUGH MONEY YOU COULD COMMISSION GOURMET HUNTERS FOR HIGH-END INGREDIENTS AND PUT OUT A WHOLE NEW MENU.
THEN YOUR RESTAU-RANT WOULD DO EVEN BETTER.
THE IGO'S REPUTATION WOULD GET A BOOST AND YOU MIGHT EVEN ADD ANOTHER STAR TO YOUR RATING.
I... NEVER THOUGHT OF THAT...
IT'S THE TRUTH!
!
...HAS TO SELL FOOD.
A PROFES-SIONAL CHEF...

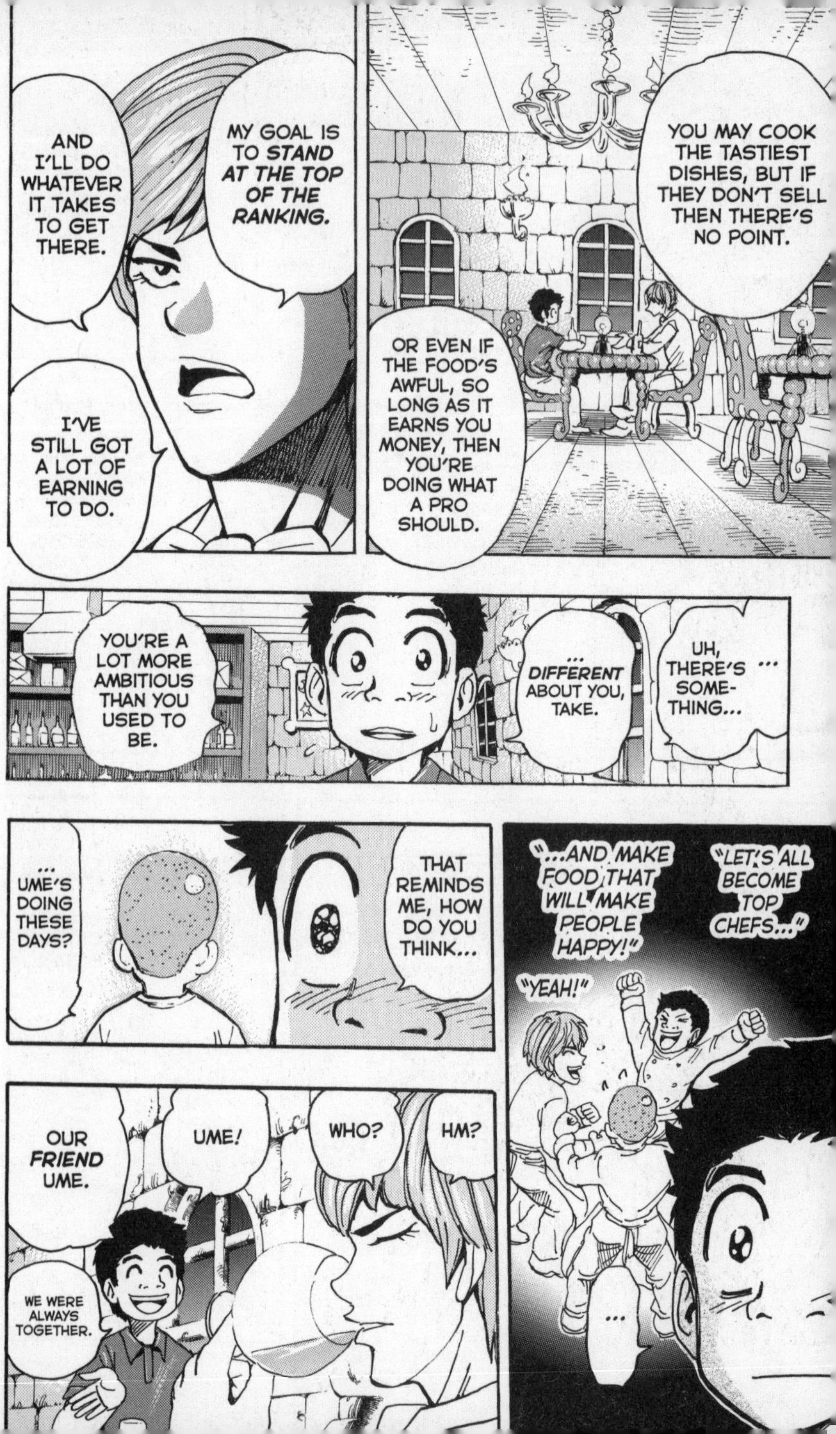
YOU MAY COOK THE TASTIEST DISHES, BUT IF THEY DON'T SELL THEN THERE'S NO POINT.
OR EVEN IF THE FOOD'S AWFUL, SO LONG AS IT EARNS YOU MONEY, THEN YOU'RE DOING WHAT A PRO SHOULD.
MY GOAL IS TO *STAND AT THE TOP OF THE RANKING.*
AND I'LL DO WHATEVER IT TAKES TO GET THERE.
I'VE STILL GOT A LOT OF EARNING TO DO.
UH, THERE'S SOME-THING...
...
... *DIFFERENT* ABOUT YOU, TAKE.
YOU'RE A LOT MORE AMBITIOUS THAN YOU USED TO BE.
"LET'S ALL BECOME TOP CHEFS..."
"...AND MAKE FOOD THAT WILL MAKE PEOPLE HAPPY!"
"YEAH!"
...
THAT REMINDS ME, HOW DO YOU THINK...
... UME'S DOING THESE DAYS?
HM?
WHO?
UME!
OUR *FRIEND* UME.
WE WERE ALWAYS TOGETHER.

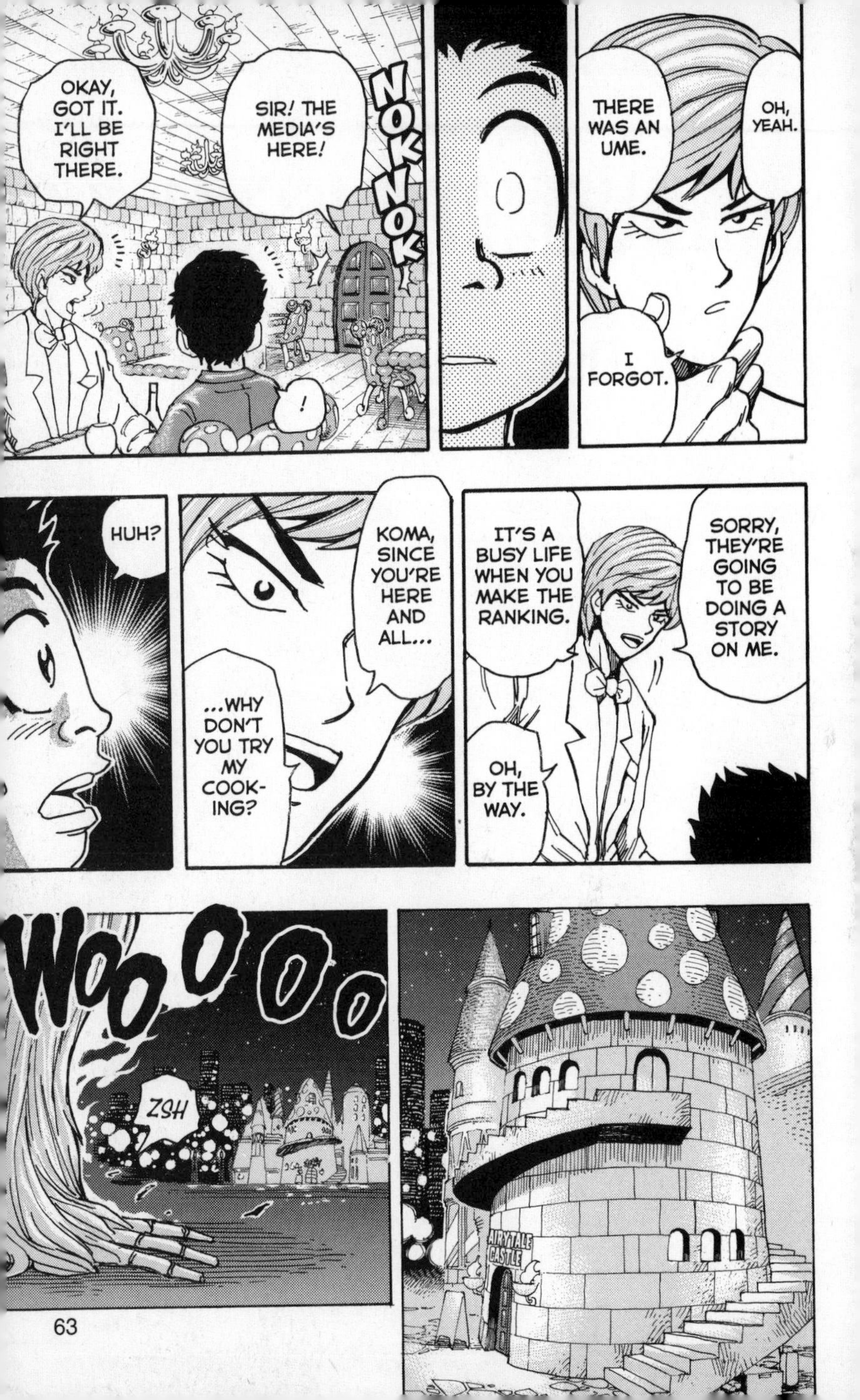
OH, YEAH.
THERE WAS AN UME.
I FORGOT.
NOK NOK
SIR! THE MEDIA'S HERE!
OKAY, GOT IT. I'LL BE RIGHT THERE.
!
SORRY, THEY'RE GOING TO BE DOING A STORY ON ME.
IT'S A BUSY LIFE WHEN YOU MAKE THE RANKING.
OH, BY THE WAY.
KOMA, SINCE YOU'RE HERE AND ALL...
...WHY DON'T YOU TRY MY COOK-ING?
HUH?
AIRYTALE CASTLE
WOOOOOO
ZSH

TORIKO

GOURMET CHECKLIST

Vol. 187

EIGHT-TAILED SCORPION
(CRUSTACEAN)

CAPTURE LEVEL: 28

HABITAT: SAND GARDEN (ALSO
    ARTIFICIALLY BRED AS A WEAPON)

LENGTH: 15 METERS

HEIGHT: ---

WEIGHT: 12 TONS

PRICE: 100 G OF MEAT FROM DETOXIFIED

TAIL / 150,000 YEN

SCALE

A GIANT SCORPION WITH EIGHT TAILS. EACH TAIL CONTAINS A DIFFERENT POISON, WHICH MAKES THE CHANCE OF RECEIVING THE CORRECT ANTIDOTE AFTER BEING STUNG QUITE LOW. FOR THAT REASON, IT IS ALSO USED AS A WEAPON IN MILITARY OPERATIONS. BECAUSE IT CAN KILL ALMOST ANY CREATURE AND WREAK HAVOC ON AN ECOSYSTEM, IT HAS BEEN DESIGNATED AN ISOLATED SPECIMEN AND A LEVEL-2 DANGEROUS CREATURE. CAPTURING IT FOR CONSUMPTION IS HIGHLY DANGEROUS, BUT THE FLESH BENEATH ITS TOUGH OUTER SHELL IS RATHER TASTY AND THE MEAT FROM ITS DETOXIFIED TAIL IS SAID TO BE EVEN MORE DELICIOUS.

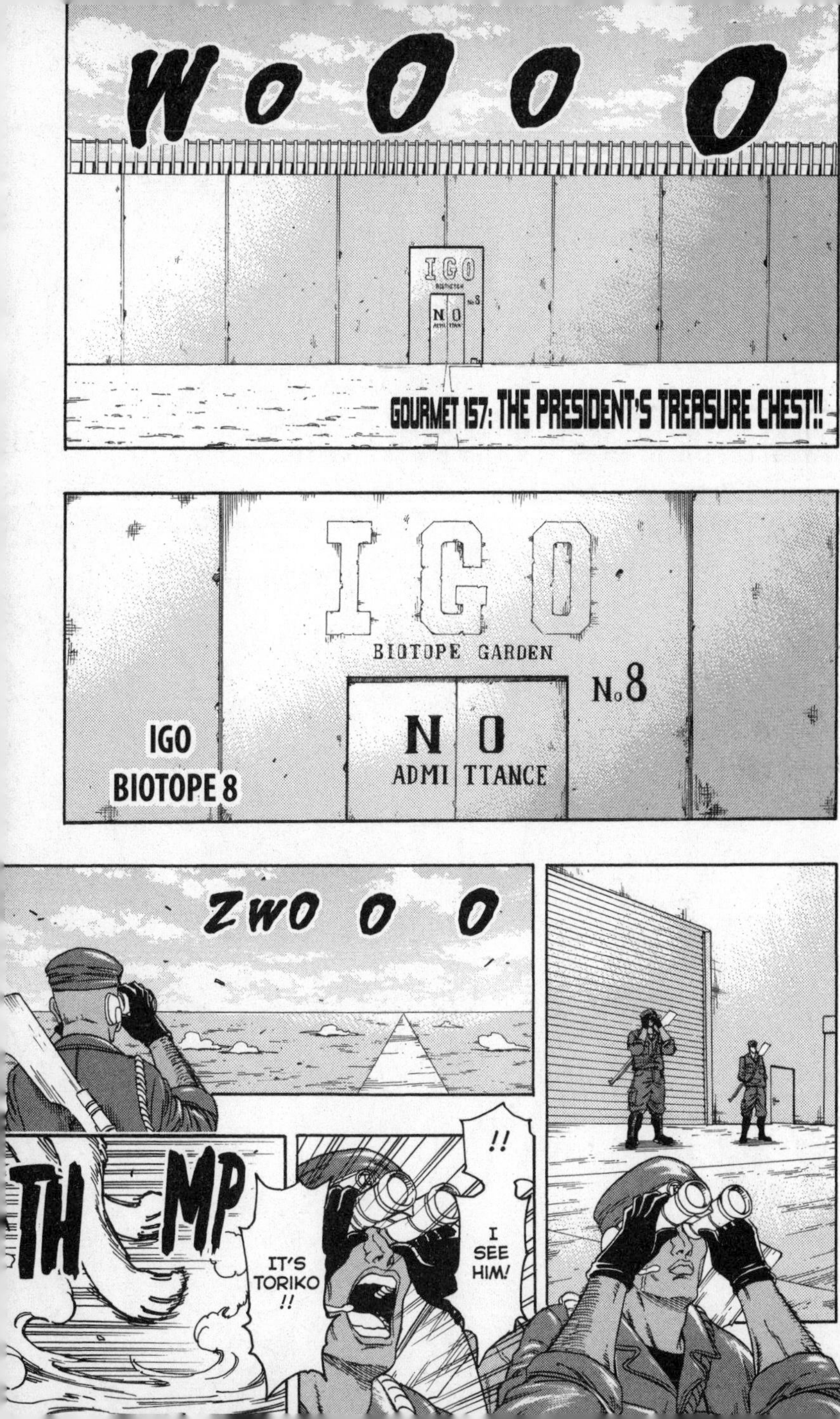
WOOOO
IGO
NO
ADMI TTANCE
No 8
GOURMET 157: THE PRESIDENT'S TREASURE CHEST!!
IGO
BIOTOPE GARDEN
No 8
NO
ADMI TTANCE
IGO BIOTOPE 8
I SEE HIM!
ZWOOO
!!
IT'S TORIKO!!
THMP

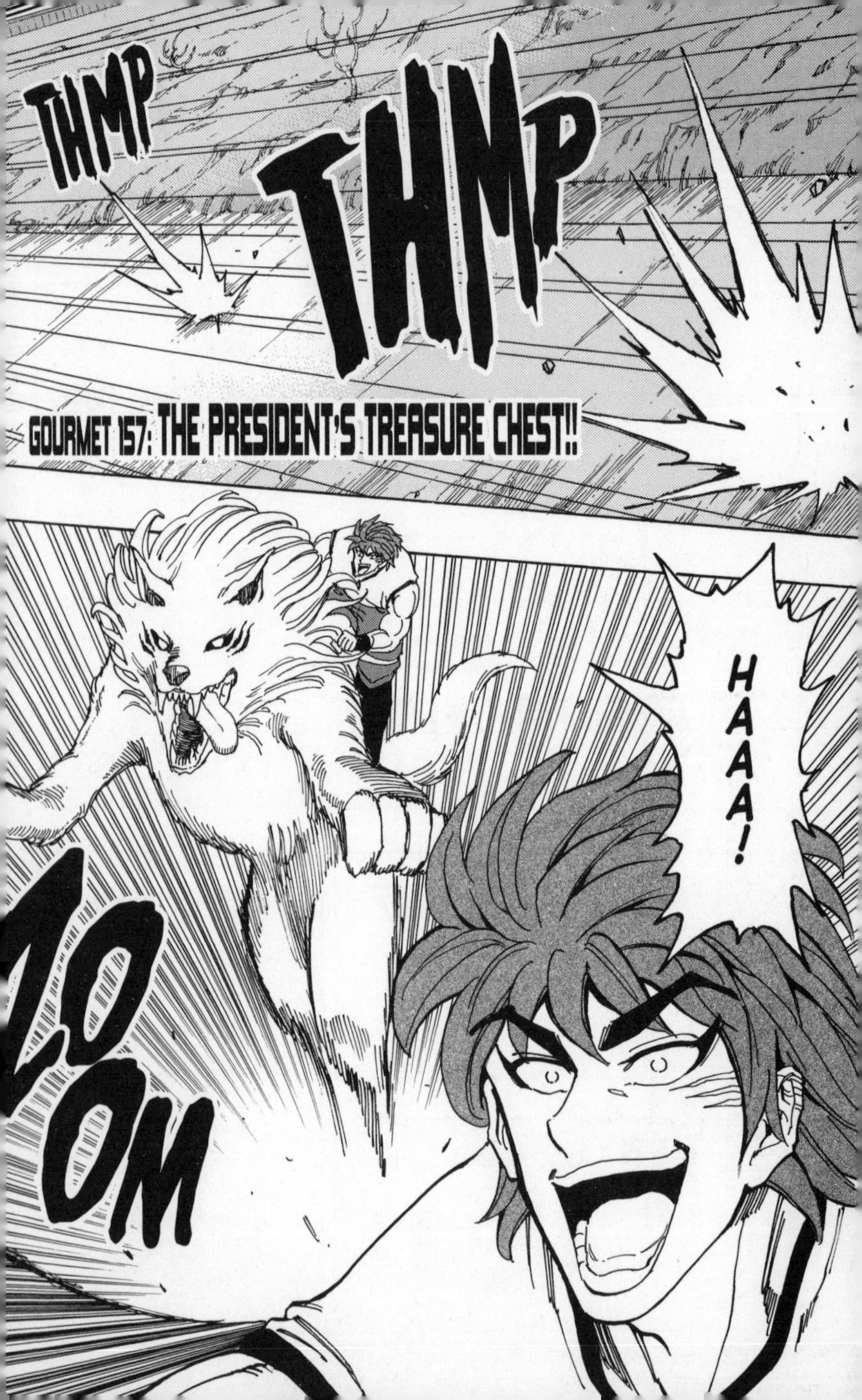
THMP
THMP
GOURMET 157: THE PRESIDENT'S TREASURE CHEST!!
HAAA!
ZOOM

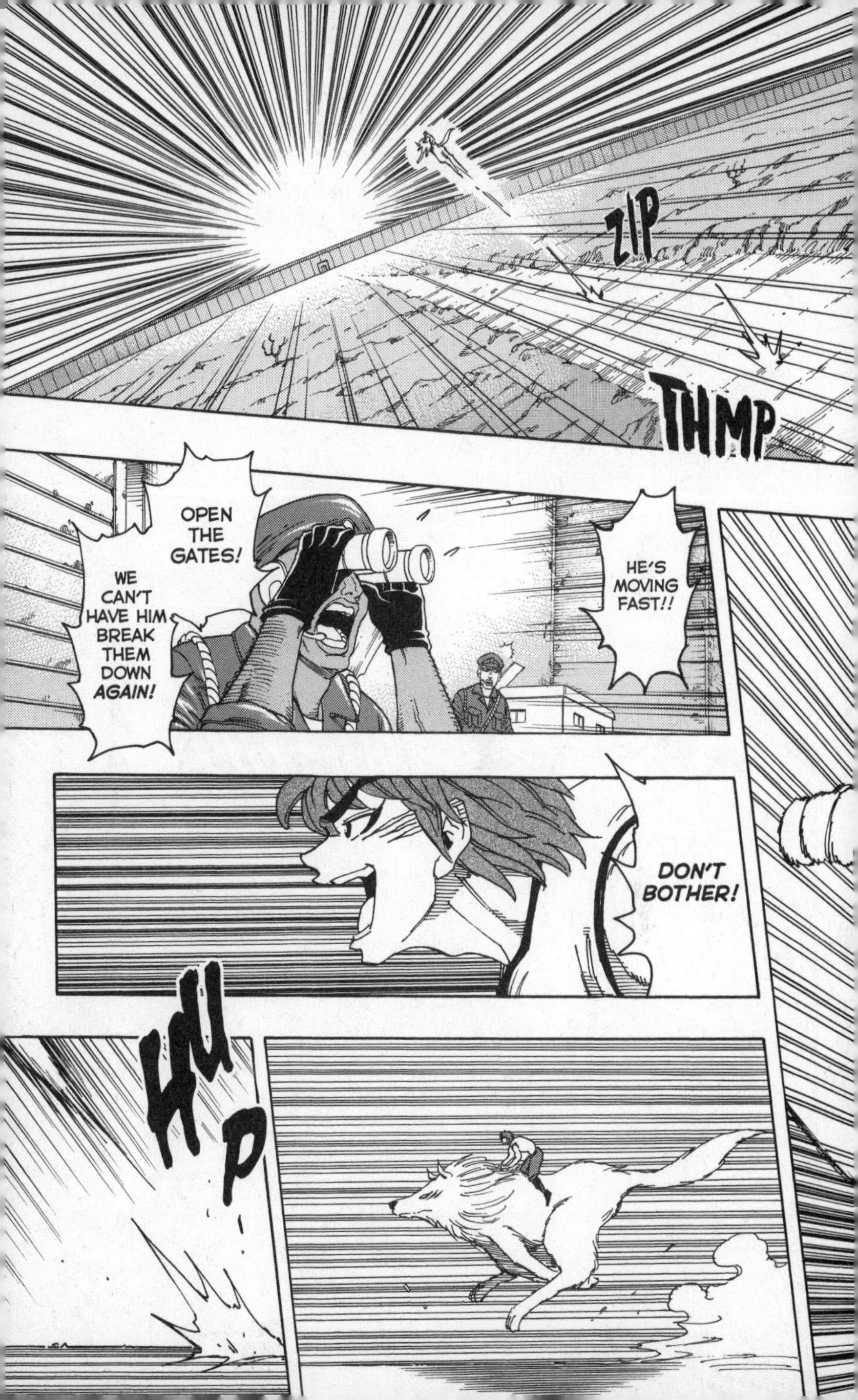
ZIP
THMP
HE'S MOVING FAST!!
OPEN THE GATES!
WE CAN'T HAVE HIM BREAK THEM DOWN AGAIN!
DON'T BOTHER!
HUP

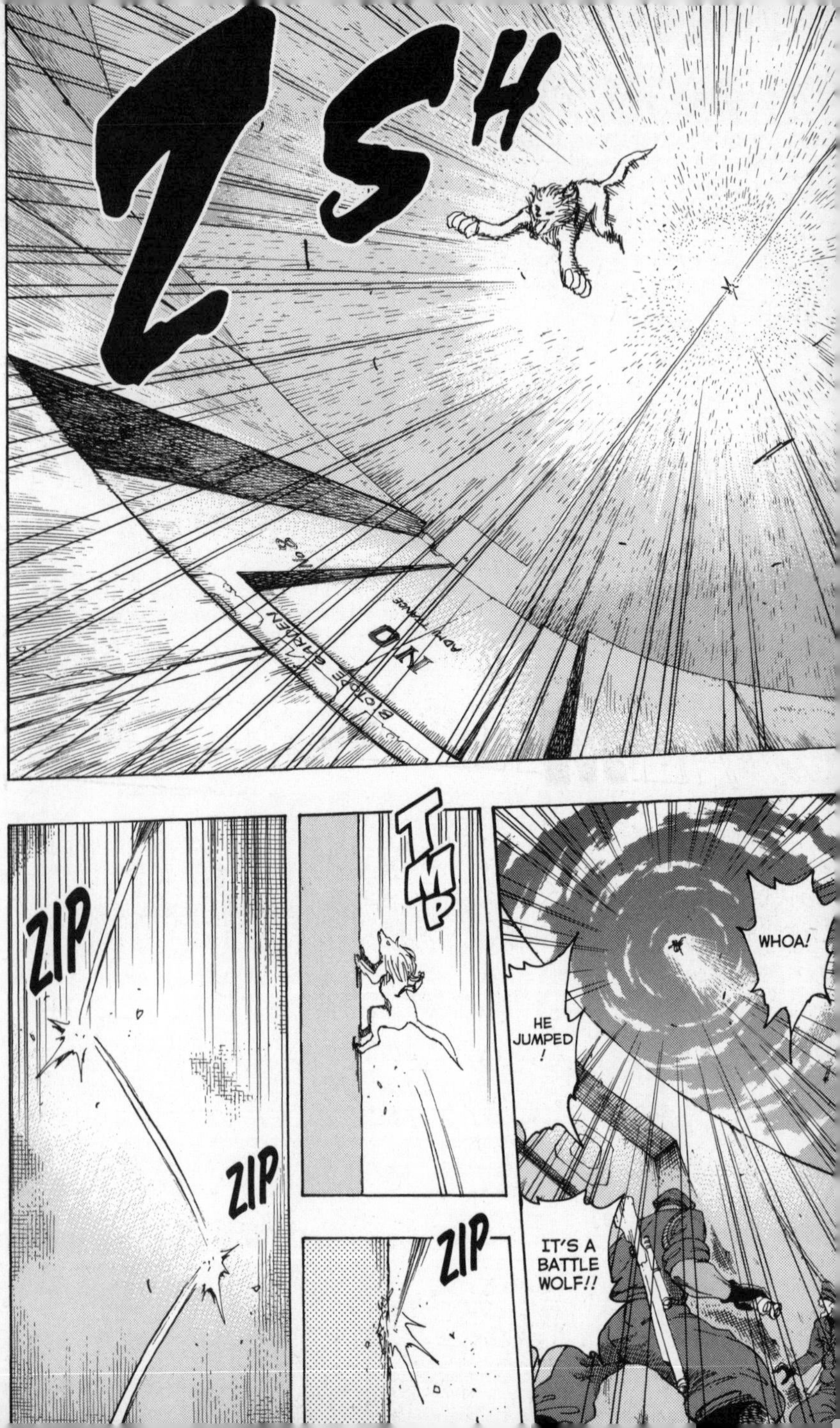
ZSH
WHOA!
HE JUMPED!
IT'S A BATTLE WOLF!!
TMP
ZIP
ZIP
ZIP

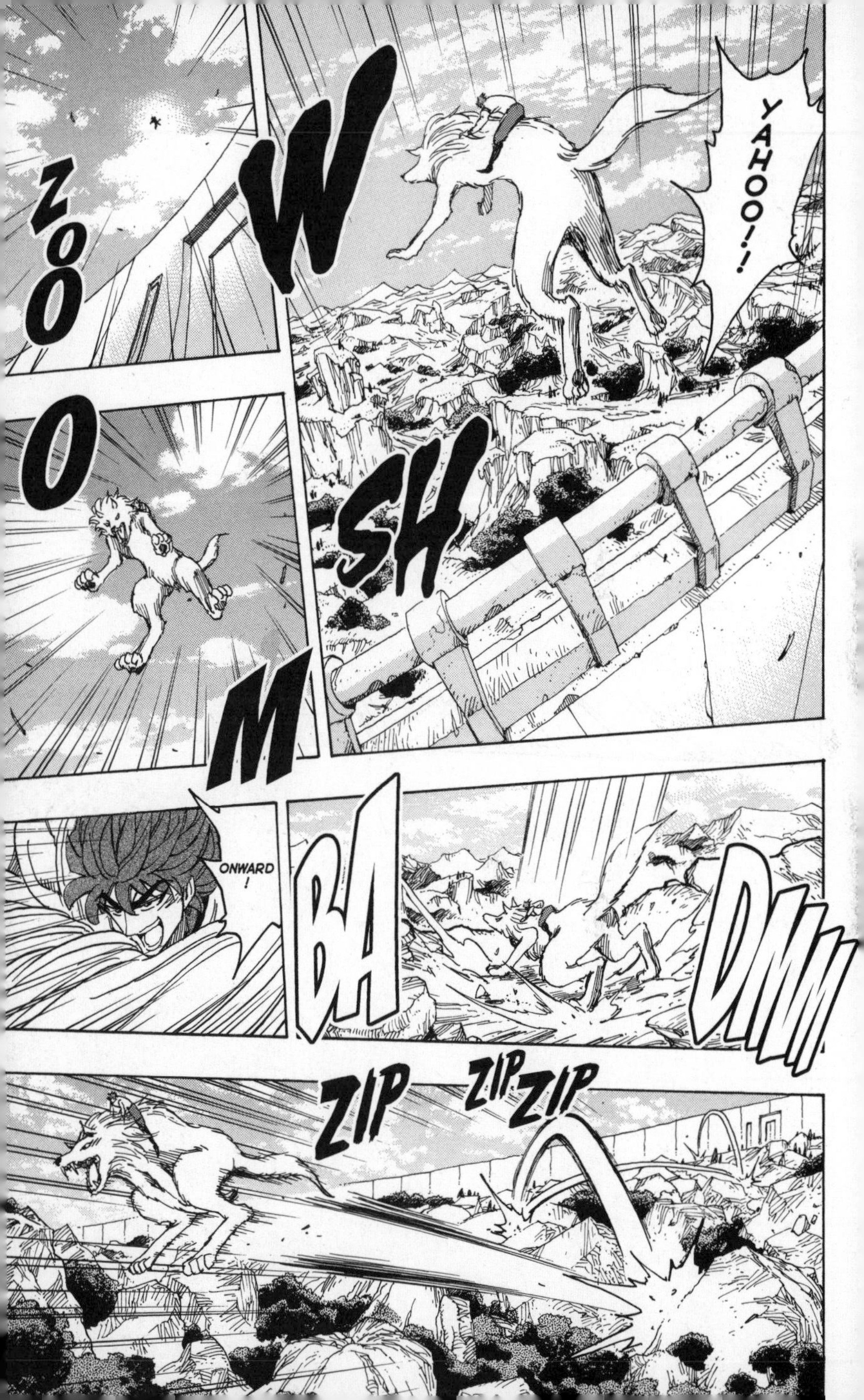

YAHOO!!
W
SH
ZOO
O
M
DMM
BA
ONWARD!
ZIP ZIP ZIP

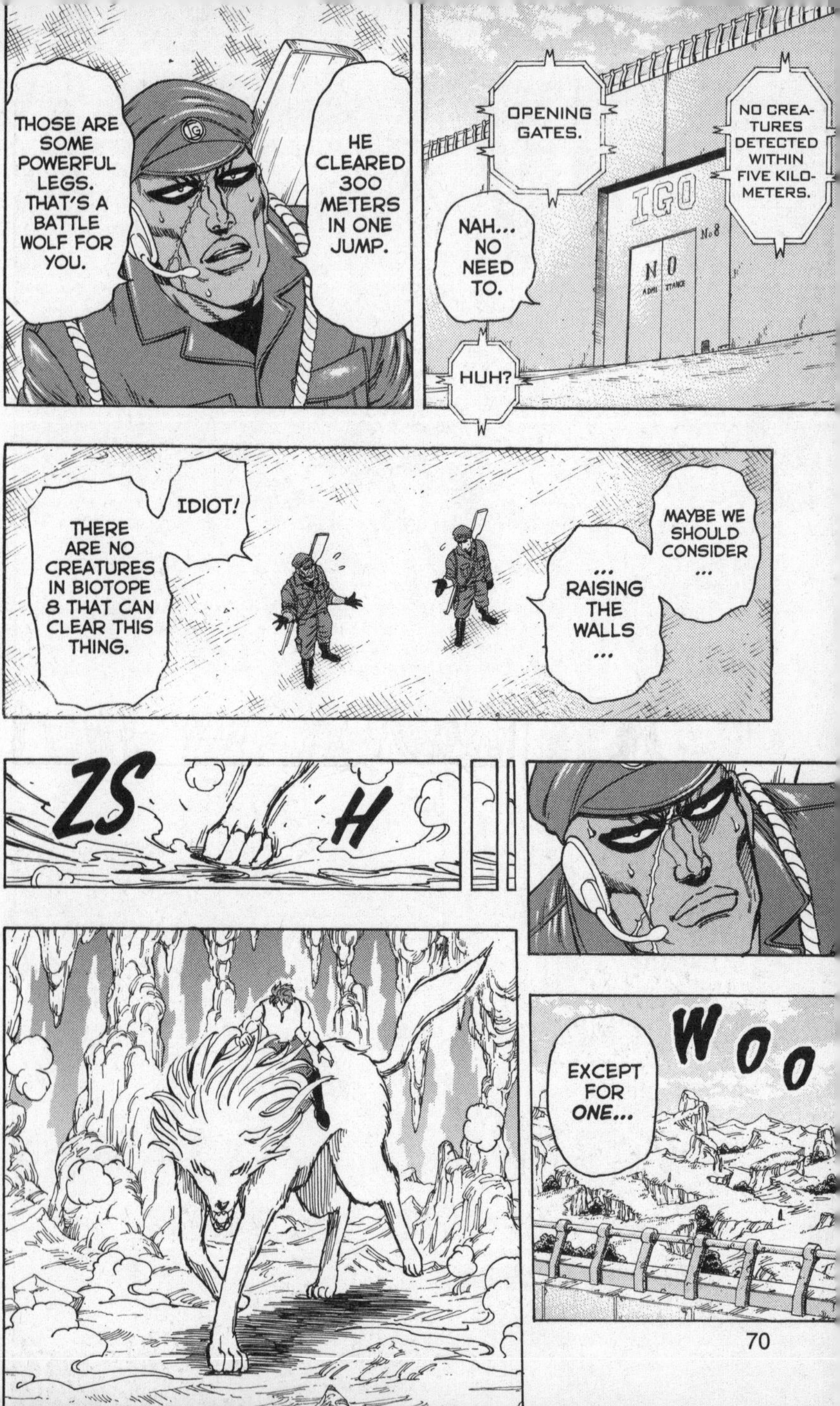
NO CREA-TURES DETECTED WITHIN FIVE KILO-METERS.
OPENING GATES.
IGO
No 8
NAH... NO NEED TO.
HUH?
HE CLEARED 300 METERS IN ONE JUMP.
THOSE ARE SOME POWERFUL LEGS. THAT'S A BATTLE WOLF FOR YOU.
MAYBE WE SHOULD CONSIDER ...
... RAISING THE WALLS ...
IDIOT!
THERE ARE NO CREATURES IN BIOTOPE 8 THAT CAN CLEAR THIS THING.
ZS
H
WOO
EXCEPT FOR ONE...

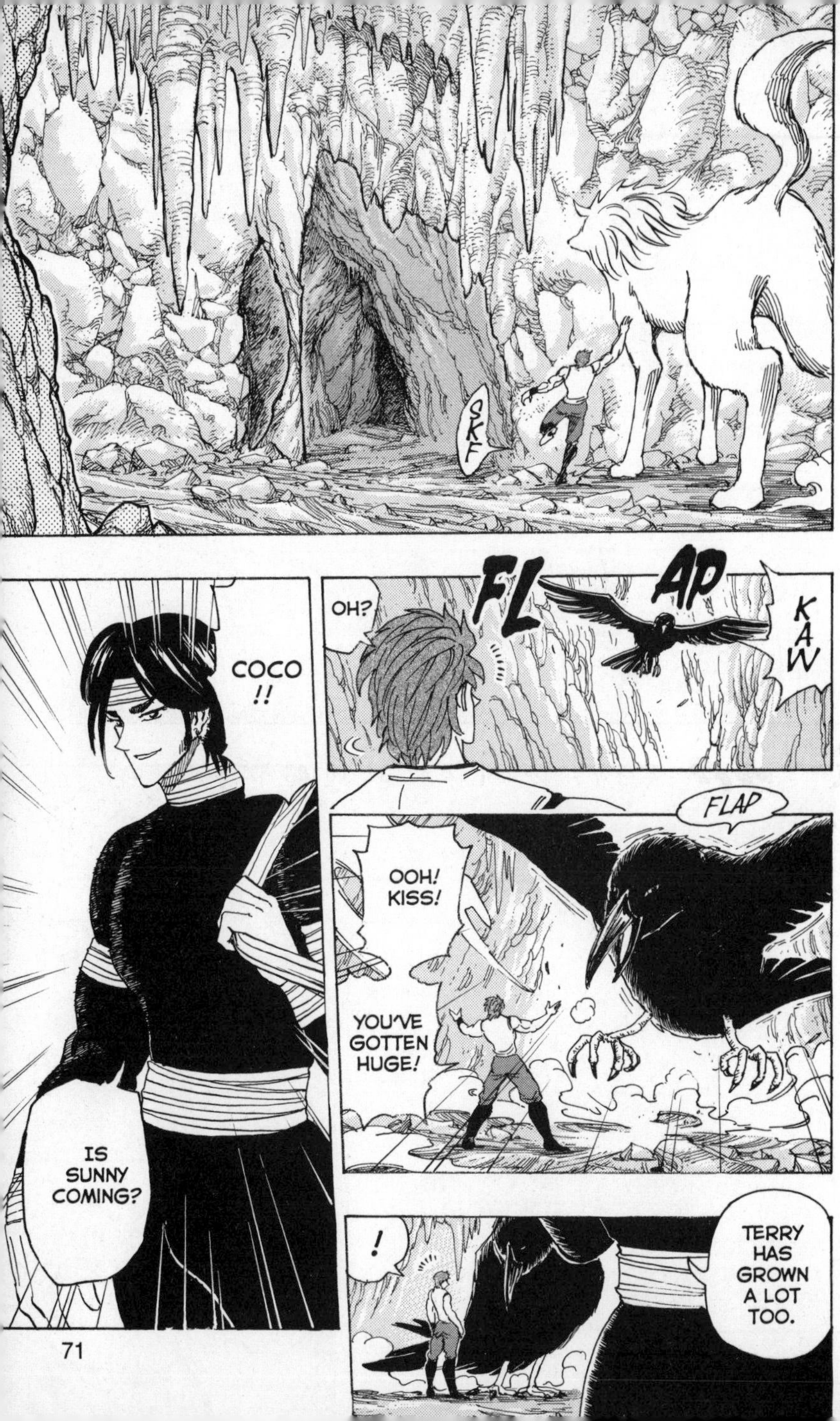
SKF
FLAP
KAW
OH?
FLAP
OOH! KISS!
YOU'VE GOTTEN HUGE!
TERRY HAS GROWN A LOT TOO.
!
COCO!!
IS SUNNY COMING?

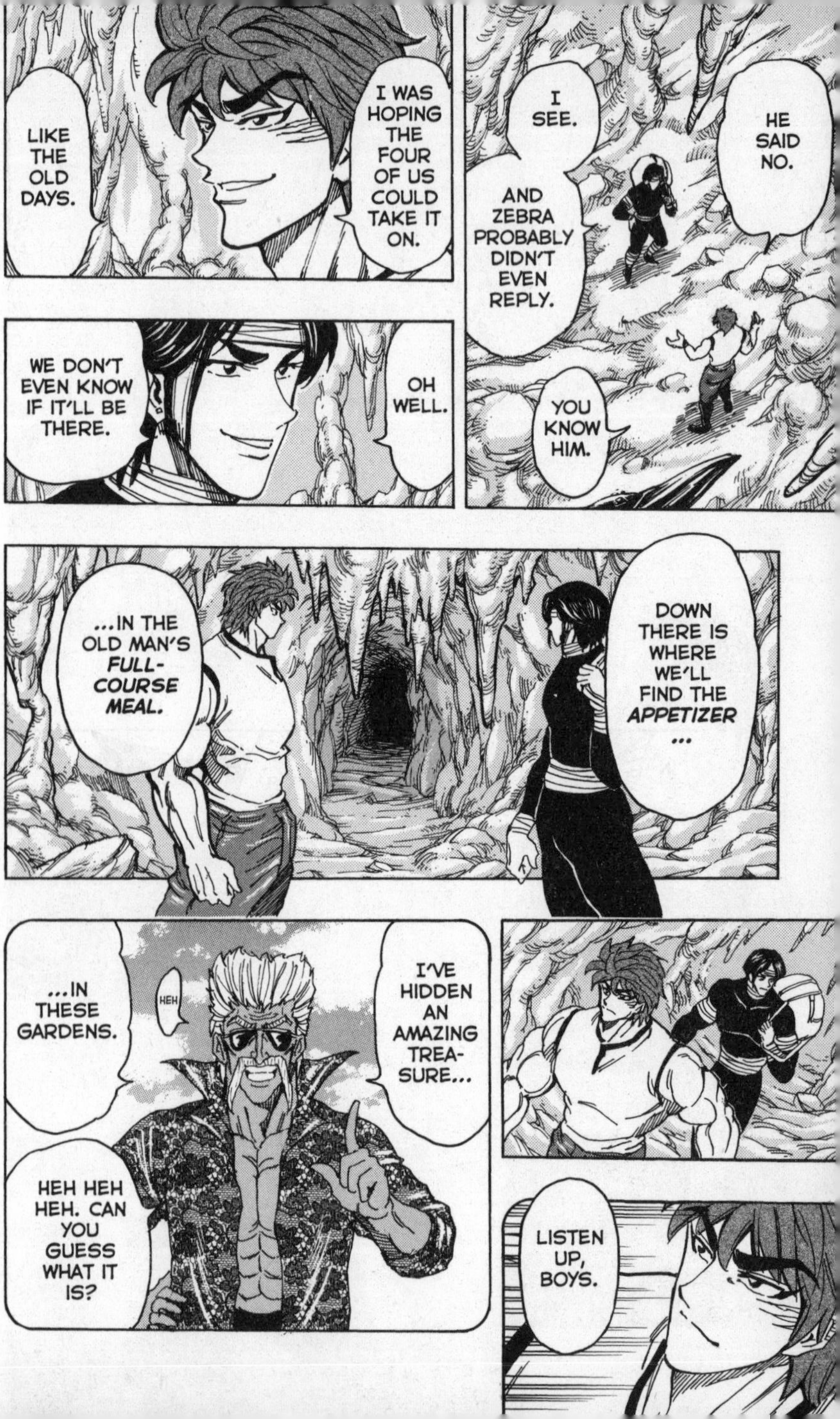
HE SAID NO.
I SEE.
AND ZEBRA PROBABLY DIDN'T EVEN REPLY.
YOU KNOW HIM.
I WAS HOPING THE FOUR OF US COULD TAKE IT ON.
LIKE THE OLD DAYS.
OH WELL.
WE DON'T EVEN KNOW IF IT'LL BE THERE.
DOWN THERE IS WHERE WE'LL FIND THE *APPETIZER* ...
...IN THE OLD MAN'S *FULL-COURSE MEAL.*
LISTEN UP, BOYS.
I'VE HIDDEN AN AMAZING TREASURE...
HEH
...IN THESE GARDENS.
HEH HEH HEH. CAN YOU GUESS WHAT IT IS?

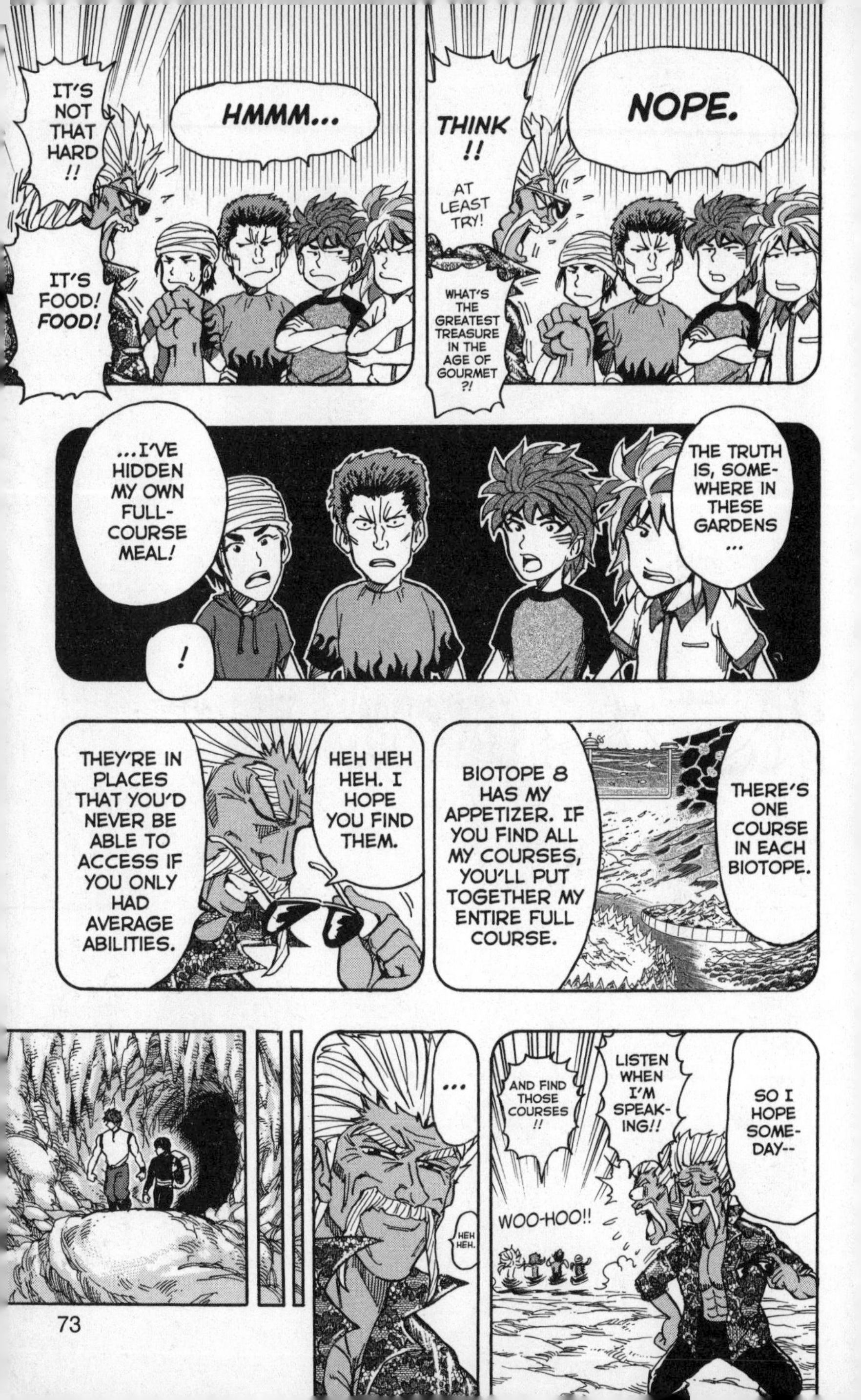
NOPE.
THINK!!
AT LEAST TRY!
WHAT'S THE GREATEST TREASURE IN THE AGE OF GOURMET?!
HMMM...
IT'S NOT THAT HARD!!
IT'S FOOD! FOOD!
THE TRUTH IS, SOME-WHERE IN THESE GARDENS...
...I'VE HIDDEN MY OWN FULL-COURSE MEAL!
!
THERE'S ONE COURSE IN EACH BIOTOPE.
BIOTOPE 8 HAS MY APPETIZER. IF YOU FIND ALL MY COURSES, YOU'LL PUT TOGETHER MY ENTIRE FULL COURSE.
HEH HEH HEH. I HOPE YOU FIND THEM.
THEY'RE IN PLACES THAT YOU'D NEVER BE ABLE TO ACCESS IF YOU ONLY HAD AVERAGE ABILITIES.
SO I HOPE SOME-DAY--
LISTEN WHEN I'M SPEAK-ING!!
AND FIND THOSE COURSES!!
WOO-HOO!!
...
HEH HEH.

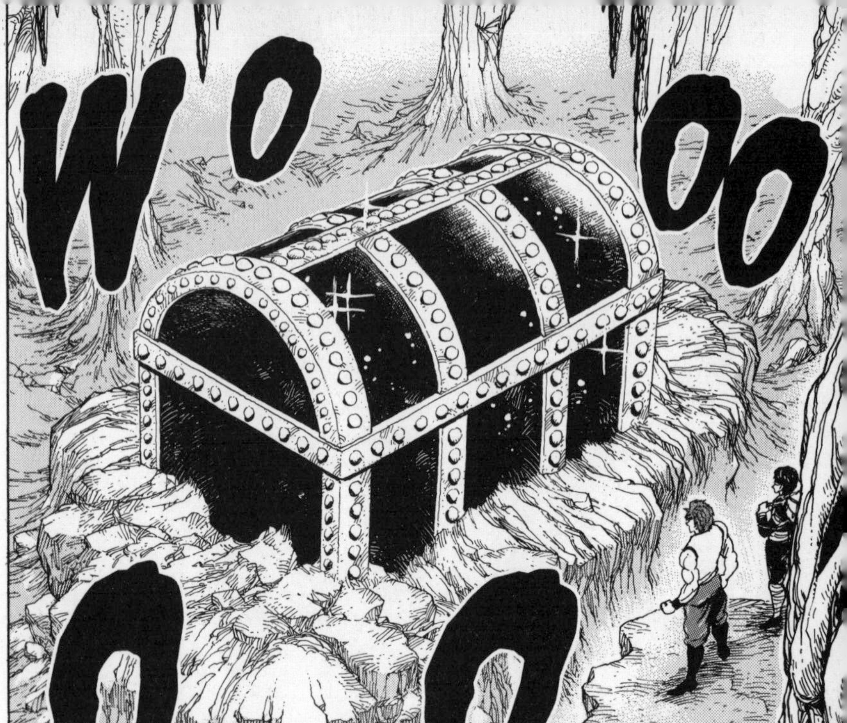
WOOOOOO

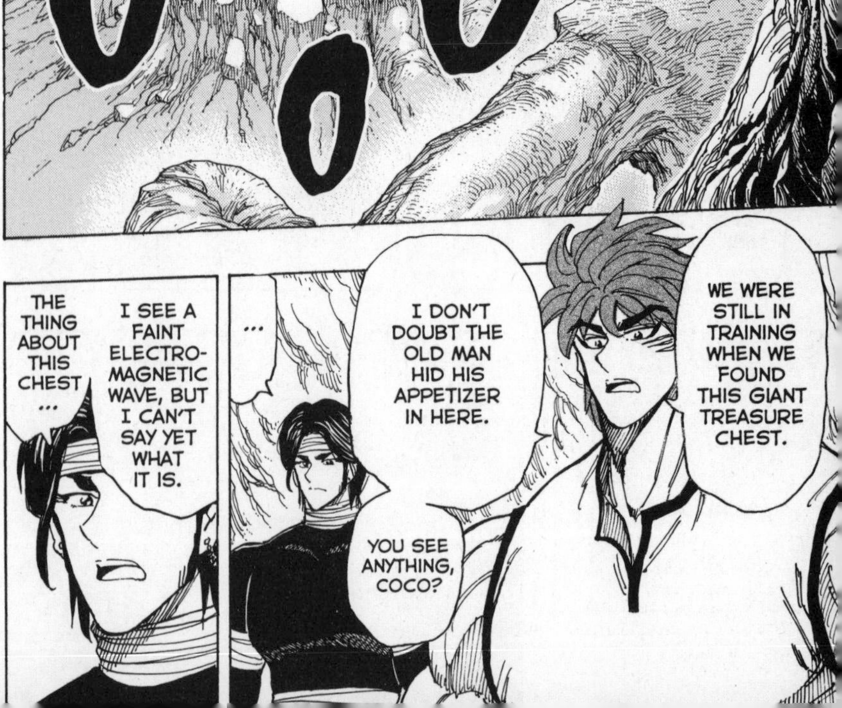
WE WERE STILL IN TRAINING WHEN WE FOUND THIS GIANT TREASURE CHEST.
I DON'T DOUBT THE OLD MAN HID HIS APPETIZER IN HERE.
YOU SEE ANYTHING, COCO?
...
I SEE A FAINT ELECTRO-MAGNETIC WAVE, BUT I CAN'T SAY YET WHAT IT IS.
THE THING ABOUT THIS CHEST ...

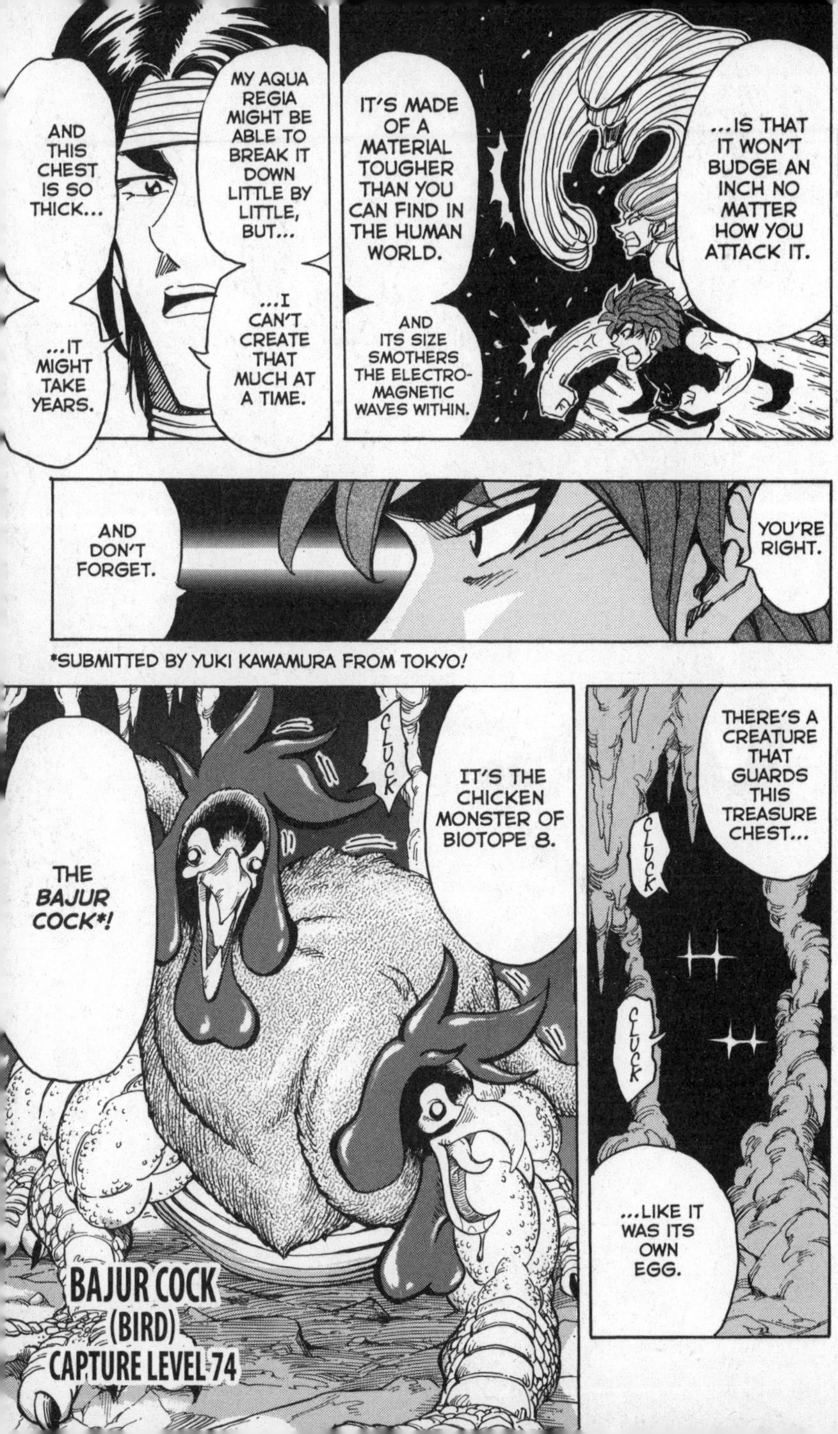
...IS THAT IT WON'T BUDGE AN INCH NO MATTER HOW YOU ATTACK IT.
IT'S MADE OF A MATERIAL TOUGHER THAN YOU CAN FIND IN THE HUMAN WORLD.
AND ITS SIZE SMOTHERS THE ELECTRO-MAGNETIC WAVES WITHIN.
MY AQUA REGIA MIGHT BE ABLE TO BREAK IT DOWN LITTLE BY LITTLE, BUT...
...I CAN'T CREATE THAT MUCH AT A TIME.
AND THIS CHEST IS SO THICK...
...IT MIGHT TAKE YEARS.
YOU'RE RIGHT.
AND DON'T FORGET.
*SUBMITTED BY YUKI KAWAMURA FROM TOKYO!
THERE'S A CREATURE THAT GUARDS THIS TREASURE CHEST...
CLUCK
CLUCK
...LIKE IT WAS ITS OWN EGG.
CLUCK
IT'S THE CHICKEN MONSTER OF BIOTOPE 8.
THE *BAJUR COCK**!
BAJUR COCK
(BIRD)
CAPTURE LEVEL 74

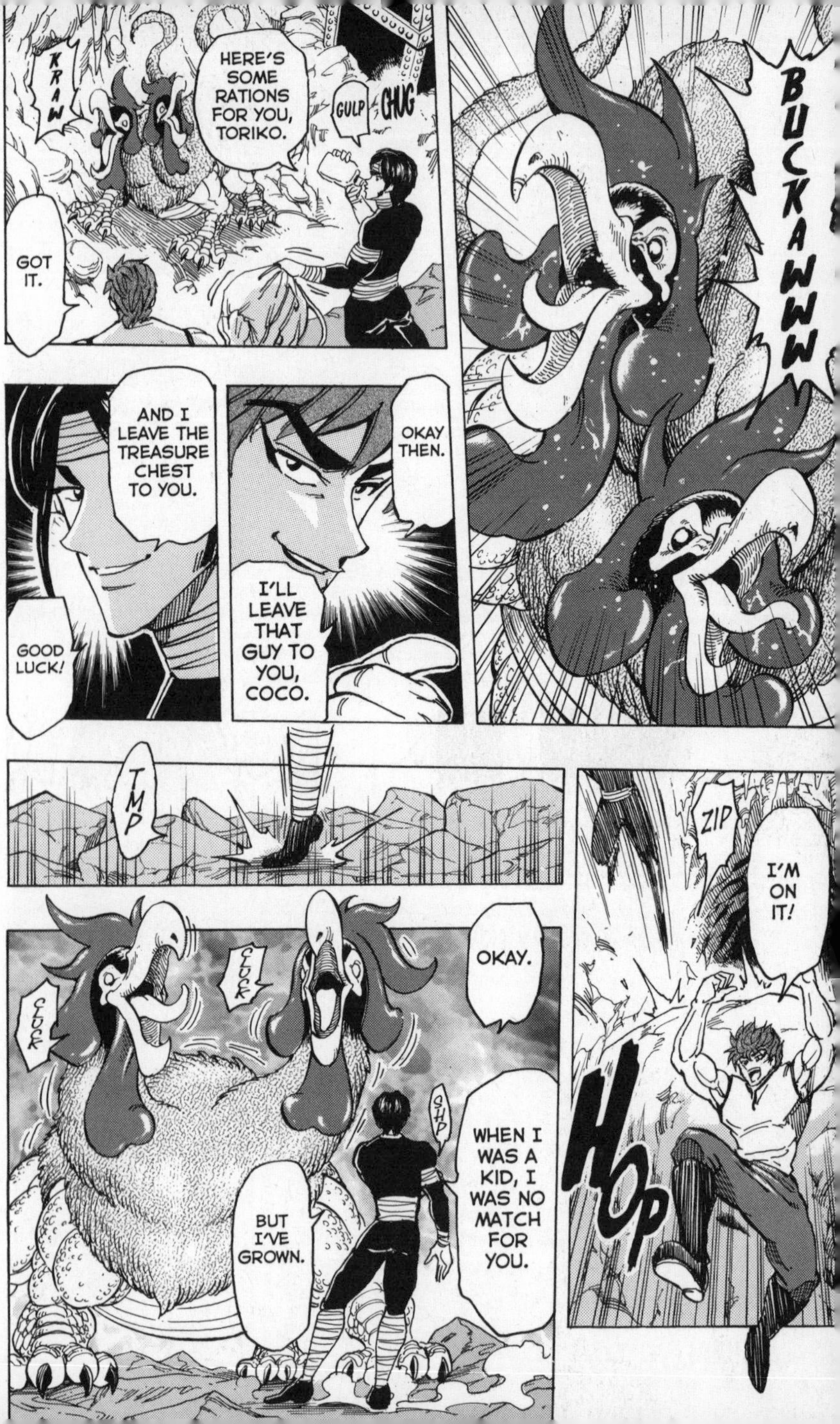

BUCKAWWWW
HERE'S SOME RATIONS FOR YOU, TORIKO.
CHUG
GULP
KRAW
GOT IT.
OKAY THEN.
I'LL LEAVE THAT GUY TO YOU, COCO.
AND I LEAVE THE TREASURE CHEST TO YOU.
GOOD LUCK!
I'M ON IT!
ZIP
HOP
TMP
OKAY.
WHEN I WAS A KID, I WAS NO MATCH FOR YOU.
SHP
CLUCK
BUT I'VE GROWN.
CLUCK

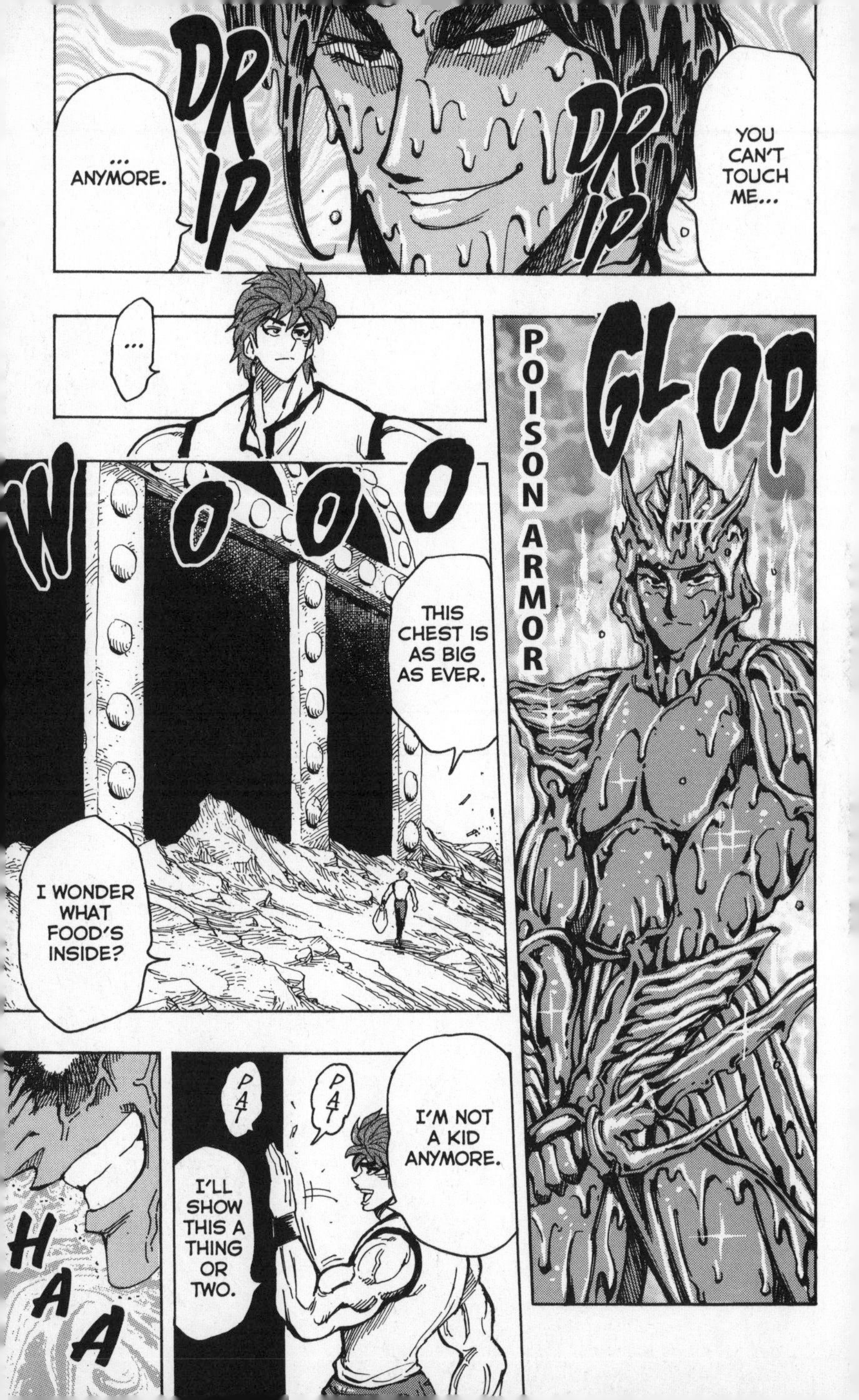
YOU CAN'T TOUCH ME...
DRIP
DRIP
... ANYMORE.
GLOP
POISON ARMOR
...
WOOOO
THIS CHEST IS AS BIG AS EVER.
I WONDER WHAT FOOD'S INSIDE?
I'M NOT A KID ANYMORE.
PAT
PAT
I'LL SHOW THIS A THING OR TWO.
HAA

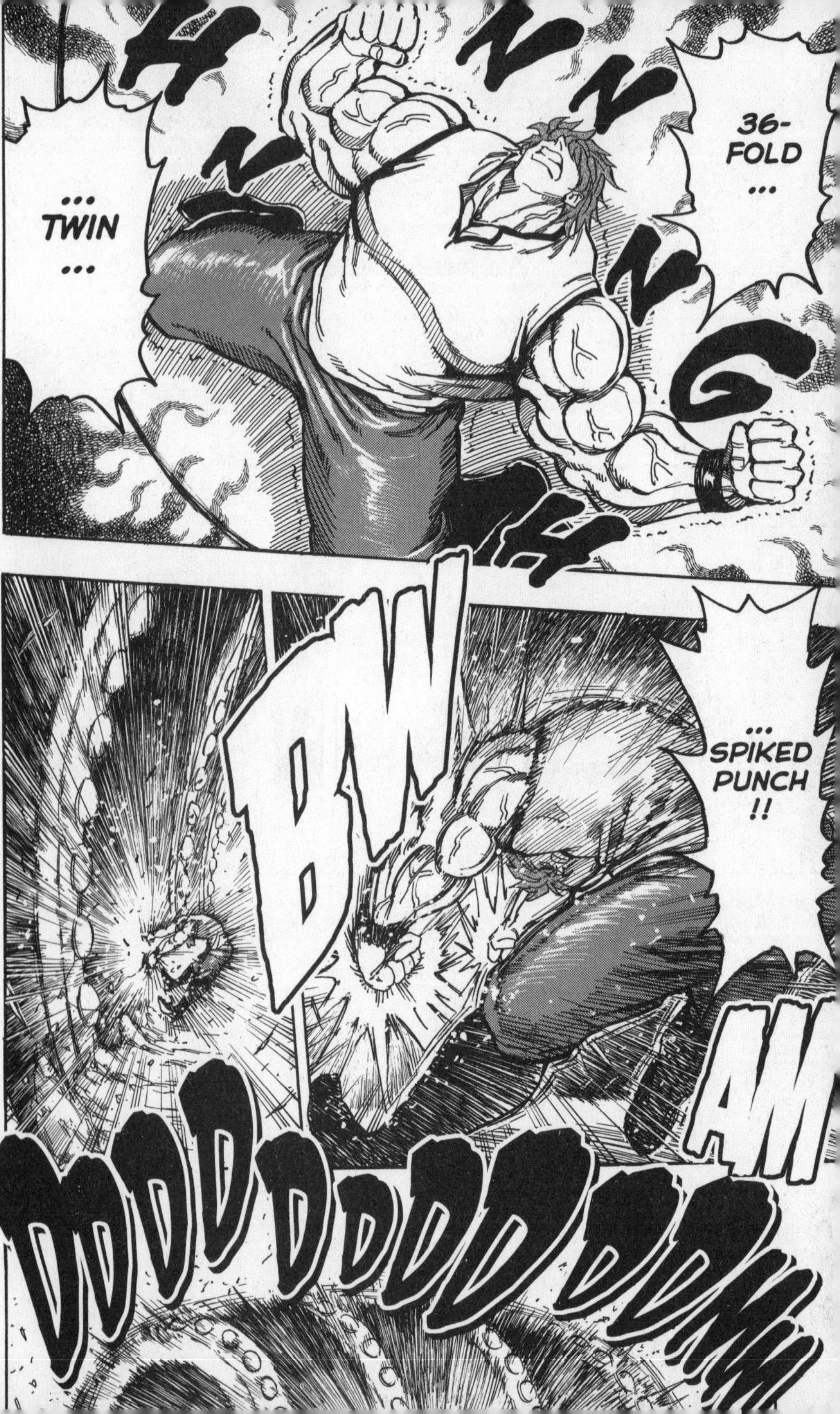
36-FOLD ...
... TWIN ...
HNNNNNGH
... SPIKED PUNCH !!
BAM
DOOOOOOOOOOM

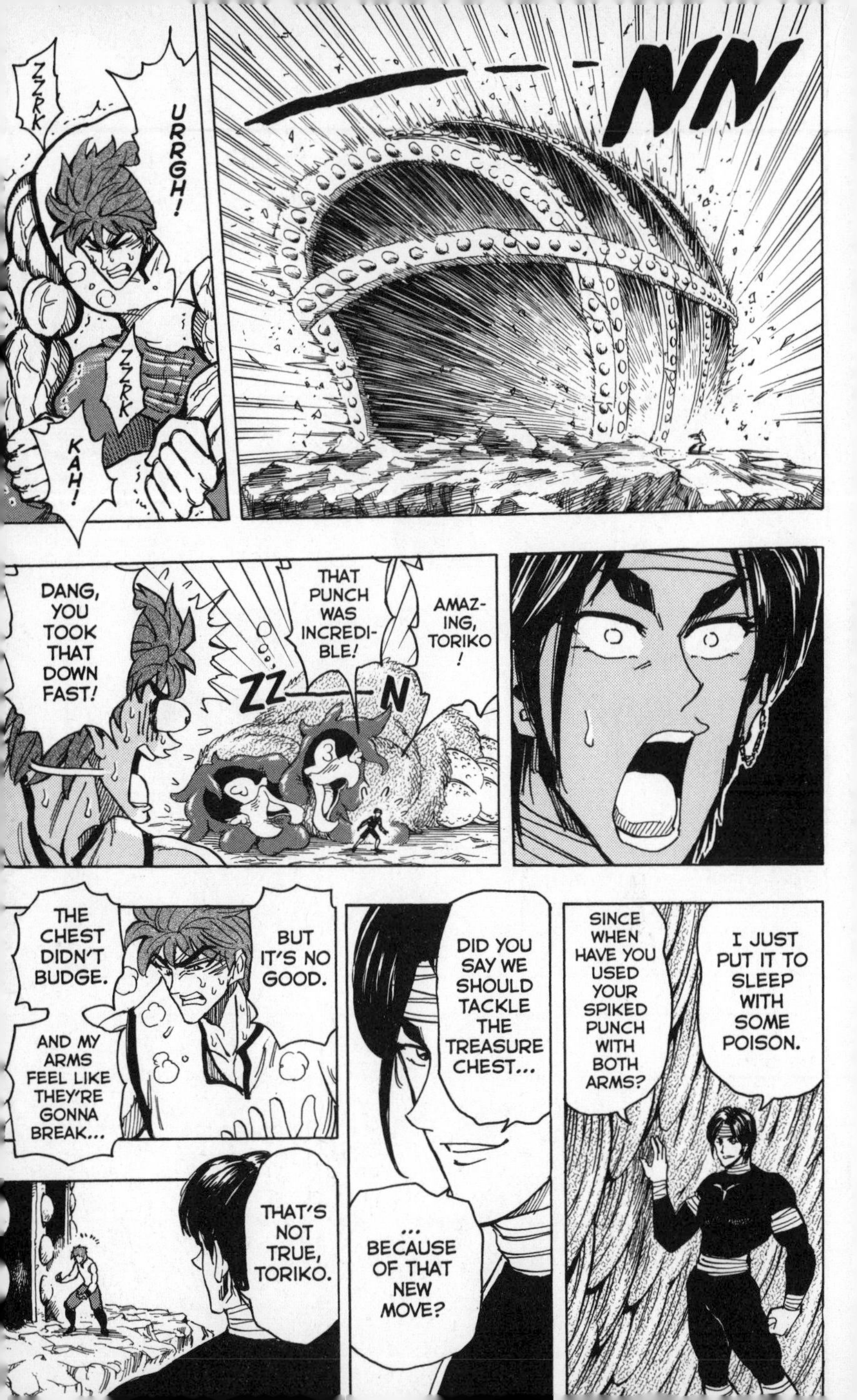

——NN
URRGH!
ZZZRK
ZZRK
KAH!
AMAZ-ING, TORIKO!
THAT PUNCH WAS INCREDIBLE!
ZZ—N
DANG, YOU TOOK THAT DOWN FAST!
I JUST PUT IT TO SLEEP WITH SOME POISON.
SINCE WHEN HAVE YOU USED YOUR SPIKED PUNCH WITH BOTH ARMS?
DID YOU SAY WE SHOULD TACKLE THE TREASURE CHEST...
...BECAUSE OF THAT NEW MOVE?
BUT IT'S NO GOOD.
THE CHEST DIDN'T BUDGE.
AND MY ARMS FEEL LIKE THEY'RE GONNA BREAK...
THAT'S NOT TRUE, TORIKO.

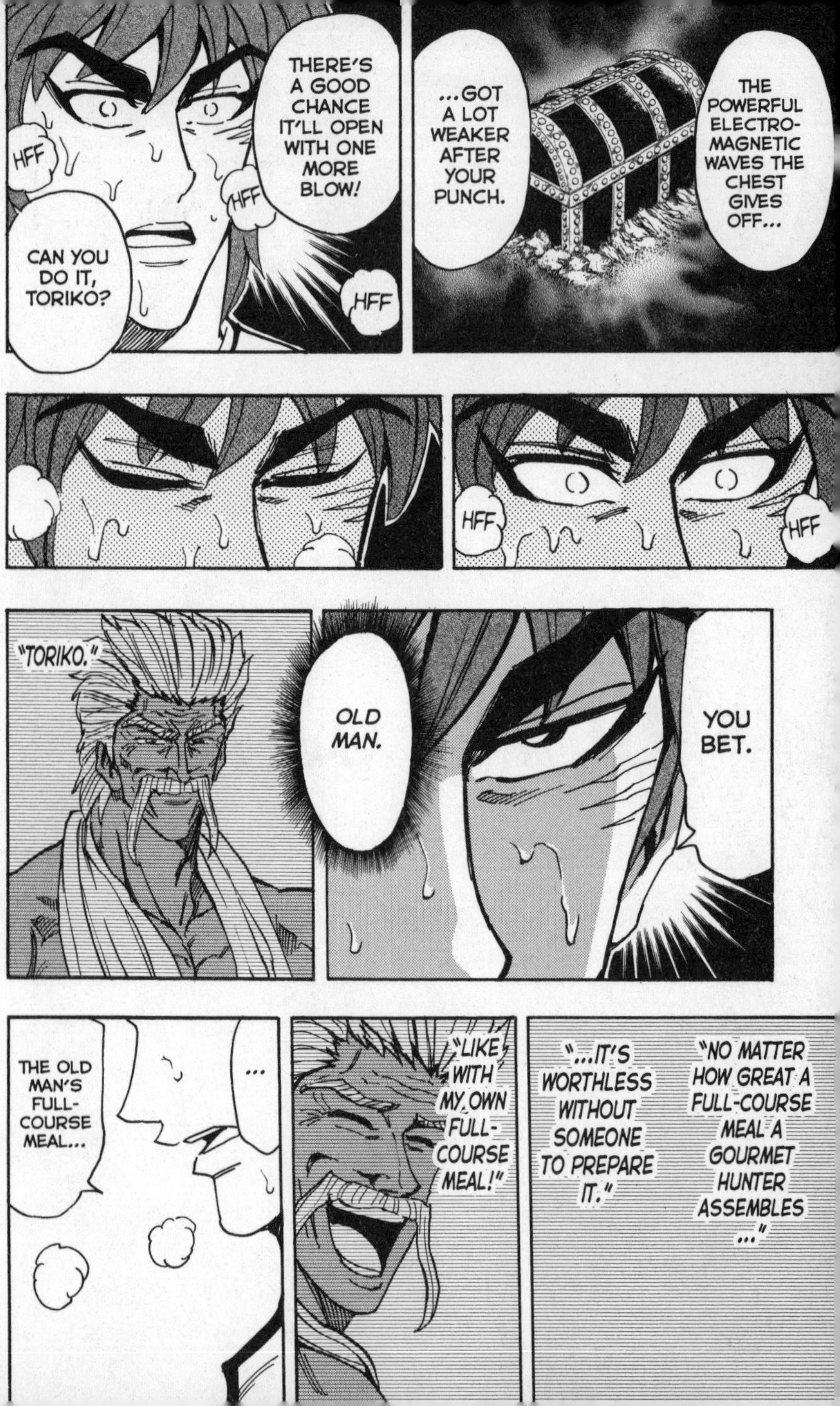
THE POWERFUL ELECTRO-MAGNETIC WAVES THE CHEST GIVES OFF...
...GOT A LOT WEAKER AFTER YOUR PUNCH.
HFF
HFF
THERE'S A GOOD CHANCE IT'LL OPEN WITH ONE MORE BLOW!
HFF
CAN YOU DO IT, TORIKO?
HFF
HFF
YOU BET.
OLD MAN.
"TORIKO."
"NO MATTER HOW GREAT A FULL-COURSE MEAL A GOURMET HUNTER ASSEMBLES ..."
"...IT'S WORTHLESS WITHOUT SOMEONE TO PREPARE IT."
"LIKE WITH MY OWN FULL-COURSE MEAL!"
...
THE OLD MAN'S FULL-COURSE MEAL...

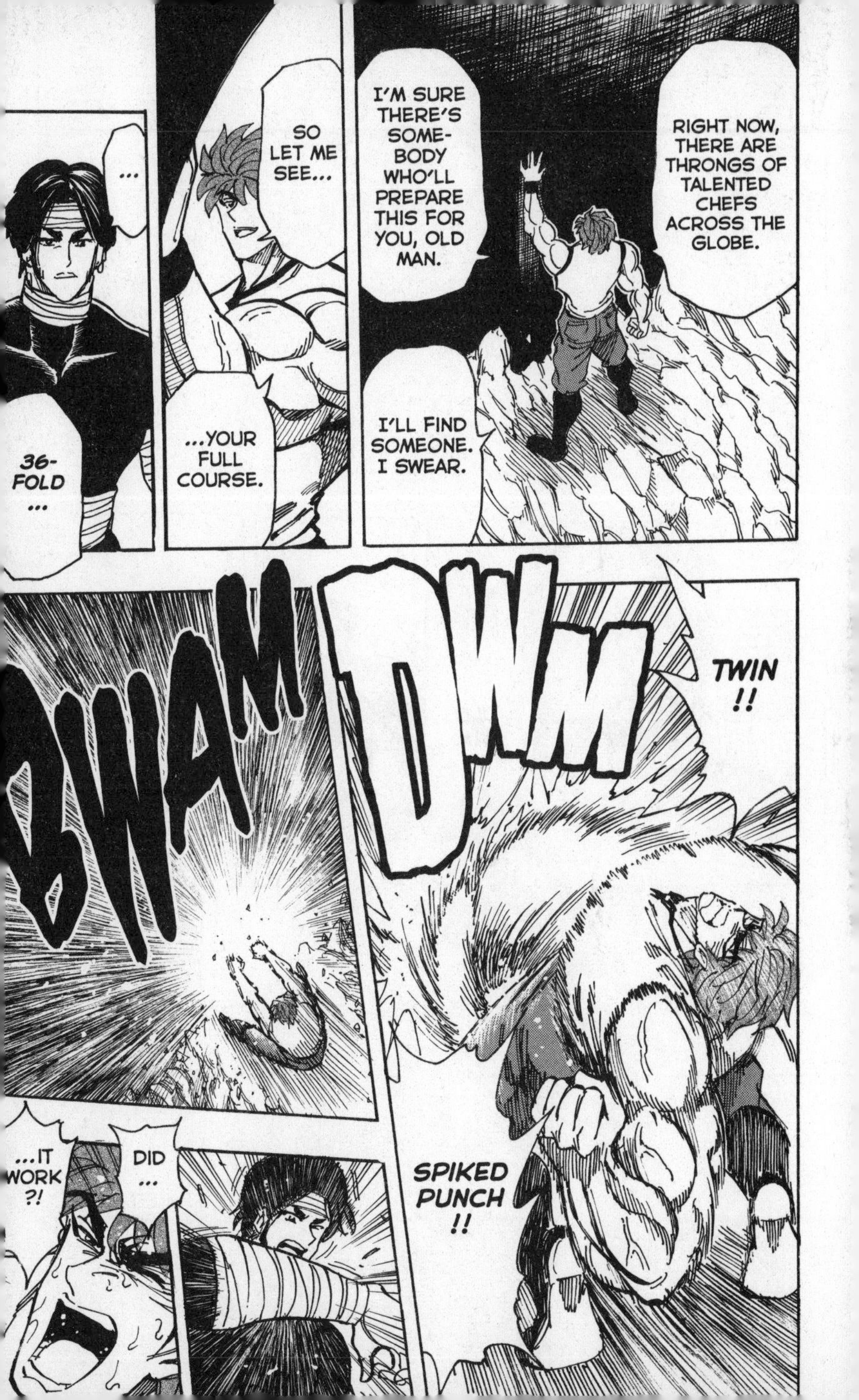
RIGHT NOW, THERE ARE THRONGS OF TALENTED CHEFS ACROSS THE GLOBE.
I'M SURE THERE'S SOME-BODY WHO'LL PREPARE THIS FOR YOU, OLD MAN.
I'LL FIND SOMEONE. I SWEAR.
SO LET ME SEE...
...YOUR FULL COURSE.
...
36-FOLD ...
DWM
TWIN !!
SPIKED PUNCH !!
BWAM
DID ...
...IT WORK ?!

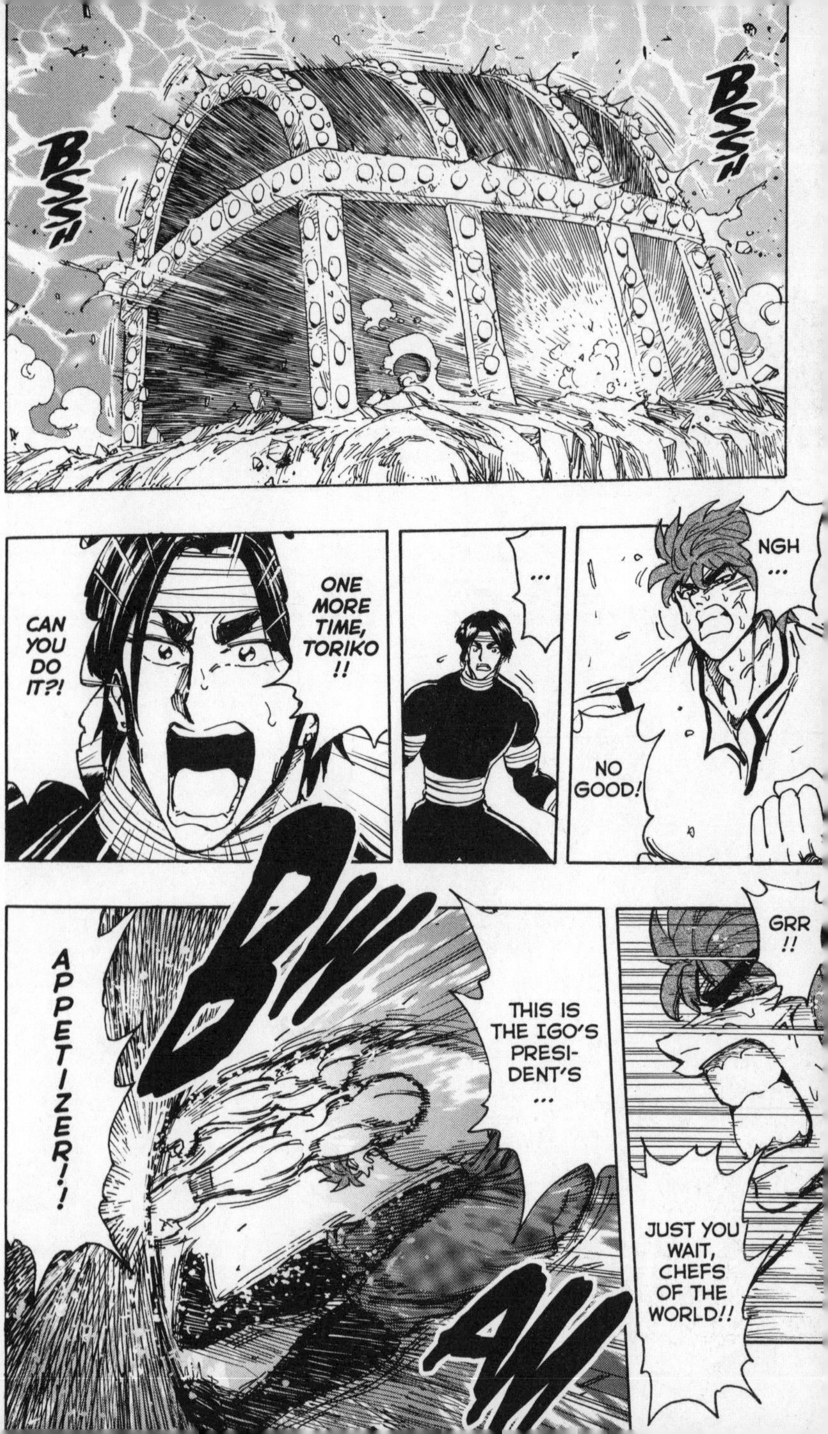
BSSH
BSSH
NGH...
NO GOOD!
...
ONE MORE TIME, TORIKO!!
CAN YOU DO IT?!
GRR!!
JUST YOU WAIT, CHEFS OF THE WORLD!!
THIS IS THE IGO'S PRESIDENT'S...
APPETIZER!!
BWAM

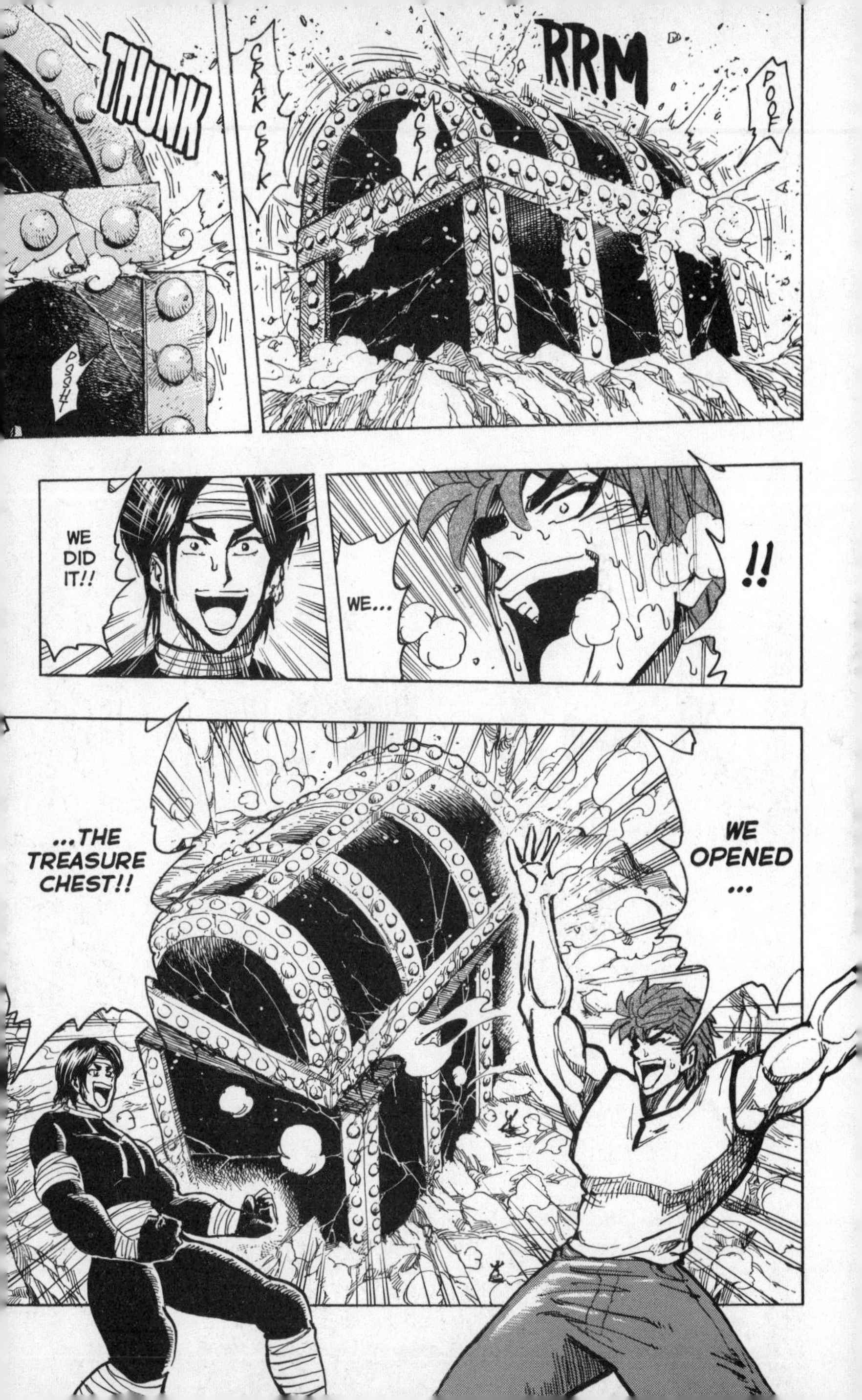
POOF
RRM
CRIK
CRAK CRIK
THUNK
POOSH!
!!
WE...
WE DID IT!!
WE OPENED ...
...THE TREASURE CHEST!!

TORIKO

GOURMET CHECKLIST

Vol. 188
RESERVOIR CAMEL
(MAMMAL)

CAPTURE LEVEL: 2
HABITAT: SAND GARDEN
LENGTH: 4 METERS
HEIGHT: 3 METERS
WEIGHT: 5 TONS
PRICE: MEAT NOT FIT FOR CONSUMPTION;
1 LITER OF WATER FROM ITS HUMP / 500 YEN

SCALE

A MAMMAL IN THE CAMEL FAMILY. IT LIVES IN THE DESERT AND HAS A LARGE BUILD, BROWN FUR, LONG LEGS AND NECK, AND A HUMP ON ITS BACK. ITS HUMP CAN STORE APPROXIMATELY 2,000 LITERS OF WATER. THIS RARE CREATURE IS RATHER HELPFUL IN A DESERT BECAUSE YOU CAN DRINK WATER FROM THE FAUCETS ON ITS SIDE. TAKE THIS TRAVELING COMPANION ALONG ON YOUR NEXT TRIP TO THE DESERT.

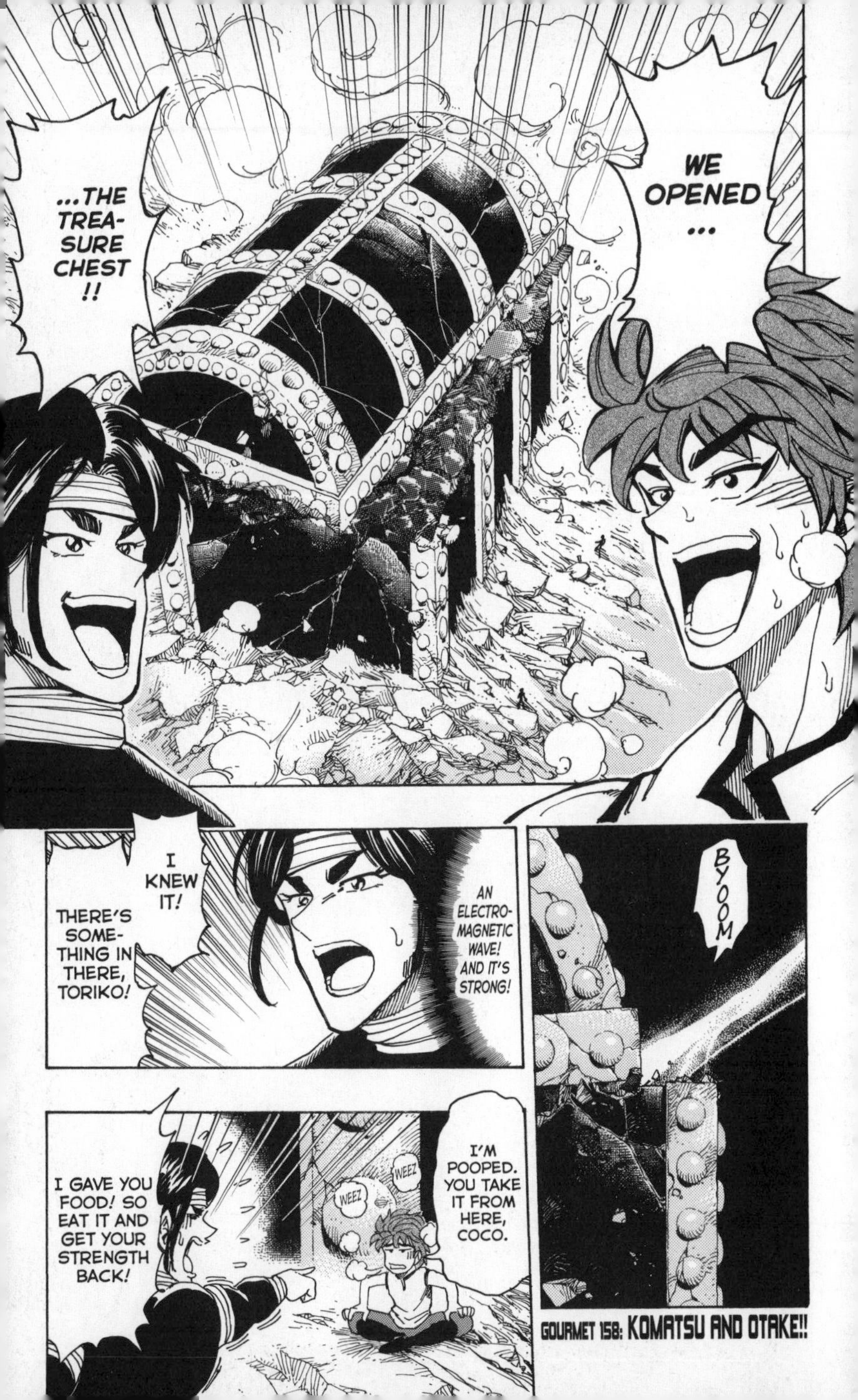
WE OPENED ...
...THE TREASURE CHEST!!
BYOOM
GOURMET 158: KOMATSU AND OTAKE!!
AN ELECTROMAGNETIC WAVE! AND IT'S STRONG!
I KNEW IT!
THERE'S SOMETHING IN THERE, TORIKO!
I'M POOPED. YOU TAKE IT FROM HERE, COCO.
WEEZ
WEEZ
I GAVE YOU FOOD! SO EAT IT AND GET YOUR STRENGTH BACK!

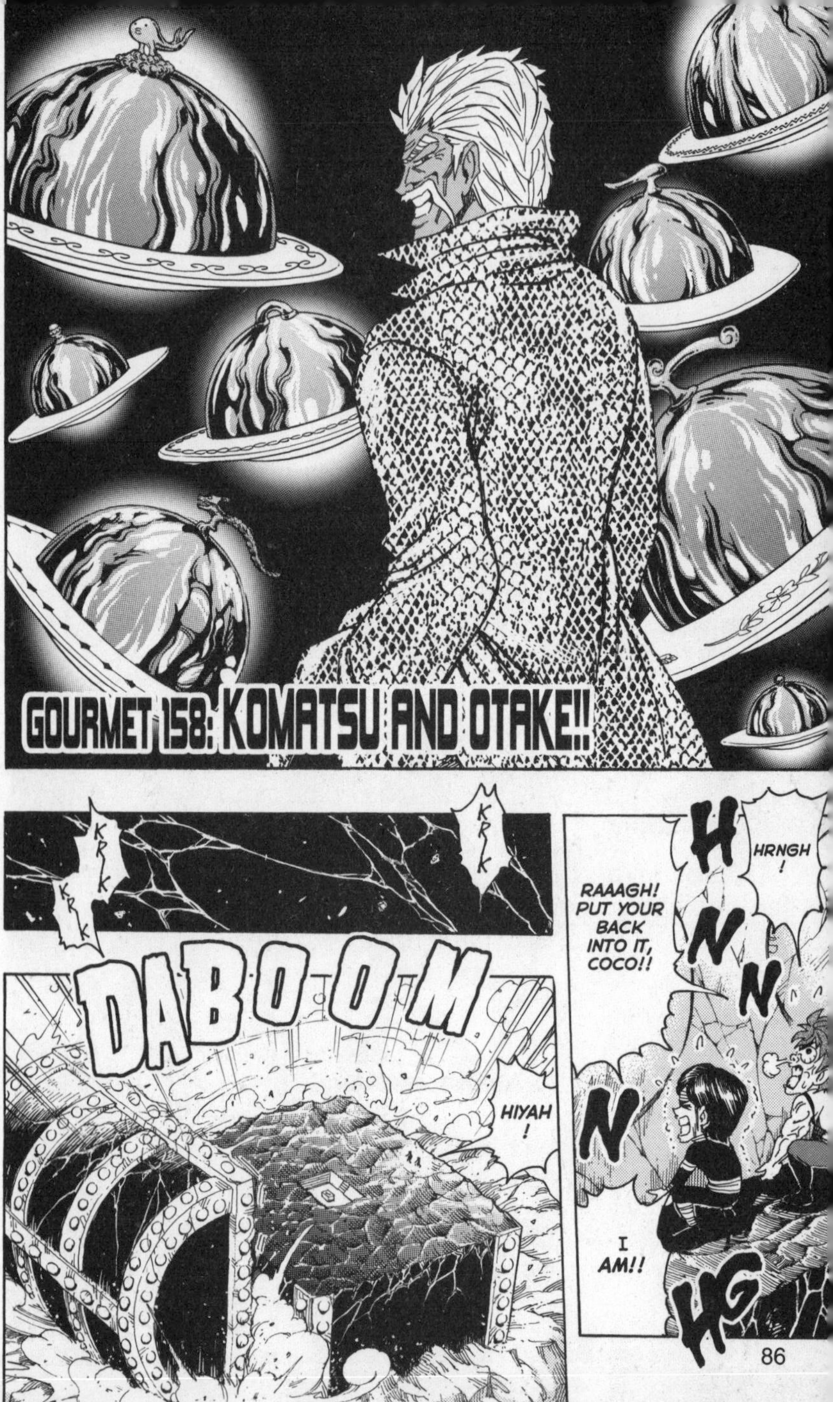
GOURMET 158: KOMATSU AND OTAKE!!
HRNGH!
HNNN
RAAAGH! PUT YOUR BACK INTO IT, COCO!!
I AM!!
HG
KRK
KRK
KRK
DABOOM
HIYAH!

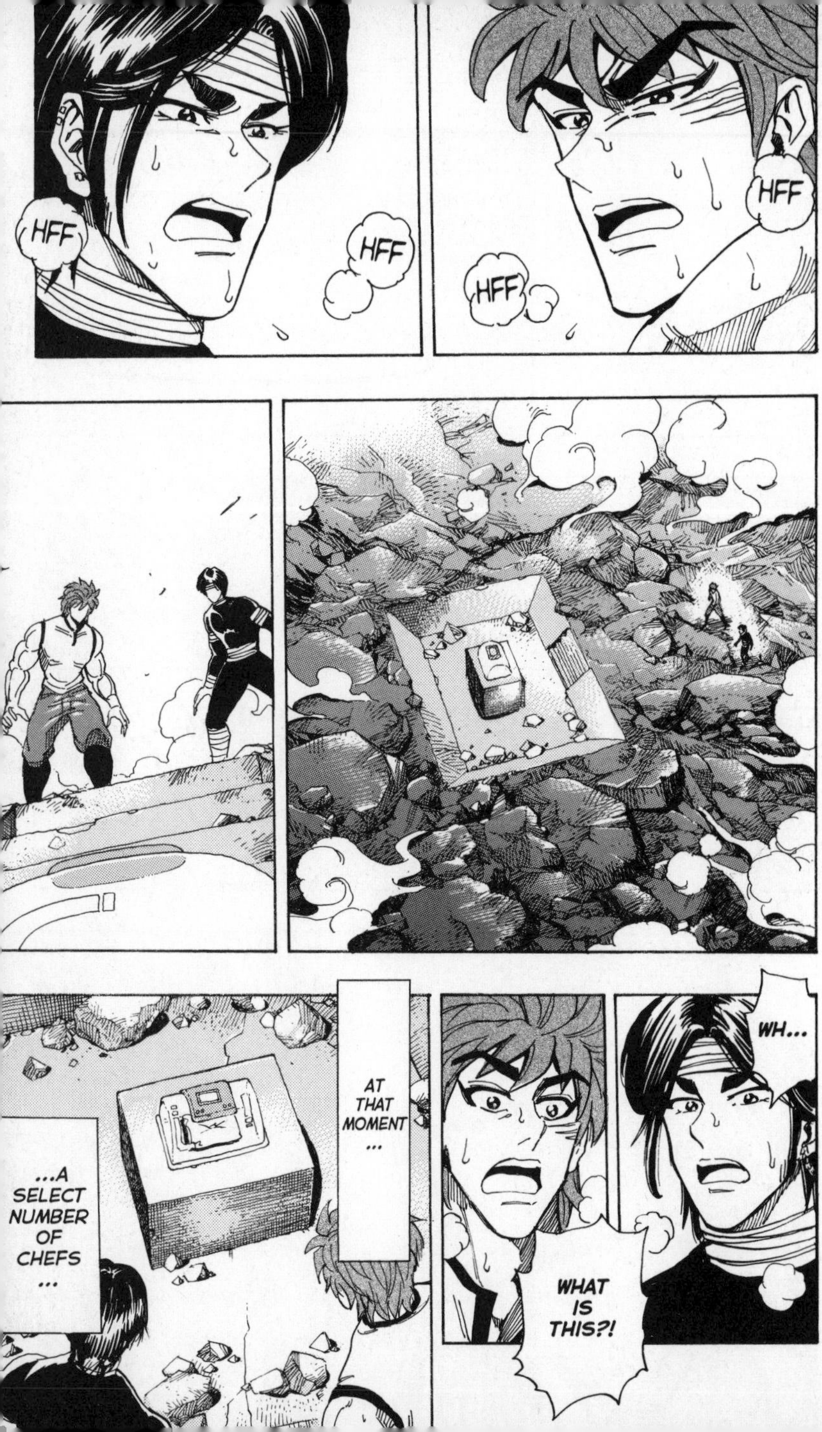
HFF
HFF
HFF
HFF
WH...
WHAT IS THIS?!
AT THAT MOMENT...
...A SELECT NUMBER OF CHEFS...

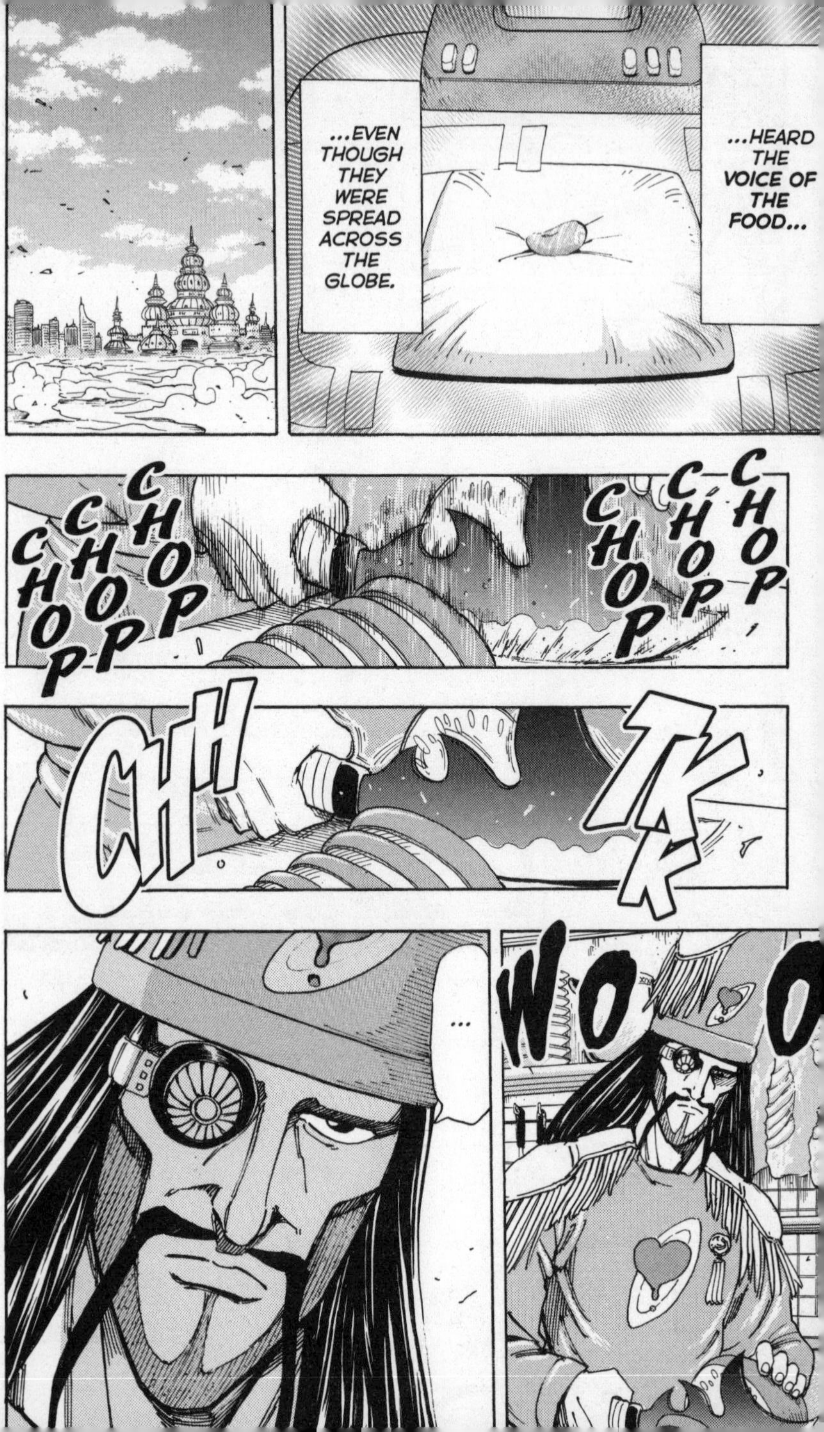
...HEARD THE VOICE OF THE FOOD...
...EVEN THOUGH THEY WERE SPREAD ACROSS THE GLOBE.
CHOP CHOP CHOP
CHOP CHOP CHOP
TK
CHH
WOO
...

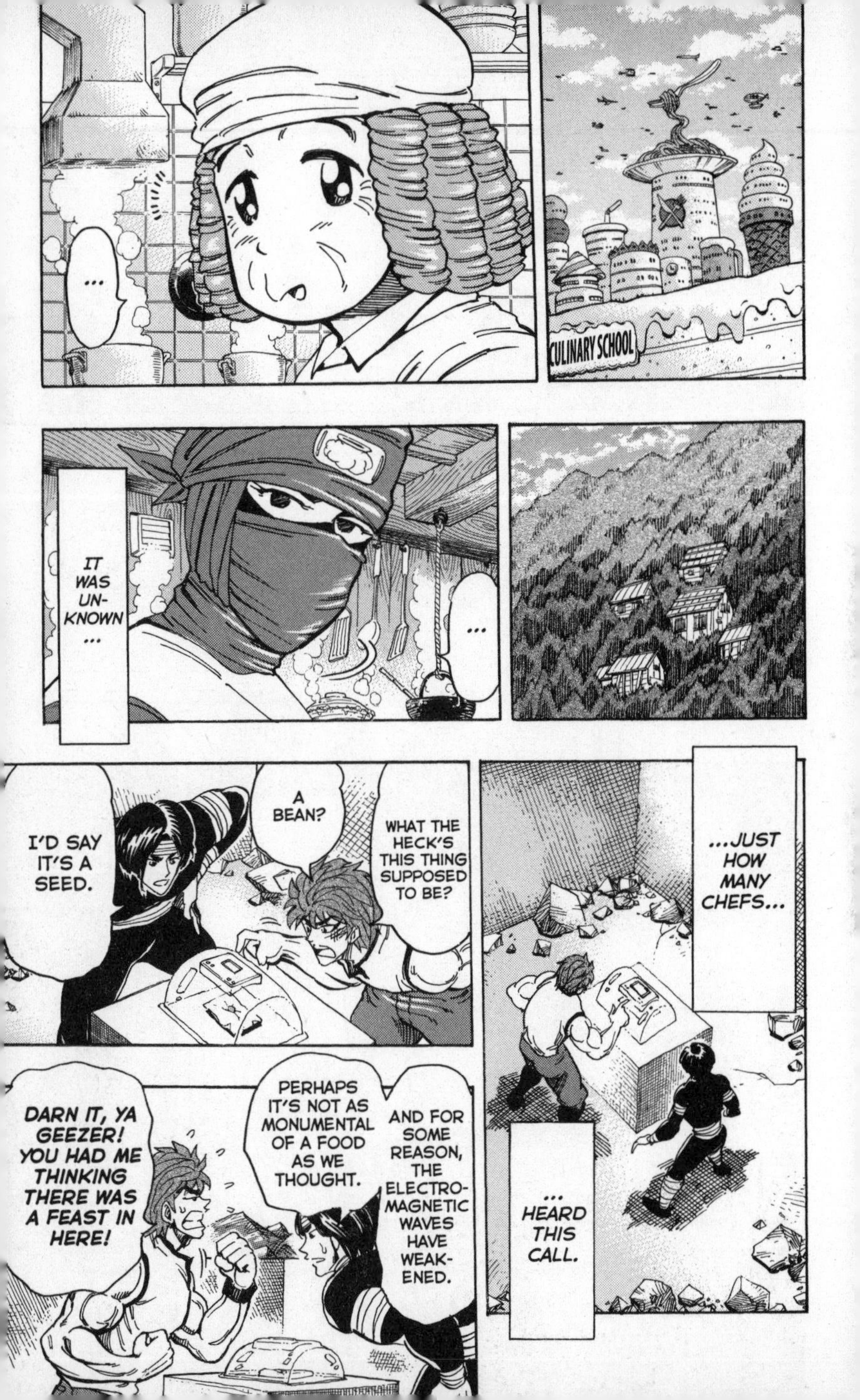
CULINARY SCHOOL
...
...
IT WAS UNKNOWN...
...JUST HOW MANY CHEFS...
...HEARD THIS CALL.
WHAT THE HECK'S THIS THING SUPPOSED TO BE?
A BEAN?
I'D SAY IT'S A SEED.
AND FOR SOME REASON, THE ELECTROMAGNETIC WAVES HAVE WEAKENED.
PERHAPS IT'S NOT AS MONUMENTAL OF A FOOD AS WE THOUGHT.
DARN IT, YA GEEZER! YOU HAD ME THINKING THERE WAS A FEAST IN HERE!

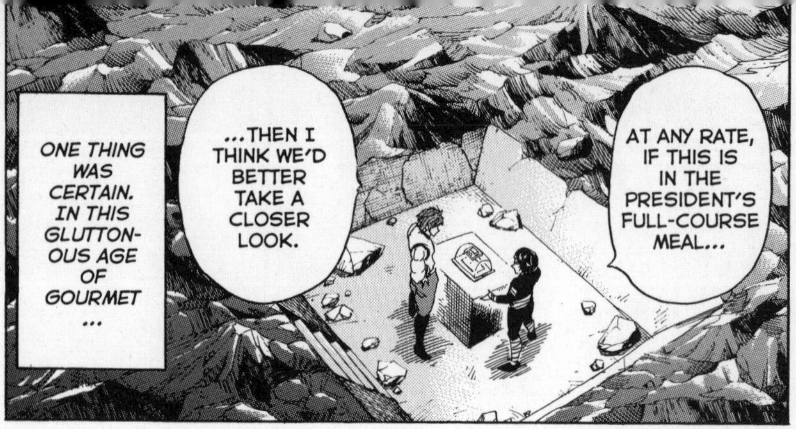
AT ANY RATE, IF THIS IS IN THE PRESIDENT'S FULL-COURSE MEAL...
...THEN I THINK WE'D BETTER TAKE A CLOSER LOOK.
ONE THING WAS CERTAIN. IN THIS GLUTTON-OUS AGE OF GOURMET ...
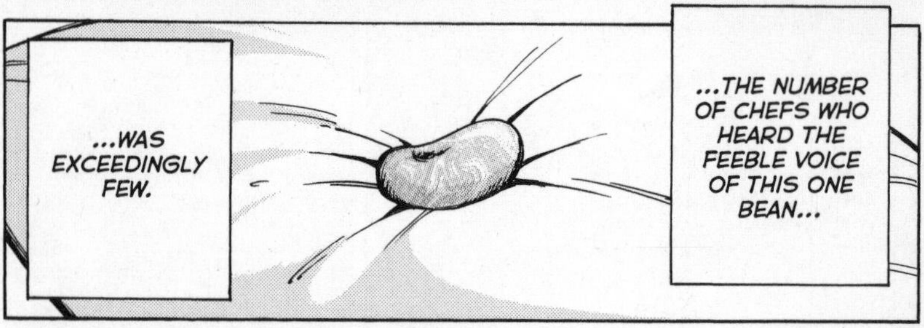
...THE NUMBER OF CHEFS WHO HEARD THE FEEBLE VOICE OF THIS ONE BEAN...
...WAS EXCEEDINGLY FEW.
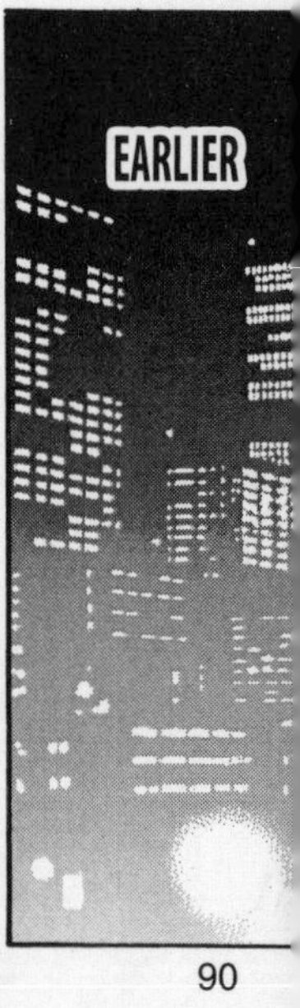
EARLIER
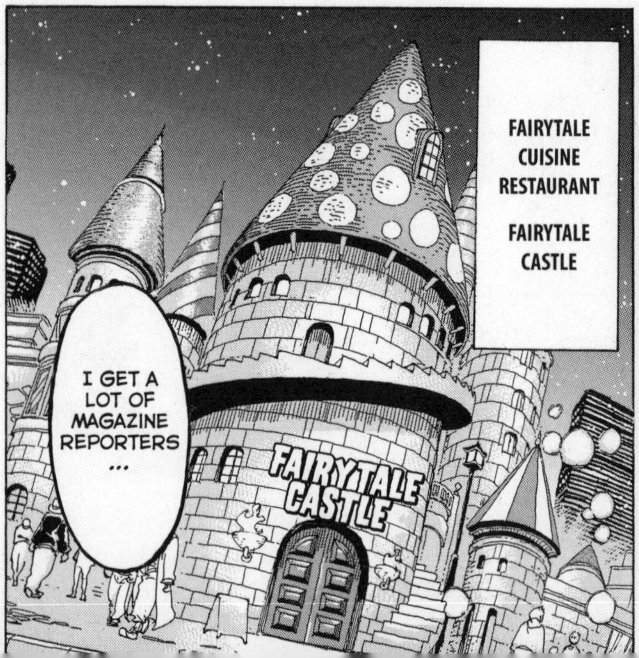
FAIRYTALE CUISINE RESTAURANT
FAIRYTALE CASTLE
FAIRYTALE CASTLE
I GET A LOT OF MAGAZINE REPORTERS ...

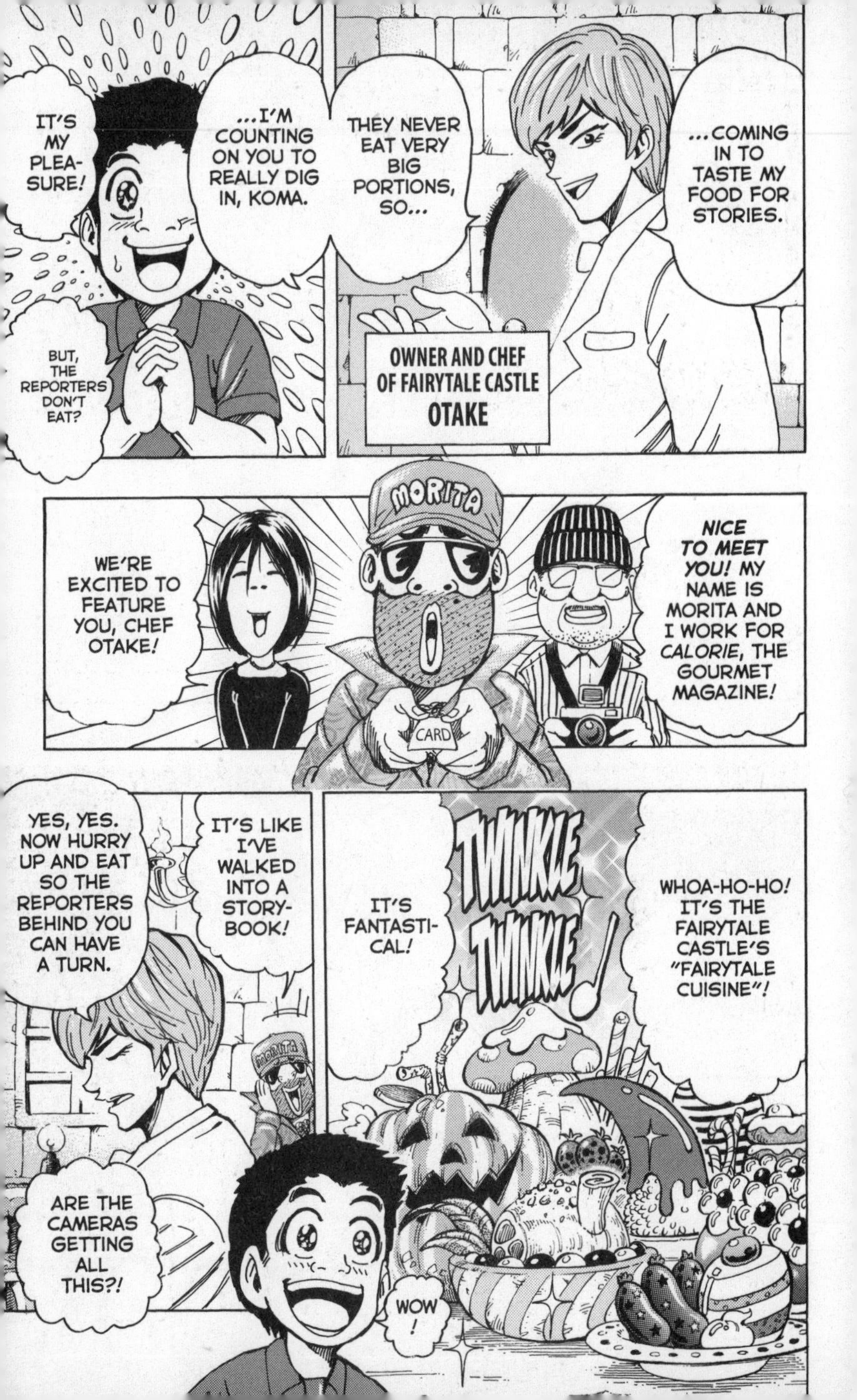
...COMING IN TO TASTE MY FOOD FOR STORIES.
THEY NEVER EAT VERY BIG PORTIONS, SO...
OWNER AND CHEF OF FAIRYTALE CASTLE
OTAKE
...I'M COUNTING ON YOU TO REALLY DIG IN, KOMA.
IT'S MY PLEA-SURE!
BUT, THE REPORTERS DON'T EAT?
NICE TO MEET YOU! MY NAME IS MORITA AND I WORK FOR *CALORIE*, THE GOURMET MAGAZINE!
MORITA
CARD
WE'RE EXCITED TO FEATURE YOU, CHEF OTAKE!
WHOA-HO-HO! IT'S THE FAIRYTALE CASTLE'S "FAIRYTALE CUISINE"!
TWINKLE TWINKLE
IT'S FANTASTI-CAL!
WOW!
IT'S LIKE I'VE WALKED INTO A STORY-BOOK!
YES, YES. NOW HURRY UP AND EAT SO THE REPORTERS BEHIND YOU CAN HAVE A TURN.
MORITA
ARE THE CAMERAS GETTING ALL THIS?!

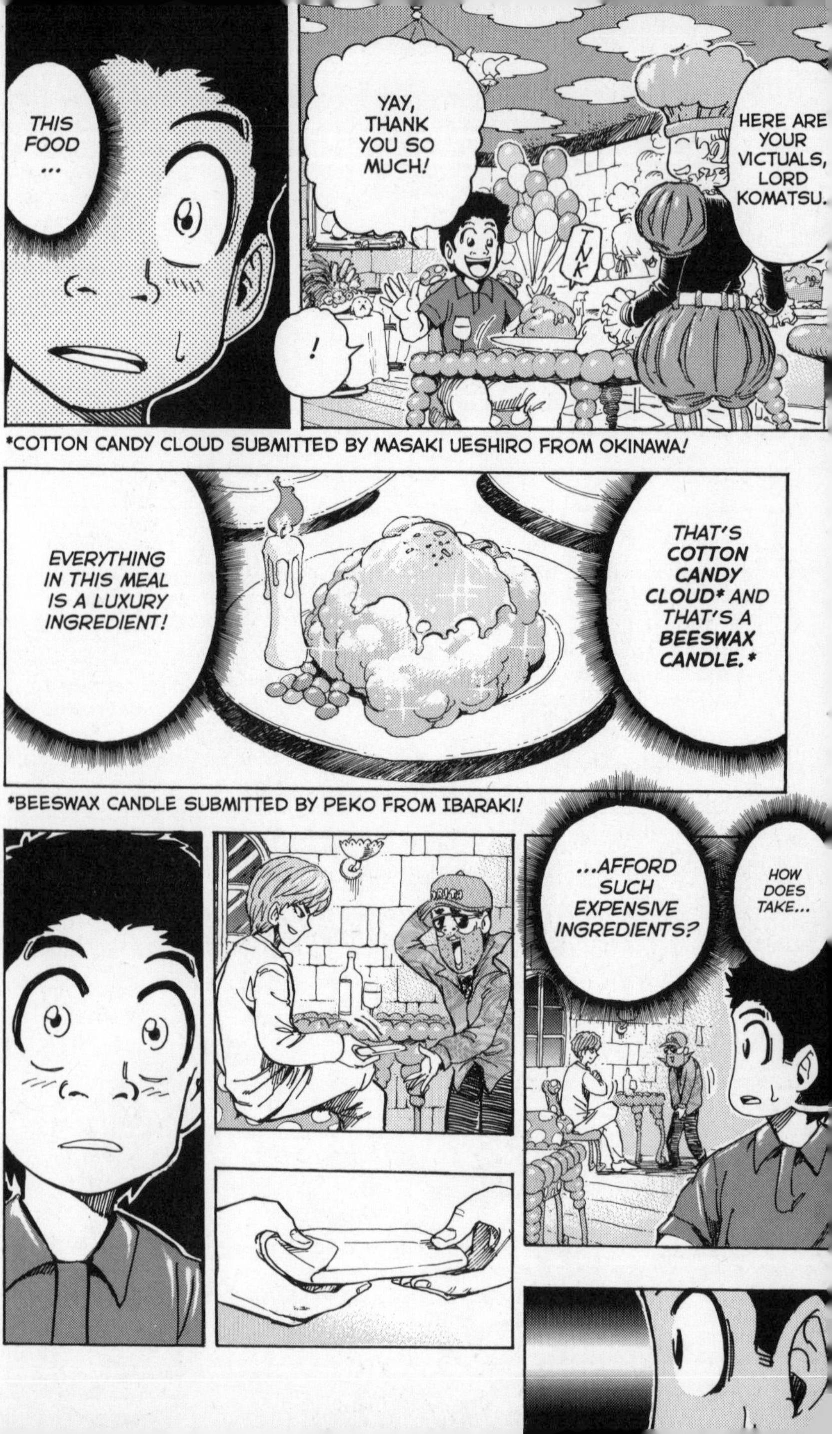
HERE ARE YOUR VICTUALS, LORD KOMATSU.
TNK
YAY, THANK YOU SO MUCH!
!
THIS FOOD ...
THAT'S COTTON CANDY CLOUD* AND THAT'S A BEESWAX CANDLE.*
EVERYTHING IN THIS MEAL IS A LUXURY INGREDIENT!
HOW DOES TAKE...
...AFFORD SUCH EXPENSIVE INGREDIENTS?
*COTTON CANDY CLOUD SUBMITTED BY MASAKI UESHIRO FROM OKINAWA!

*BEESWAX CANDLE SUBMITTED BY PEKO FROM IBARAKI!

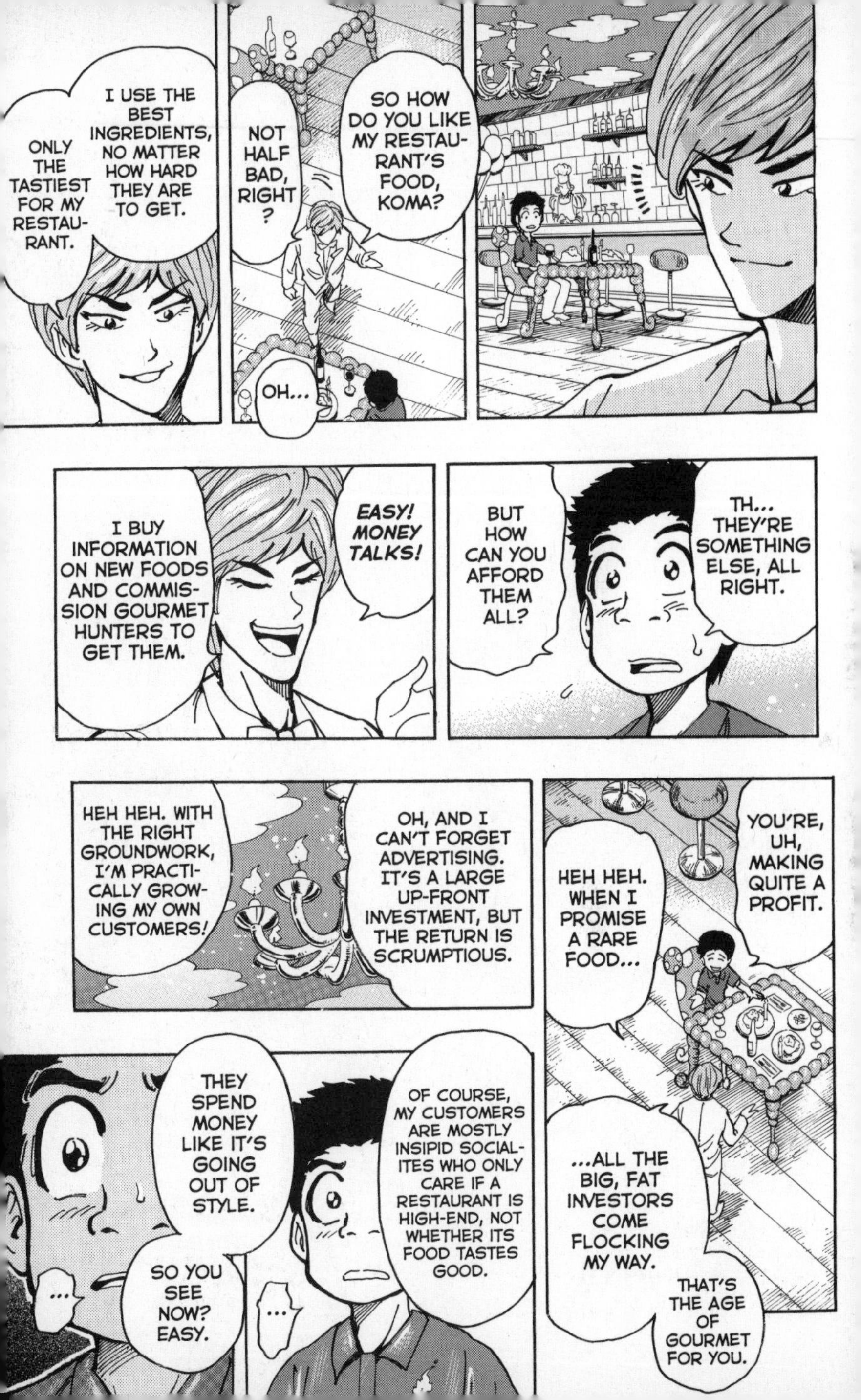
SO HOW DO YOU LIKE MY RESTAURANT'S FOOD, KOMA?
NOT HALF BAD, RIGHT?
OH...
I USE THE BEST INGREDIENTS, NO MATTER HOW HARD THEY ARE TO GET.
ONLY THE TASTIEST FOR MY RESTAURANT.
TH... THEY'RE SOMETHING ELSE, ALL RIGHT.
BUT HOW CAN YOU AFFORD THEM ALL?
EASY! MONEY TALKS!
I BUY INFORMATION ON NEW FOODS AND COMMISSION GOURMET HUNTERS TO GET THEM.
YOU'RE, UH, MAKING QUITE A PROFIT.
HEH HEH. WHEN I PROMISE A RARE FOOD...
...ALL THE BIG, FAT INVESTORS COME FLOCKING MY WAY.
THAT'S THE AGE OF GOURMET FOR YOU.
OH, AND I CAN'T FORGET ADVERTISING. IT'S A LARGE UP-FRONT INVESTMENT, BUT THE RETURN IS SCRUMPTIOUS.
HEH HEH. WITH THE RIGHT GROUNDWORK, I'M PRACTICALLY GROWING MY OWN CUSTOMERS!
OF COURSE, MY CUSTOMERS ARE MOSTLY INSIPID SOCIALITES WHO ONLY CARE IF A RESTAURANT IS HIGH-END, NOT WHETHER ITS FOOD TASTES GOOD.
...
THEY SPEND MONEY LIKE IT'S GOING OUT OF STYLE.
SO YOU SEE NOW? EASY.
...

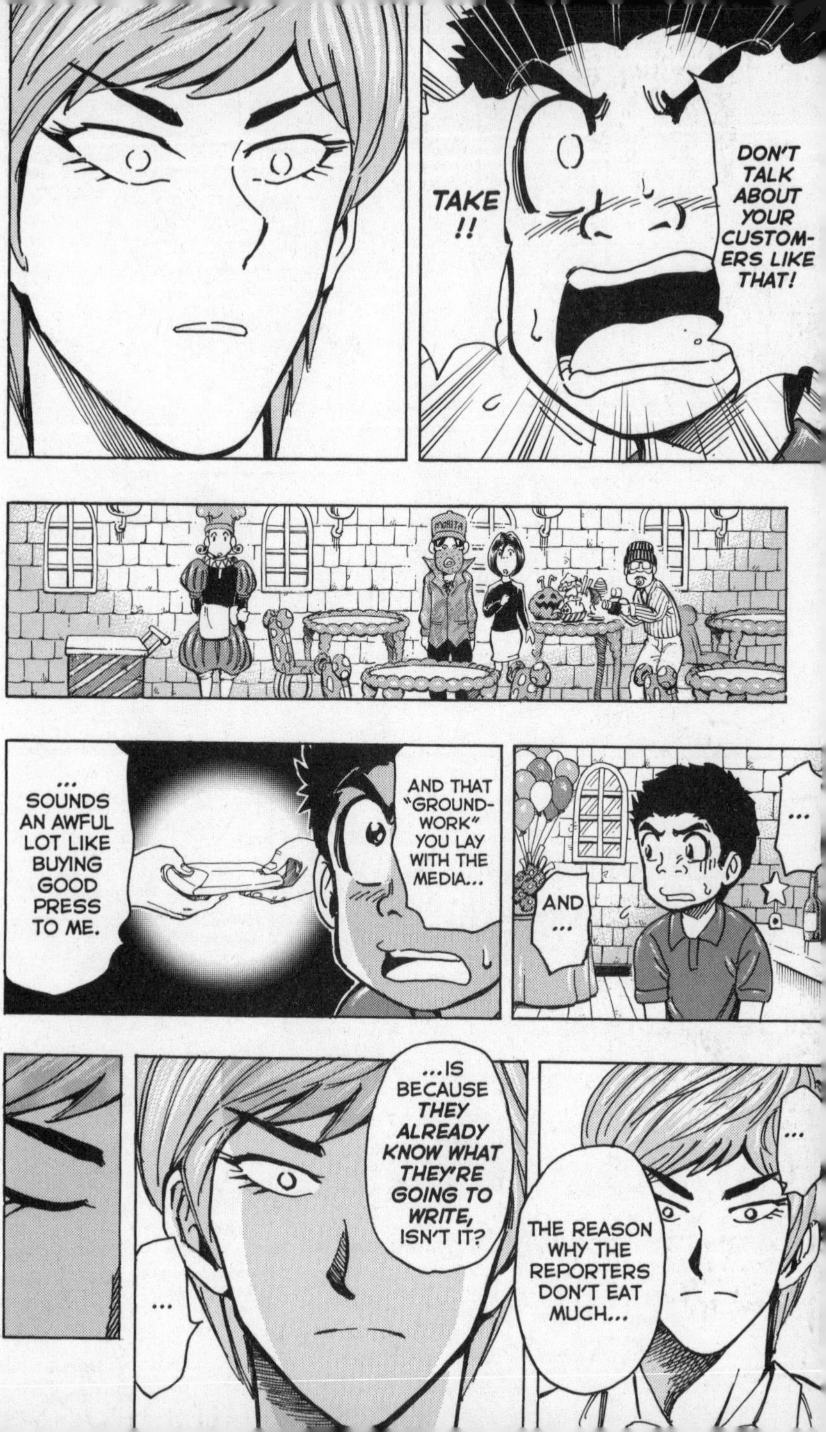
DON'T TALK ABOUT YOUR CUSTOMERS LIKE THAT!
TAKE!!
...
AND...
AND THAT "GROUNDWORK" YOU LAY WITH THE MEDIA...
...SOUNDS AN AWFUL LOT LIKE BUYING GOOD PRESS TO ME.
...
THE REASON WHY THE REPORTERS DON'T EAT MUCH...
...IS BECAUSE THEY ALREADY KNOW WHAT THEY'RE GOING TO WRITE, ISN'T IT?
...

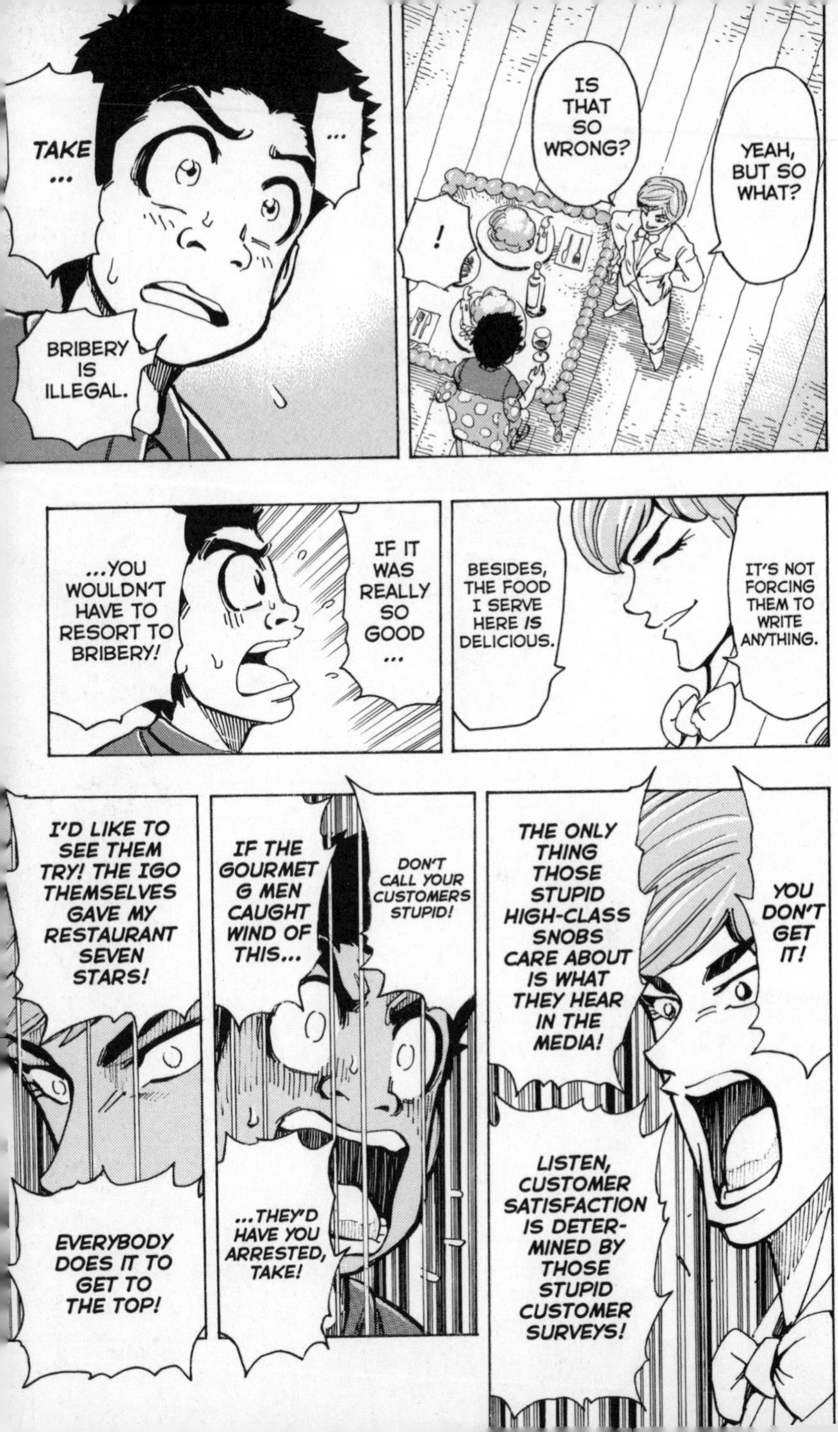
YEAH, BUT SO WHAT?
IS THAT SO WRONG?
!
...
TAKE ...
BRIBERY IS ILLEGAL.
IT'S NOT FORCING THEM TO WRITE ANYTHING.
BESIDES, THE FOOD I SERVE HERE IS DELICIOUS.
IF IT WAS REALLY SO GOOD ...
...YOU WOULDN'T HAVE TO RESORT TO BRIBERY!
YOU DON'T GET IT!
THE ONLY THING THOSE STUPID HIGH-CLASS SNOBS CARE ABOUT IS WHAT THEY HEAR IN THE MEDIA!
LISTEN, CUSTOMER SATISFACTION IS DETER-MINED BY THOSE STUPID CUSTOMER SURVEYS!
DON'T CALL YOUR CUSTOMERS STUPID!
IF THE GOURMET G MEN CAUGHT WIND OF THIS...
...THEY'D HAVE YOU ARRESTED, TAKE!
I'D LIKE TO SEE THEM TRY! THE IGO THEMSELVES GAVE MY RESTAURANT SEVEN STARS!
EVERYBODY DOES IT TO GET TO THE TOP!

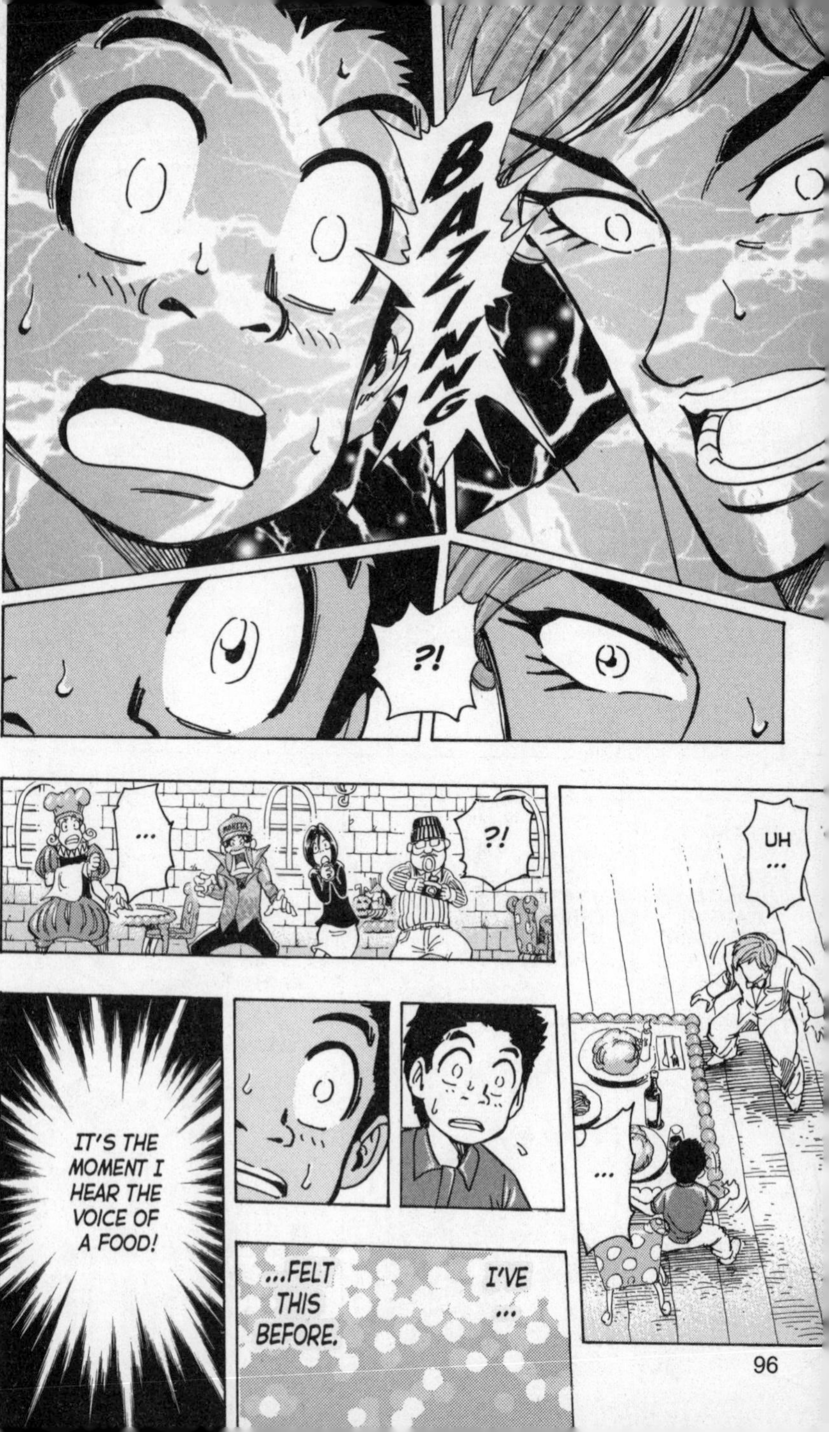
BAZINNNG
?!
UH ...
...
?!
...
I'VE ...
...FELT THIS BEFORE.
IT'S THE MOMENT I HEAR THE VOICE OF A FOOD!

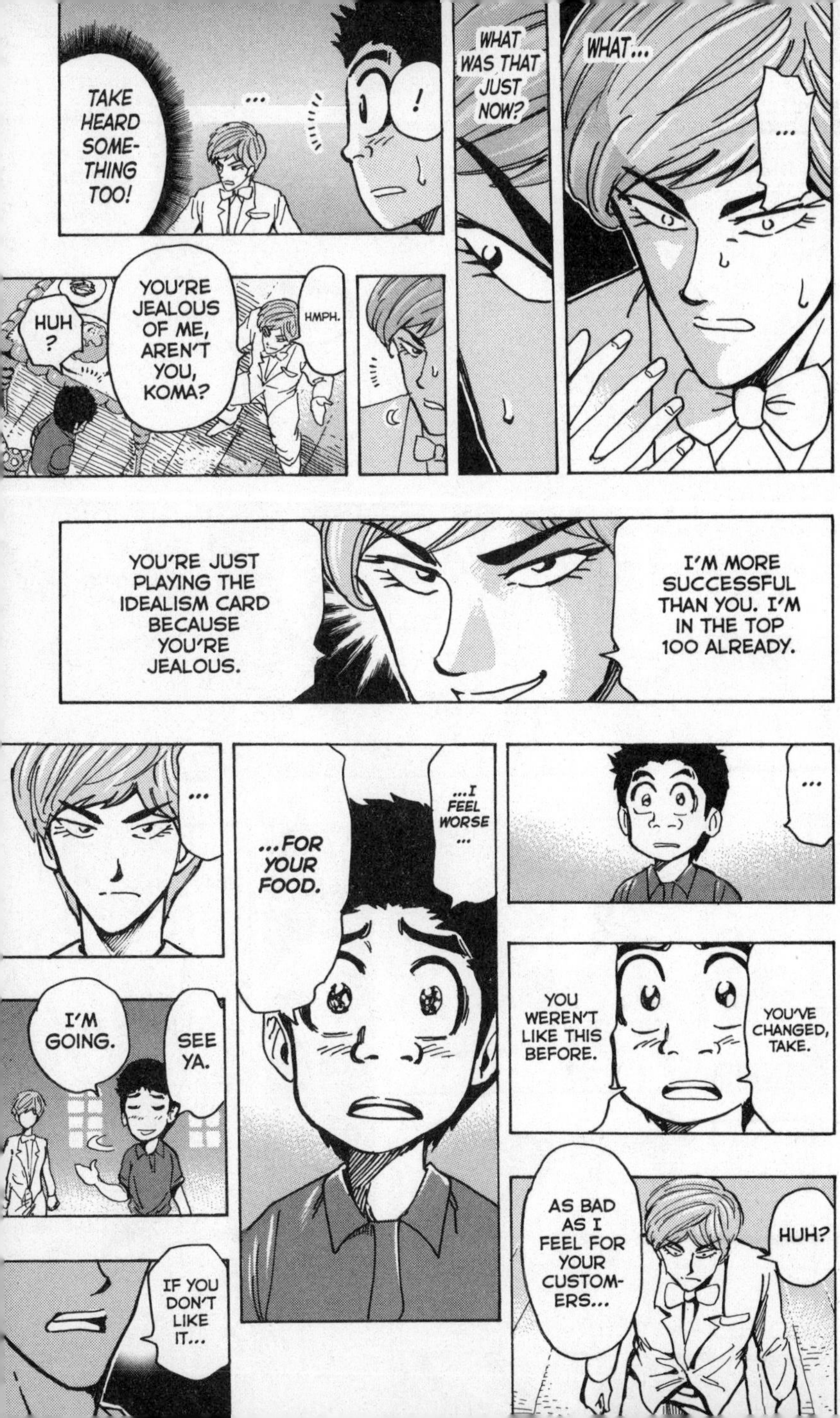
WHAT...
...
WHAT WAS THAT JUST NOW?
!
...
TAKE HEARD SOMETHING TOO!
HMPH.
YOU'RE JEALOUS OF ME, AREN'T YOU, KOMA?
HUH?
I'M MORE SUCCESSFUL THAN YOU. I'M IN THE TOP 100 ALREADY.
YOU'RE JUST PLAYING THE IDEALISM CARD BECAUSE YOU'RE JEALOUS.
...
YOU'VE CHANGED, TAKE.
YOU WEREN'T LIKE THIS BEFORE.
HUH?
AS BAD AS I FEEL FOR YOUR CUSTOMERS...
...I FEEL WORSE...
...FOR YOUR FOOD.
...
SEE YA.
I'M GOING.
IF YOU DON'T LIKE IT...

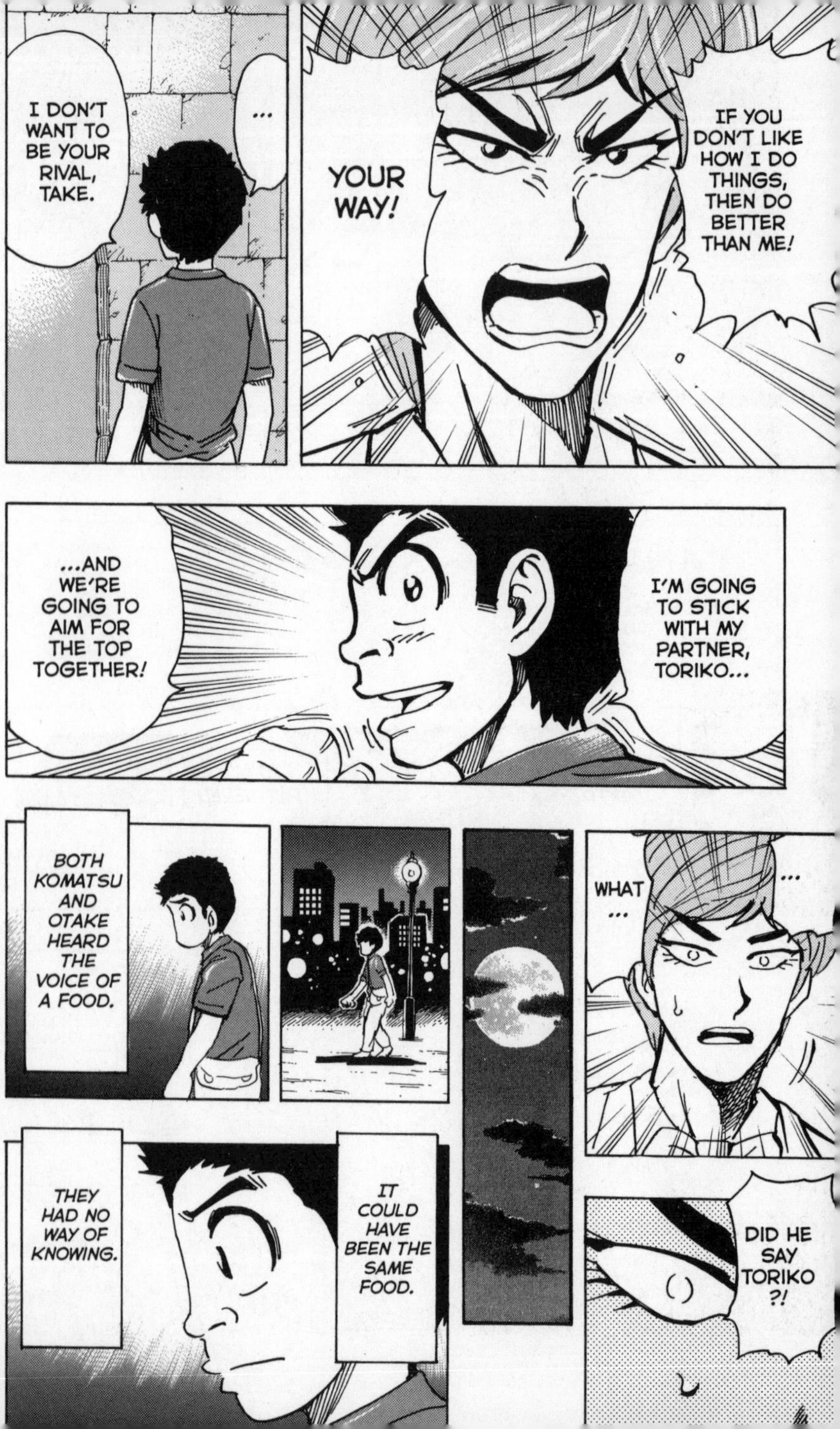
IF YOU DON'T LIKE HOW I DO THINGS, THEN DO BETTER THAN ME!
YOUR WAY!
...
I DON'T WANT TO BE YOUR RIVAL, TAKE.
I'M GOING TO STICK WITH MY PARTNER, TORIKO...
...AND WE'RE GOING TO AIM FOR THE TOP TOGETHER!
...
WHAT...
DID HE SAY TORIKO?!
BOTH KOMATSU AND OTAKE HEARD THE VOICE OF A FOOD.
IT COULD HAVE BEEN THE SAME FOOD.
THEY HAD NO WAY OF KNOWING.

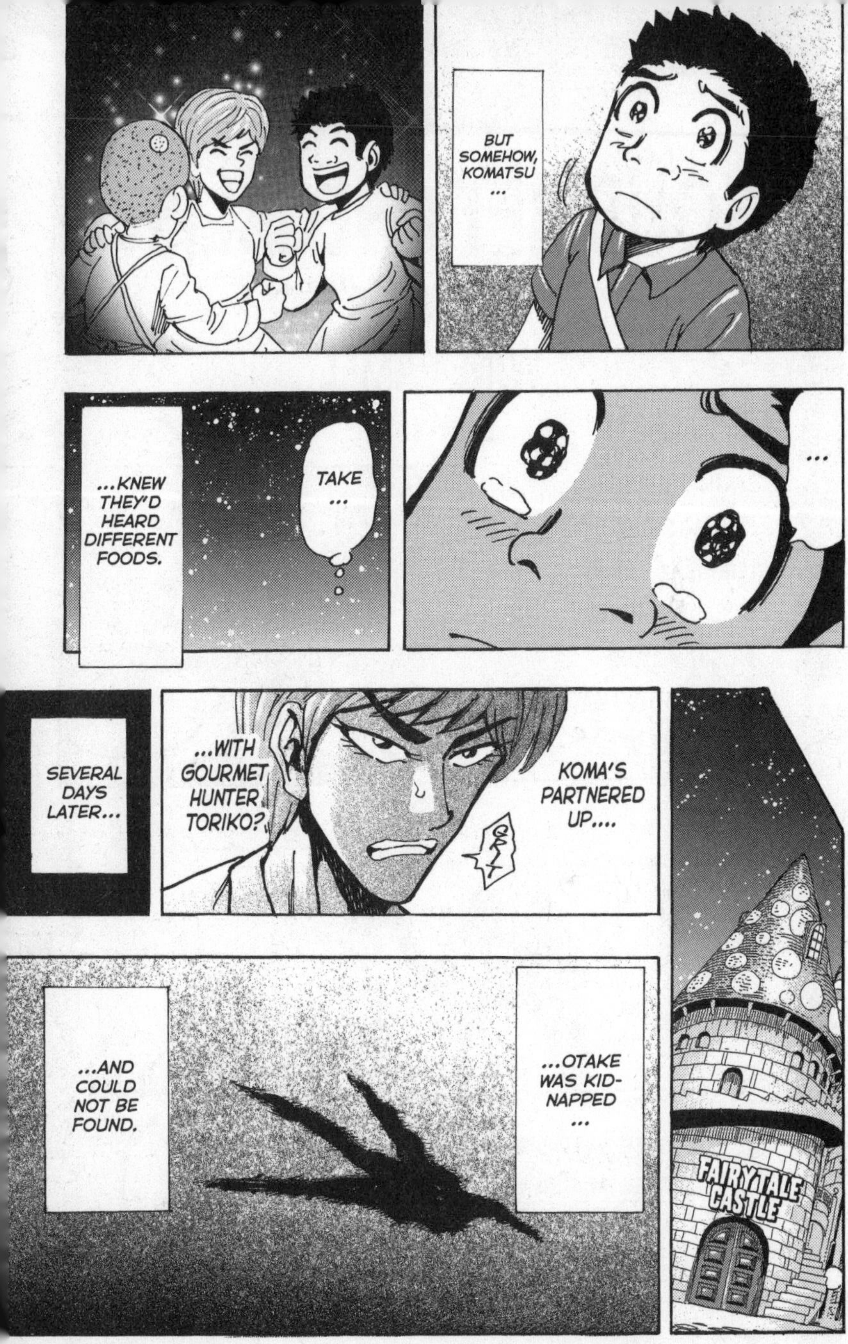
BUT SOMEHOW, KOMATSU ...
...
TAKE ...
...KNEW THEY'D HEARD DIFFERENT FOODS.
FAIRYTALE CASTLE
KOMA'S PARTNERED UP....
GRIT
...WITH GOURMET HUNTER TORIKO?
SEVERAL DAYS LATER...
...OTAKE WAS KID-NAPPED ...
...AND COULD NOT BE FOUND.

GOURMET CHECKLIST

Vol. 189
WINE CAMEL
(MAMMAL)

CAPTURE LEVEL: 17

HABITAT: SAND GARDEN (RARE)

LENGTH: 4.5 METERS

HEIGHT: 3.2 METERS

WEIGHT: 5.2 TONS

PRICE: 100 G OF MEAT / 10,000 YEN;
1 BOTTLE OF WINE / 20,000 YEN

SCALE

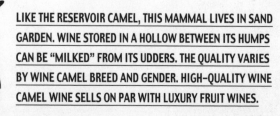

LIKE THE RESERVOIR CAMEL, THIS MAMMAL LIVES IN SAND
GARDEN. WINE STORED IN A HOLLOW BETWEEN ITS HUMPS
CAN BE "MILKED" FROM ITS UDDERS. THE QUALITY VARIES
BY WINE CAMEL BREED AND GENDER. HIGH-QUALITY WINE
CAMEL WINE SELLS ON PAR WITH LUXURY FRUIT WINES.

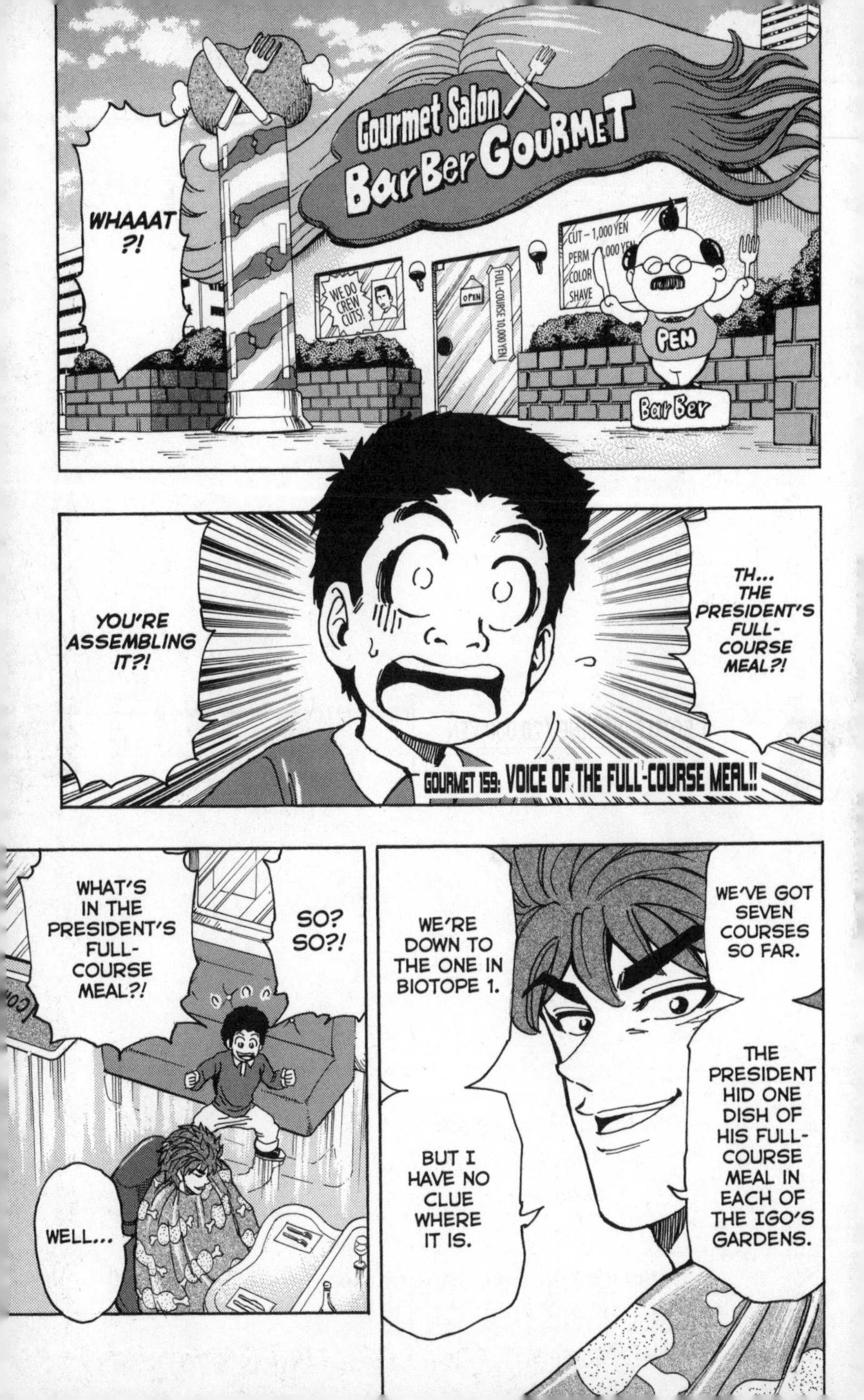
Gourmet Salon
BarBer GOURMET
CUT – 1,000 YEN
PERM
COLOR
SHAVE
FULL-COURSE 10,000 YEN
OPEN
WE DO CREW CUTS!
PEN
BarBer
WHAAAT ?!
TH... THE PRESIDENT'S FULL-COURSE MEAL?!
YOU'RE ASSEMBLING IT?!
GOURMET 159: VOICE OF THE FULL-COURSE MEAL!!
WE'VE GOT SEVEN COURSES SO FAR.
WE'RE DOWN TO THE ONE IN BIOTOPE 1.
THE PRESIDENT HID ONE DISH OF HIS FULL-COURSE MEAL IN EACH OF THE IGO'S GARDENS.
BUT I HAVE NO CLUE WHERE IT IS.
SO? SO?!
WHAT'S IN THE PRESIDENT'S FULL-COURSE MEAL?!
WELL...

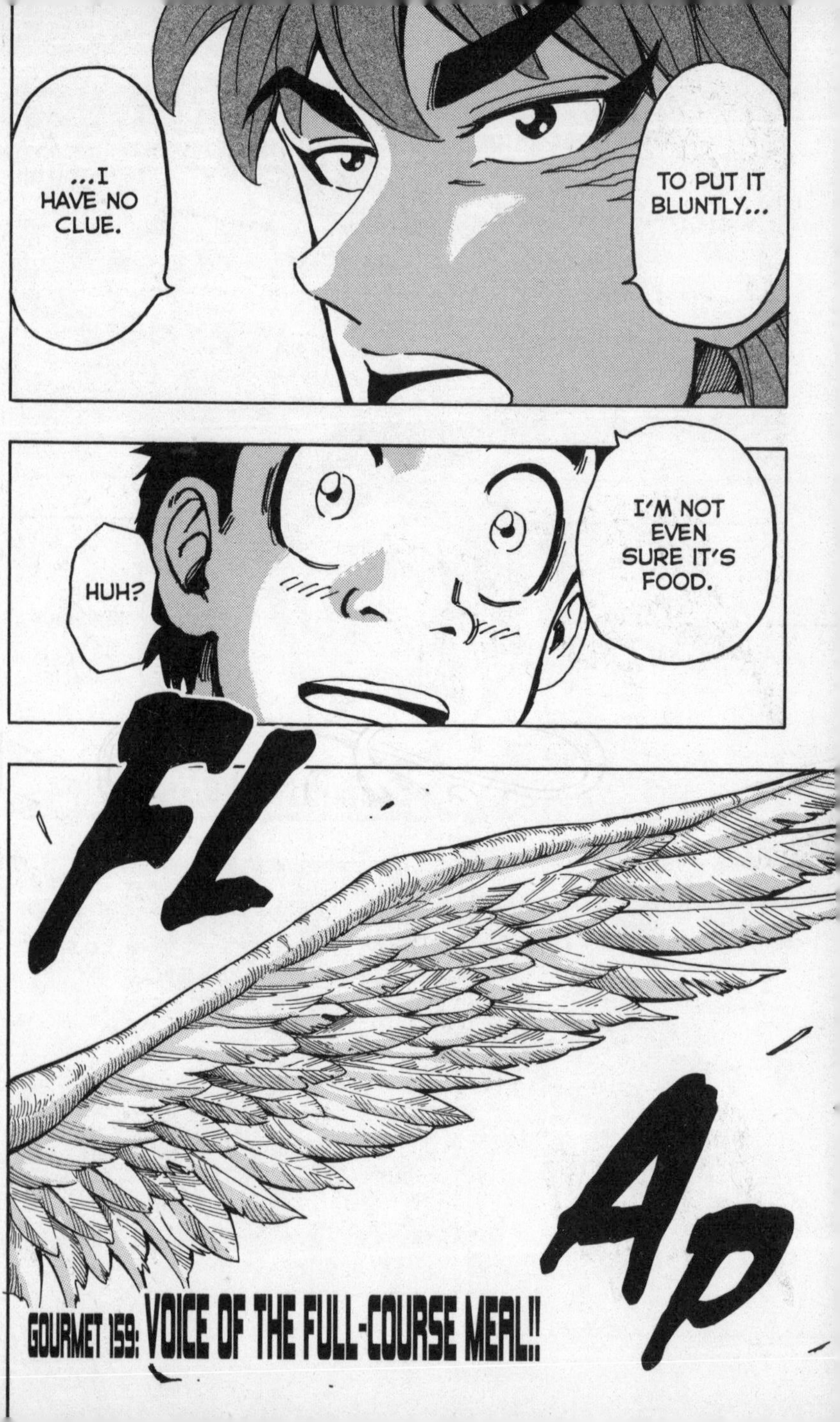
TO PUT IT BLUNTLY...
...I HAVE NO CLUE.
I'M NOT EVEN SURE IT'S FOOD.
HUH?
FLAP
GOURMET 159: VOICE OF THE FULL-COURSE MEAL!!

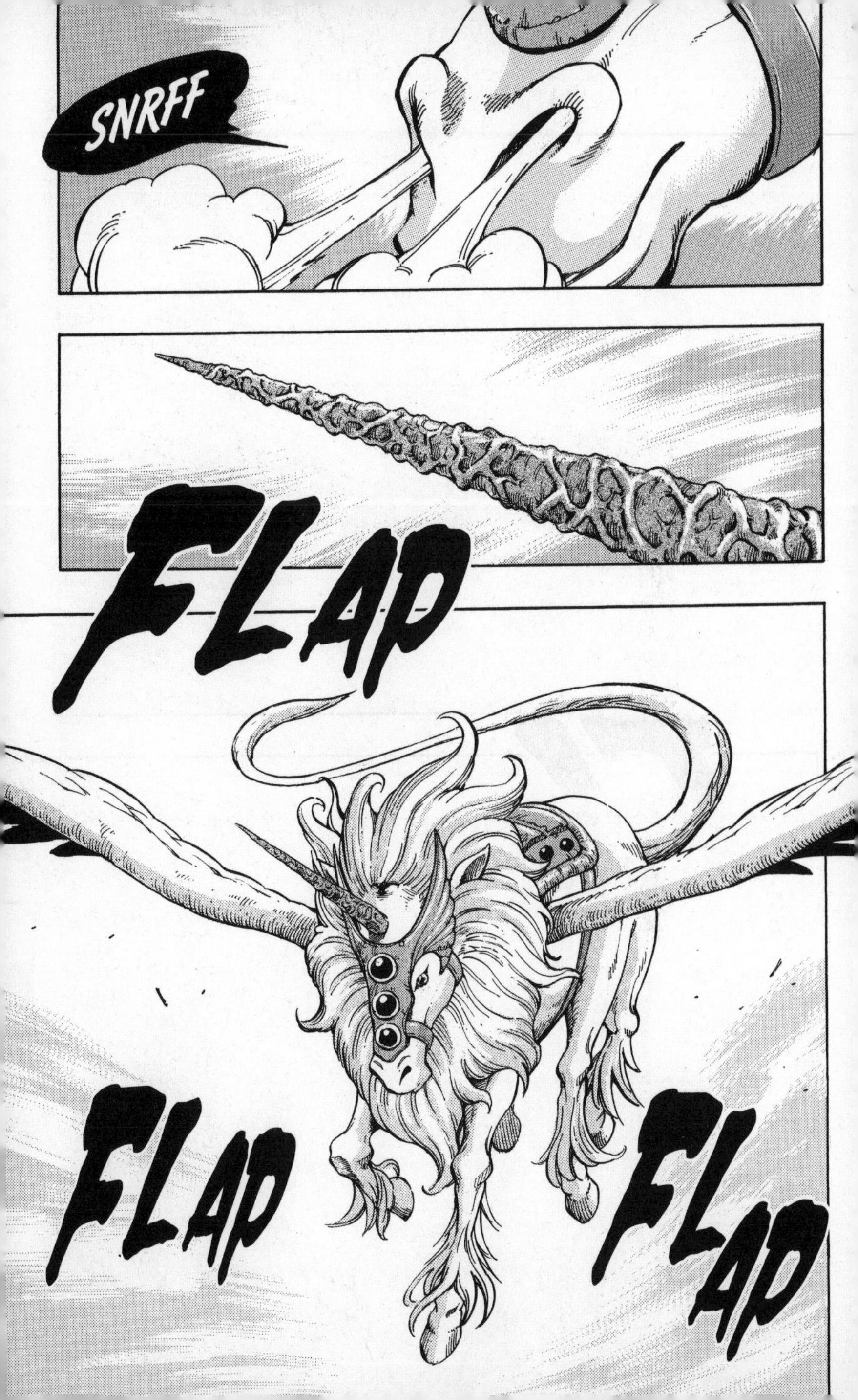
SNRFF
FLAP
FLAP
FLAP

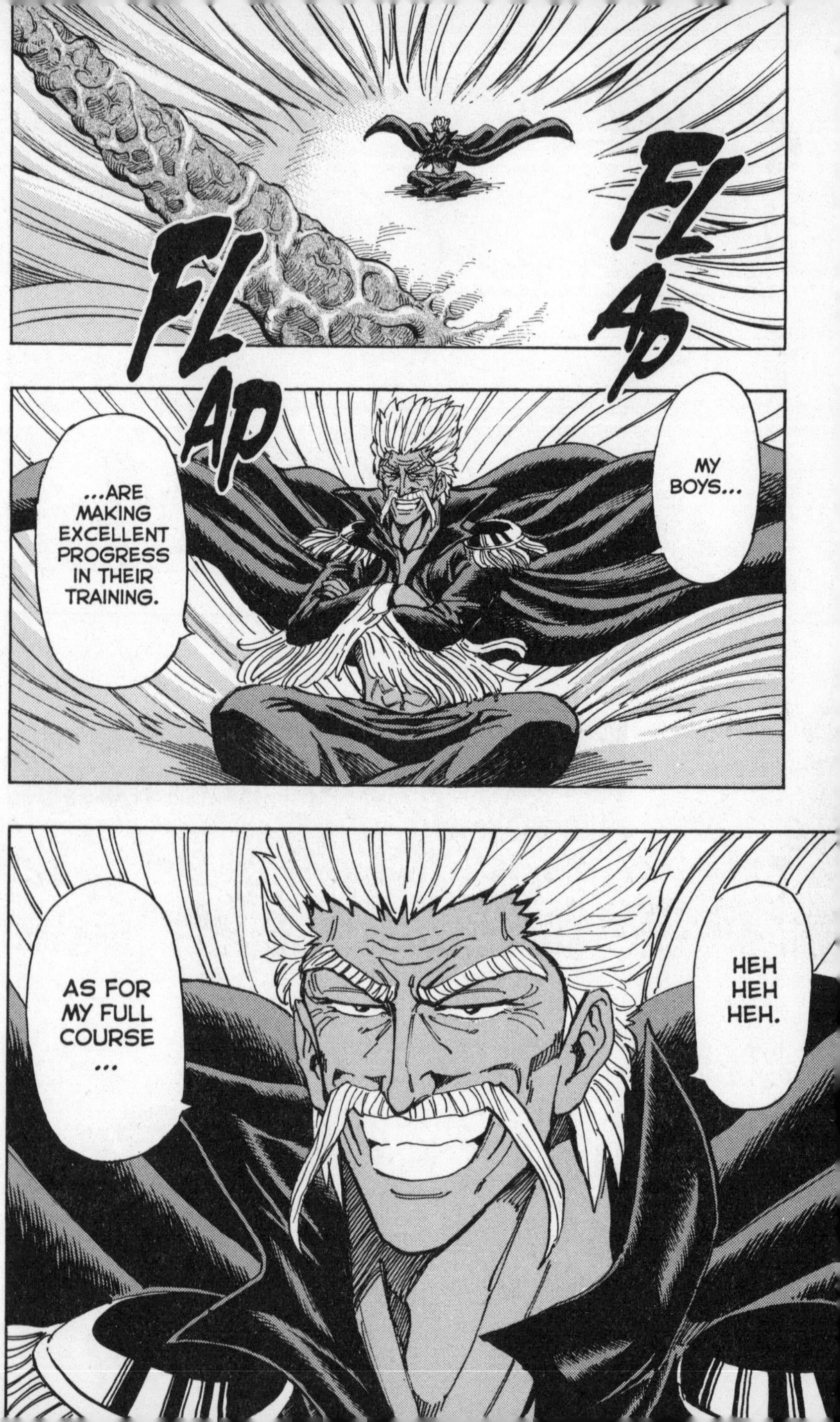
FLAP
FLAP
MY BOYS...
...ARE MAKING EXCELLENT PROGRESS IN THEIR TRAINING.
HEH HEH HEH.
AS FOR MY FULL COURSE ...

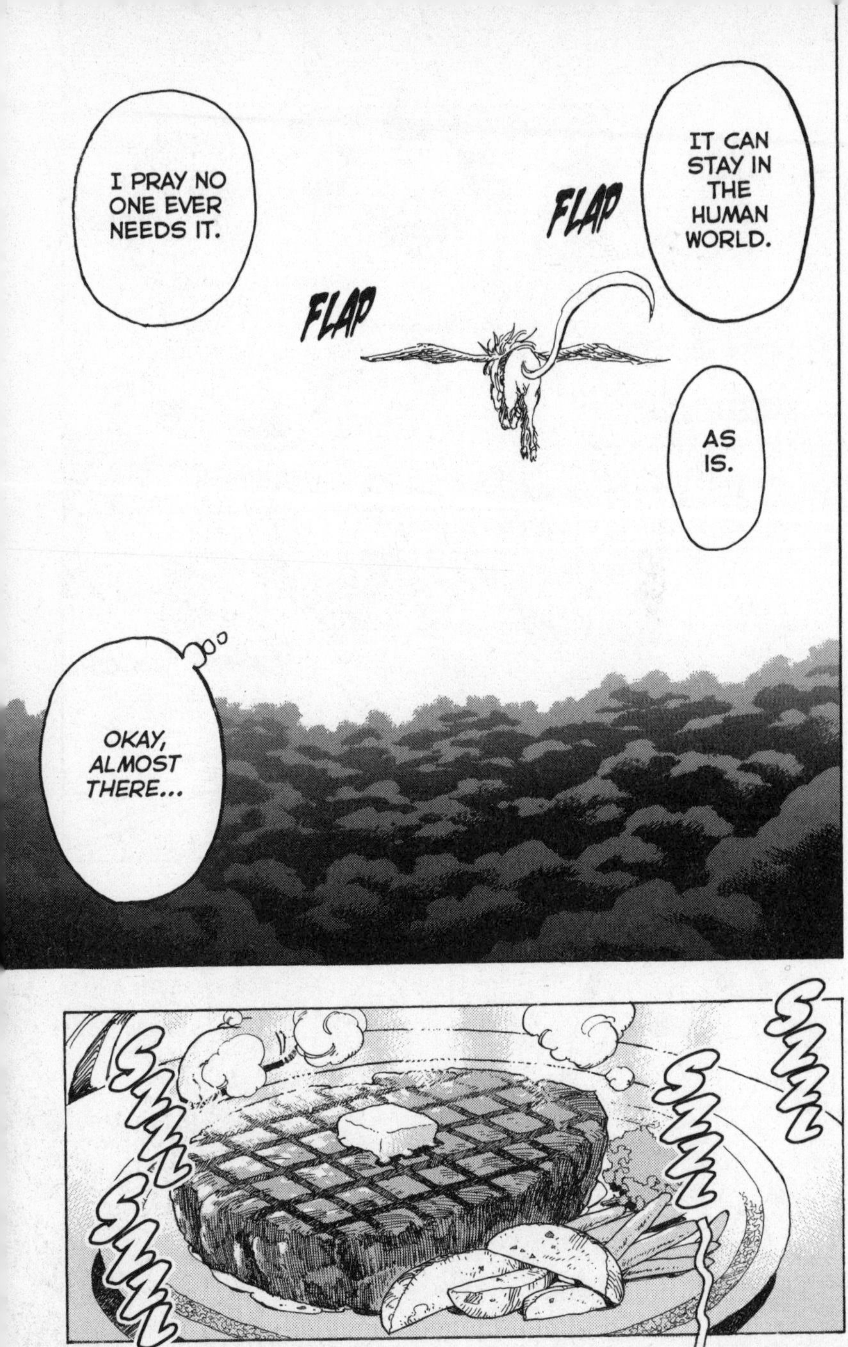
IT CAN STAY IN THE HUMAN WORLD.
FLAP
AS IS.
FLAP
I PRAY NO ONE EVER NEEDS IT.
OKAY, ALMOST THERE...

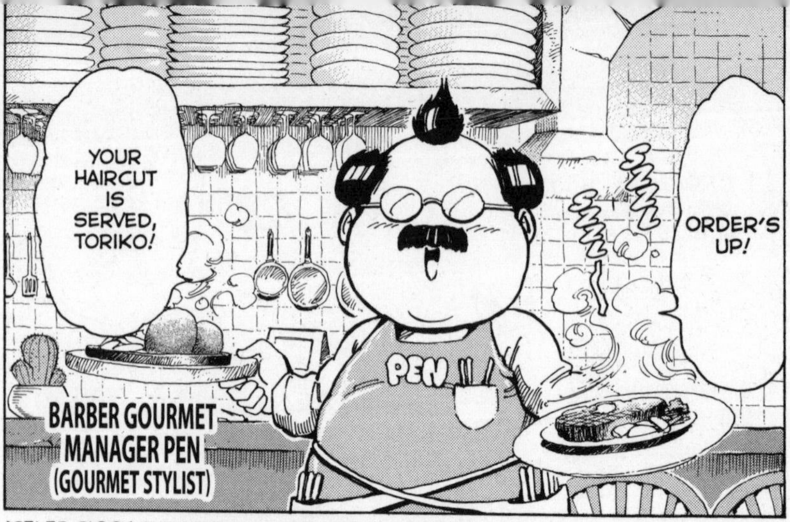
ORDER'S UP!
SZZL SZZL
YOUR HAIRCUT IS SERVED, TORIKO!
BARBER GOURMET MANAGER PEN (GOURMET STYLIST)

*CELEB-PIGGY SUBMITTED BY ODEN FROM OSAKA!

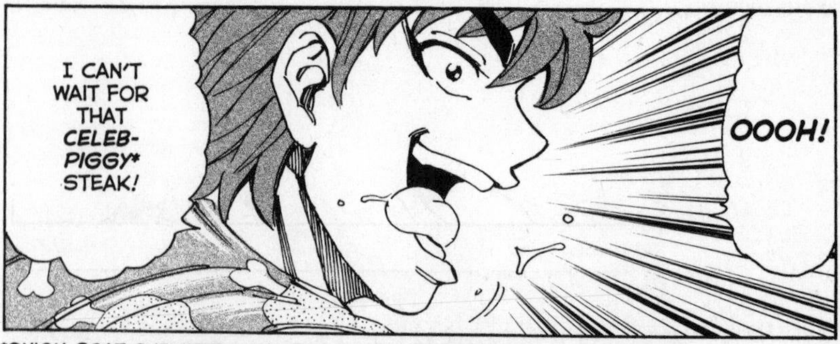
OOOH!
I CAN'T WAIT FOR THAT CELEB-PIGGY* STEAK!

*ONION GOAT SUBMITTED BY KENGO NISHI FROM HYOGA!

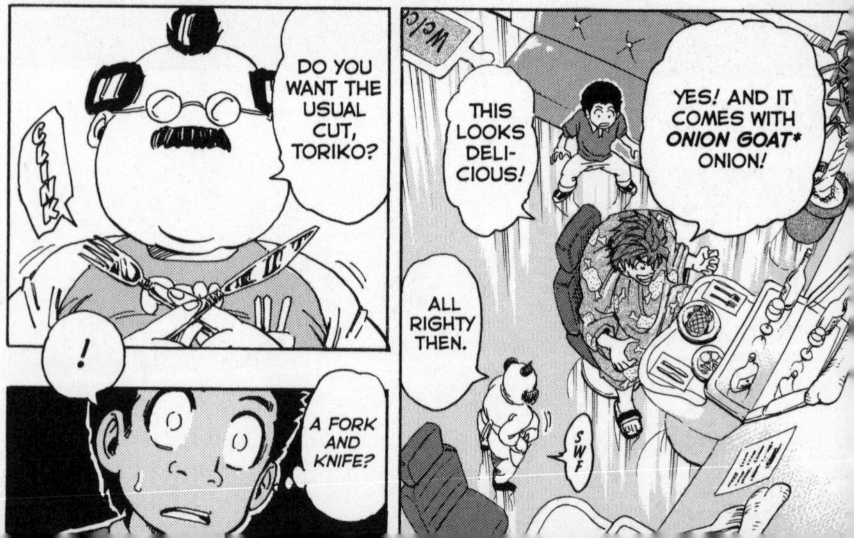
YES! AND IT COMES WITH ONION GOAT* ONION!
THIS LOOKS DELI-CIOUS!
ALL RIGHTY THEN.
SWF
DO YOU WANT THE USUAL CUT, TORIKO?
CLINK
!
A FORK AND KNIFE?

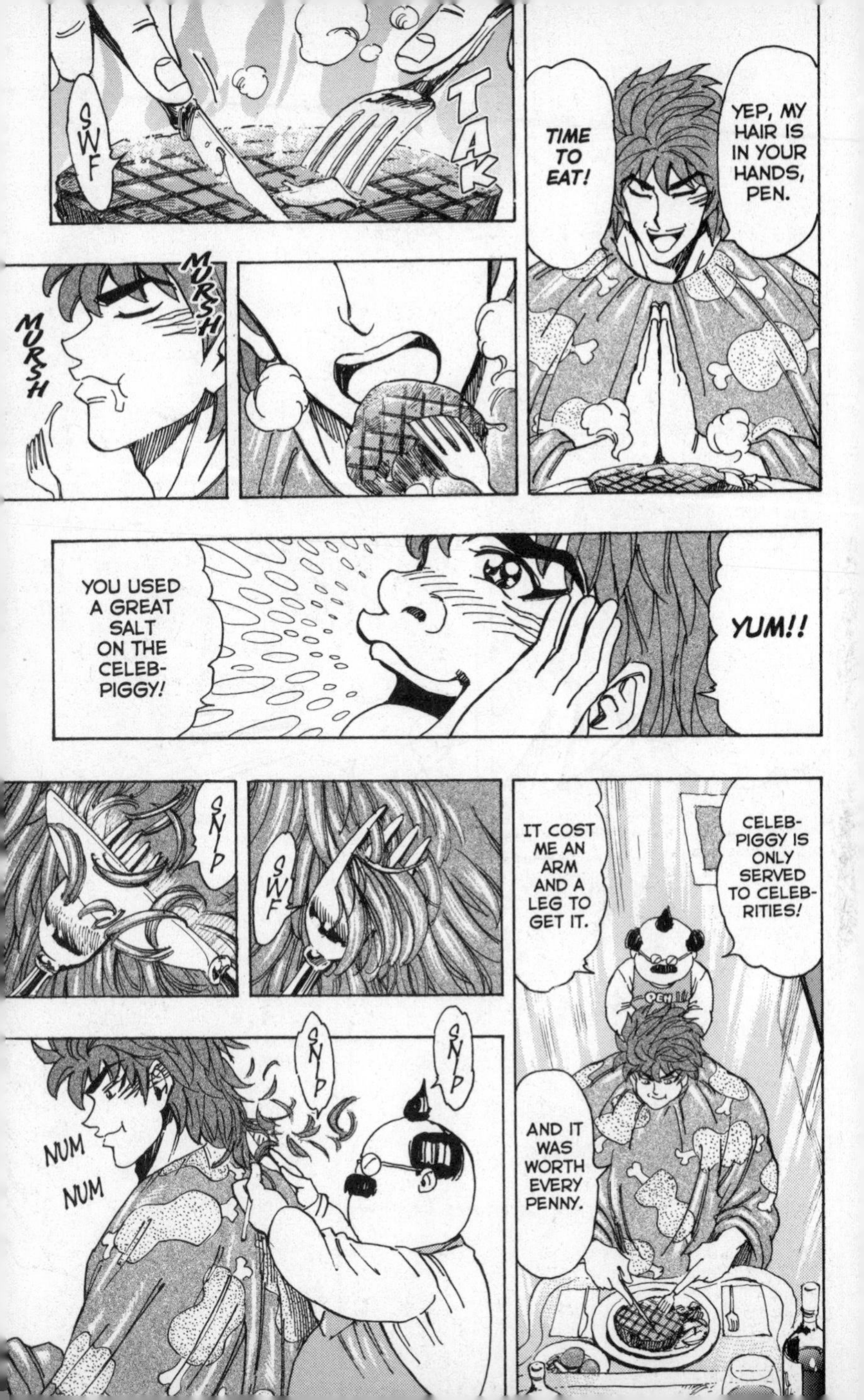
SWF
TAK
YEP, MY HAIR IS IN YOUR HANDS, PEN.
TIME TO EAT!
MURSH
MURSH
YUM!!
YOU USED A GREAT SALT ON THE CELEB-PIGGY!
CELEB-PIGGY IS ONLY SERVED TO CELEBRITIES!
IT COST ME AN ARM AND A LEG TO GET IT.
AND IT WAS WORTH EVERY PENNY.
SWF
SNIP
SNIP
SNIP
NUM
NUM

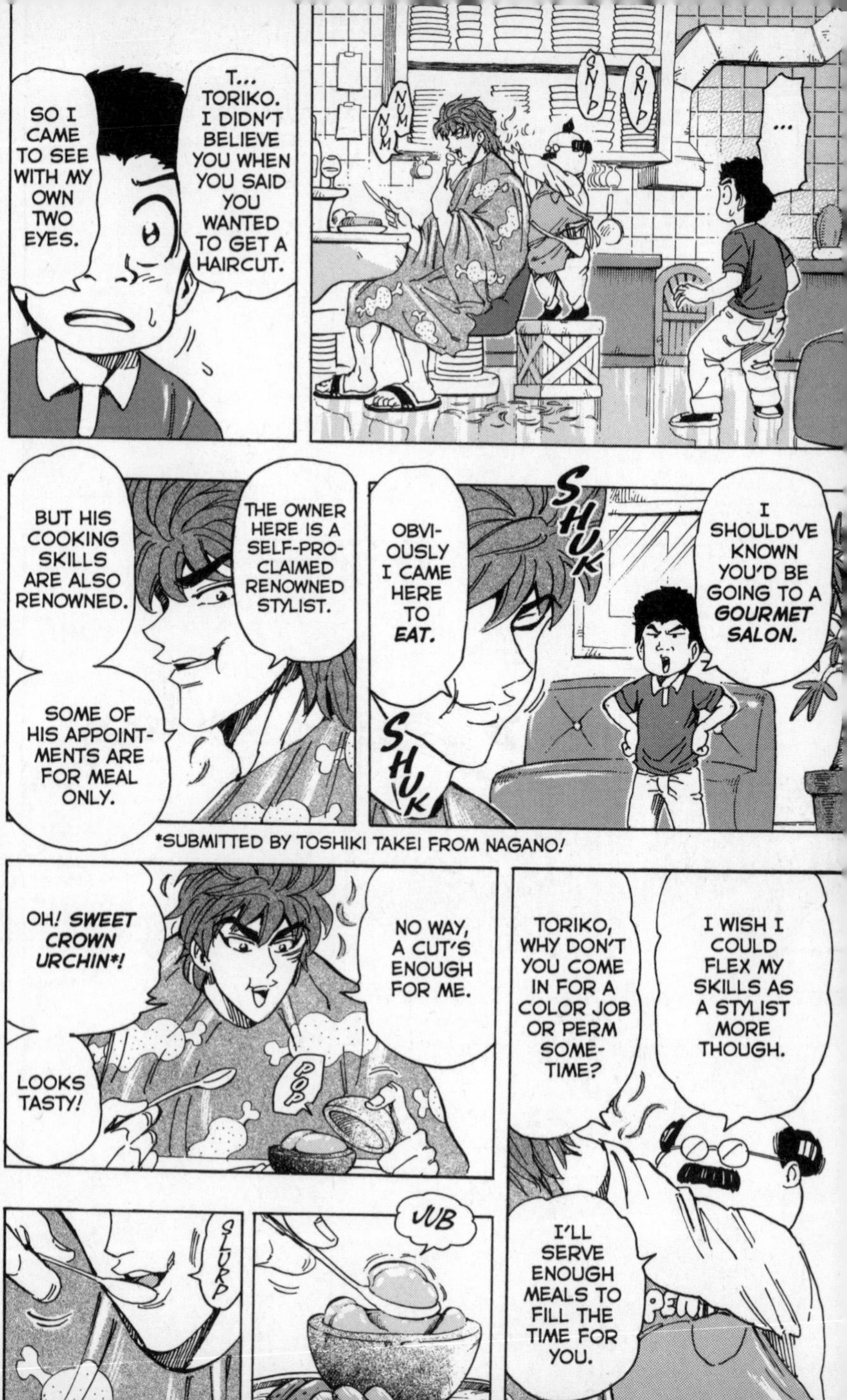
SNIP
SNIP
NUM NUM
...
T... TORIKO. I DIDN'T BELIEVE YOU WHEN YOU SAID YOU WANTED TO GET A HAIRCUT.
SO I CAME TO SEE WITH MY OWN TWO EYES.
I SHOULD'VE KNOWN YOU'D BE GOING TO A GOURMET SALON.
SHUK
OBVI-OUSLY I CAME HERE TO EAT.
SHUK
THE OWNER HERE IS A SELF-PRO-CLAIMED RENOWNED STYLIST.
BUT HIS COOKING SKILLS ARE ALSO RENOWNED.
SOME OF HIS APPOINT-MENTS ARE FOR MEAL ONLY.
I WISH I COULD FLEX MY SKILLS AS A STYLIST MORE THOUGH.
TORIKO, WHY DON'T YOU COME IN FOR A COLOR JOB OR PERM SOME-TIME?
I'LL SERVE ENOUGH MEALS TO FILL THE TIME FOR YOU.
NO WAY, A CUT'S ENOUGH FOR ME.
OH! SWEET CROWN URCHIN*!
POP
LOOKS TASTY!
JUB
SLURP

*SUBMITTED BY TOSHIKI TAKEI FROM NAGANO!

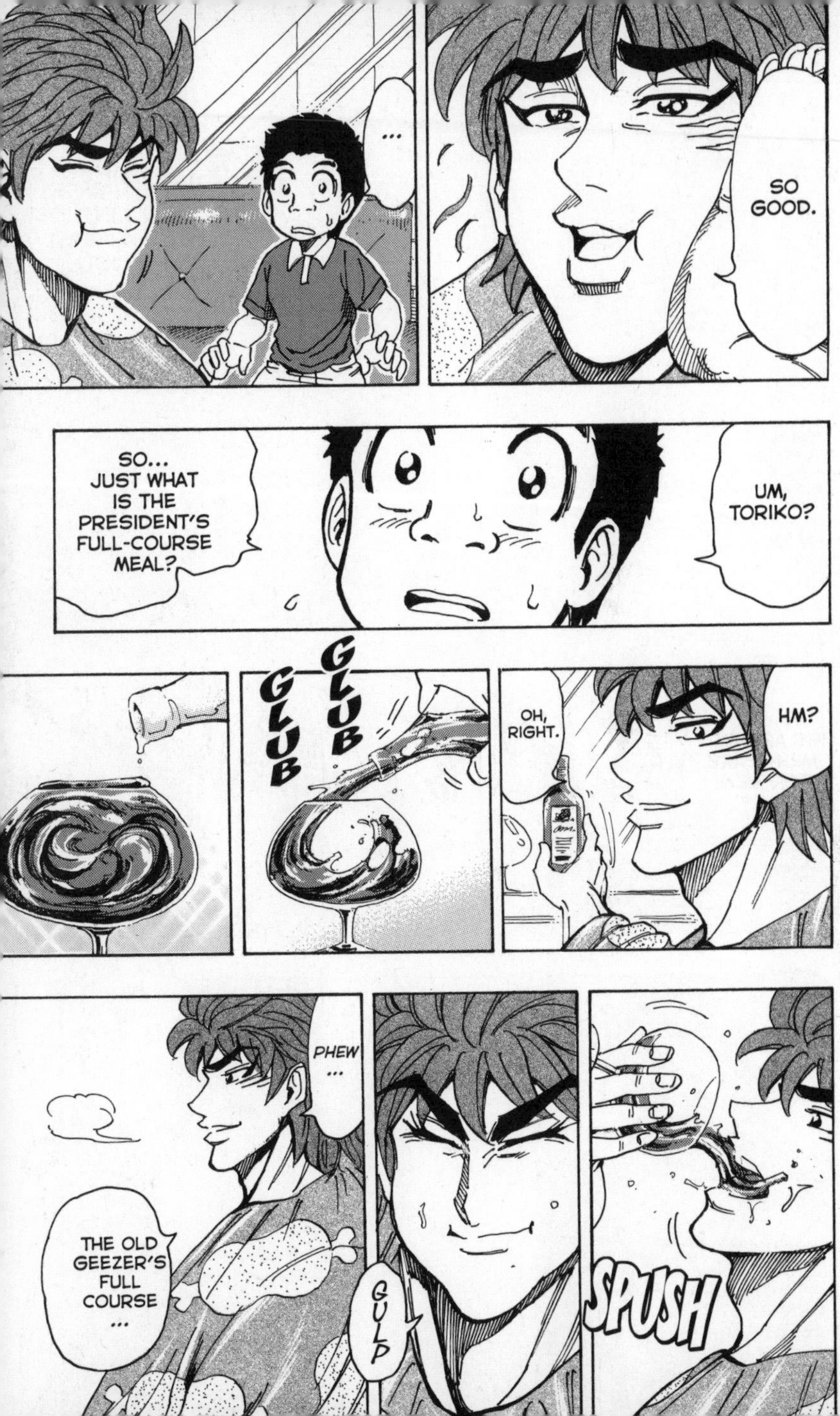
SO GOOD.
...
UM, TORIKO?
SO... JUST WHAT IS THE PRESIDENT'S FULL-COURSE MEAL?
HM?
OH, RIGHT.
GLUB GLUB
SPUSH
GULP
PHEW ...
THE OLD GEEZER'S FULL COURSE ...

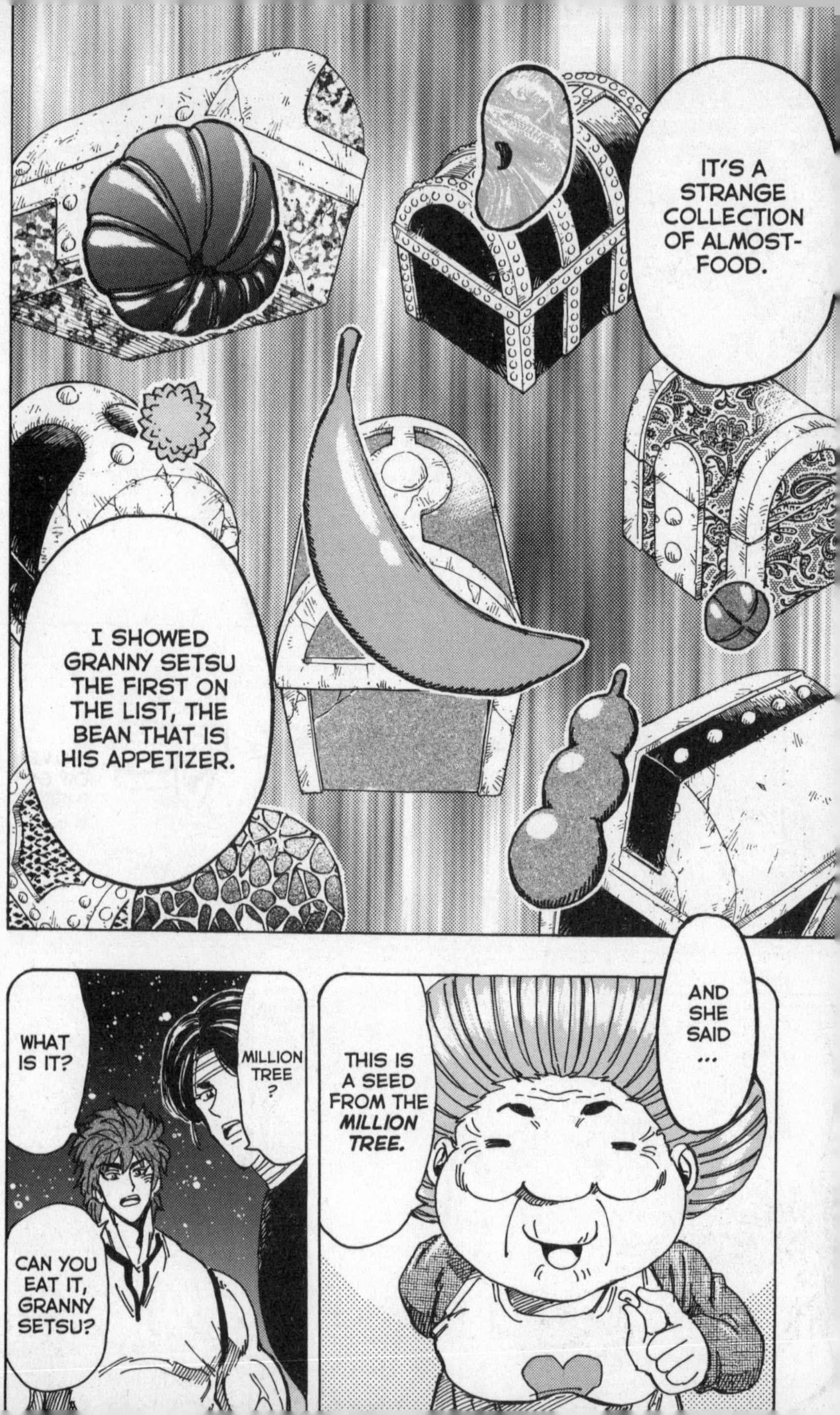
IT'S A STRANGE COLLECTION OF ALMOST-FOOD.
I SHOWED GRANNY SETSU THE FIRST ON THE LIST, THE BEAN THAT IS HIS APPETIZER.
AND SHE SAID ...
THIS IS A SEED FROM THE *MILLION TREE.*
MILLION TREE ?
WHAT IS IT?
CAN YOU EAT IT, GRANNY SETSU?

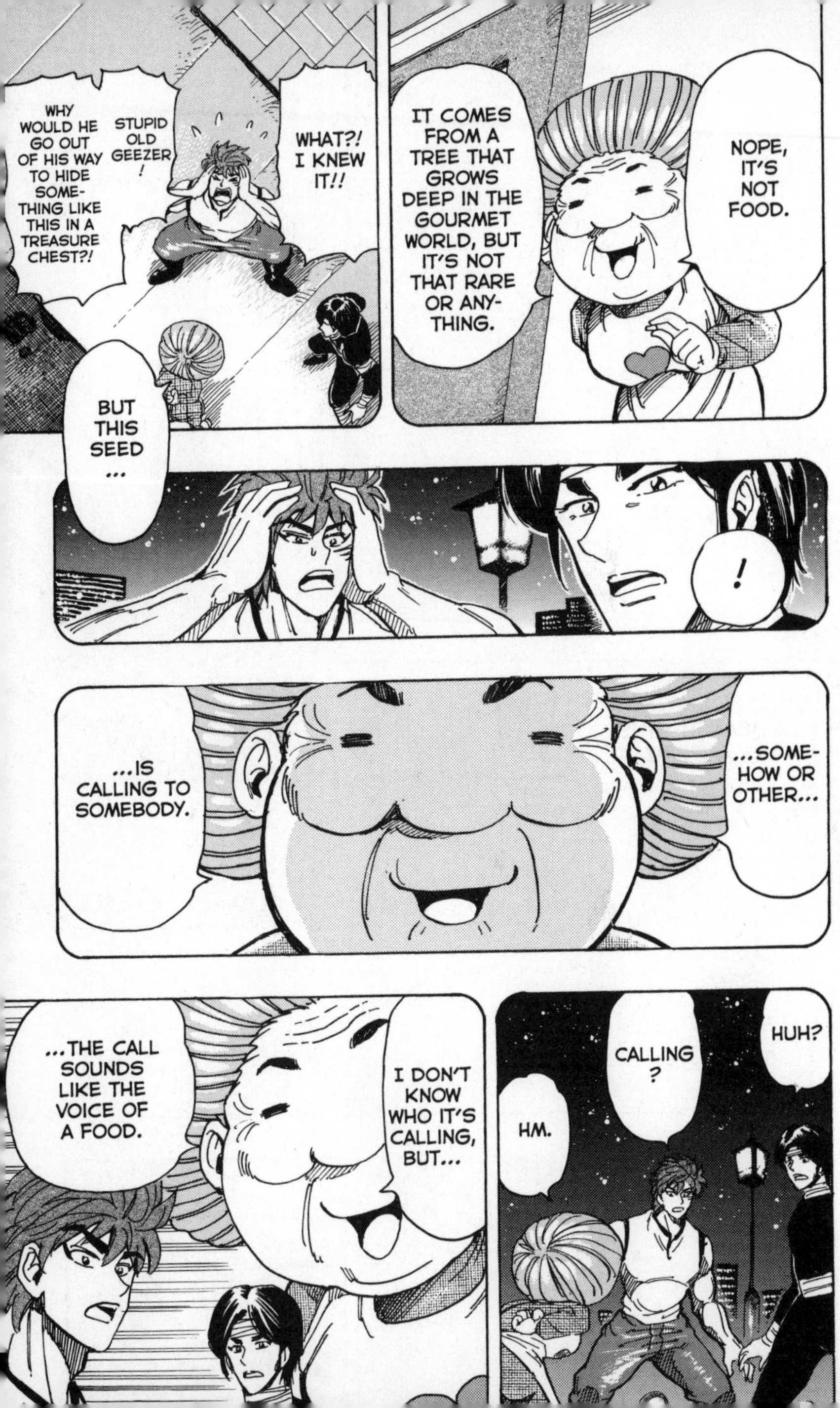
NOPE, IT'S NOT FOOD.
IT COMES FROM A TREE THAT GROWS DEEP IN THE GOURMET WORLD, BUT IT'S NOT THAT RARE OR ANY-THING.
WHAT?! I KNEW IT!!
STUPID OLD GEEZER!
WHY WOULD HE GO OUT OF HIS WAY TO HIDE SOME-THING LIKE THIS IN A TREASURE CHEST?!
BUT THIS SEED...
!
...SOME-HOW OR OTHER...
...IS CALLING TO SOMEBODY.
HUH?
CALLING?
HM.
I DON'T KNOW WHO IT'S CALLING, BUT...
...THE CALL SOUNDS LIKE THE VOICE OF A FOOD.

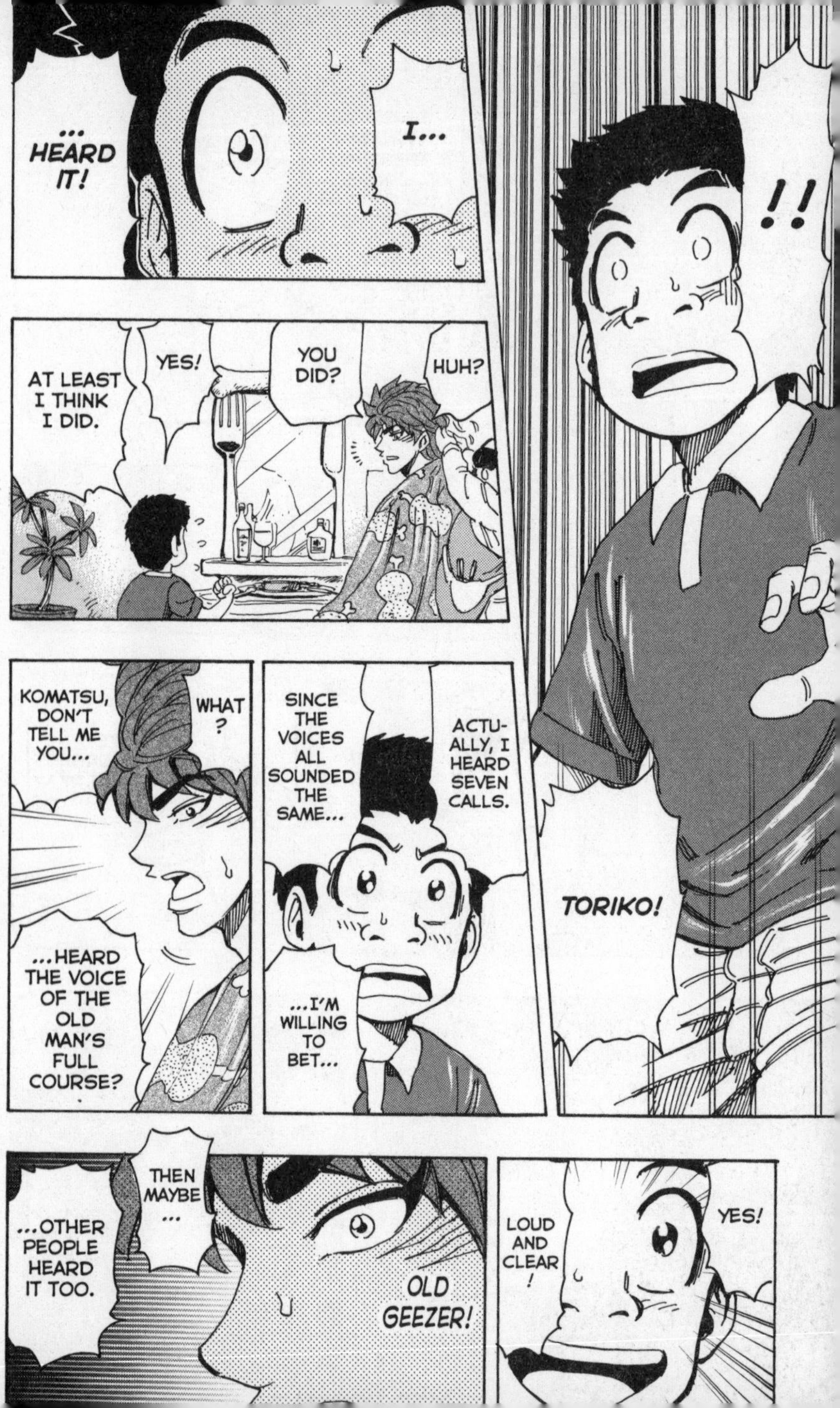
!!
TORIKO!
I...
...HEARD IT!
HUH?
YOU DID?
YES!
AT LEAST I THINK I DID.
ACTU-ALLY, I HEARD SEVEN CALLS.
SINCE THE VOICES ALL SOUNDED THE SAME...
...I'M WILLING TO BET...
WHAT?
KOMATSU, DON'T TELL ME YOU...
...HEARD THE VOICE OF THE OLD MAN'S FULL COURSE?
YES!
LOUD AND CLEAR!
OLD GEEZER!
THEN MAYBE...
...OTHER PEOPLE HEARD IT TOO.

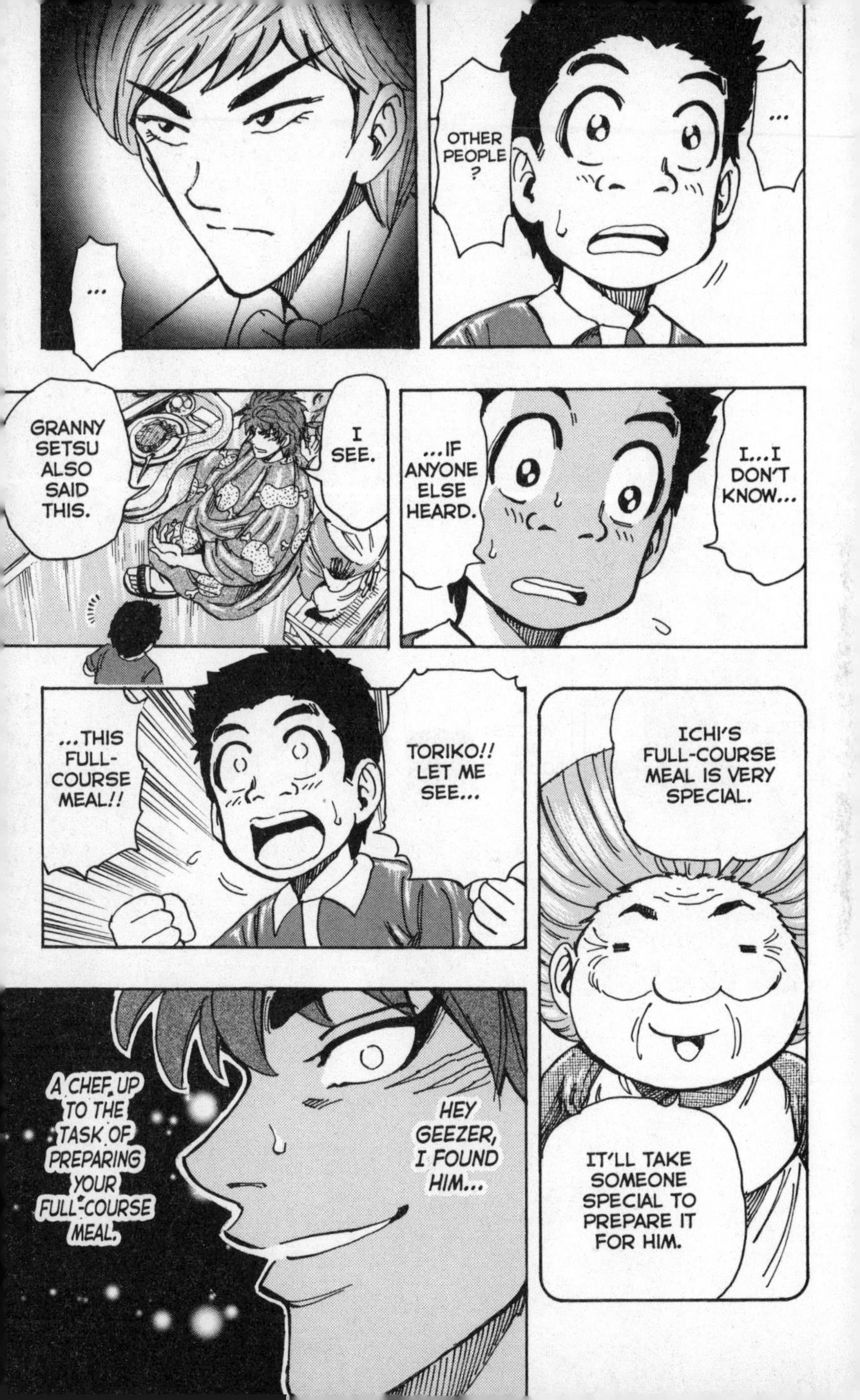
...
OTHER PEOPLE?
...
I...I DON'T KNOW...
...IF ANYONE ELSE HEARD.
I SEE.
GRANNY SETSU ALSO SAID THIS.
ICHI'S FULL-COURSE MEAL IS VERY SPECIAL.
IT'LL TAKE SOMEONE SPECIAL TO PREPARE IT FOR HIM.
TORIKO!! LET ME SEE...
...THIS FULL-COURSE MEAL!!
HEY GEEZER, I FOUND HIM...
A CHEF UP TO THE TASK OF PREPARING YOUR FULL-COURSE MEAL.

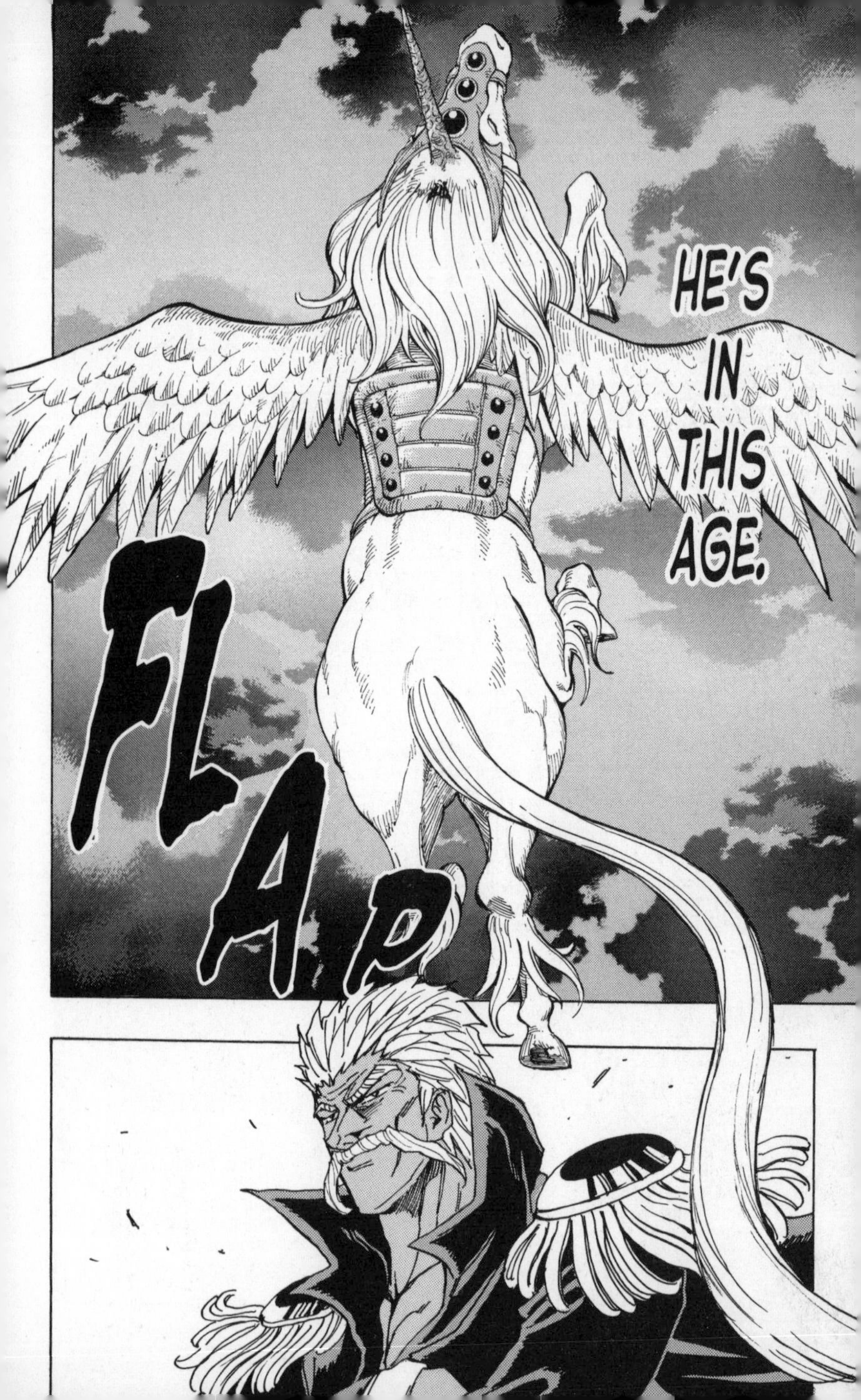
HE'S IN THIS AGE.
FLAP

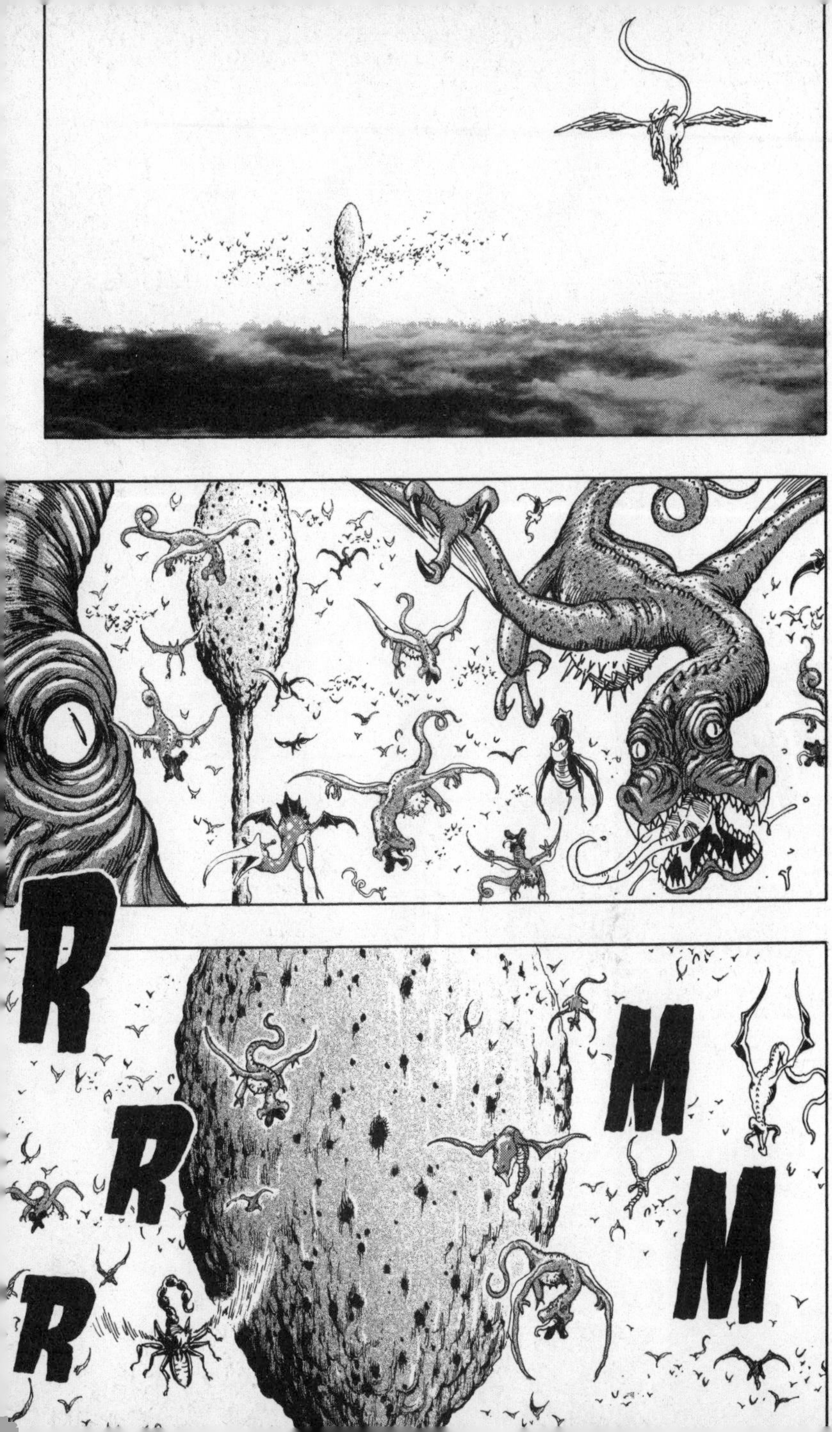
RRRMM

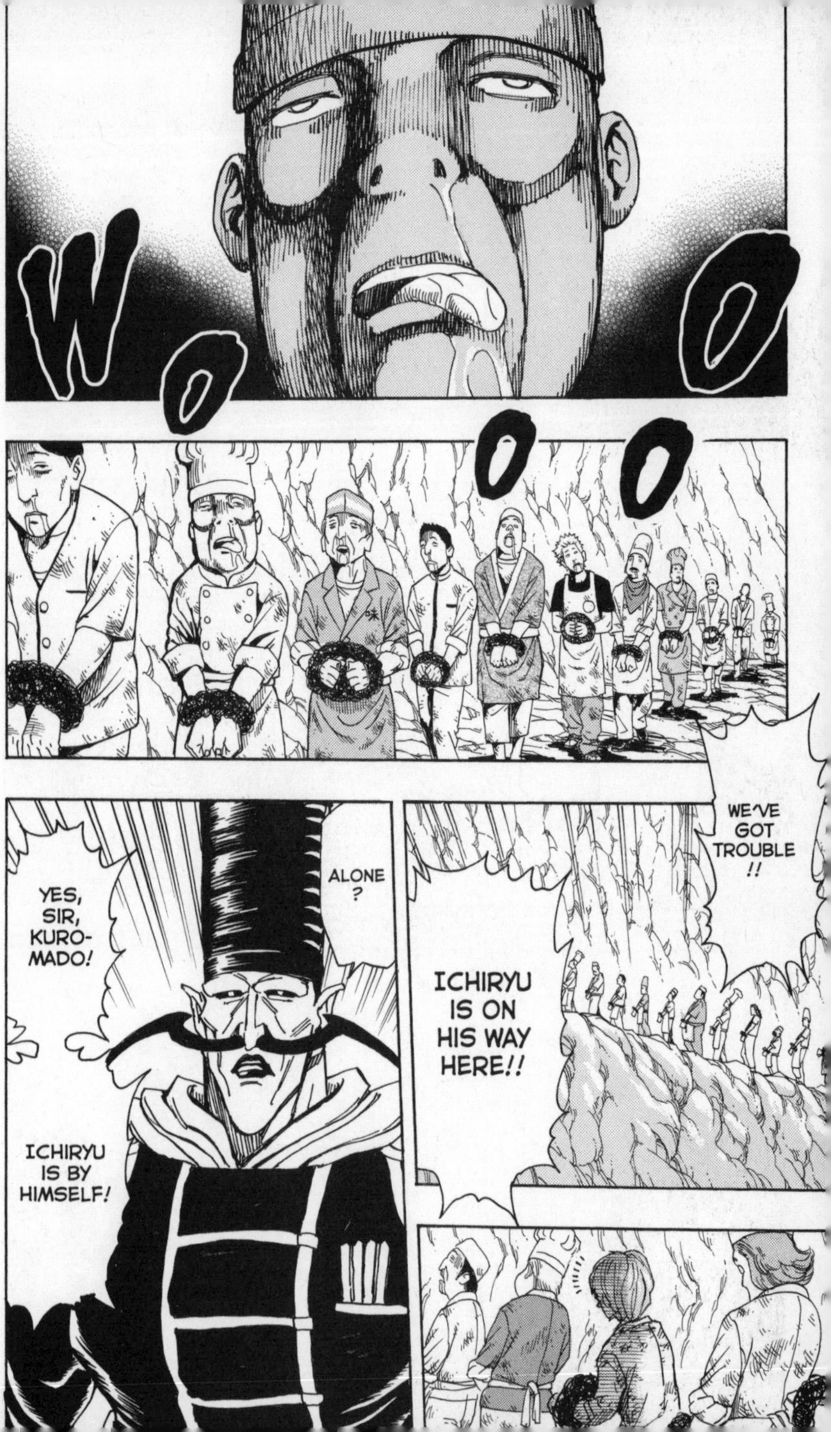
WOOOOO
WE'VE GOT TROUBLE!!
ICHIRYU IS ON HIS WAY HERE!!
ALONE?
YES, SIR, KURO-MADO!
ICHIRYU IS BY HIMSELF!

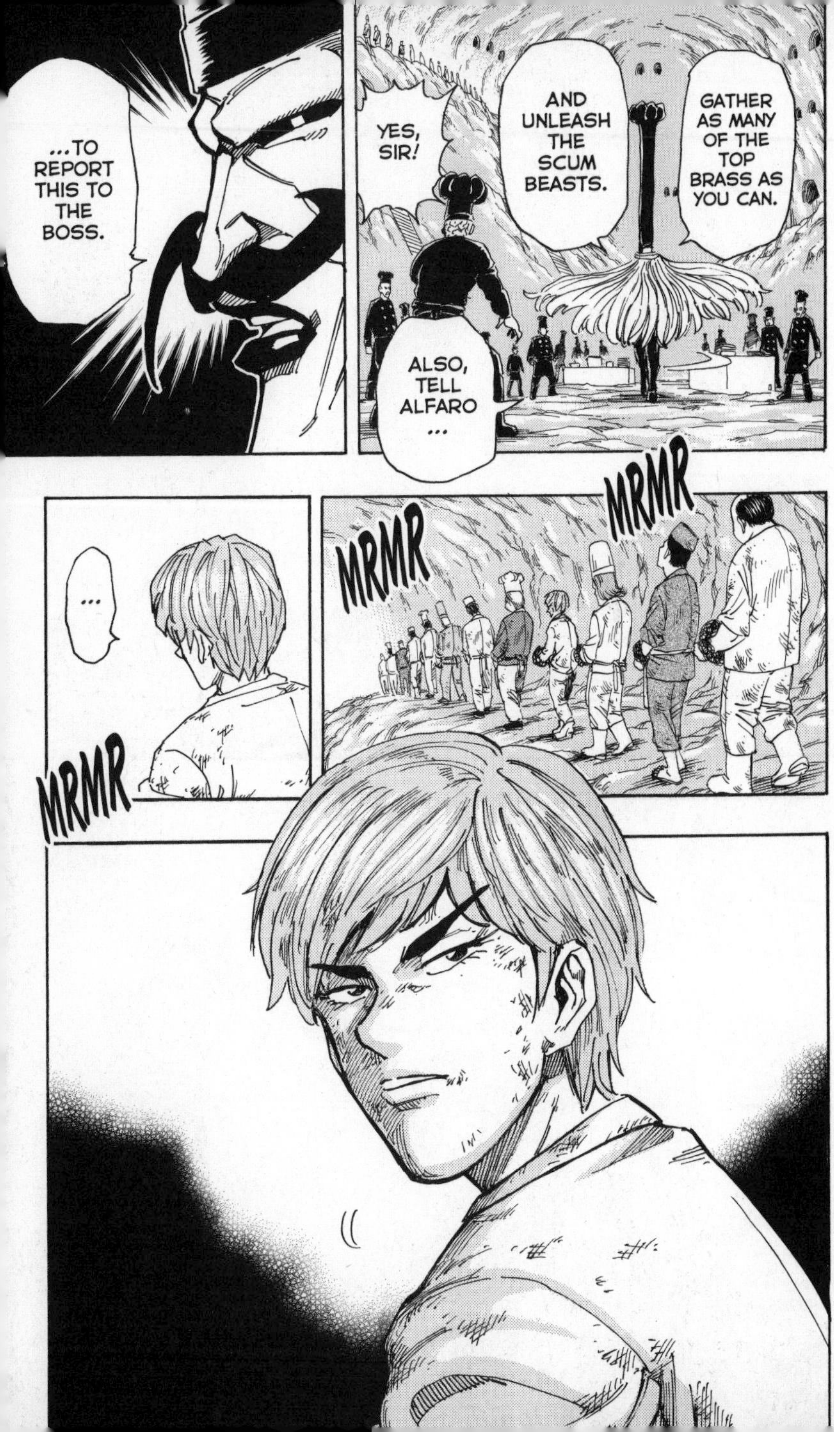
GATHER AS MANY OF THE TOP BRASS AS YOU CAN.
AND UNLEASH THE SCUM BEASTS.
YES, SIR!
ALSO, TELL ALFARO ...
...TO REPORT THIS TO THE BOSS.
MRMR
MRMR
...
MRMR

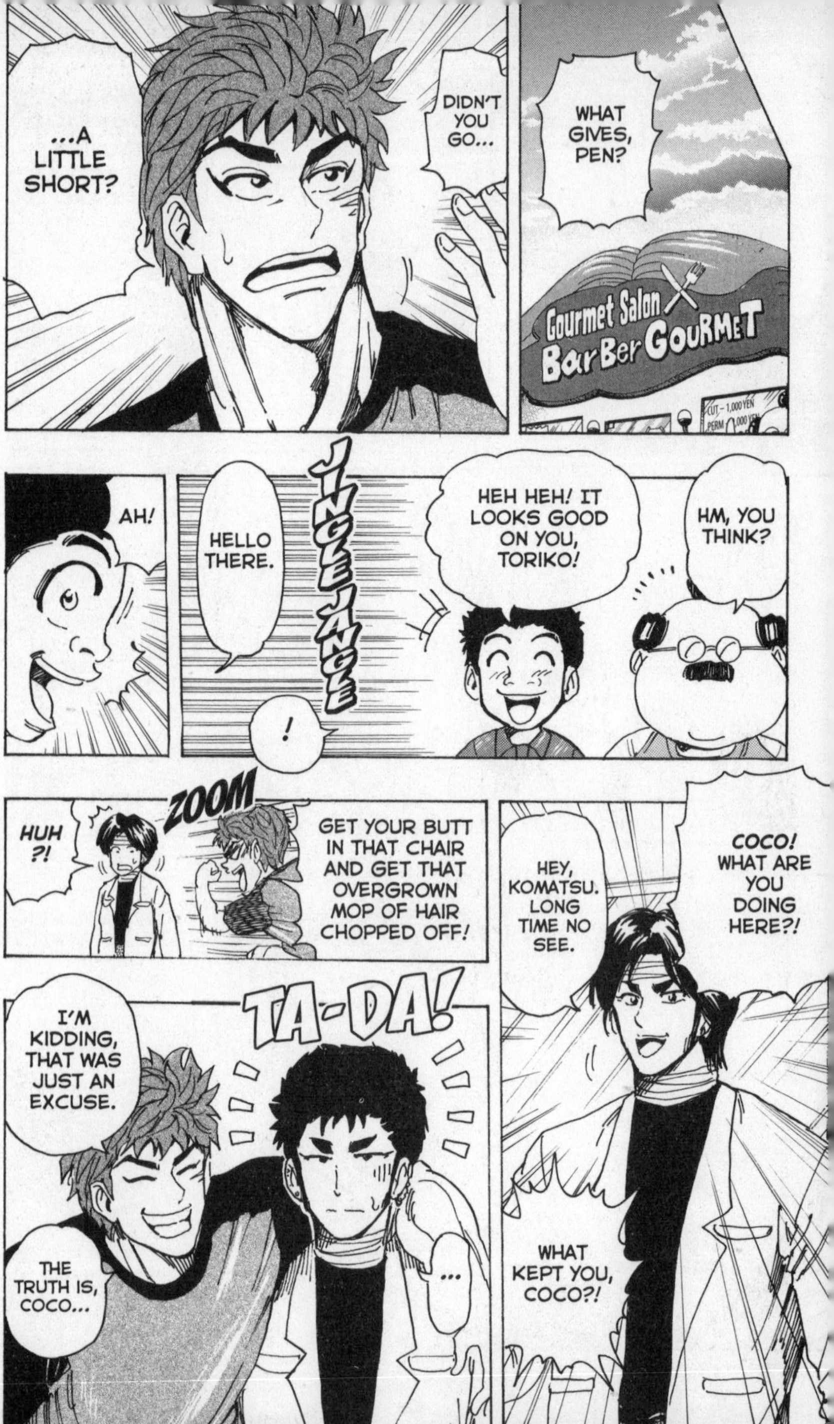
WHAT GIVES, PEN?
Gourmet Salon
BarBer GOURMET
CUT – 1,000 YEN
DIDN'T YOU GO...
...A LITTLE SHORT?
HM, YOU THINK?
HEH HEH! IT LOOKS GOOD ON YOU, TORIKO!
JINGLE JANGLE
HELLO THERE.
!
AH!
COCO! WHAT ARE YOU DOING HERE?!
HEY, KOMATSU. LONG TIME NO SEE.
WHAT KEPT YOU, COCO?!
GET YOUR BUTT IN THAT CHAIR AND GET THAT OVERGROWN MOP OF HAIR CHOPPED OFF!
ZOOM
HUH ?!
TA-DA!
I'M KIDDING, THAT WAS JUST AN EXCUSE.
...
THE TRUTH IS, COCO...

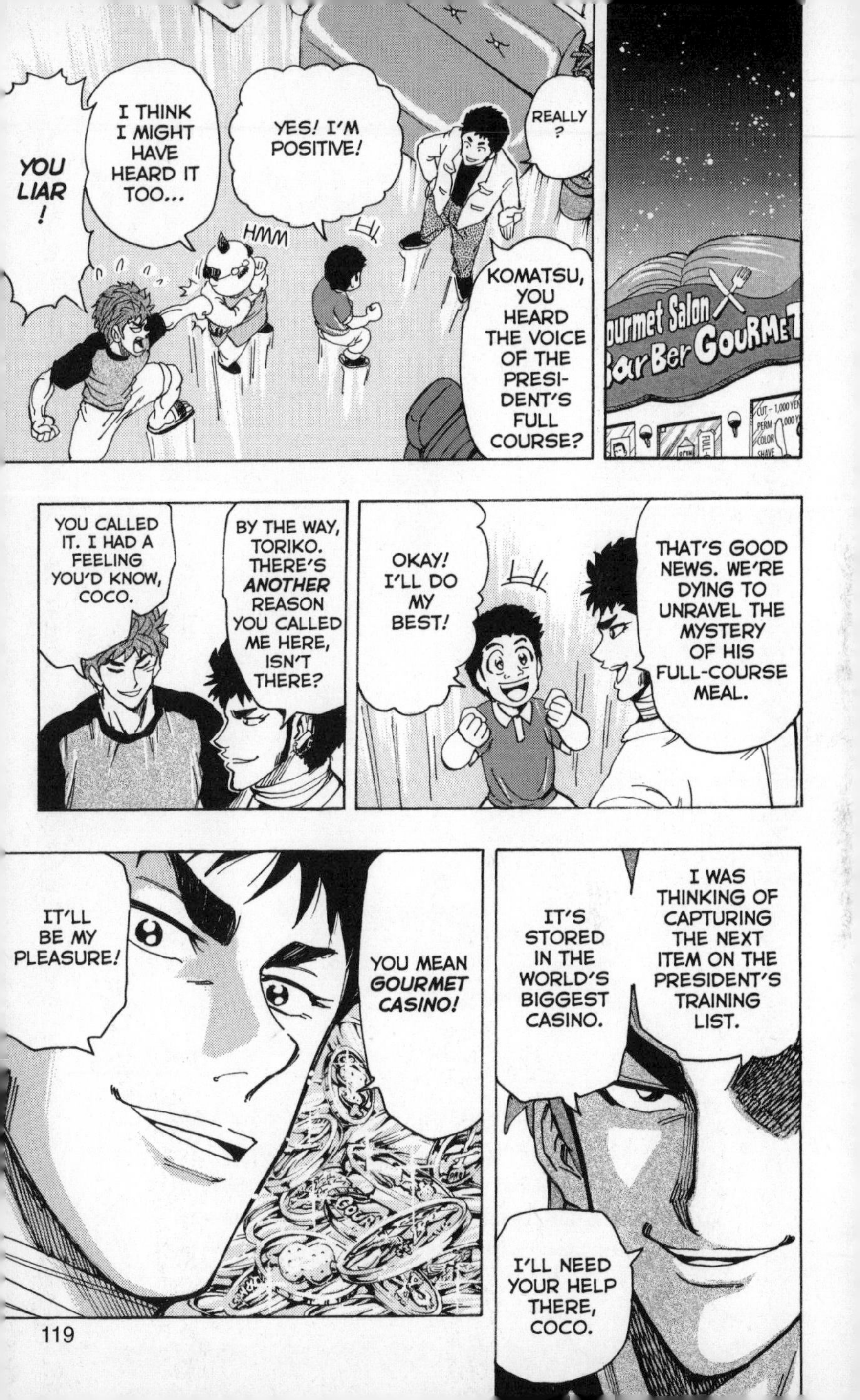
CUT – 1,000 YEN
KOMATSU, YOU HEARD THE VOICE OF THE PRESIDENT'S FULL COURSE?
YES! I'M POSITIVE!
I THINK I MIGHT HAVE HEARD IT TOO...
HMM
YOU LIAR!
REALLY?
THAT'S GOOD NEWS. WE'RE DYING TO UNRAVEL THE MYSTERY OF HIS FULL-COURSE MEAL.
OKAY! I'LL DO MY BEST!
BY THE WAY, TORIKO. THERE'S ANOTHER REASON YOU CALLED ME HERE, ISN'T THERE?
YOU CALLED IT. I HAD A FEELING YOU'D KNOW, COCO.
I WAS THINKING OF CAPTURING THE NEXT ITEM ON THE PRESIDENT'S TRAINING LIST.
IT'S STORED IN THE WORLD'S BIGGEST CASINO.
I'LL NEED YOUR HELP THERE, COCO.
YOU MEAN GOURMET CASINO!
IT'LL BE MY PLEASURE!

TORIKO

GOURMET CHECKLIST

Vol. 190

DESERT SHARK

(FISH)

CAPTURE LEVEL: 8

HABITAT: SAND GARDEN

LENGTH: 18 METERS

HEIGHT: ---

WEIGHT: 22 TONS

PRICE: DORSAL FIN / 700 MILLION YEN; MEAT HAS NO VALUE AS A FOODSTUFF

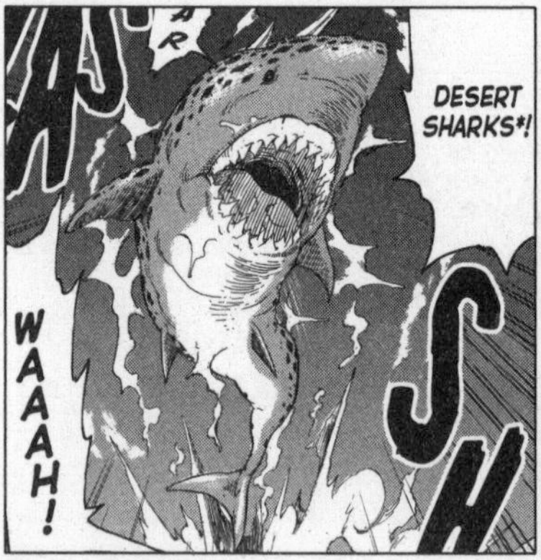
DESERT SHARKS*!
WAAAAH!

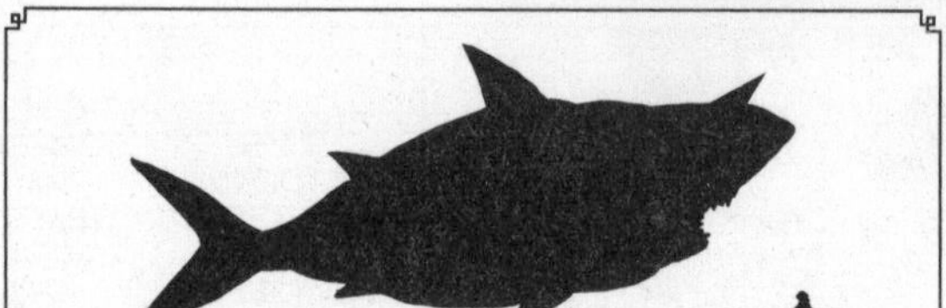

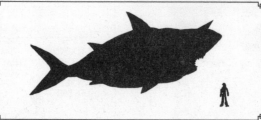

SCALE

A RARE BREED OF SHARK THAT LIVES IN THE SHIFTING DESERT SANDS OF SAND GARDEN. ITS TEETH ARE COATED WITH SCORPION-LIKE POISON AND ITS DORSAL FIN IS SHARP ENOUGH TO CUT THROUGH ROCK. ITS MEAT IS TOO TOUGH TOO EAT, BUT ITS DORSAL FIN IS KNOWN AS ONE OF THE DESERT'S DELICACIES. DESERT SHARK DORSAL FIN IS QUITE POPULAR WHEN IT MAKES A RARE APPEARANCE ON THE MARKET.

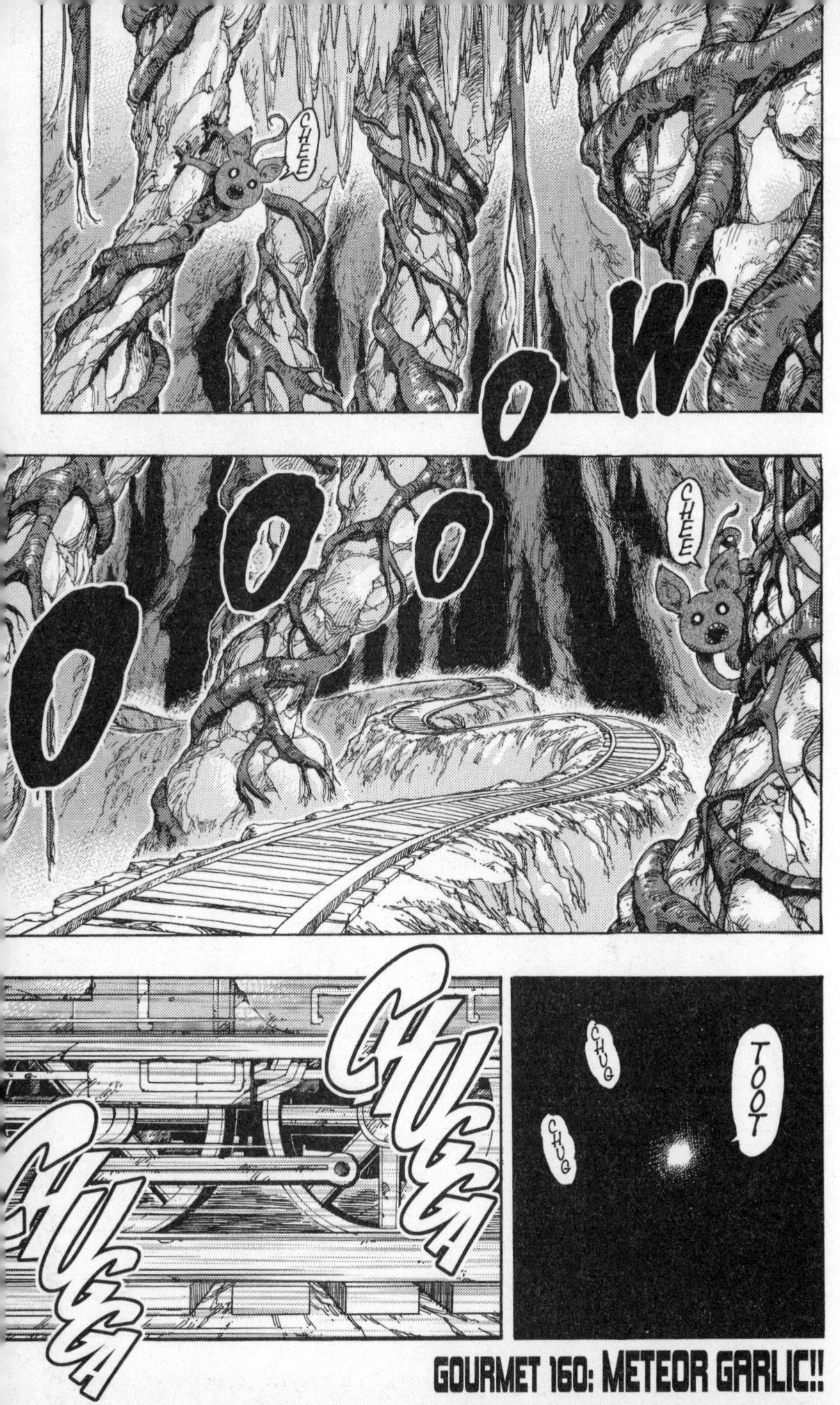
CHEE
WOOOO
CHEE
TOOT
CHUG
CHUG
CHUGGA
CHUGGA

GOURMET 160: METEOR GARLIC!!

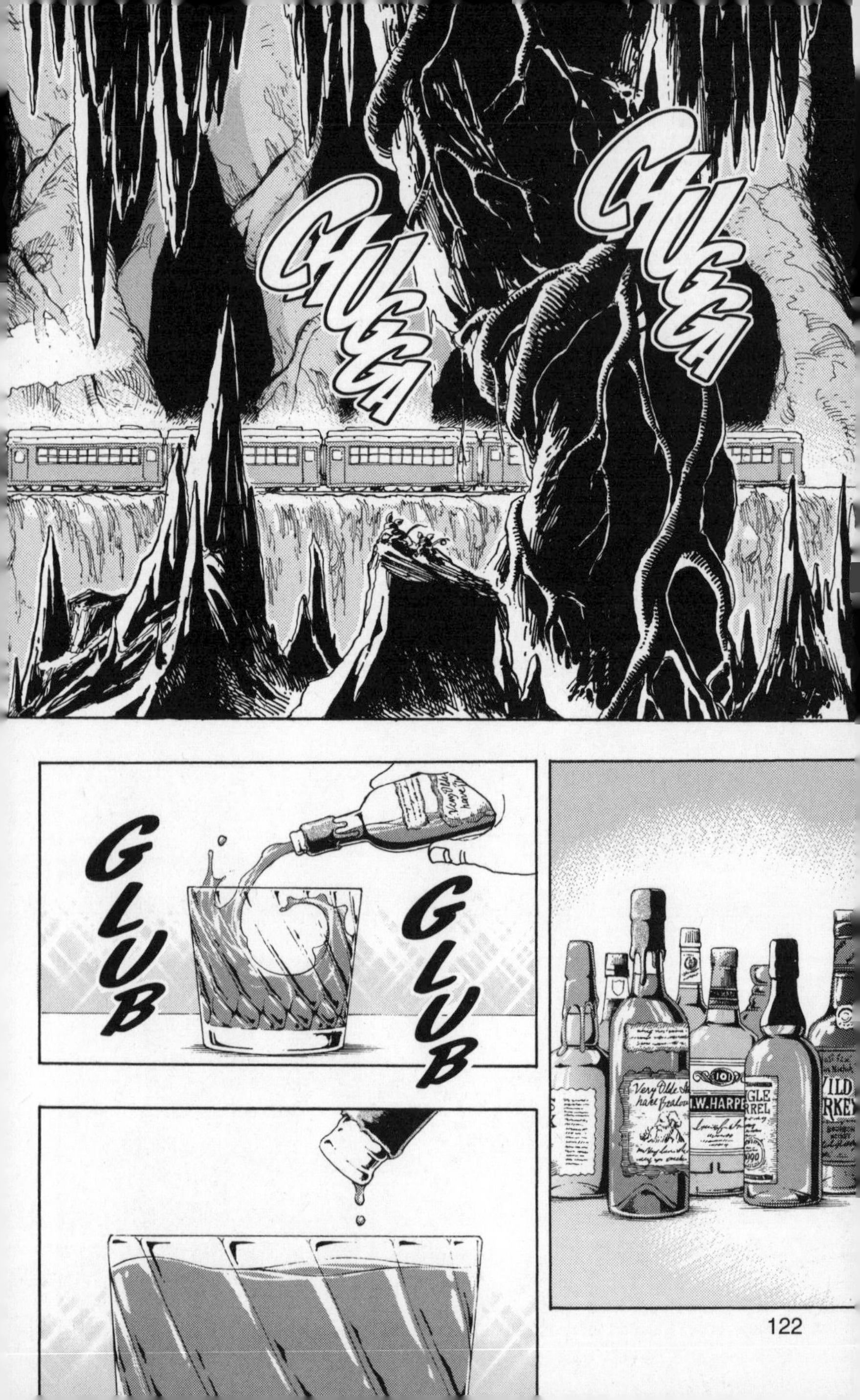
CHUGGA
CHUGGA
GLUB
GLUB

GOURMET 160: METEOR GARLIC!!

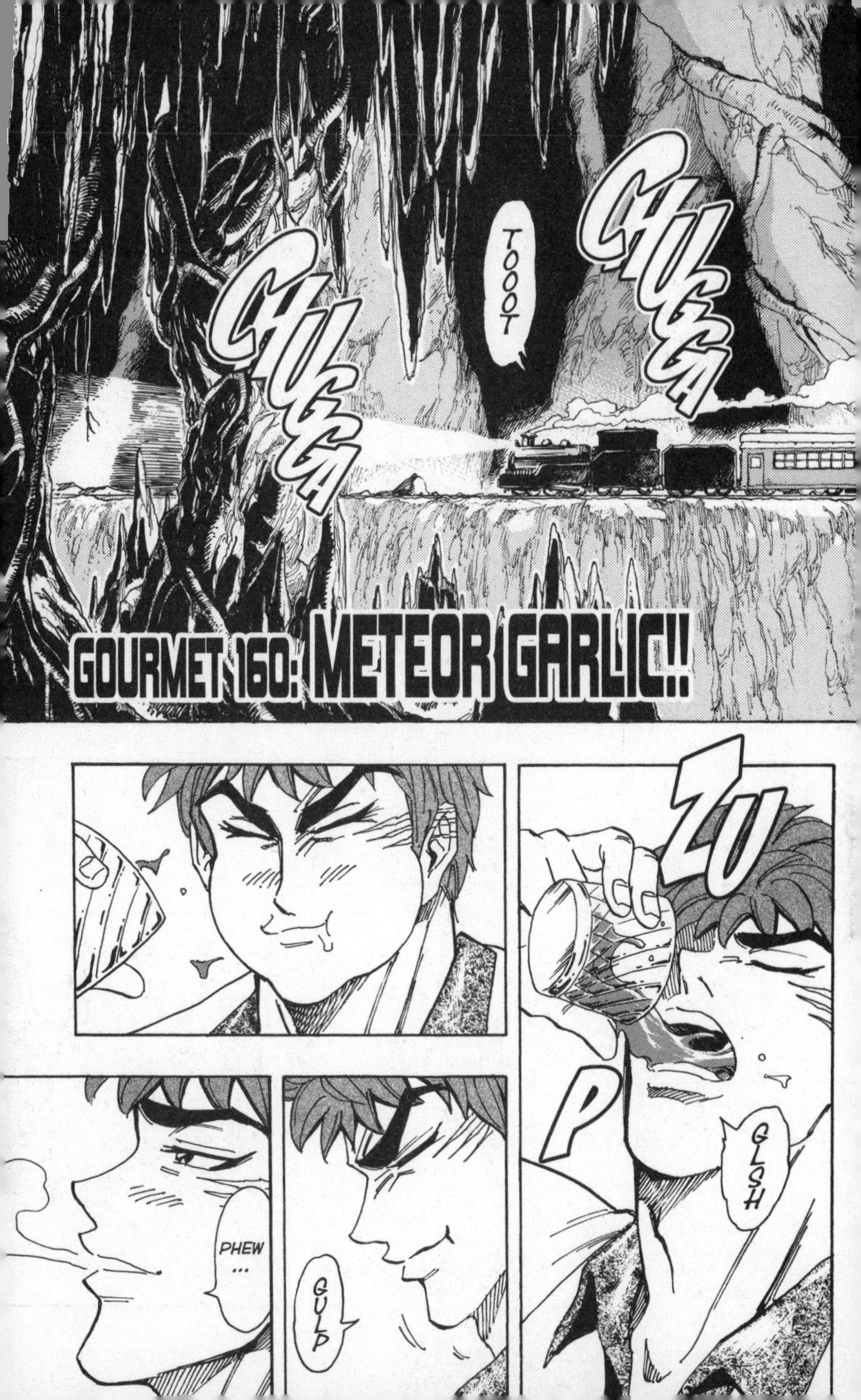
CHUGGA
TOOOT
CHUGGA
ZU
P
GLSH
GULP
PHEW...

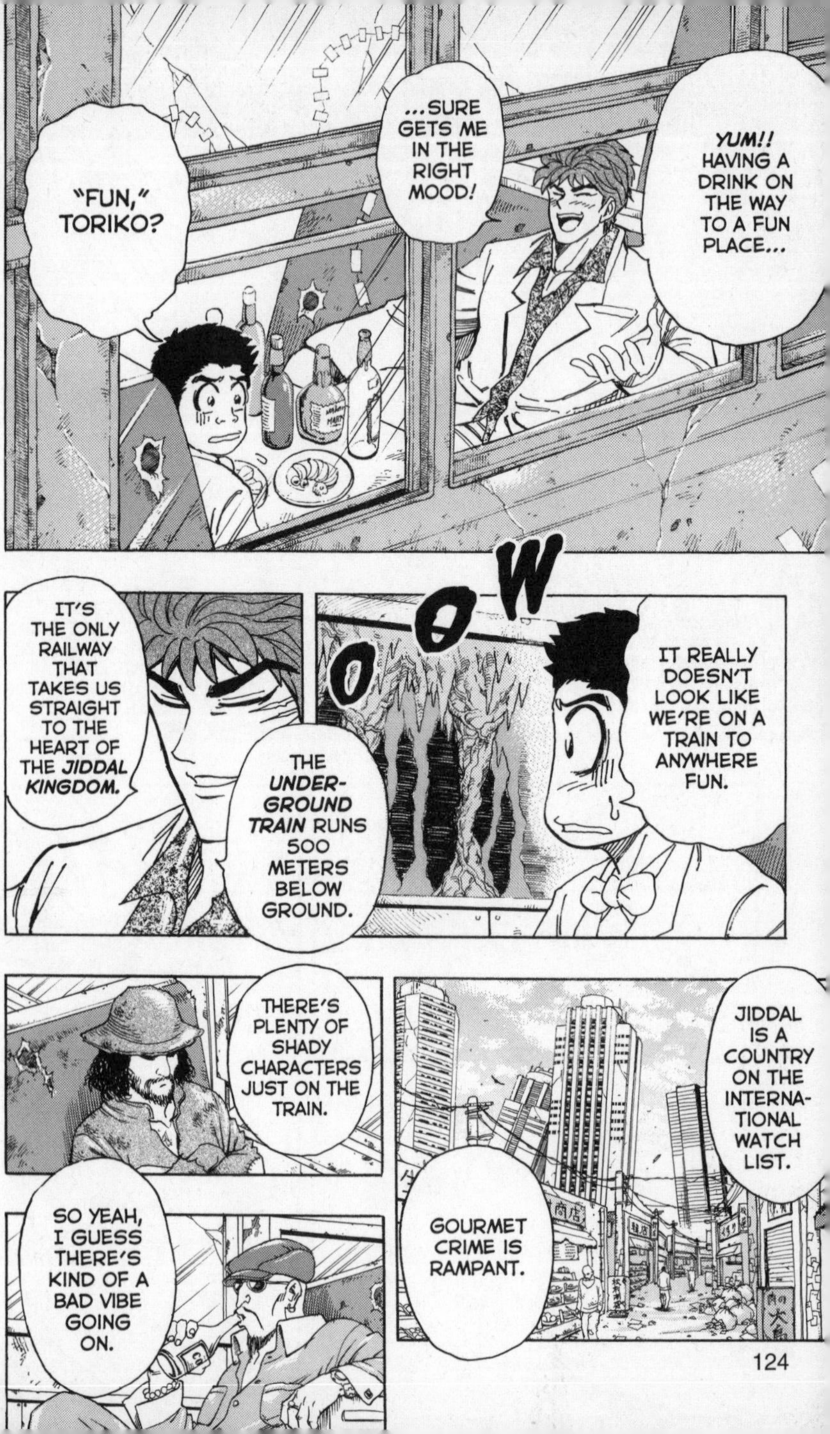
YUM!! HAVING A DRINK ON THE WAY TO A FUN PLACE...
...SURE GETS ME IN THE RIGHT MOOD!
"FUN," TORIKO?
OOW
IT REALLY DOESN'T LOOK LIKE WE'RE ON A TRAIN TO ANYWHERE FUN.
THE UNDER-GROUND TRAIN RUNS 500 METERS BELOW GROUND.
IT'S THE ONLY RAILWAY THAT TAKES US STRAIGHT TO THE HEART OF THE JIDDAL KINGDOM.
JIDDAL IS A COUNTRY ON THE INTERNA-TIONAL WATCH LIST.
GOURMET CRIME IS RAMPANT.
THERE'S PLENTY OF SHADY CHARACTERS JUST ON THE TRAIN.
SO YEAH, I GUESS THERE'S KIND OF A BAD VIBE GOING ON.

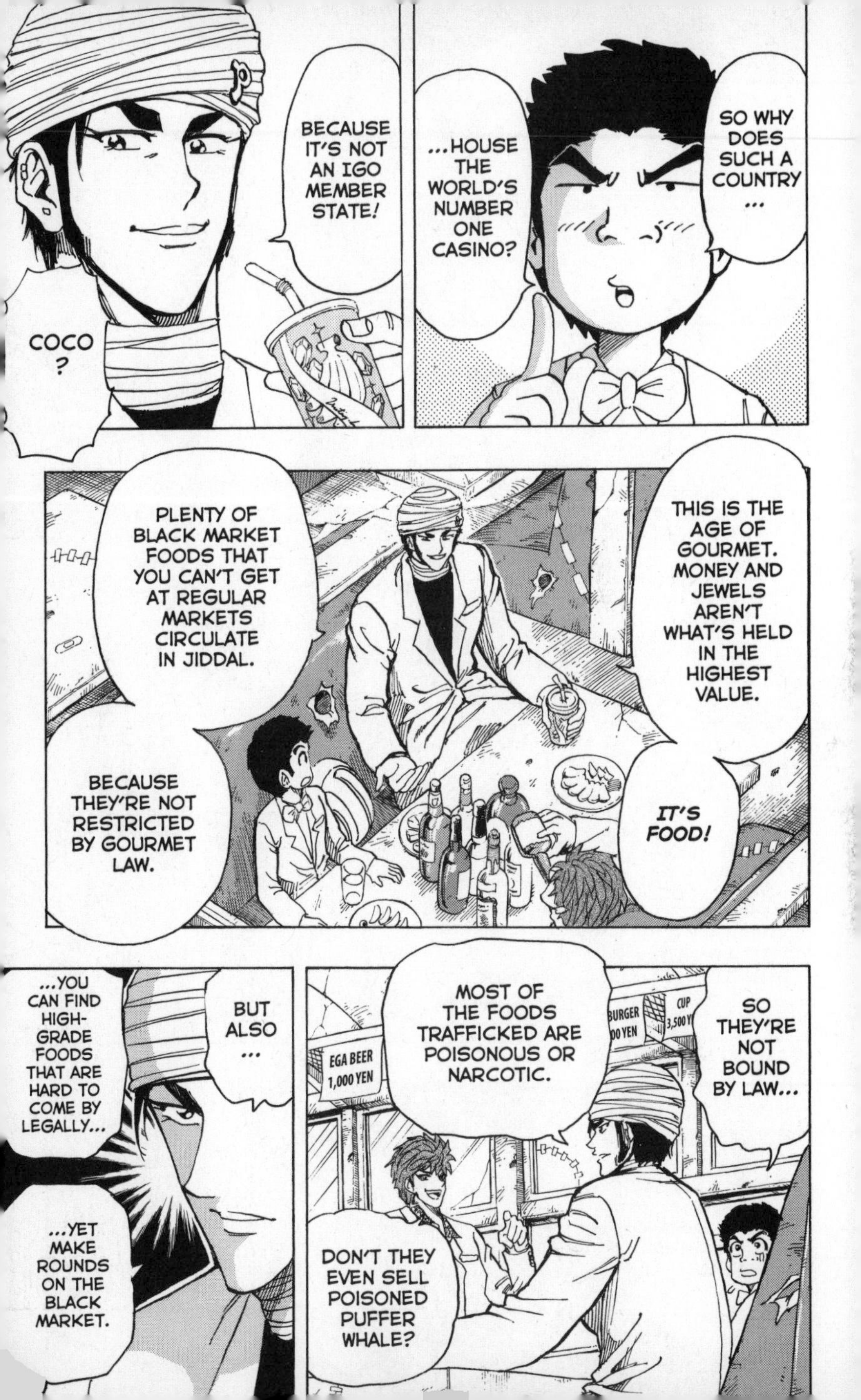
SO WHY DOES SUCH A COUNTRY ...
...HOUSE THE WORLD'S NUMBER ONE CASINO?
BECAUSE IT'S NOT AN IGO MEMBER STATE!
COCO ?
THIS IS THE AGE OF GOURMET. MONEY AND JEWELS AREN'T WHAT'S HELD IN THE HIGHEST VALUE.
IT'S FOOD!
PLENTY OF BLACK MARKET FOODS THAT YOU CAN'T GET AT REGULAR MARKETS CIRCULATE IN JIDDAL.
BECAUSE THEY'RE NOT RESTRICTED BY GOURMET LAW.
SO THEY'RE NOT BOUND BY LAW...
CUP
BURGER
MOST OF THE FOODS TRAFFICKED ARE POISONOUS OR NARCOTIC.
EGA BEER 1,000 YEN
DON'T THEY EVEN SELL POISONED PUFFER WHALE?
BUT ALSO ...
...YOU CAN FIND HIGH-GRADE FOODS THAT ARE HARD TO COME BY LEGALLY...
...YET MAKE ROUNDS ON THE BLACK MARKET.

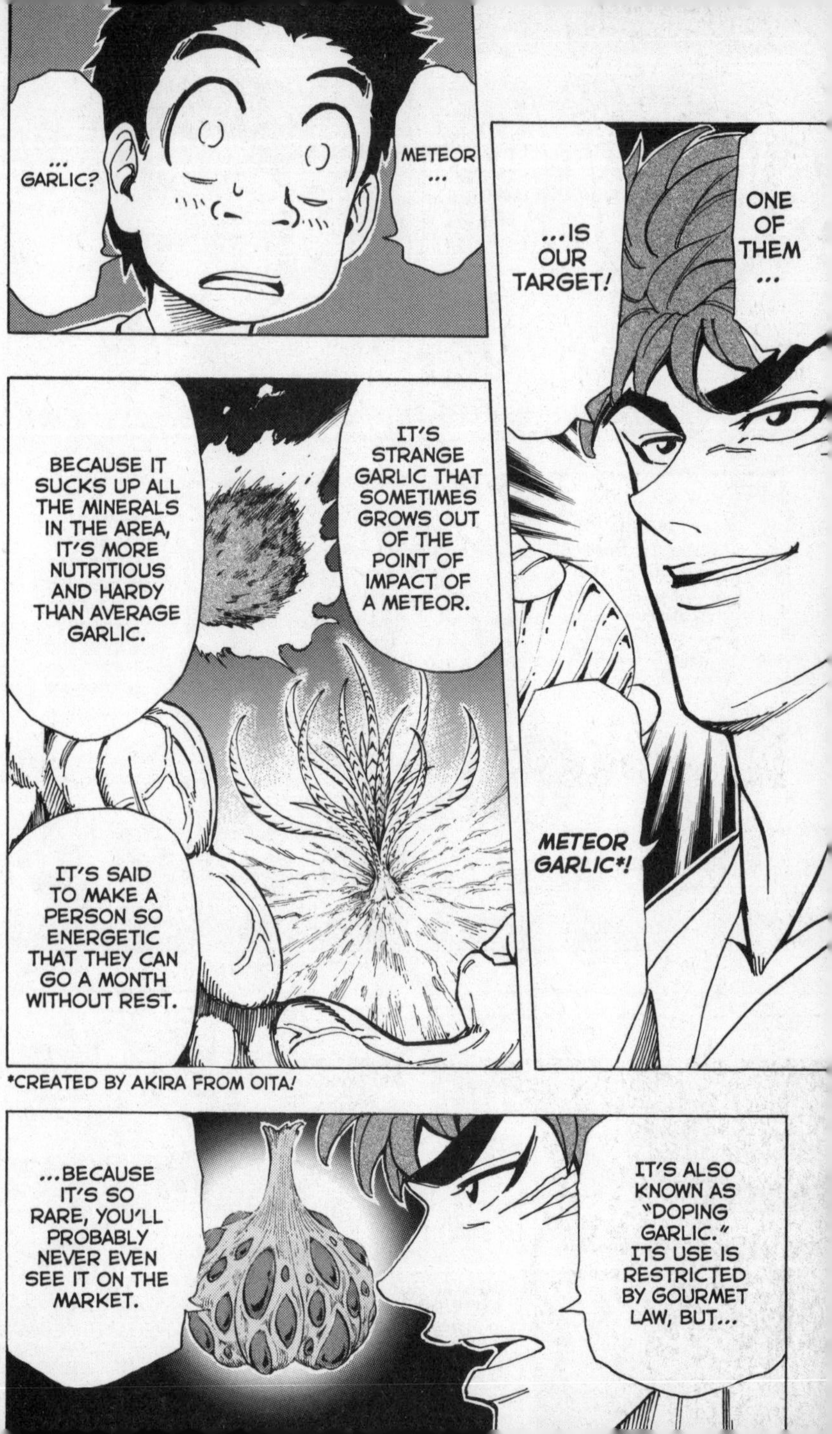
ONE OF THEM ...
...IS OUR TARGET!
METEOR GARLIC*!
METEOR ...
... GARLIC?
IT'S STRANGE GARLIC THAT SOMETIMES GROWS OUT OF THE POINT OF IMPACT OF A METEOR.
BECAUSE IT SUCKS UP ALL THE MINERALS IN THE AREA, IT'S MORE NUTRITIOUS AND HARDY THAN AVERAGE GARLIC.
IT'S SAID TO MAKE A PERSON SO ENERGETIC THAT THEY CAN GO A MONTH WITHOUT REST.
IT'S ALSO KNOWN AS "DOPING GARLIC." ITS USE IS RESTRICTED BY GOURMET LAW, BUT...
...BECAUSE IT'S SO RARE, YOU'LL PROBABLY NEVER EVEN SEE IT ON THE MARKET.

*CREATED BY AKIRA FROM OITA!

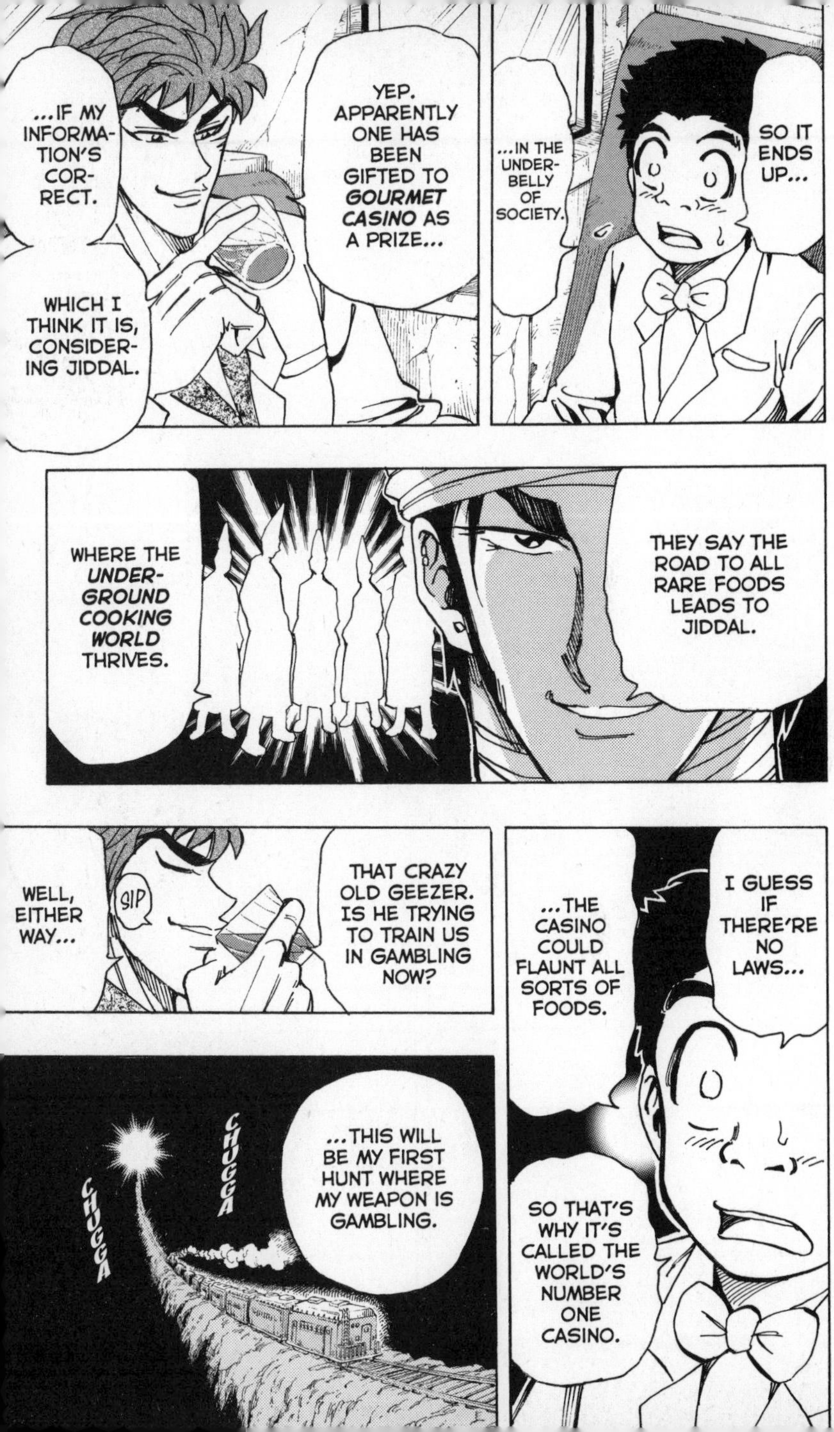
SO IT ENDS UP...
...IN THE UNDERBELLY OF SOCIETY.
YEP. APPARENTLY ONE HAS BEEN GIFTED TO GOURMET CASINO AS A PRIZE...
...IF MY INFORMATION'S CORRECT.
WHICH I THINK IT IS, CONSIDERING JIDDAL.
THEY SAY THE ROAD TO ALL RARE FOODS LEADS TO JIDDAL.
WHERE THE UNDERGROUND COOKING WORLD THRIVES.
I GUESS IF THERE'RE NO LAWS...
...THE CASINO COULD FLAUNT ALL SORTS OF FOODS.
SO THAT'S WHY IT'S CALLED THE WORLD'S NUMBER ONE CASINO.
THAT CRAZY OLD GEEZER. IS HE TRYING TO TRAIN US IN GAMBLING NOW?
SIP
WELL, EITHER WAY...
...THIS WILL BE MY FIRST HUNT WHERE MY WEAPON IS GAMBLING.
CHUGGA
CHUGGA

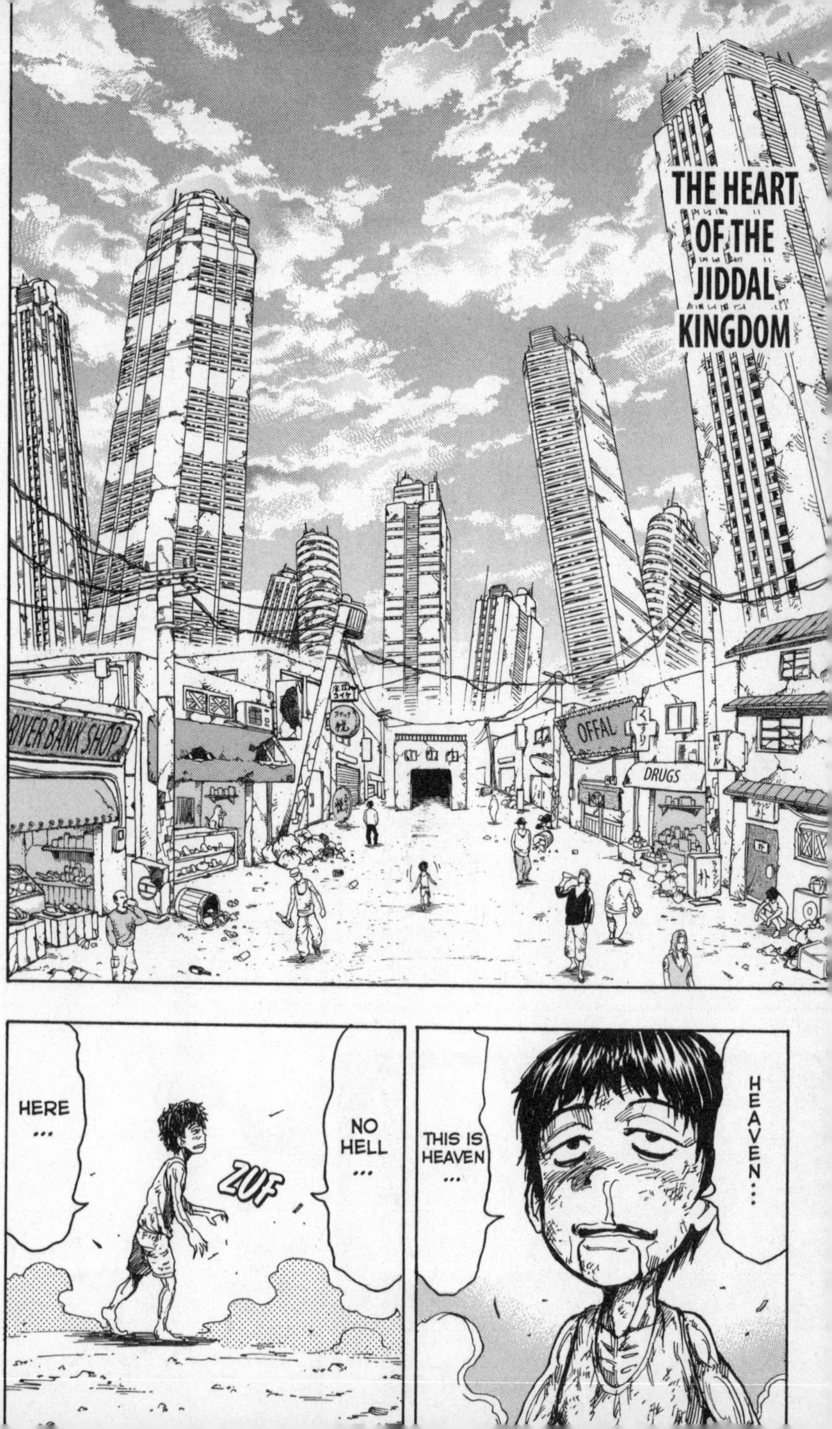
THE HEART OF THE JIDDAL KINGDOM
RIVER BANK SHOP
OFFAL
くすり
DRUGS
HEAVEN...
THIS IS HEAVEN...
NO HELL...
ZUF
HERE...

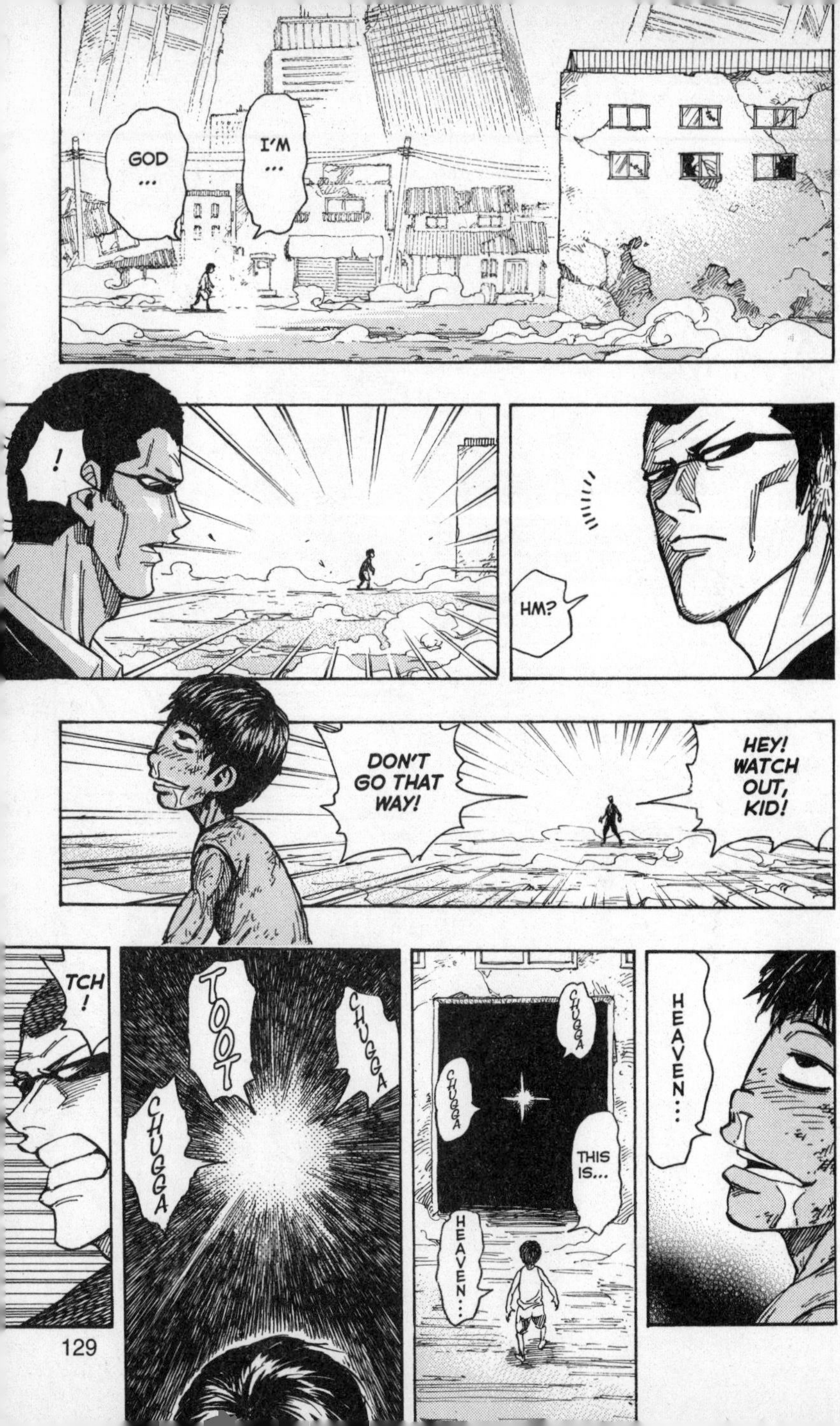
I'M ...
GOD ...
HM?
!
HEY! WATCH OUT, KID!
DON'T GO THAT WAY!
HEAVEN...
CHUGGA
CHUGGA
THIS IS...
HEAVEN...
CHUGGA
TOOT
CHUGGA
TCH!

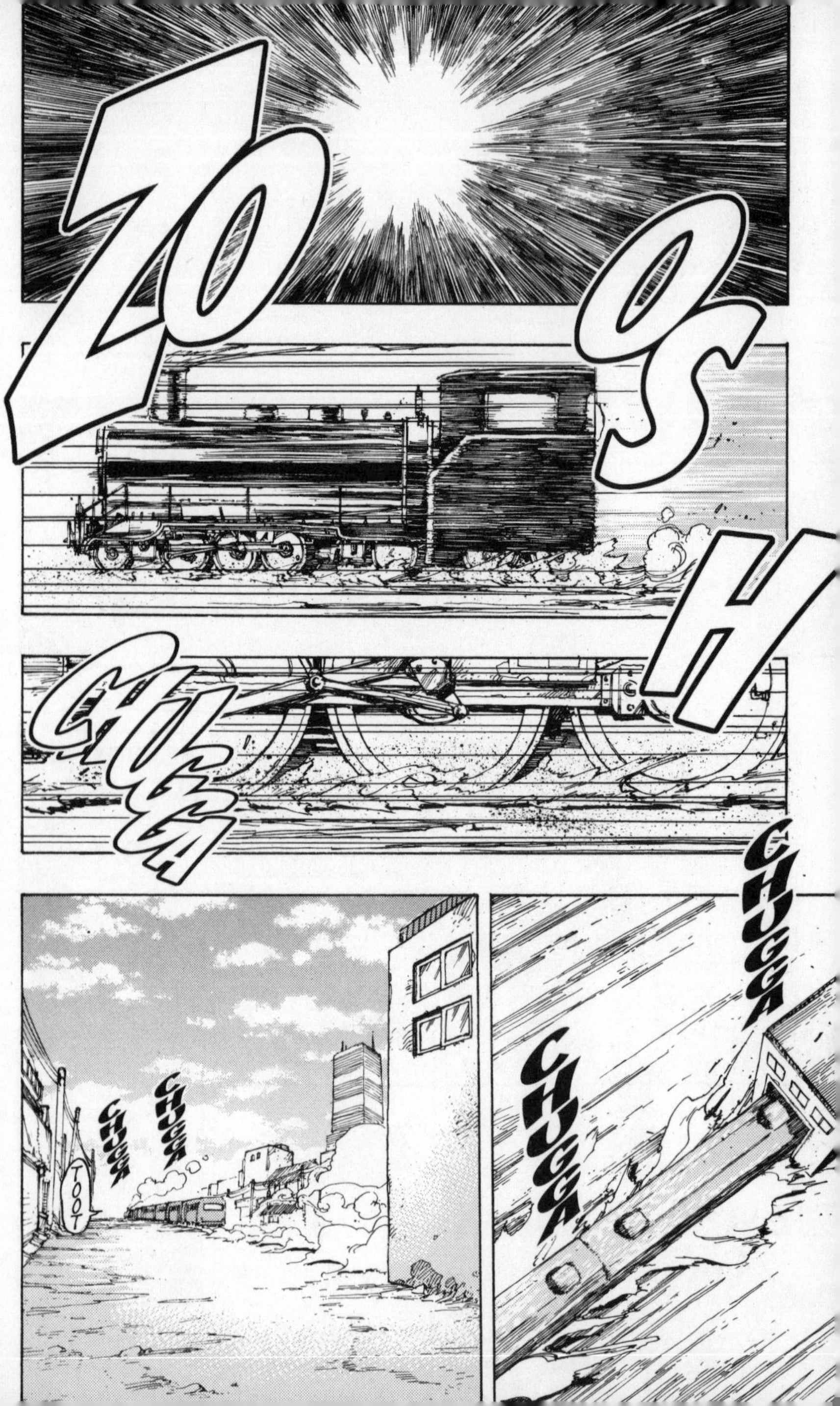
ZOOSH
CHUGGA
CHUGGA CHUGGA
CHUGGA CHUGGA
TOOT

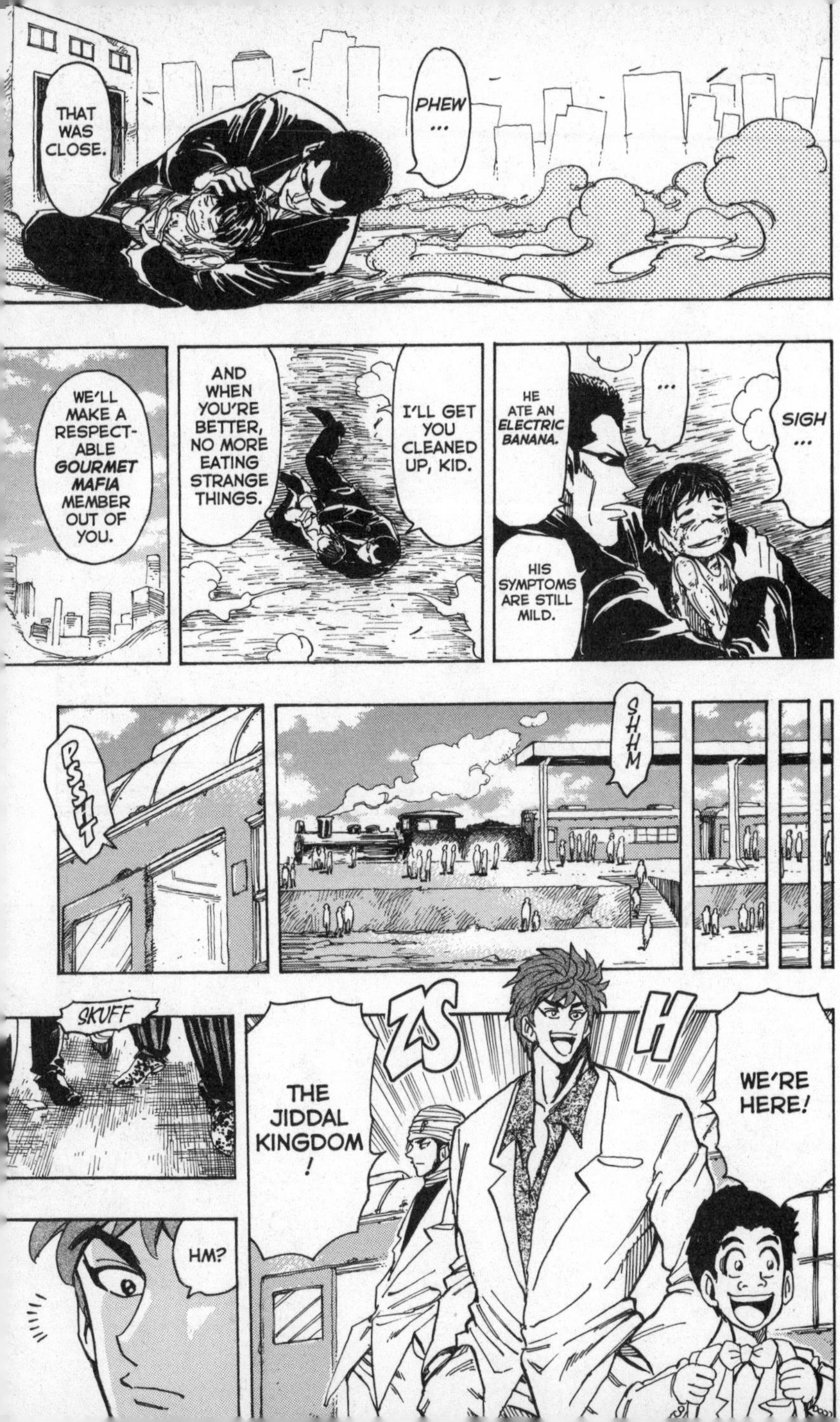
PHEW...
THAT WAS CLOSE.
SIGH...
...
HE ATE AN ELECTRIC BANANA.
HIS SYMPTOMS ARE STILL MILD.
I'LL GET YOU CLEANED UP, KID.
AND WHEN YOU'RE BETTER, NO MORE EATING STRANGE THINGS.
WE'LL MAKE A RESPECTABLE GOURMET MAFIA MEMBER OUT OF YOU.
SHHM
PSSHT
ZSH
WE'RE HERE!
THE JIDDAL KINGDOM!
SKUFF
HM?

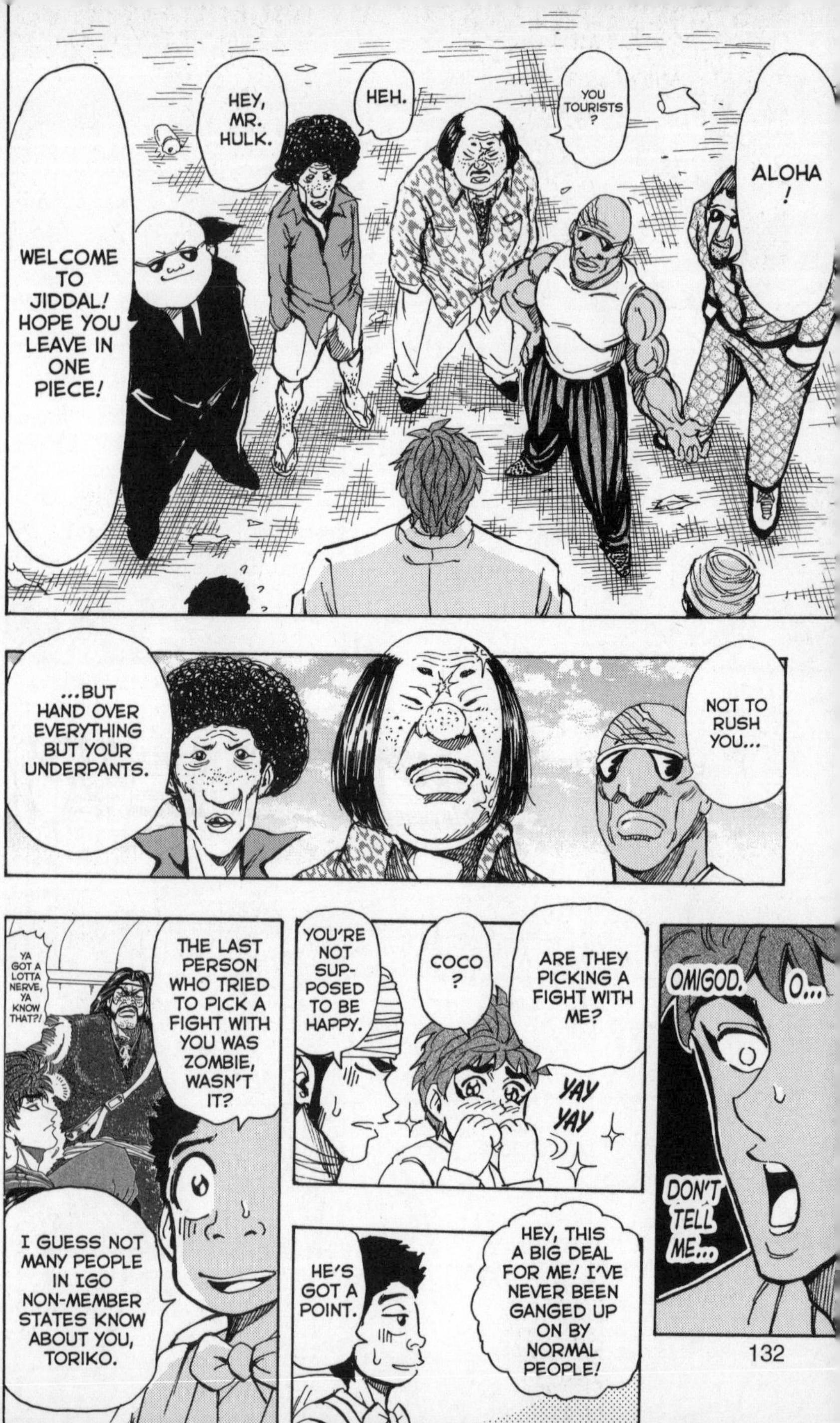
ALOHA!
YOU TOURISTS?
HEH.
HEY, MR. HULK.
WELCOME TO JIDDAL! HOPE YOU LEAVE IN ONE PIECE!
NOT TO RUSH YOU...
...BUT HAND OVER EVERYTHING BUT YOUR UNDERPANTS.
O...
OMIGOD.
DON'T TELL ME...
ARE THEY PICKING A FIGHT WITH ME?
COCO?
YOU'RE NOT SUP-POSED TO BE HAPPY.
YAY YAY
HEY, THIS A BIG DEAL FOR ME! I'VE NEVER BEEN GANGED UP ON BY NORMAL PEOPLE!
HE'S GOT A POINT.
THE LAST PERSON WHO TRIED TO PICK A FIGHT WITH YOU WAS ZOMBIE, WASN'T IT?
YA GOT A LOTTA NERVE, YA KNOW THAT?!
I GUESS NOT MANY PEOPLE IN IGO NON-MEMBER STATES KNOW ABOUT YOU, TORIKO.

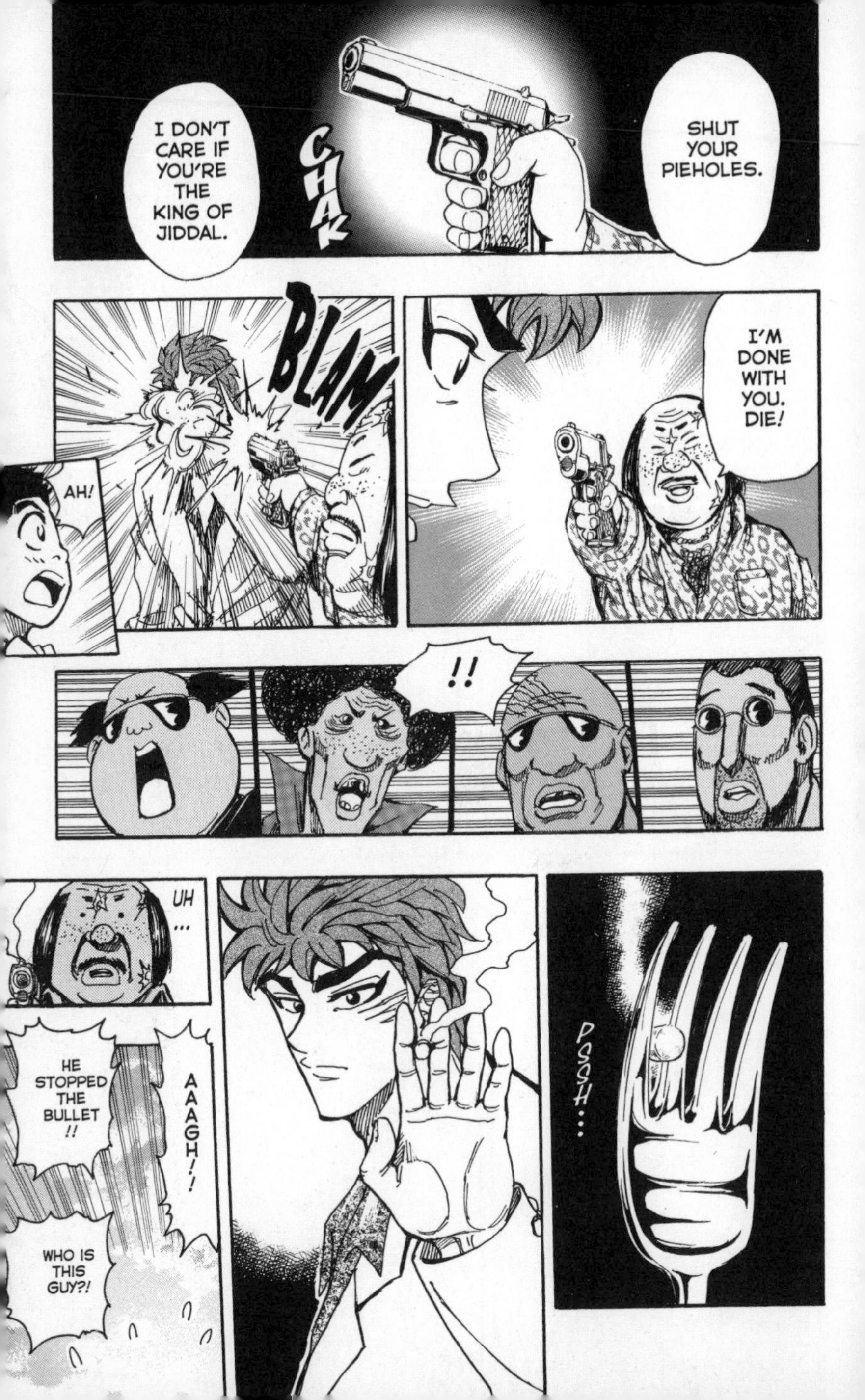
SHUT YOUR PIEHOLES.
CHAK
I DON'T CARE IF YOU'RE THE KING OF JIDDAL.
I'M DONE WITH YOU. DIE!
BLAM
AH!
!!
PSSH...
UH ...
AAAGH!!
HE STOPPED THE BULLET!!
WHO IS THIS GUY?!

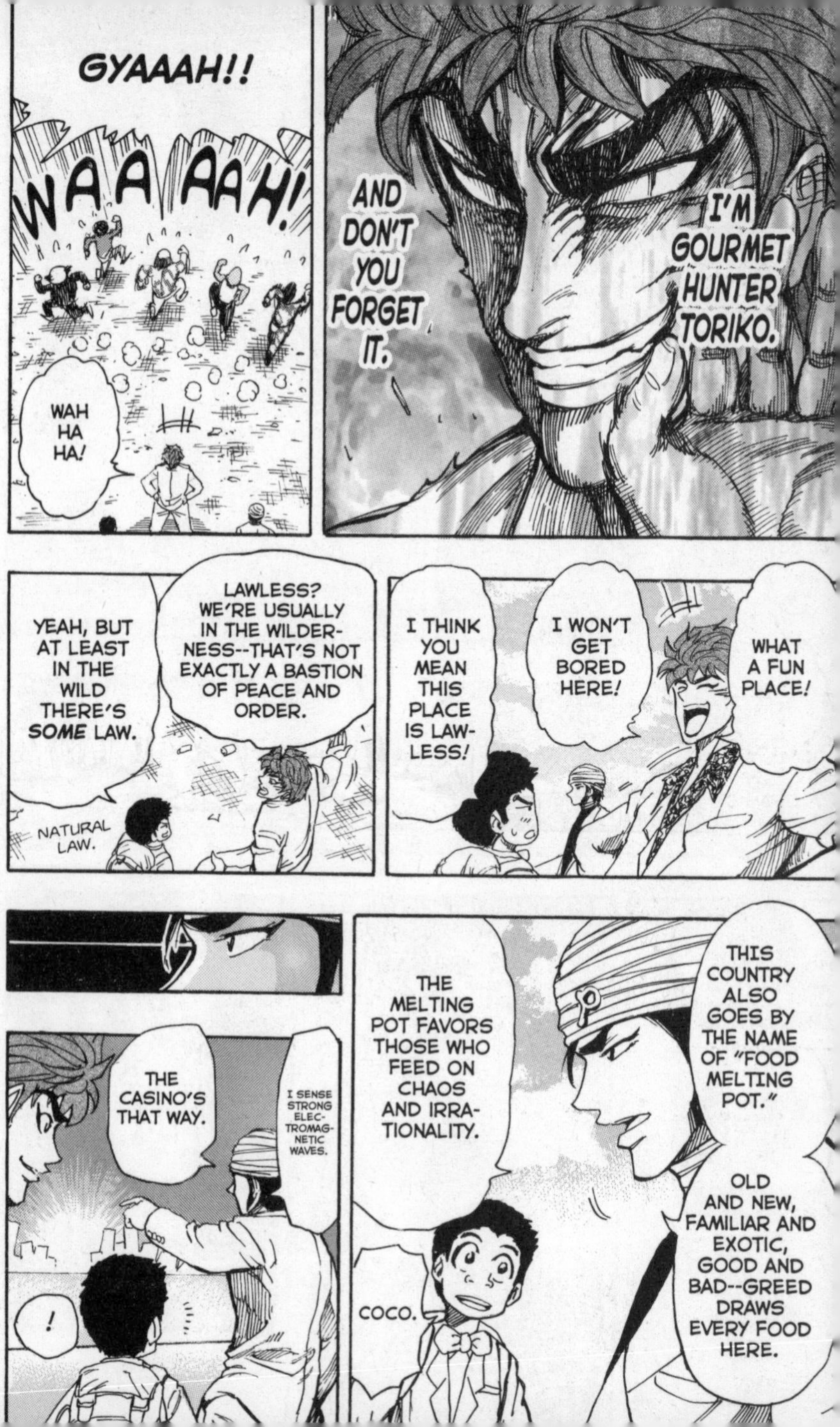
I'M GOURMET HUNTER TORIKO.
AND DON'T YOU FORGET IT.
GYAAAH!!
WAA AAH!
WAH HA HA!
WHAT A FUN PLACE!
I WON'T GET BORED HERE!
I THINK YOU MEAN THIS PLACE IS LAW-LESS!
LAWLESS? WE'RE USUALLY IN THE WILDER-NESS--THAT'S NOT EXACTLY A BASTION OF PEACE AND ORDER.
YEAH, BUT AT LEAST IN THE WILD THERE'S *SOME* LAW.
NATURAL LAW.
THIS COUNTRY ALSO GOES BY THE NAME OF "FOOD MELTING POT."
THE MELTING POT FAVORS THOSE WHO FEED ON CHAOS AND IRRA-TIONALITY.
OLD AND NEW, FAMILIAR AND EXOTIC, GOOD AND BAD--GREED DRAWS EVERY FOOD HERE.
COCO.
I SENSE STRONG ELEC-TROMAG-NETIC WAVES.
THE CASINO'S THAT WAY.
!

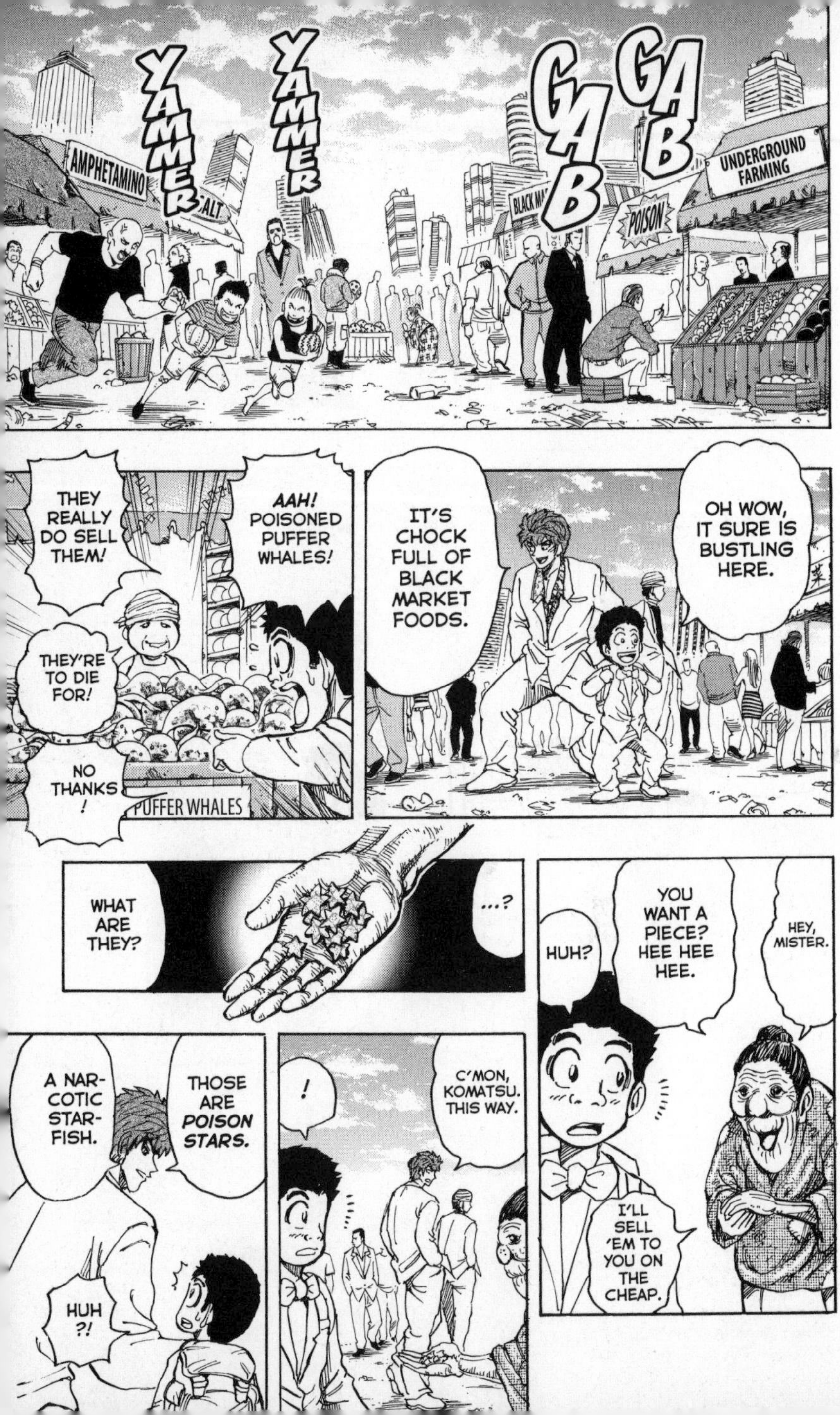
GAB
GAB
UNDERGROUND FARMING
POISON
BLACK MA
YAMMER
YAMMER
ALT
AMPHETAMINO
OH WOW, IT SURE IS BUSTLING HERE.
IT'S CHOCK FULL OF BLACK MARKET FOODS.
AAH! POISONED PUFFER WHALES!
THEY REALLY DO SELL THEM!
THEY'RE TO DIE FOR!
NO THANKS!
PUFFER WHALES
HEY, MISTER.
YOU WANT A PIECE? HEE HEE HEE.
HUH?
I'LL SELL 'EM TO YOU ON THE CHEAP.
...?
WHAT ARE THEY?
C'MON, KOMATSU. THIS WAY.
!
THOSE ARE POISON STARS.
A NAR-COTIC STAR-FISH.
HUH ?!

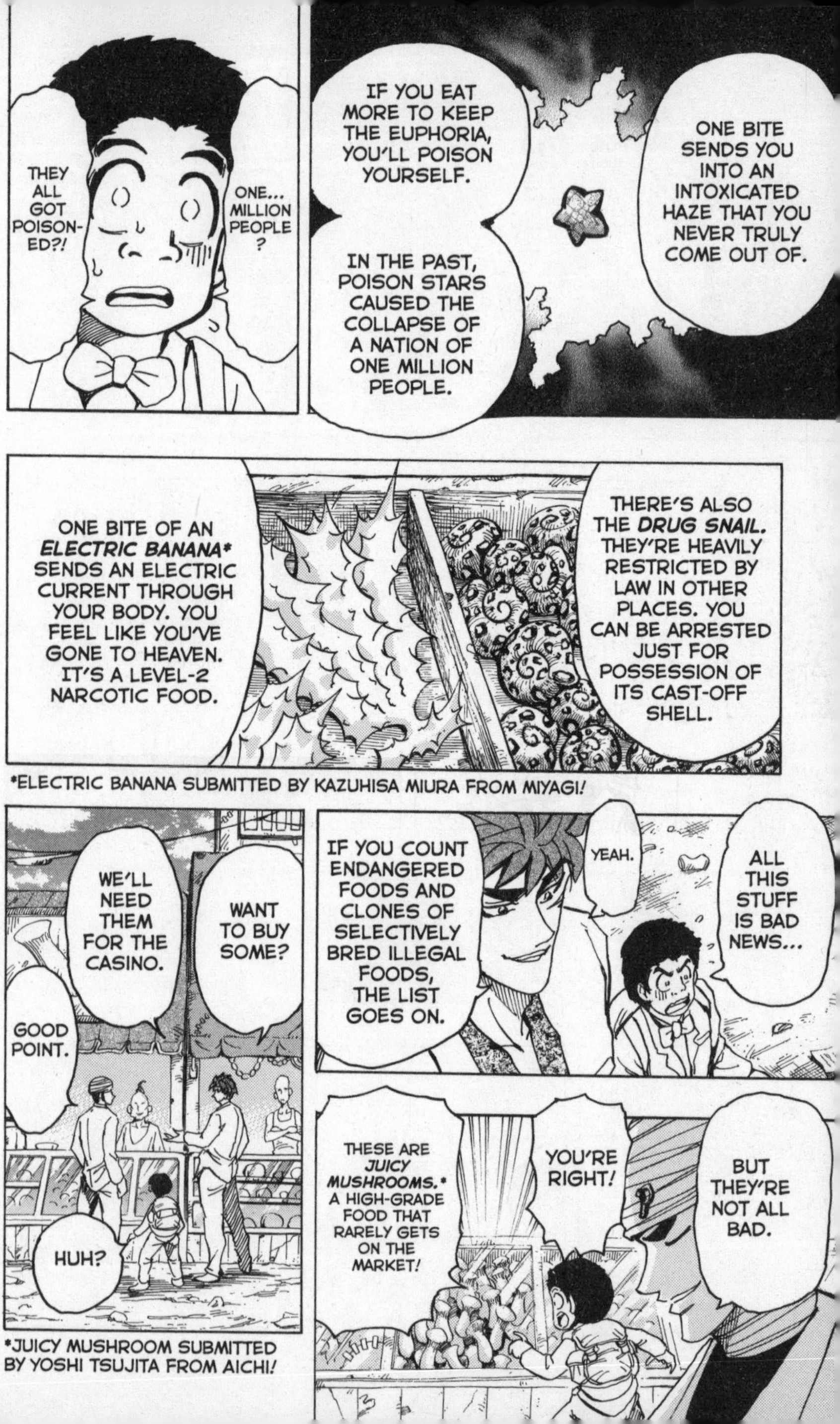
ONE BITE SENDS YOU INTO AN INTOXICATED HAZE THAT YOU NEVER TRULY COME OUT OF.
IF YOU EAT MORE TO KEEP THE EUPHORIA, YOU'LL POISON YOURSELF.
IN THE PAST, POISON STARS CAUSED THE COLLAPSE OF A NATION OF ONE MILLION PEOPLE.
ONE... MILLION PEOPLE?
THEY ALL GOT POISON-ED?!
THERE'S ALSO THE *DRUG SNAIL.* THEY'RE HEAVILY RESTRICTED BY LAW IN OTHER PLACES. YOU CAN BE ARRESTED JUST FOR POSSESSION OF ITS CAST-OFF SHELL.
ONE BITE OF AN *ELECTRIC BANANA** SENDS AN ELECTRIC CURRENT THROUGH YOUR BODY. YOU FEEL LIKE YOU'VE GONE TO HEAVEN. IT'S A LEVEL-2 NARCOTIC FOOD.
ALL THIS STUFF IS BAD NEWS...
YEAH.
IF YOU COUNT ENDANGERED FOODS AND CLONES OF SELECTIVELY BRED ILLEGAL FOODS, THE LIST GOES ON.
BUT THEY'RE NOT ALL BAD.
YOU'RE RIGHT!
THESE ARE *JUICY MUSHROOMS.** A HIGH-GRADE FOOD THAT RARELY GETS ON THE MARKET!
WANT TO BUY SOME?
WE'LL NEED THEM FOR THE CASINO.
GOOD POINT.
HUH?

*ELECTRIC BANANA SUBMITTED BY KAZUHISA MIURA FROM MIYAGI!

*JUICY MUSHROOM SUBMITTED BY YOSHI TSUJITA FROM AICHI!

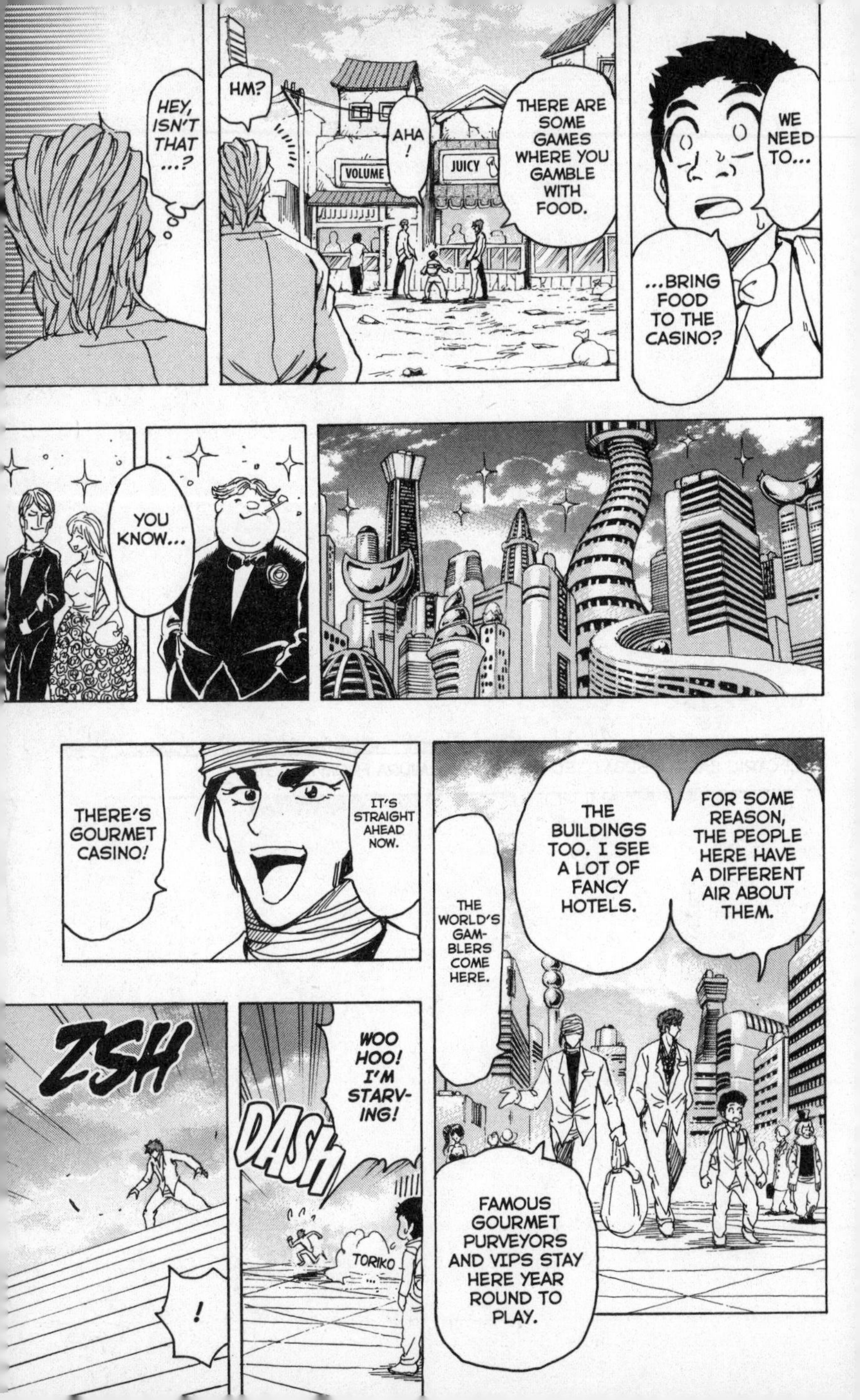
WE NEED TO...
...BRING FOOD TO THE CASINO?
THERE ARE SOME GAMES WHERE YOU GAMBLE WITH FOOD.
JUICY
AHA!
VOLUME
HM?
HEY, ISN'T THAT ...?
YOU KNOW...
FOR SOME REASON, THE PEOPLE HERE HAVE A DIFFERENT AIR ABOUT THEM.
THE BUILDINGS TOO. I SEE A LOT OF FANCY HOTELS.
THE WORLD'S GAM-BLERS COME HERE.
FAMOUS GOURMET PURVEYORS AND VIPS STAY HERE YEAR ROUND TO PLAY.
IT'S STRAIGHT AHEAD NOW.
THERE'S GOURMET CASINO!
WOO HOO! I'M STARV-ING!
DASH
TORIKO ...
ZSH
!

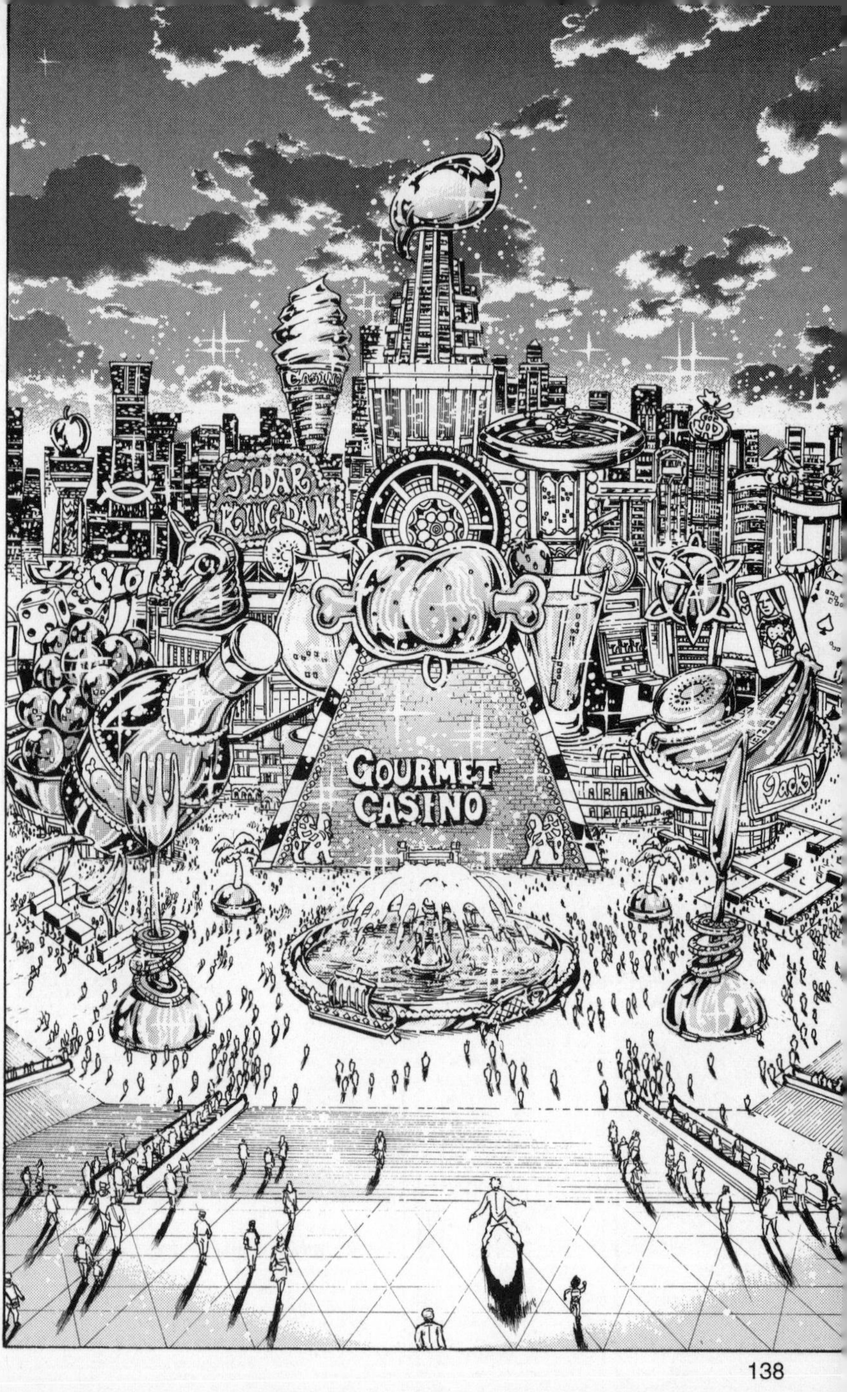

JIDAR KINGDAM
SLOT
GOURMET CASINO

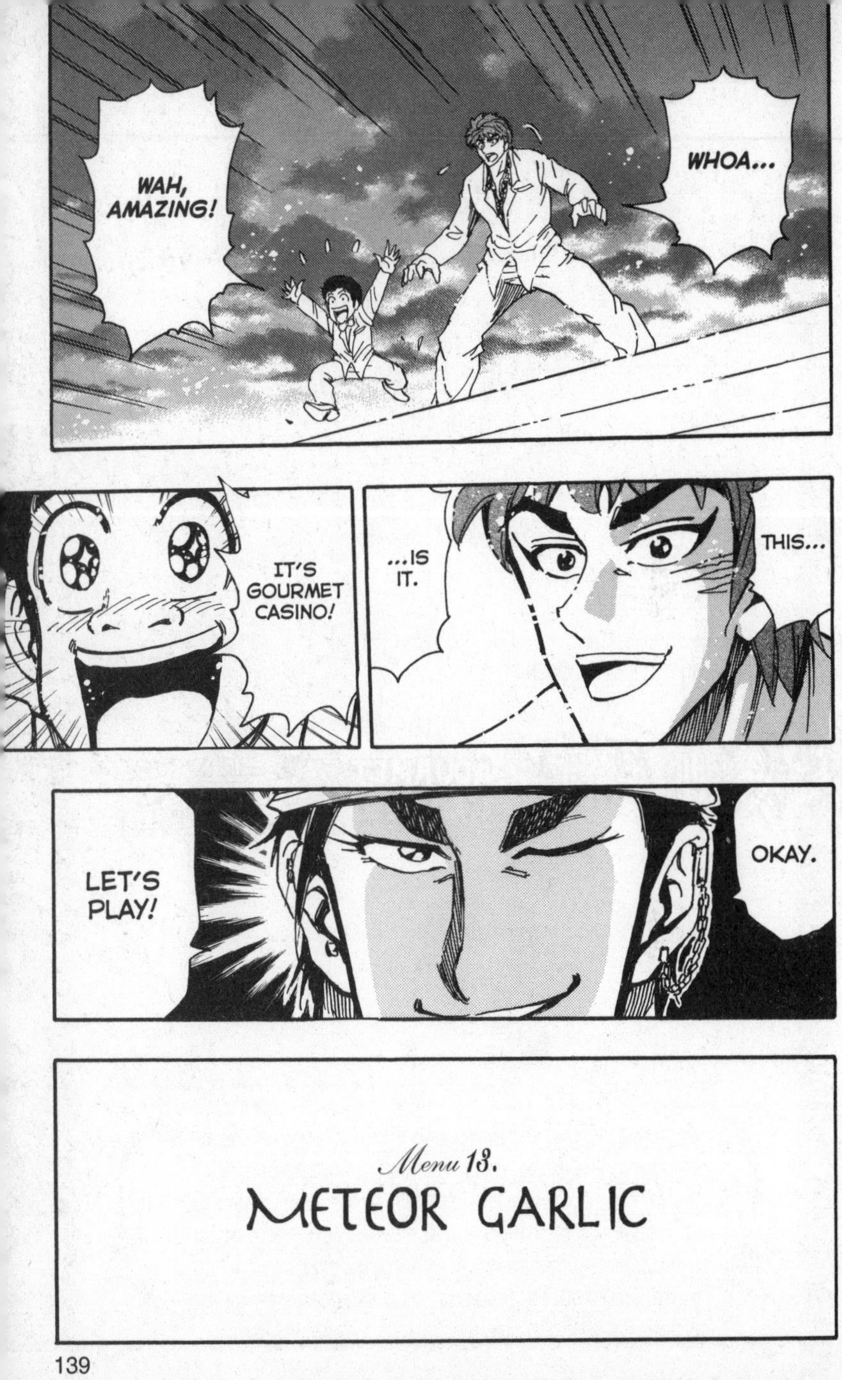
WHOA...
WAH, AMAZING!
THIS...
...IS IT.
IT'S GOURMET CASINO!
OKAY.
LET'S PLAY!

Menu 13.

METEOR GARLIC

TORIKO

GOURMET CHECKLIST

Vol. 191

FAUCET CACTUS
(PLANT)

CAPTURE LEVEL: 4

HABITAT: DESERT

LENGTH: ---

HEIGHT: 8 METERS

WEIGHT: ---

PRICE: NO VALUE AS A FOODSTUFF

LOOK, TORIKO!

A CACTUS!

SCALE

A CARNIVOROUS PLANT THAT ENTICES THIRSTY ANIMALS IN THE HOT DESERT TO COME DRINK ITS POISONOUS WATER. THIS THEN KILLS THEM SO THAT THE FAUCET CACTUS CAN ABSORB THE NUTRIENTS FROM THEIR CORPSES. THE FAUCET CACTUS IS NOT AGGRESSIVE AND BECAUSE IT CANNOT MOVE, IT WON'T HARM YOU AS LONG AS YOU STEER CLEAR OF ITS WATER. HOWEVER, THE NEED FOR WATER IN THE SWELTERING DESERT IS SO GREAT THAT FIGHTING OFF THE URGE TO DRINK IS MORE DIFFICULT THAN FIGHTING OFF A FEROCIOUS MONSTER.

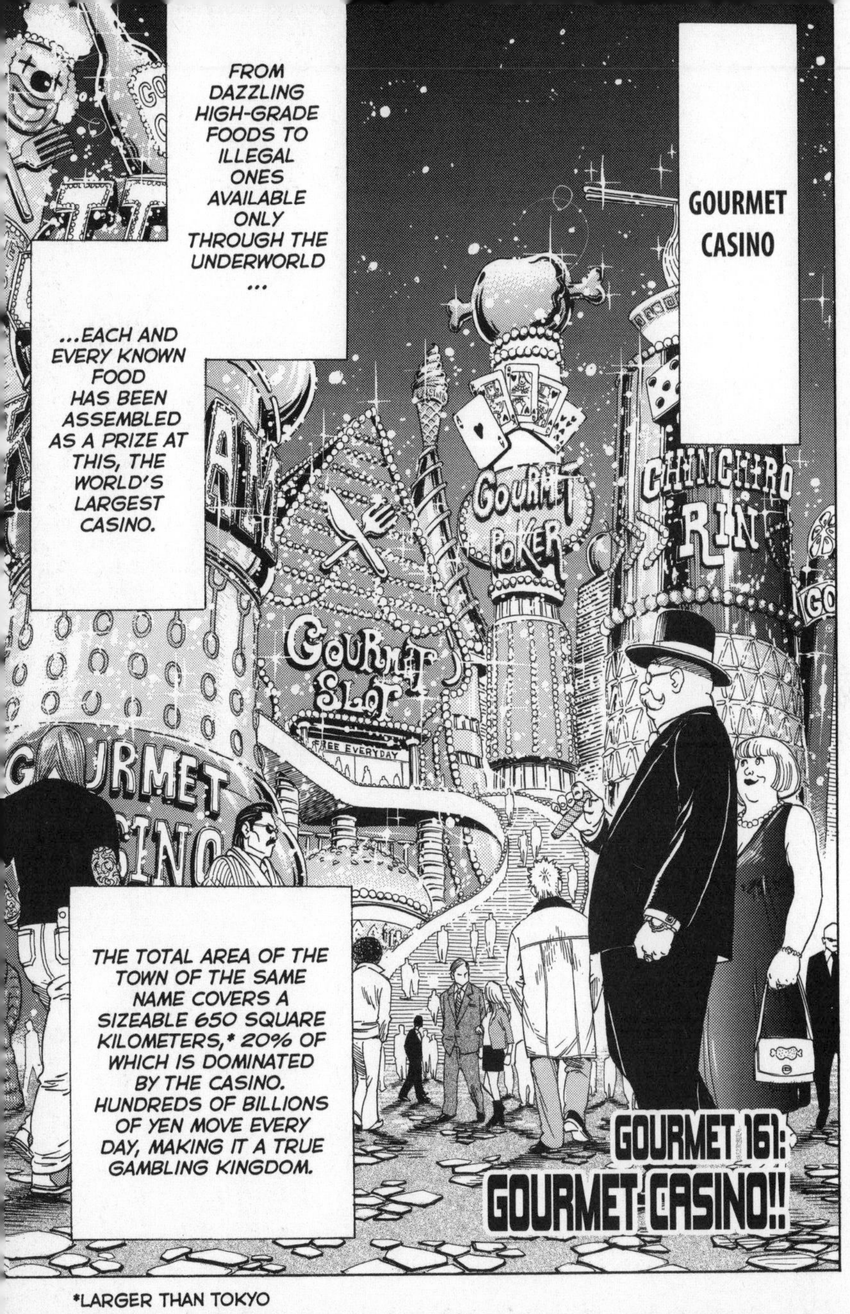
GOURMET CASINO
FROM DAZZLING HIGH-GRADE FOODS TO ILLEGAL ONES AVAILABLE ONLY THROUGH THE UNDERWORLD ...
...EACH AND EVERY KNOWN FOOD HAS BEEN ASSEMBLED AS A PRIZE AT THIS, THE WORLD'S LARGEST CASINO.
CHINCHIRO RIN
GOURMET POKER
GOURMET SLOT
FREE EVERYDAY
GOURMET 161: GOURMET CASINO!!
THE TOTAL AREA OF THE TOWN OF THE SAME NAME COVERS A SIZEABLE 650 SQUARE KILOMETERS,* 20% OF WHICH IS DOMINATED BY THE CASINO. HUNDREDS OF BILLIONS OF YEN MOVE EVERY DAY, MAKING IT A TRUE GAMBLING KINGDOM.

*LARGER THAN TOKYO

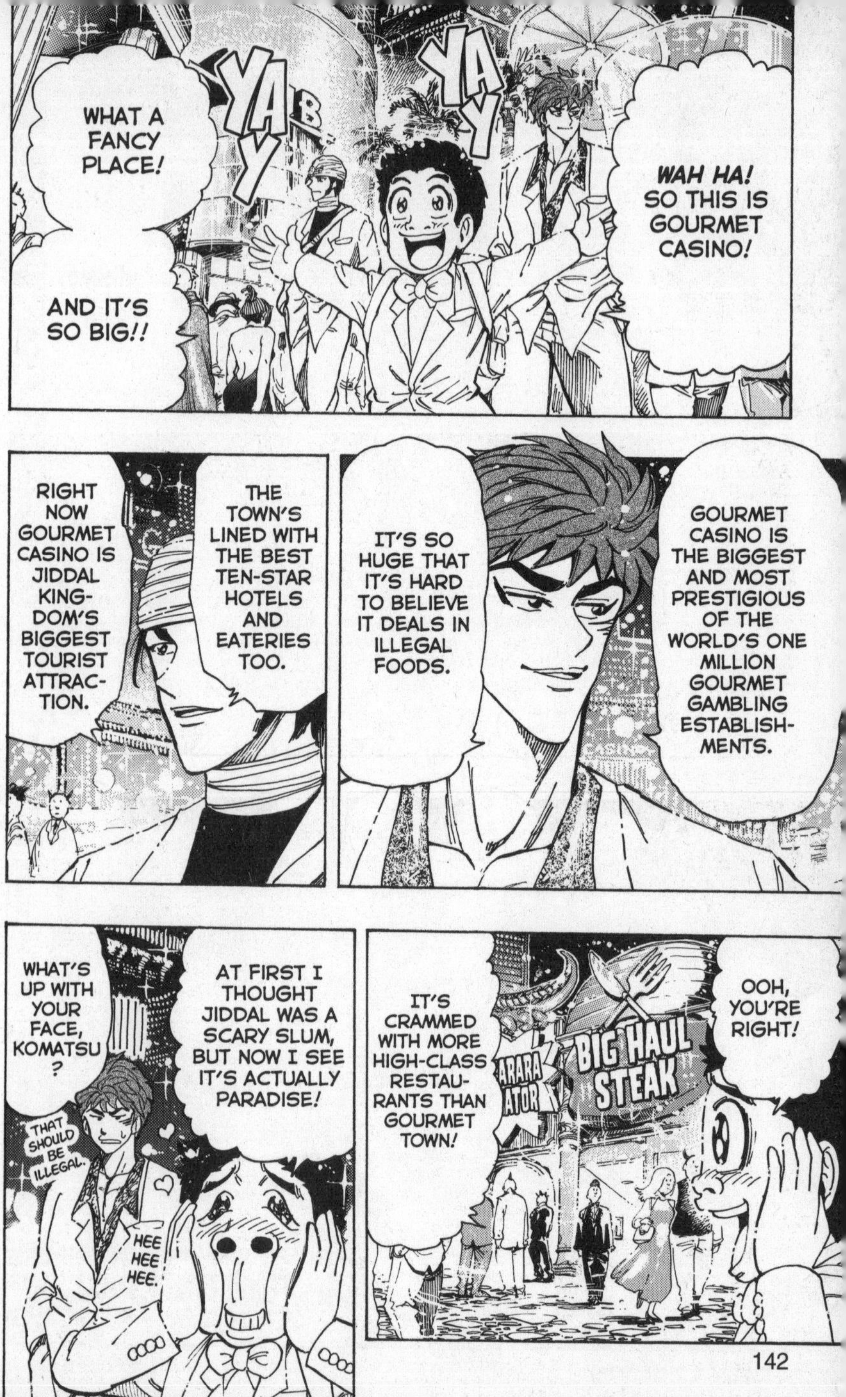
WAH HA! SO THIS IS GOURMET CASINO!
YAY
YAY
WHAT A FANCY PLACE!
AND IT'S SO BIG!!
GOURMET CASINO IS THE BIGGEST AND MOST PRESTIGIOUS OF THE WORLD'S ONE MILLION GOURMET GAMBLING ESTABLISHMENTS.
IT'S SO HUGE THAT IT'S HARD TO BELIEVE IT DEALS IN ILLEGAL FOODS.
THE TOWN'S LINED WITH THE BEST TEN-STAR HOTELS AND EATERIES TOO.
RIGHT NOW GOURMET CASINO IS JIDDAL KINGDOM'S BIGGEST TOURIST ATTRACTION.
OOH, YOU'RE RIGHT!
BIG HAUL STEAK
IT'S CRAMMED WITH MORE HIGH-CLASS RESTAURANTS THAN GOURMET TOWN!
AT FIRST I THOUGHT JIDDAL WAS A SCARY SLUM, BUT NOW I SEE IT'S ACTUALLY PARADISE!
WHAT'S UP WITH YOUR FACE, KOMATSU?
THAT SHOULD BE ILLEGAL.
HEE HEE HEE.

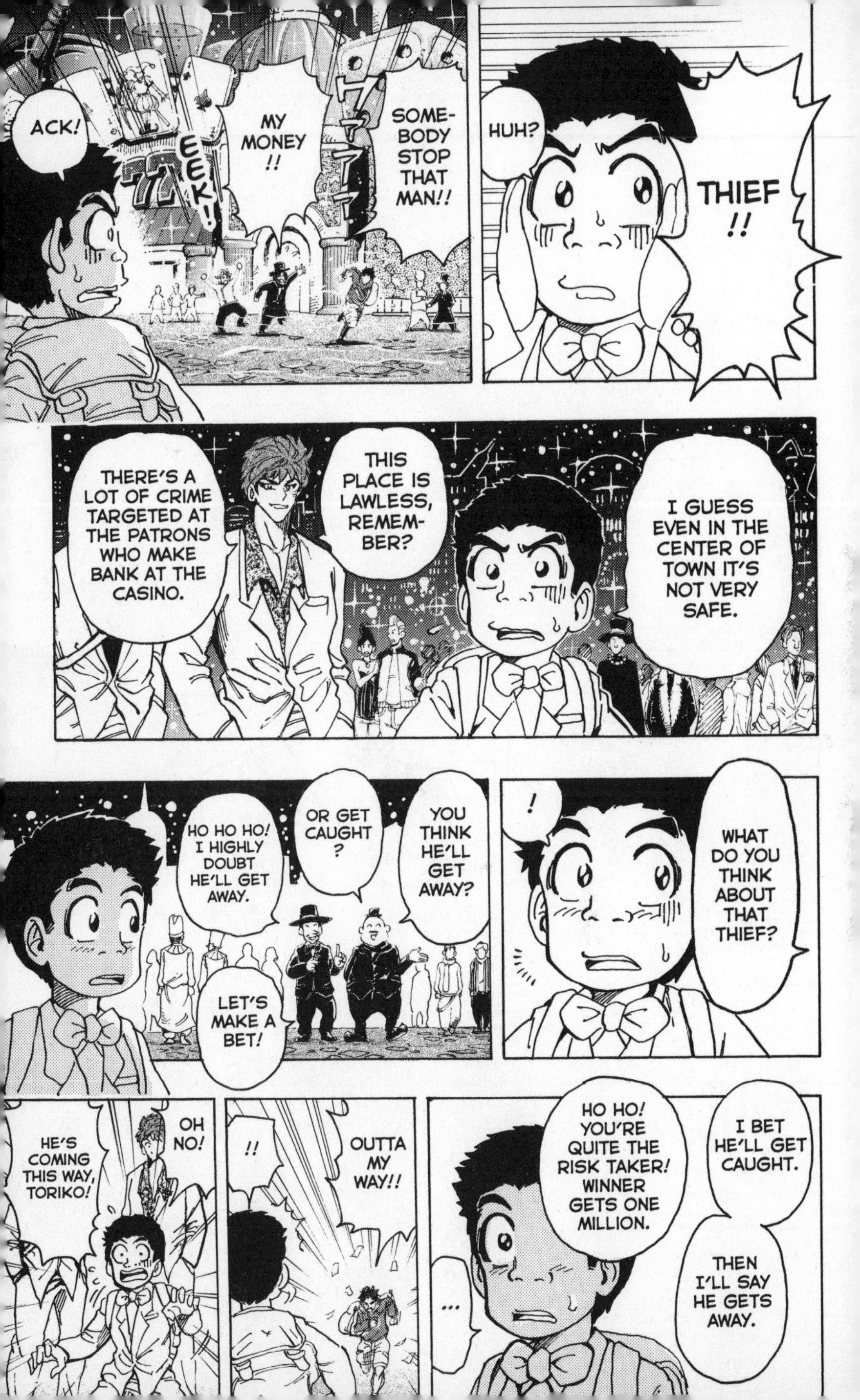
HUH?
THIEF!!
SOME-BODY STOP THAT MAN!!
MY MONEY!!
EEK!
ACK!
I GUESS EVEN IN THE CENTER OF TOWN IT'S NOT VERY SAFE.
THIS PLACE IS LAWLESS, REMEMBER?
THERE'S A LOT OF CRIME TARGETED AT THE PATRONS WHO MAKE BANK AT THE CASINO.
!
WHAT DO YOU THINK ABOUT THAT THIEF?
YOU THINK HE'LL GET AWAY?
OR GET CAUGHT?
HO HO HO! I HIGHLY DOUBT HE'LL GET AWAY.
LET'S MAKE A BET!
I BET HE'LL GET CAUGHT.
HO HO! YOU'RE QUITE THE RISK TAKER! WINNER GETS ONE MILLION.
THEN I'LL SAY HE GETS AWAY.
...
OUTTA MY WAY!!
!!
OH NO!
HE'S COMING THIS WAY, TORIKO!

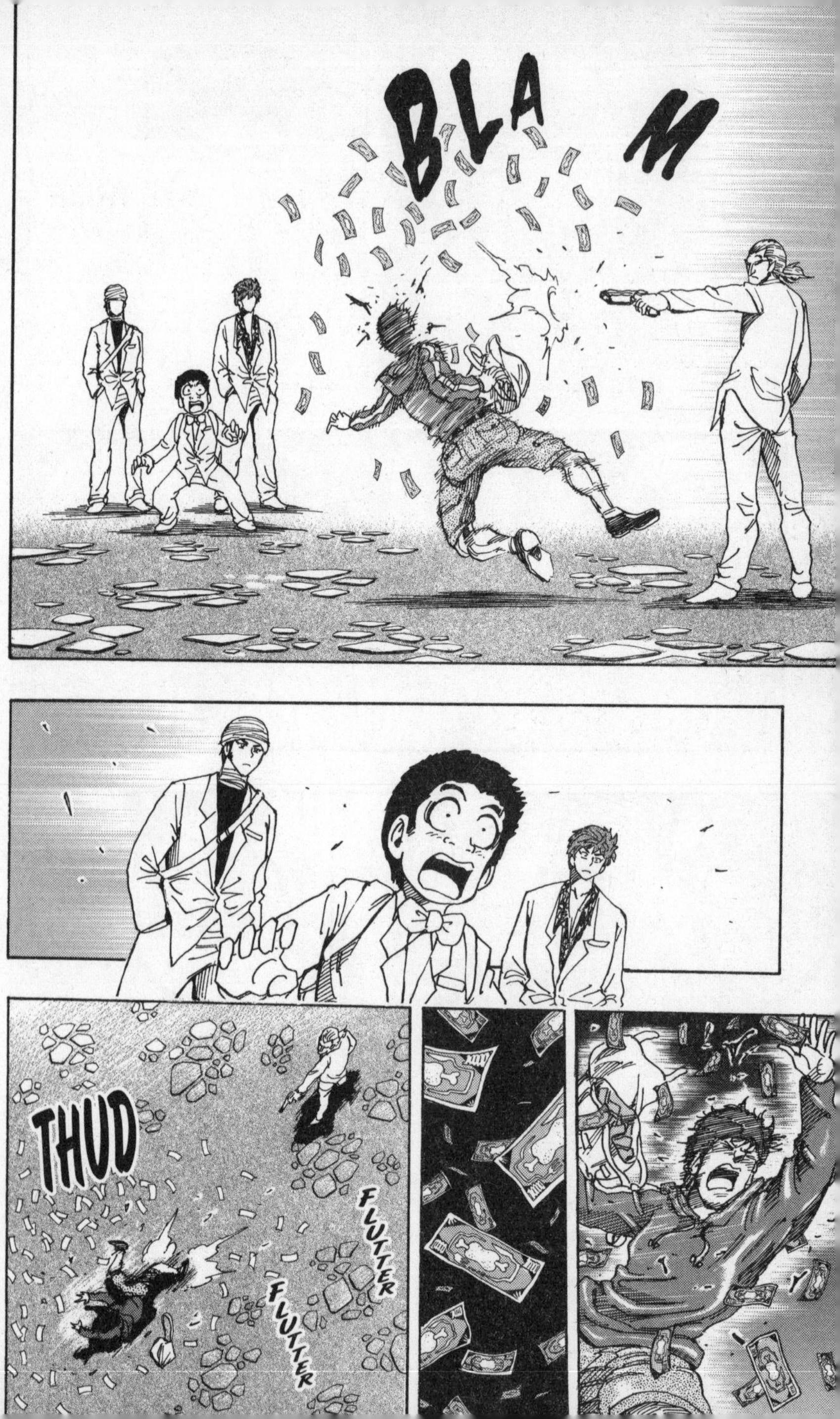
BLAM
FLUTTER
FLUTTER
THUD

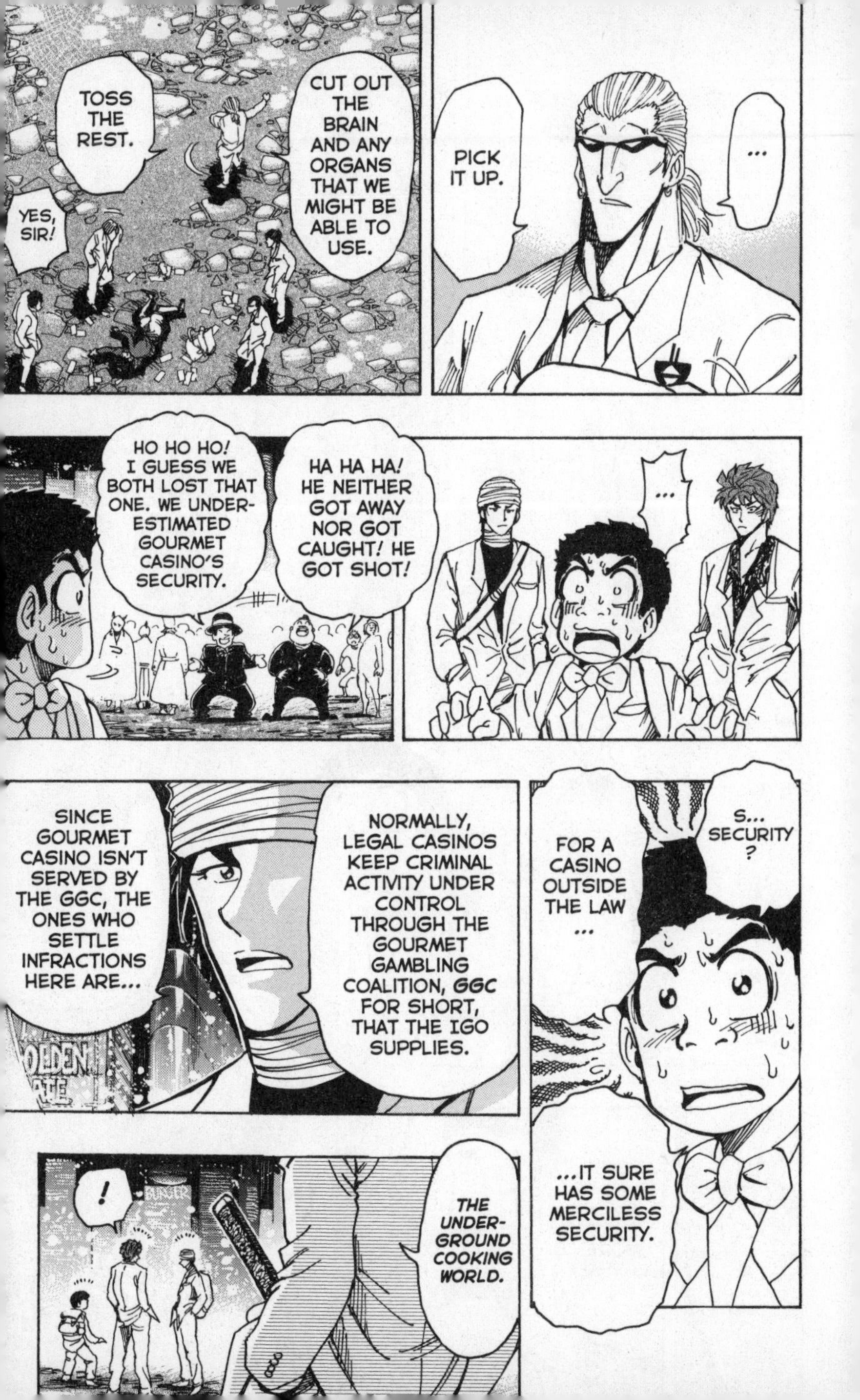
...
PICK IT UP.
CUT OUT THE BRAIN AND ANY ORGANS THAT WE MIGHT BE ABLE TO USE.
TOSS THE REST.
YES, SIR!
...
HA HA HA! HE NEITHER GOT AWAY NOR GOT CAUGHT! HE GOT SHOT!
HO HO HO! I GUESS WE BOTH LOST THAT ONE. WE UNDER-ESTIMATED GOURMET CASINO'S SECURITY.
S... SECURITY?
FOR A CASINO OUTSIDE THE LAW...
...IT SURE HAS SOME MERCILESS SECURITY.
NORMALLY, LEGAL CASINOS KEEP CRIMINAL ACTIVITY UNDER CONTROL THROUGH THE GOURMET GAMBLING COALITION, GGC FOR SHORT, THAT THE IGO SUPPLIES.
SINCE GOURMET CASINO ISN'T SERVED BY THE GGC, THE ONES WHO SETTLE INFRACTIONS HERE ARE...
THE UNDER-GROUND COOKING WORLD.
!

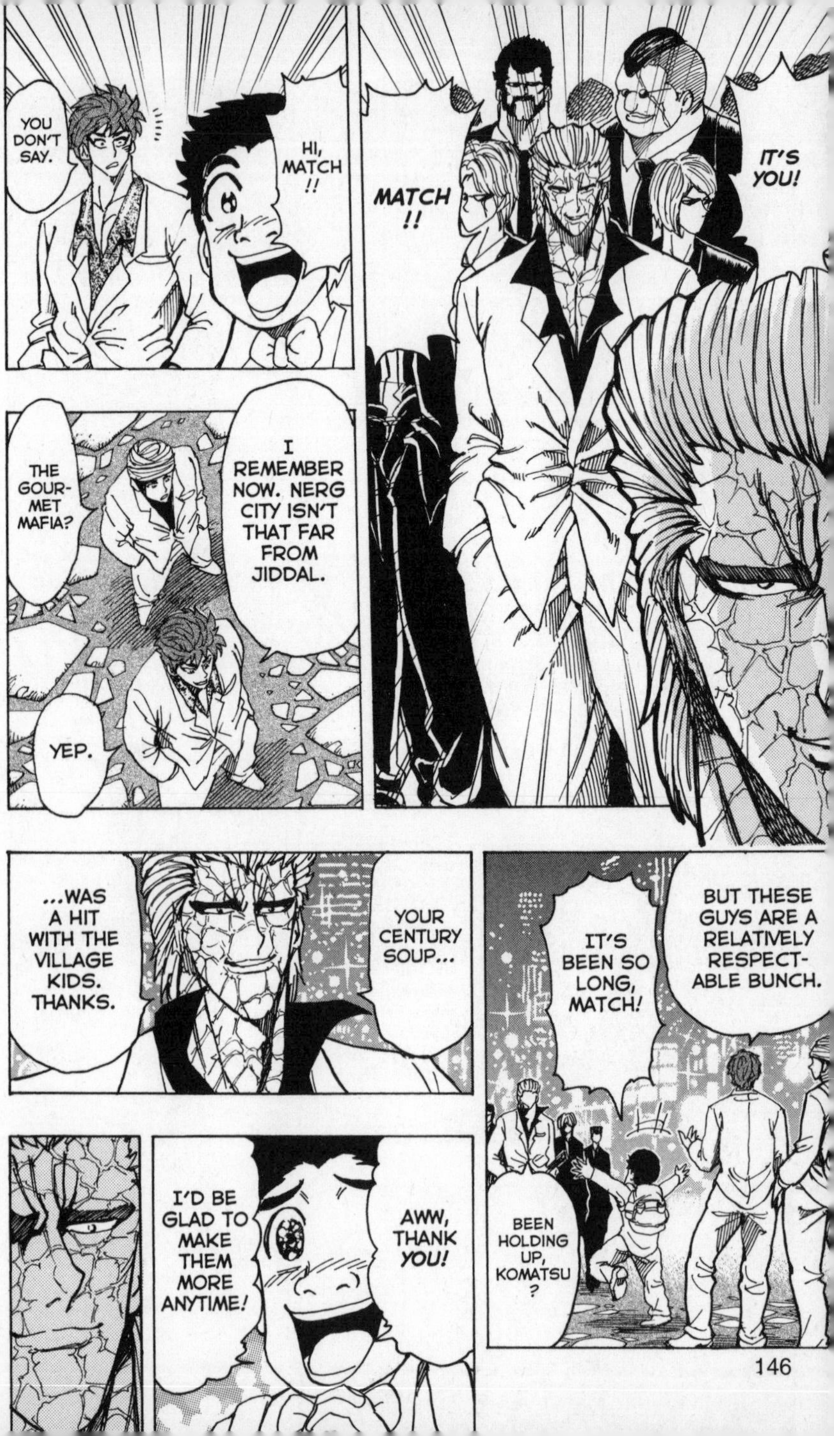
IT'S YOU!
MATCH!!
HI, MATCH!!
YOU DON'T SAY.
I REMEMBER NOW. NERG CITY ISN'T THAT FAR FROM JIDDAL.
THE GOURMET MAFIA?
YEP.
BUT THESE GUYS ARE A RELATIVELY RESPECTABLE BUNCH.
IT'S BEEN SO LONG, MATCH!
BEEN HOLDING UP, KOMATSU?
YOUR CENTURY SOUP...
...WAS A HIT WITH THE VILLAGE KIDS. THANKS.
AWW, THANK *YOU*!
I'D BE GLAD TO MAKE THEM MORE ANYTIME!

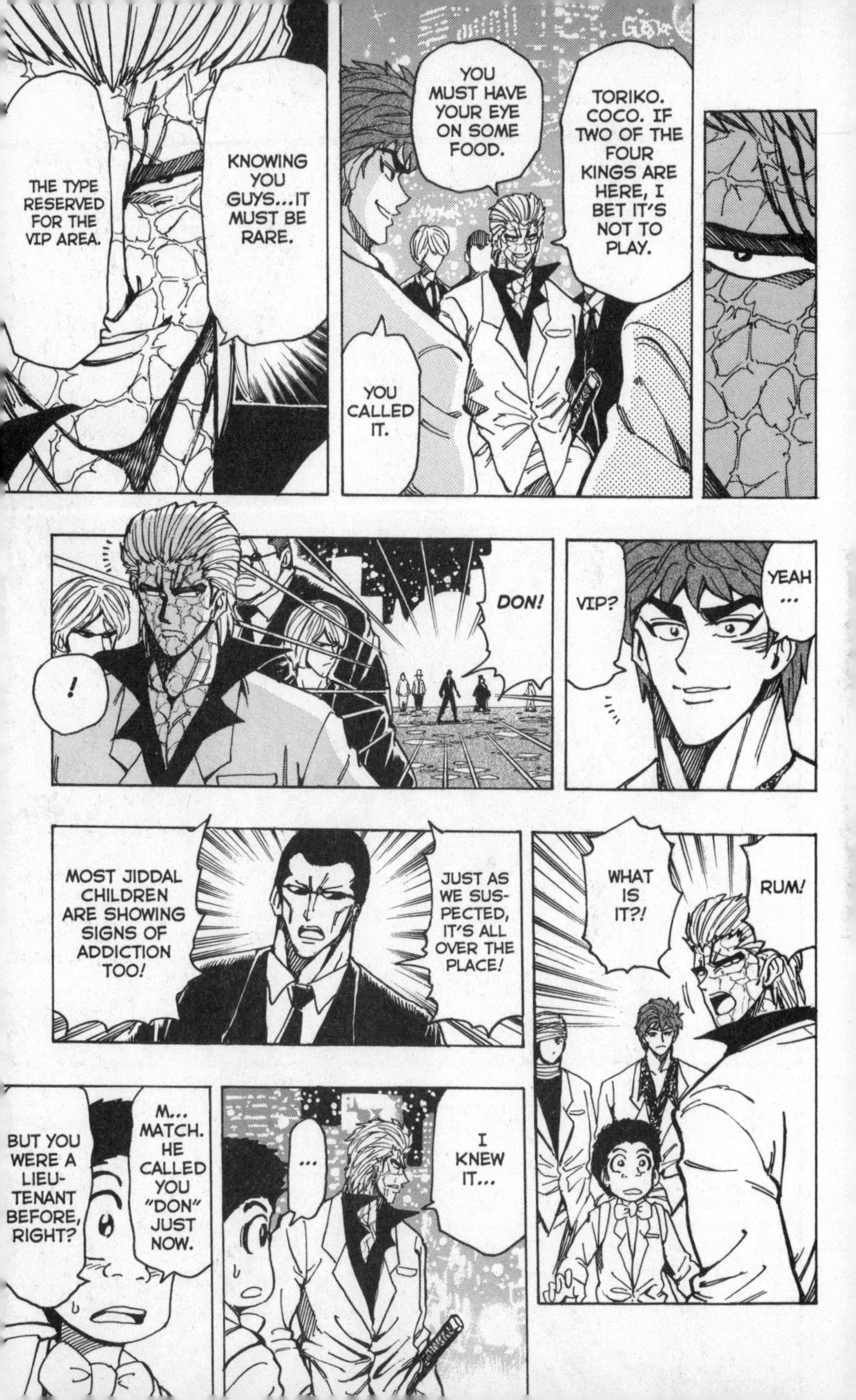
TORIKO. COCO. IF TWO OF THE FOUR KINGS ARE HERE, I BET IT'S NOT TO PLAY.
YOU MUST HAVE YOUR EYE ON SOME FOOD.
YOU CALLED IT.
KNOWING YOU GUYS...IT MUST BE RARE.
THE TYPE RESERVED FOR THE VIP AREA.
YEAH ...
VIP?
DON!
!
RUM!
WHAT IS IT?!
JUST AS WE SUS-PECTED, IT'S ALL OVER THE PLACE!
MOST JIDDAL CHILDREN ARE SHOWING SIGNS OF ADDICTION TOO!
I KNEW IT...
...
M... MATCH. HE CALLED YOU "DON" JUST NOW.
BUT YOU WERE A LIEU-TENANT BEFORE, RIGHT?

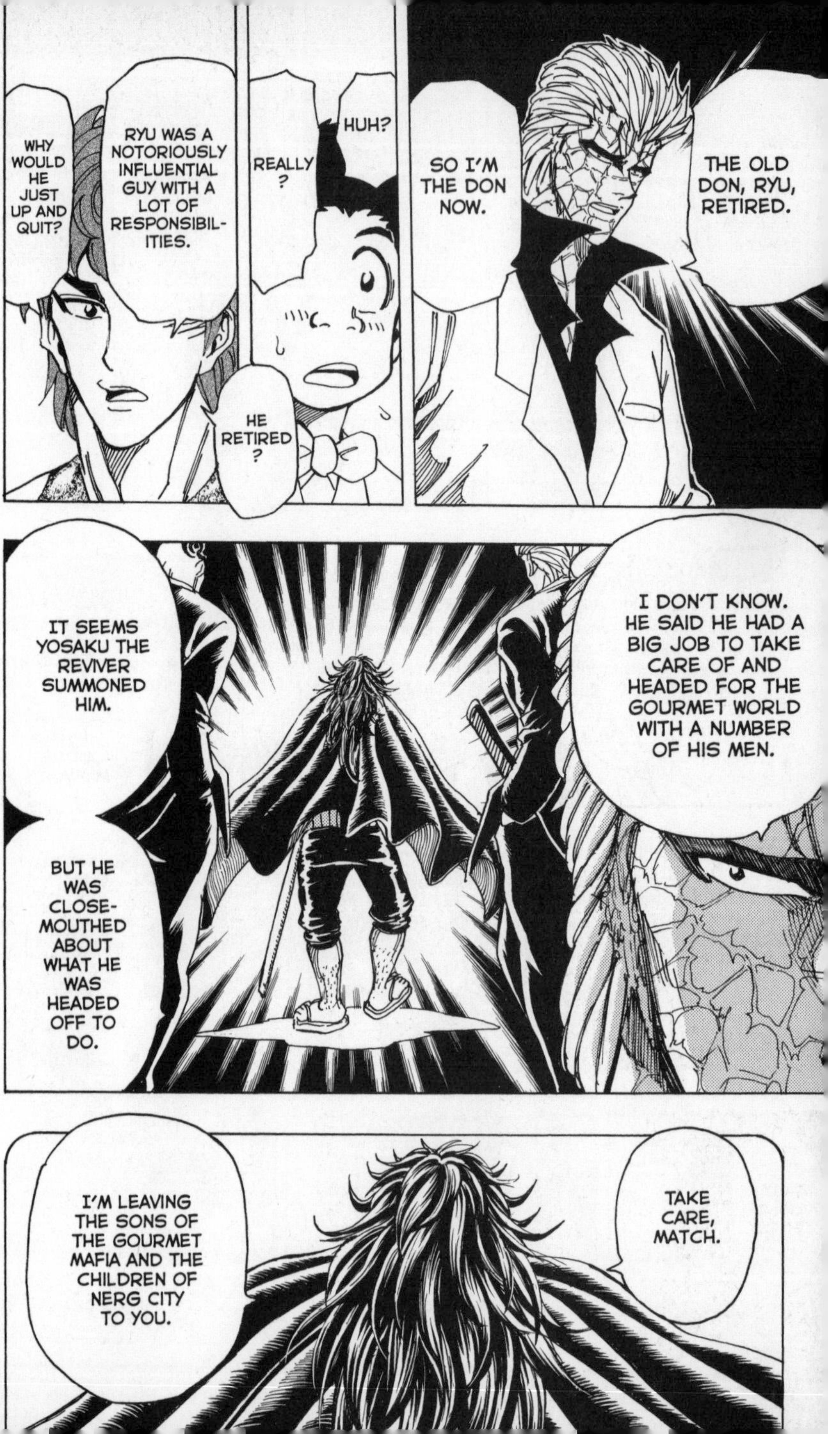
THE OLD DON, RYU, RETIRED.
SO I'M THE DON NOW.
HUH?
REALLY?
HE RETIRED?
RYU WAS A NOTORIOUSLY INFLUENTIAL GUY WITH A LOT OF RESPONSIBILITIES.
WHY WOULD HE JUST UP AND QUIT?
I DON'T KNOW. HE SAID HE HAD A BIG JOB TO TAKE CARE OF AND HEADED FOR THE GOURMET WORLD WITH A NUMBER OF HIS MEN.
IT SEEMS YOSAKU THE REVIVER SUMMONED HIM.
BUT HE WAS CLOSE-MOUTHED ABOUT WHAT HE WAS HEADED OFF TO DO.
TAKE CARE, MATCH.
I'M LEAVING THE SONS OF THE GOURMET MAFIA AND THE CHILDREN OF NERG CITY TO YOU.

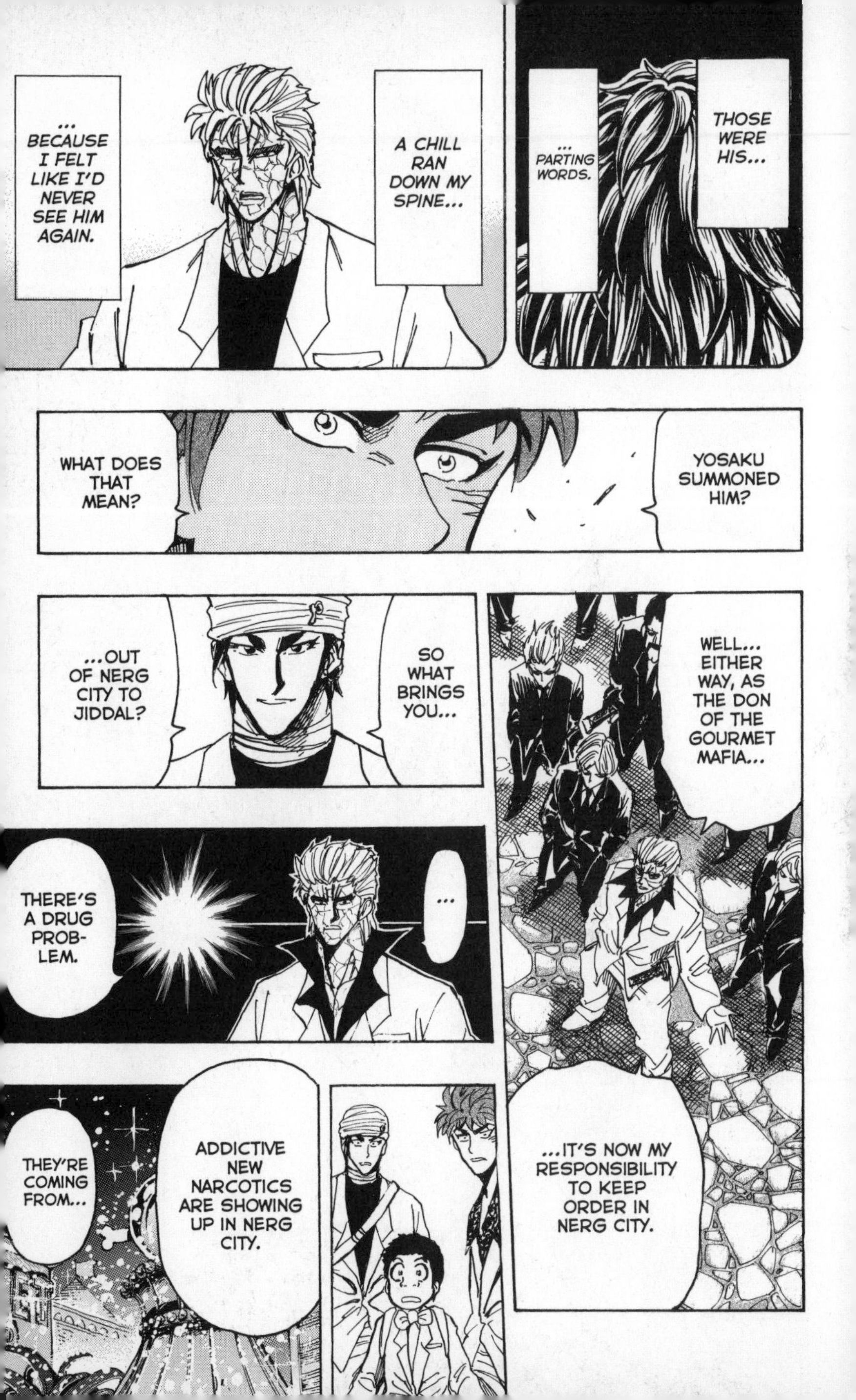

THOSE WERE HIS...
...PARTING WORDS.
A CHILL RAN DOWN MY SPINE...
...BECAUSE I FELT LIKE I'D NEVER SEE HIM AGAIN.
YOSAKU SUMMONED HIM?
WHAT DOES THAT MEAN?
WELL... EITHER WAY, AS THE DON OF THE GOURMET MAFIA...
...IT'S NOW MY RESPONSIBILITY TO KEEP ORDER IN NERG CITY.
SO WHAT BRINGS YOU...
...OUT OF NERG CITY TO JIDDAL?
...
THERE'S A DRUG PROB-LEM.
ADDICTIVE NEW NARCOTICS ARE SHOWING UP IN NERG CITY.
THEY'RE COMING FROM...

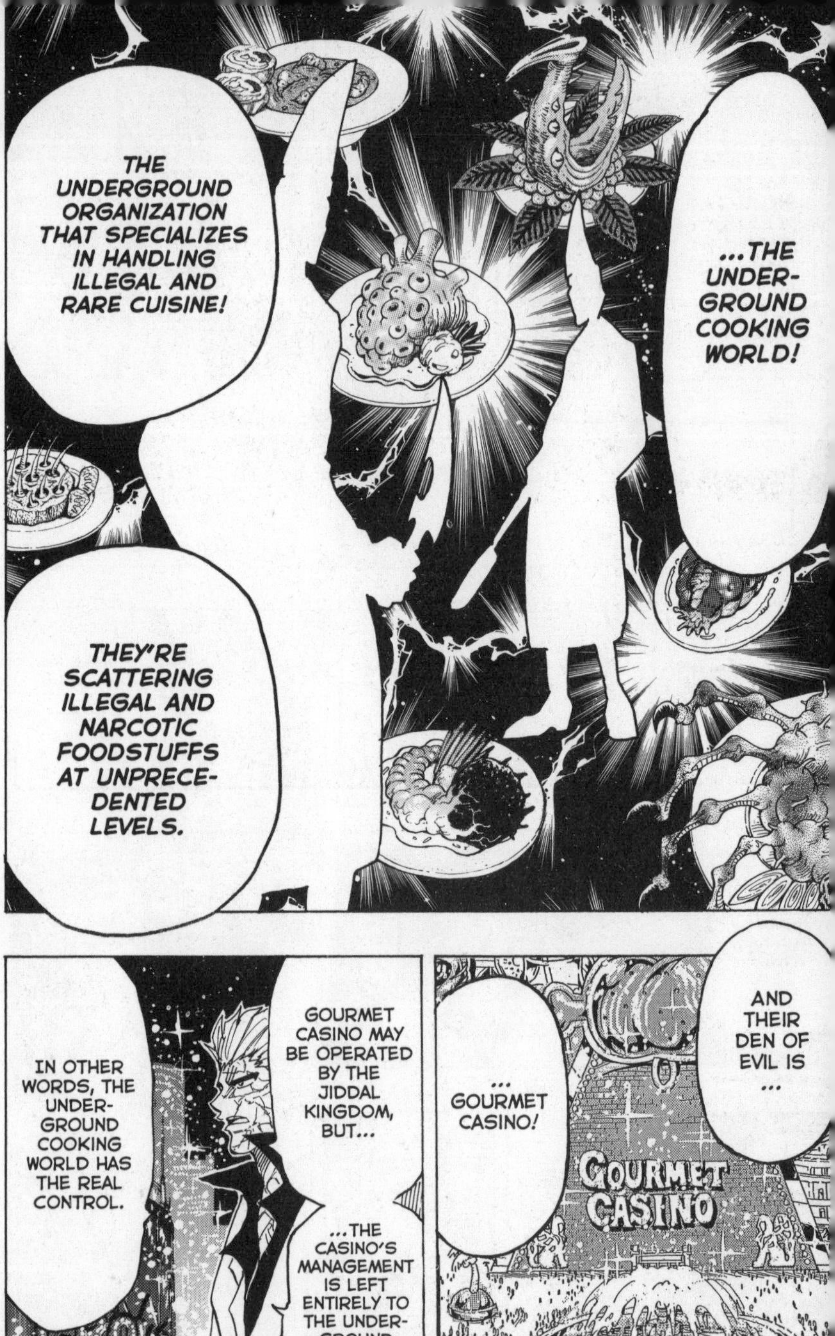
...THE UNDER-GROUND COOKING WORLD!
THE UNDERGROUND ORGANIZATION THAT SPECIALIZES IN HANDLING ILLEGAL AND RARE CUISINE!
THEY'RE SCATTERING ILLEGAL AND NARCOTIC FOODSTUFFS AT UNPRECE-DENTED LEVELS.
AND THEIR DEN OF EVIL IS ...
... GOURMET CASINO!
GOURMET CASINO
GOURMET CASINO MAY BE OPERATED BY THE JIDDAL KINGDOM, BUT...
...THE CASINO'S MANAGEMENT IS LEFT ENTIRELY TO THE UNDER-GROUND COOKING WORLD.
IN OTHER WORDS, THE UNDER-GROUND COOKING WORLD HAS THE REAL CONTROL.

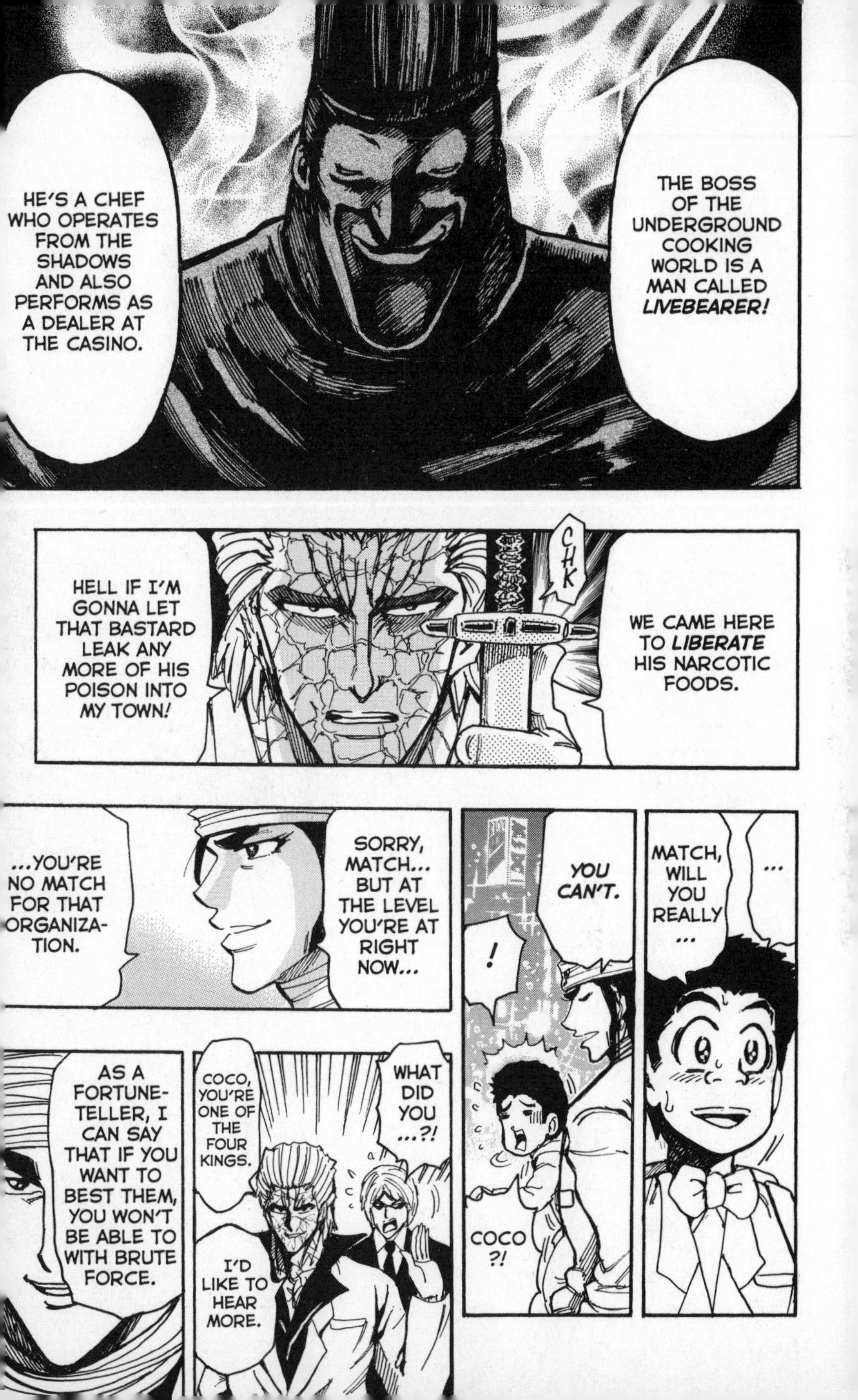
THE BOSS OF THE UNDERGROUND COOKING WORLD IS A MAN CALLED *LIVEBEARER!*
HE'S A CHEF WHO OPERATES FROM THE SHADOWS AND ALSO PERFORMS AS A DEALER AT THE CASINO.
WE CAME HERE TO *LIBERATE* HIS NARCOTIC FOODS.
CHK
HELL IF I'M GONNA LET THAT BASTARD LEAK ANY MORE OF HIS POISON INTO MY TOWN!
...
MATCH, WILL YOU REALLY ...
YOU CAN'T.
!
COCO ?!
SORRY, MATCH... BUT AT THE LEVEL YOU'RE AT RIGHT NOW...
...YOU'RE NO MATCH FOR THAT ORGANIZA-TION.
WHAT DID YOU ...?!
COCO, YOU'RE ONE OF THE FOUR KINGS.
I'D LIKE TO HEAR MORE.
AS A FORTUNE-TELLER, I CAN SAY THAT IF YOU WANT TO BEST THEM, YOU WON'T BE ABLE TO WITH BRUTE FORCE.

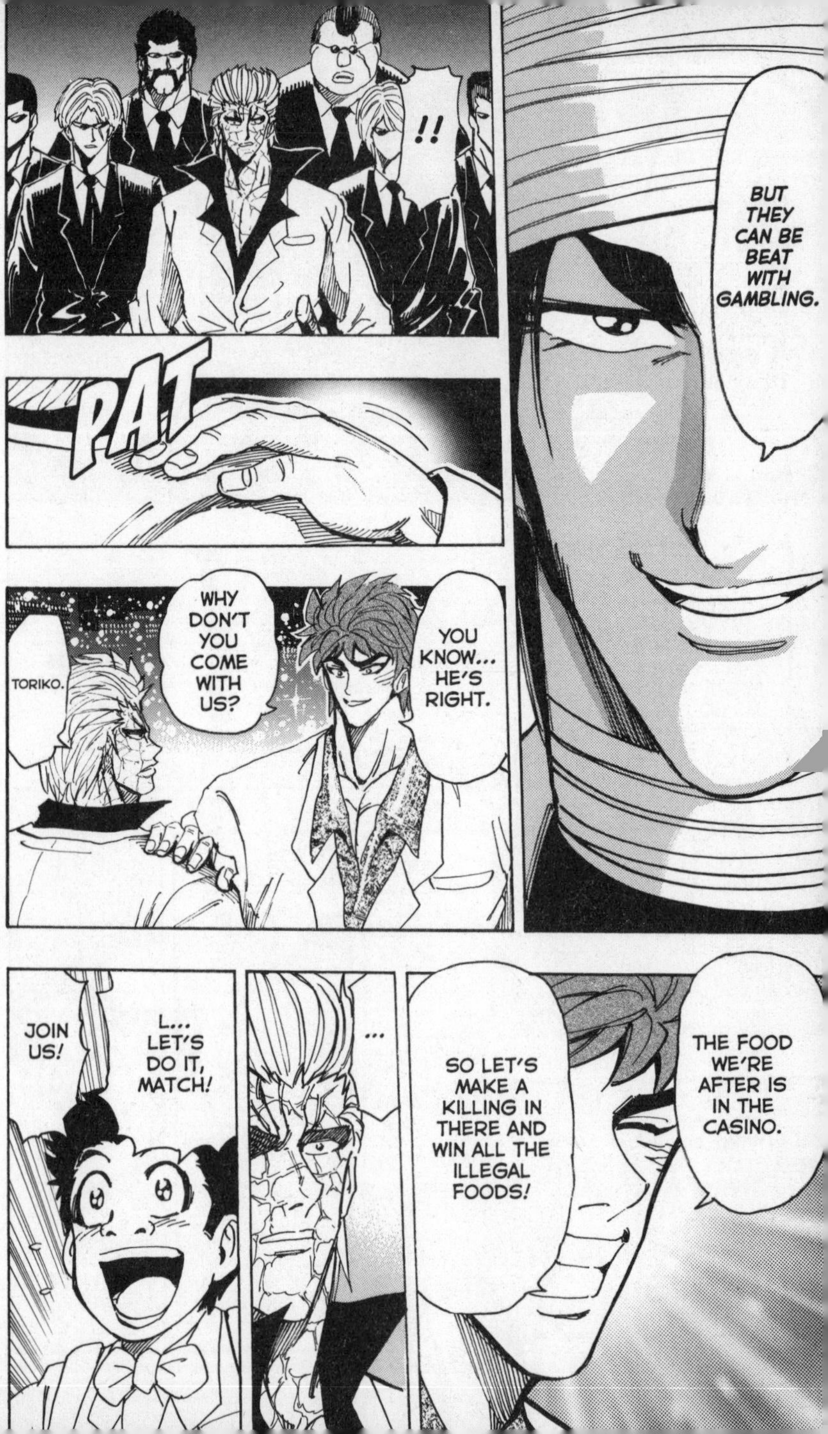
BUT THEY CAN BE BEAT WITH GAMBLING.
!!
PAT
YOU KNOW... HE'S RIGHT.
WHY DON'T YOU COME WITH US?
TORIKO.
THE FOOD WE'RE AFTER IS IN THE CASINO.
SO LET'S MAKE A KILLING IN THERE AND WIN ALL THE ILLEGAL FOODS!
...
L... LET'S DO IT, MATCH!
JOIN US!

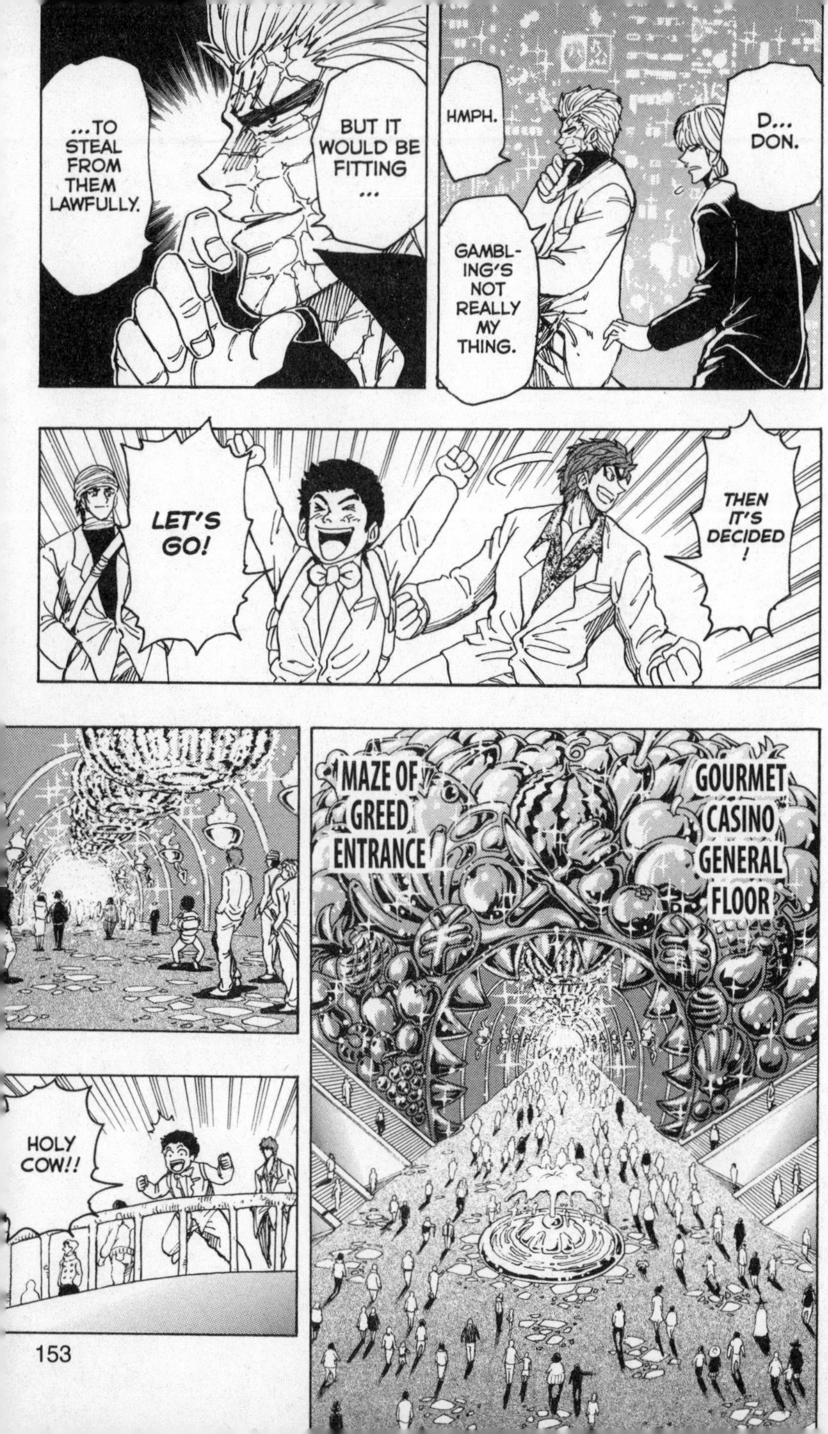
D... DON.
HMPH.
GAMBLING'S NOT REALLY MY THING.
BUT IT WOULD BE FITTING ...
...TO STEAL FROM THEM LAWFULLY.
THEN IT'S DECIDED!
LET'S GO!
GOURMET CASINO GENERAL FLOOR
MAZE OF GREED ENTRANCE
HOLY COW!!

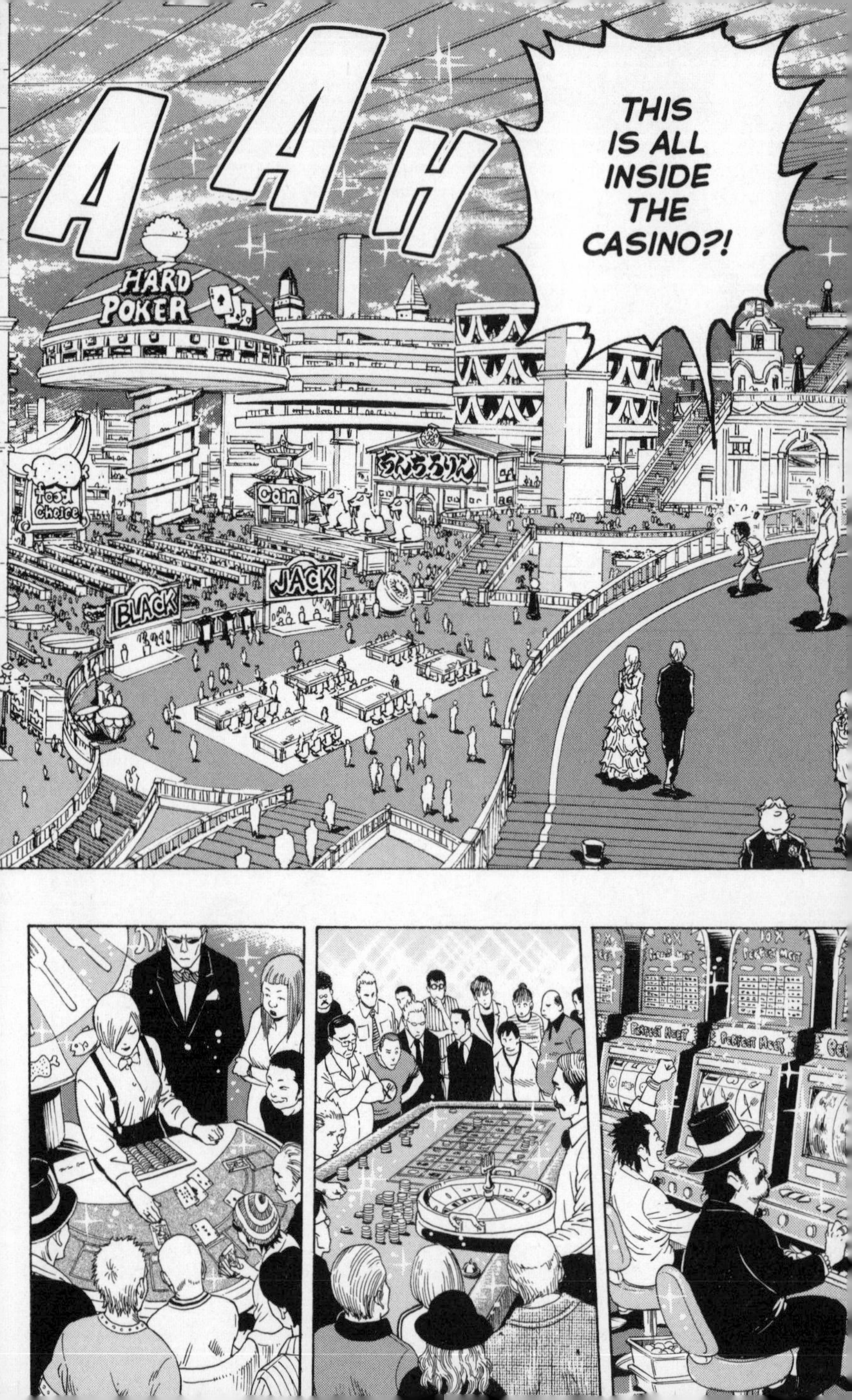
THIS IS ALL INSIDE THE CASINO?!
AAH
HARD POKER
Food Choice
Coin
ちんちろりん
BLACK
JACK
PERFECT MEET
PERFECT MEET

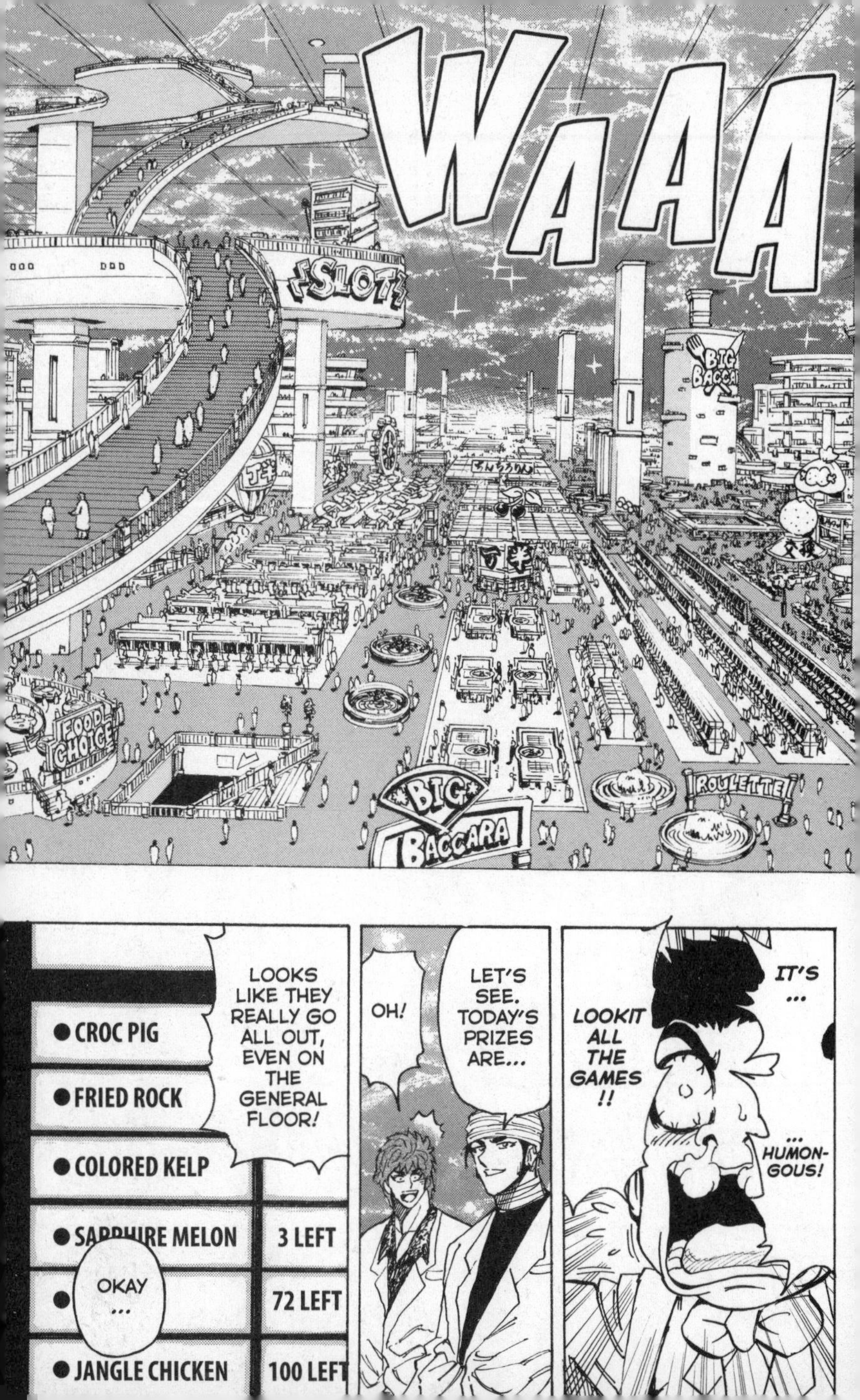
WAAA
SLOT
FOOD CHOICE
ROULETTE
BIG BACCARA
IT'S ...
LOOKIT ALL THE GAMES!!
...HUMONGOUS!
LET'S SEE. TODAY'S PRIZES ARE...
OH!
LOOKS LIKE THEY REALLY GO ALL OUT, EVEN ON THE GENERAL FLOOR!
● CROC PIG
● FRIED ROCK
● COLORED KELP
● SAPPHIRE MELON 3 LEFT
● 72 LEFT
● JANGLE CHICKEN 100 LEFT
OKAY ...

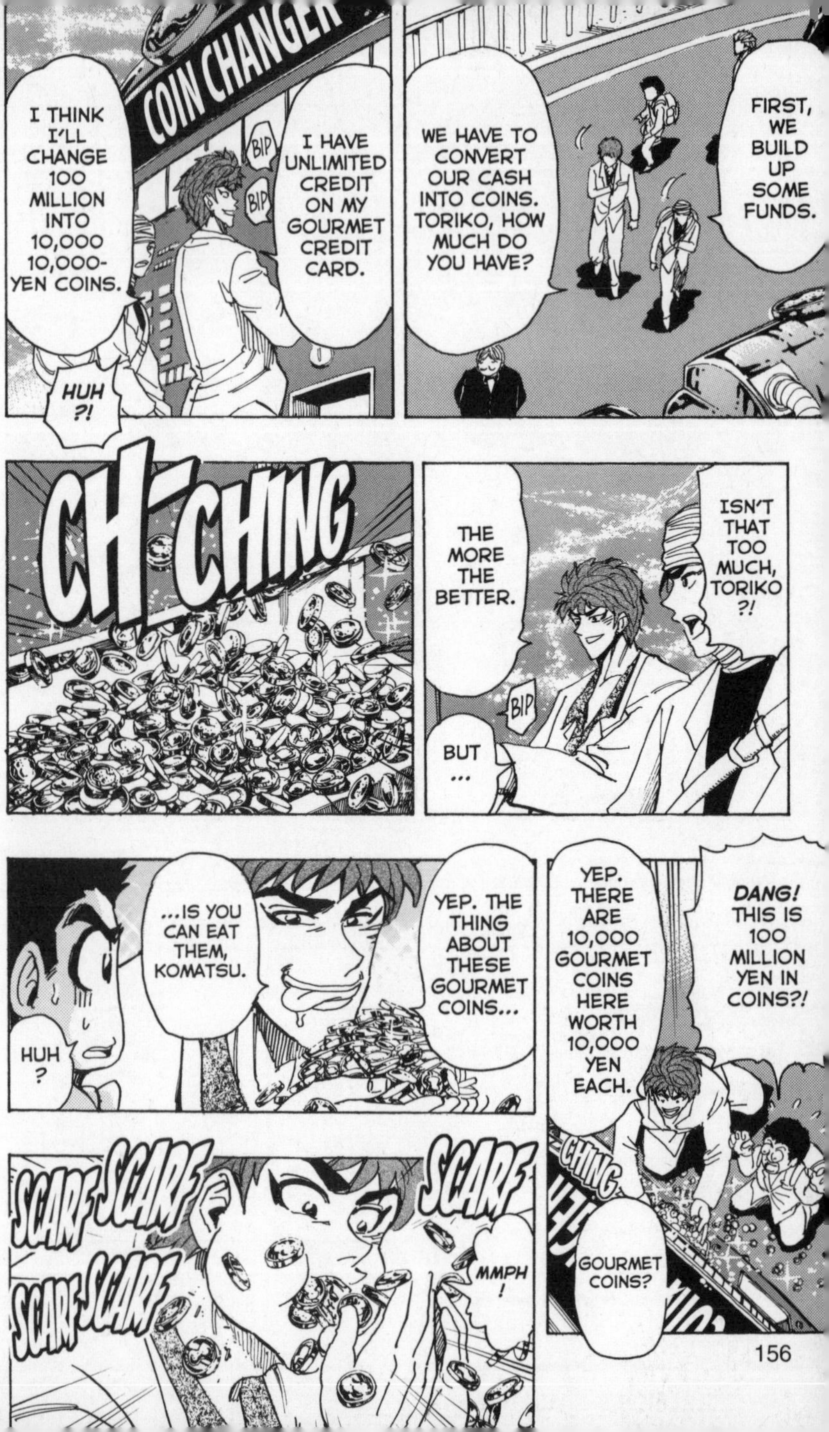
FIRST, WE BUILD UP SOME FUNDS.
WE HAVE TO CONVERT OUR CASH INTO COINS. TORIKO, HOW MUCH DO YOU HAVE?
COIN CHANGER
I HAVE UNLIMITED CREDIT ON MY GOURMET CREDIT CARD.
BIP
BIP
I THINK I'LL CHANGE 100 MILLION INTO 10,000 10,000-YEN COINS.
HUH ?!
ISN'T THAT TOO MUCH, TORIKO ?!
THE MORE THE BETTER.
BIP
BUT ...
CH-CHING
DANG! THIS IS 100 MILLION YEN IN COINS?!
YEP. THERE ARE 10,000 GOURMET COINS HERE WORTH 10,000 YEN EACH.
CHING
GOURMET COINS?
YEP. THE THING ABOUT THESE GOURMET COINS...
...IS YOU CAN EAT THEM, KOMATSU.
HUH ?
SCARF
SCARF SCARF
MMPH !
SCARF SCARF

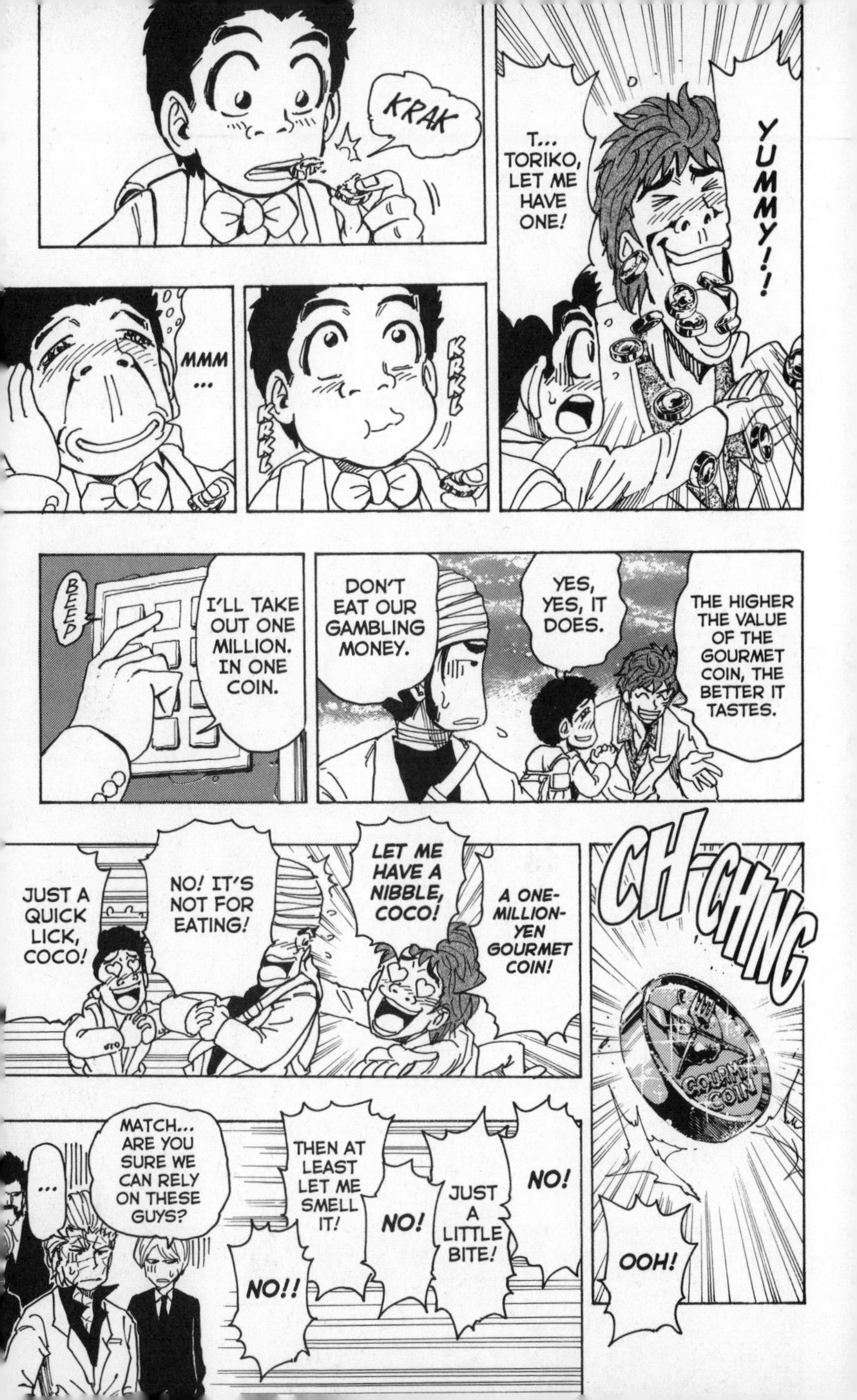
YUMMY!!
T... TORIKO, LET ME HAVE ONE!
KRAK
KRKL KRKL
MMM...
THE HIGHER THE VALUE OF THE GOURMET COIN, THE BETTER IT TASTES.
YES, YES, IT DOES.
DON'T EAT OUR GAMBLING MONEY.
I'LL TAKE OUT ONE MILLION. IN ONE COIN.
BEEP
CH-CHING
GOURMET COIN
OOH!
A ONE-MILLION-YEN GOURMET COIN!
LET ME HAVE A NIBBLE, COCO!
NO! IT'S NOT FOR EATING!
JUST A QUICK LICK, COCO!
NO!
JUST A LITTLE BITE!
NO!
THEN AT LEAST LET ME SMELL IT!
NO!!
MATCH... ARE YOU SURE WE CAN RELY ON THESE GUYS?
...

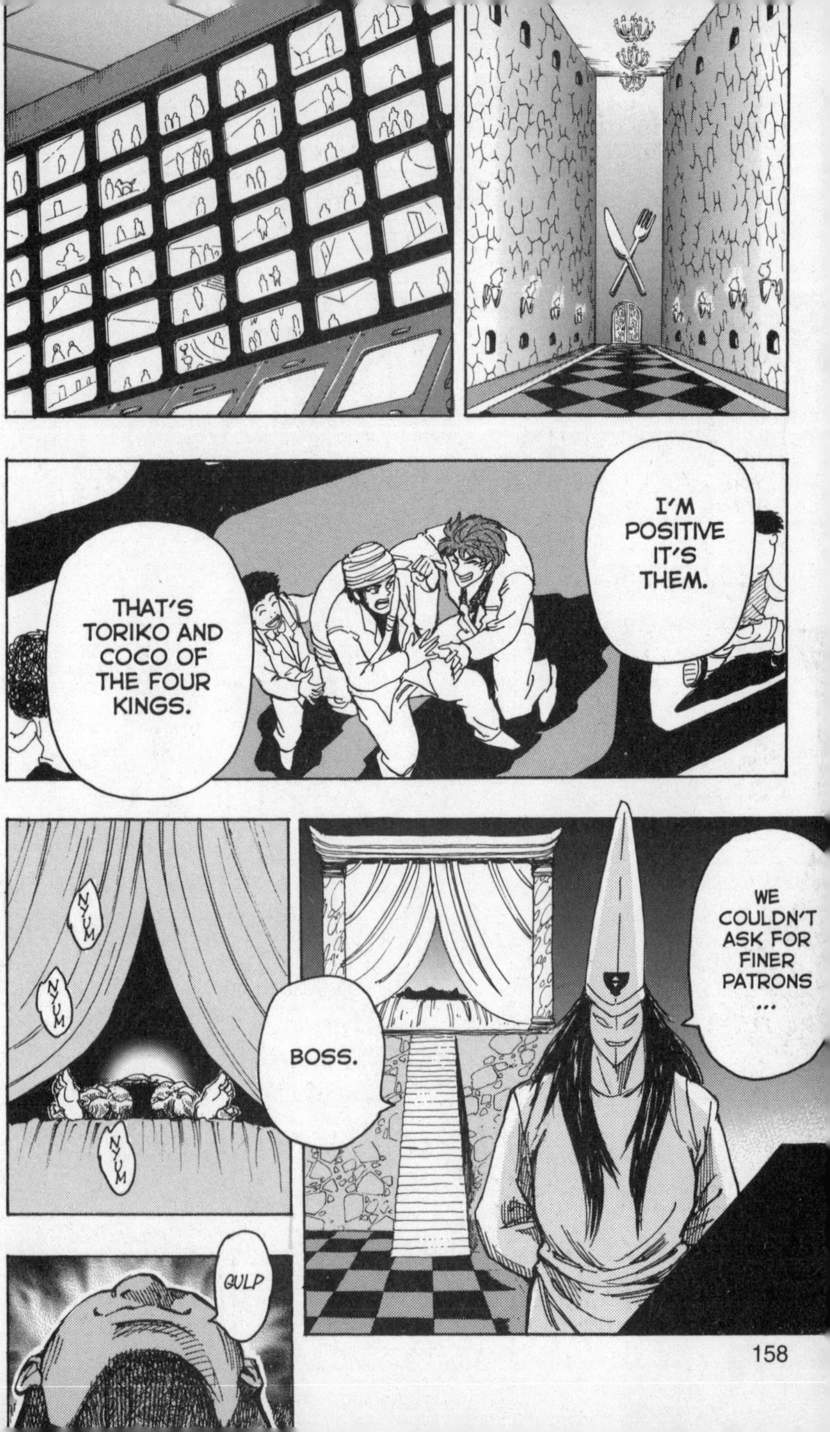
I'M POSITIVE IT'S THEM.
THAT'S TORIKO AND COCO OF THE FOUR KINGS.
WE COULDN'T ASK FOR FINER PATRONS...
BOSS.
NYUM
NYUM
NYUM
GULP

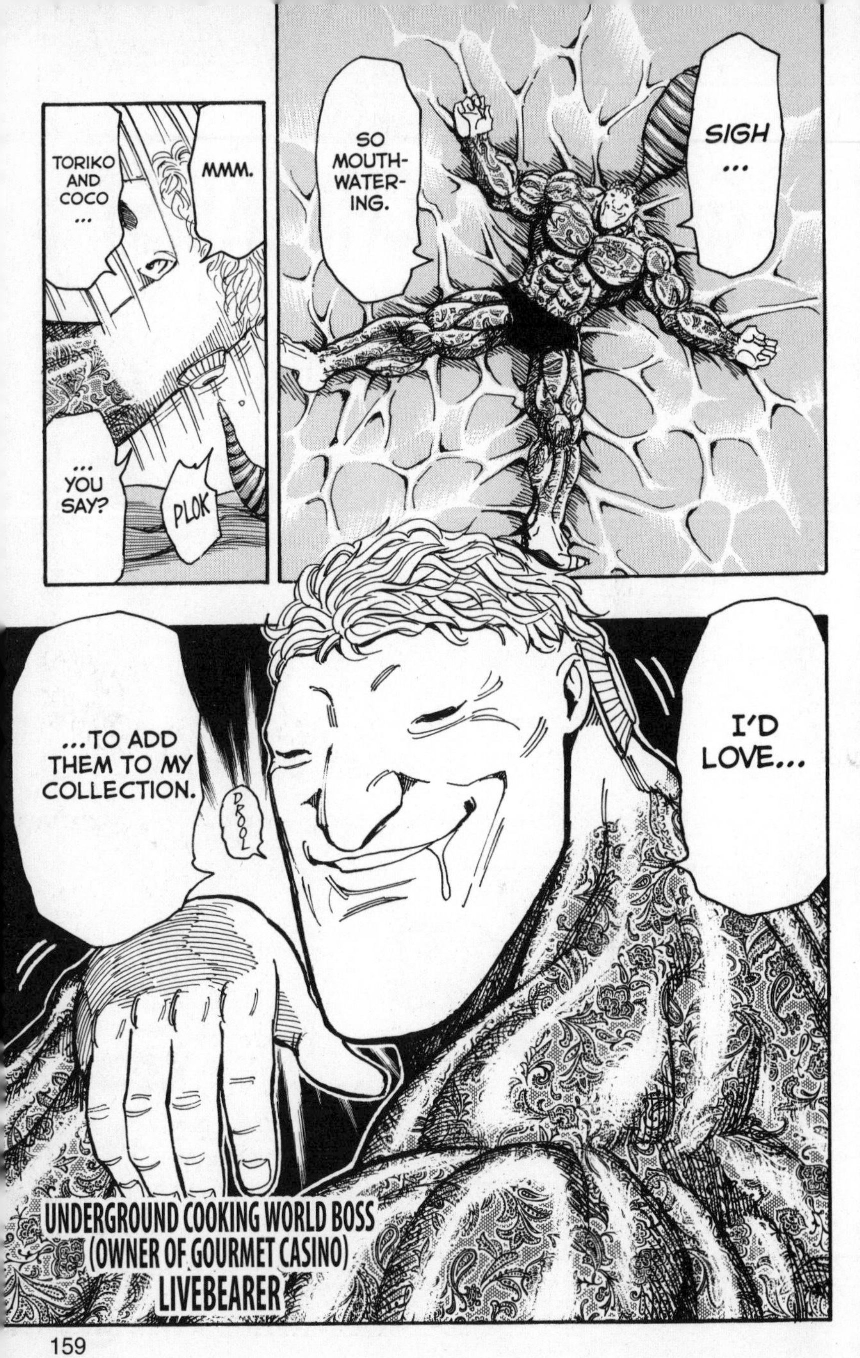
SIGH ...
SO MOUTH-WATER-ING.
MMM.
TORIKO AND COCO ...
... YOU SAY?
PLOK
I'D LOVE...
...TO ADD THEM TO MY COLLECTION.
DROOL
UNDERGROUND COOKING WORLD BOSS (OWNER OF GOURMET CASINO) LIVEBEARER

TORIKO

GOURMET CHECKLIST

Vol. 192

SANDFLOWER FISH
(FISH)

CAPTURE LEVEL: 9

HABITAT: DESERT

LENGTH: 13 METERS

HEIGHT: ---

WEIGHT: 14 TONS

PRICE: 100 G OF MEAT / 10,000 YEN

SCORE! A SAND-FLOWER FISH*!!

SCALE

NORMALLY LIVING IN THE COOLER SUBTERRANEAN SANDS OF THE SWELTERING DESERT LABYRINTH, THE SANDFLOWER FISH ONLY SURFACES TO HUNT. MORE SNEAKY THAN AGGRESSIVE, THIS FISH ONLY ATTACKS CREATURES EXHAUSTED BY THE INTENSE HEAT OF DESERT LABYRINTH OR MESMERIZED BY THE FAUX FLOWER GROWING FROM ITS HEAD. IF ITS SURPRISE ATTACK FAILS, IT'S EASILY KILLED. A DEAD SANDFLOWER FISH'S FLESH AND BLOOD ARE A PRECIOUS SOURCE OF NOURISHMENT FOR ANYONE TRAVELING THROUGH DESERT LABYRINTH.

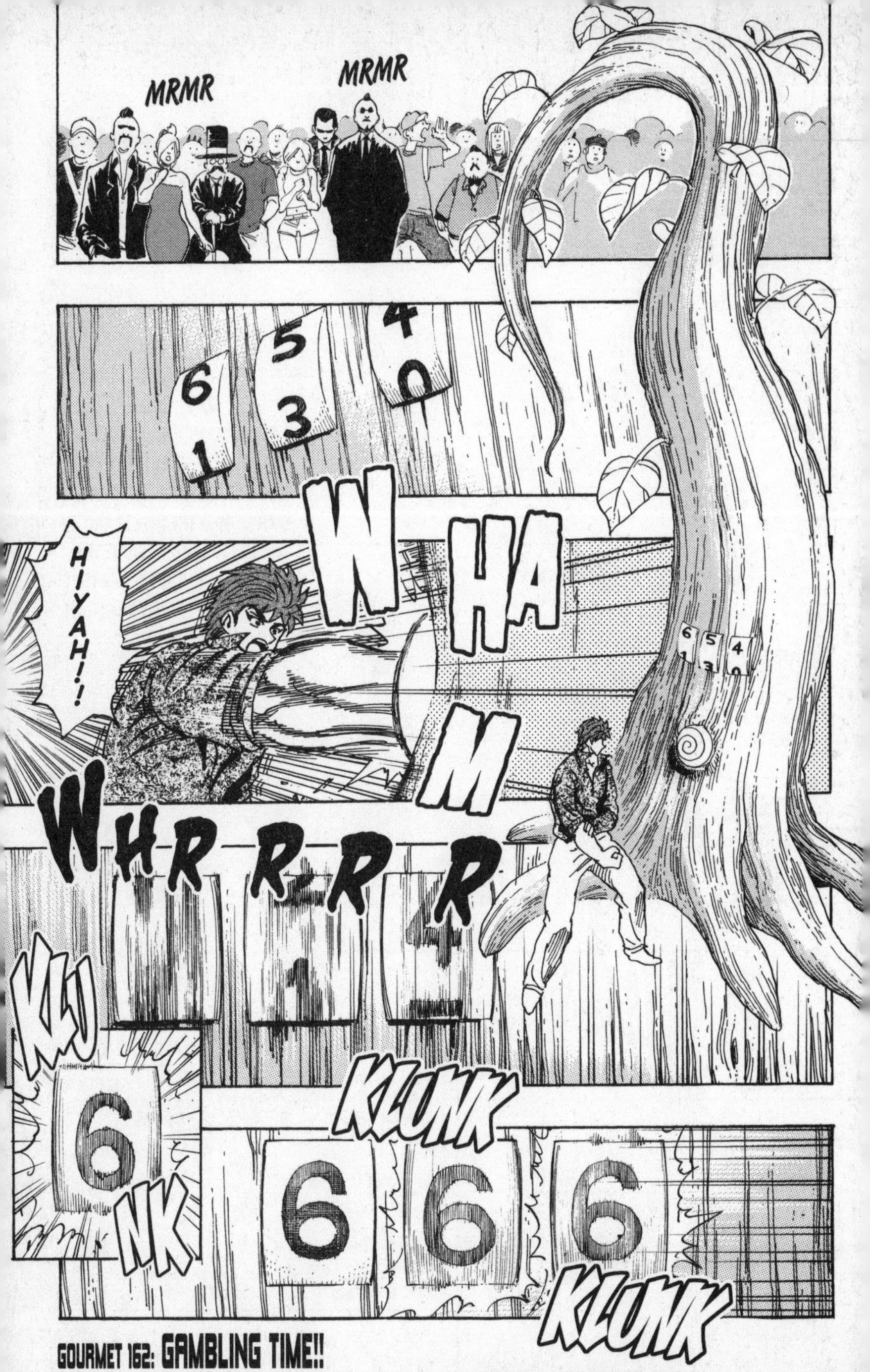
MRMR
MRMR
6 5 4
1 3 0
WHAM
HIYAH!!
WHRRRR
KLONK
6 6 6
KLONK
KLUNK
6

GOURMET 162: GAMBLING TIME!!

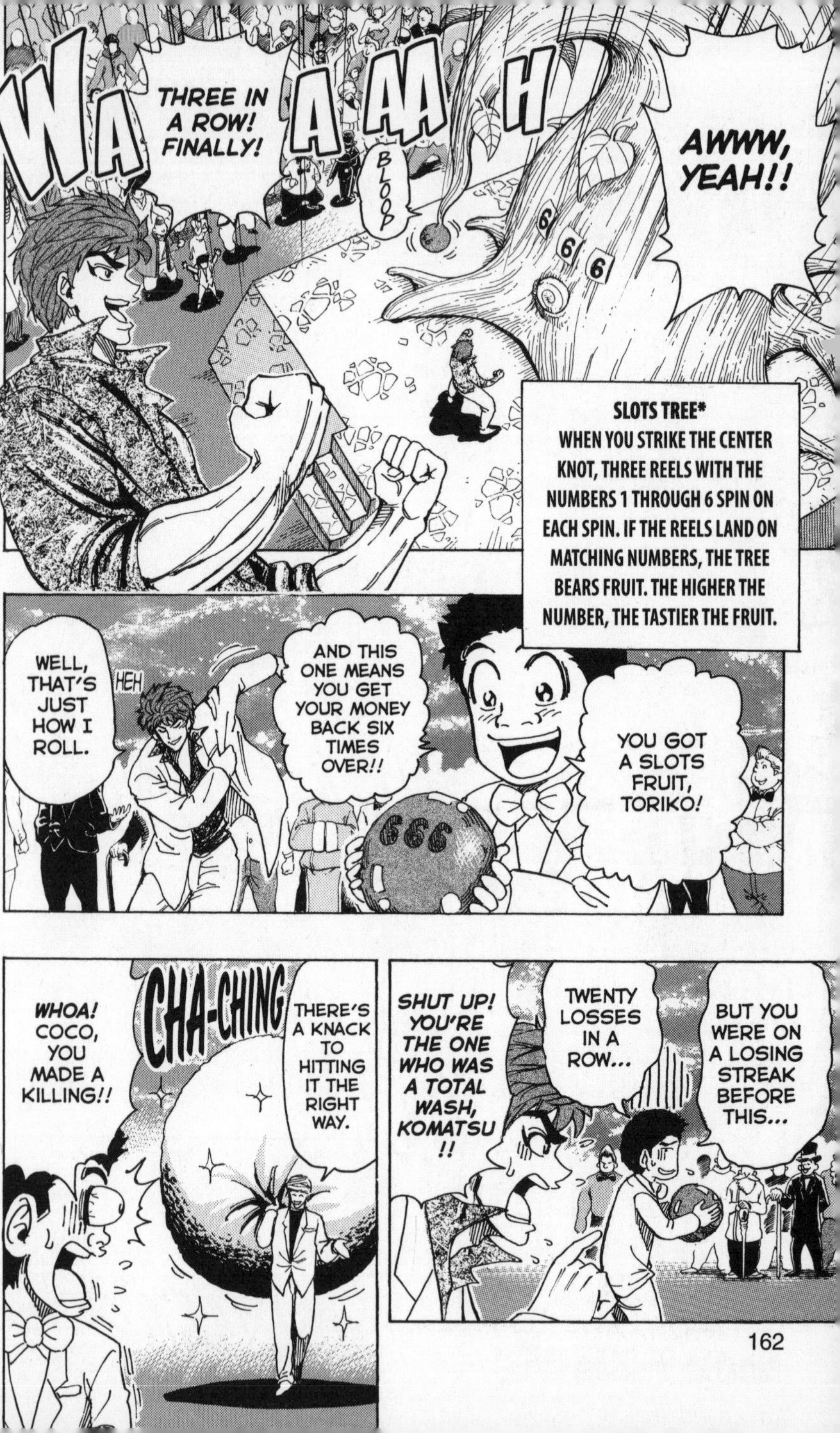
WAAAAH
AWWW, YEAH!!
THREE IN A ROW! FINALLY!
BLOOP
666
SLOTS TREE* WHEN YOU STRIKE THE CENTER KNOT, THREE REELS WITH THE NUMBERS 1 THROUGH 6 SPIN ON EACH SPIN. IF THE REELS LAND ON MATCHING NUMBERS, THE TREE BEARS FRUIT. THE HIGHER THE NUMBER, THE TASTIER THE FRUIT.
YOU GOT A SLOTS FRUIT, TORIKO!
666
AND THIS ONE MEANS YOU GET YOUR MONEY BACK SIX TIMES OVER!!
HEH
WELL, THAT'S JUST HOW I ROLL.
BUT YOU WERE ON A LOSING STREAK BEFORE THIS...
TWENTY LOSSES IN A ROW...
SHUT UP! YOU'RE THE ONE WHO WAS A TOTAL WASH, KOMATSU!!
THERE'S A KNACK TO HITTING IT THE RIGHT WAY.
CHA-CHING
WHOA! COCO, YOU MADE A KILLING!!

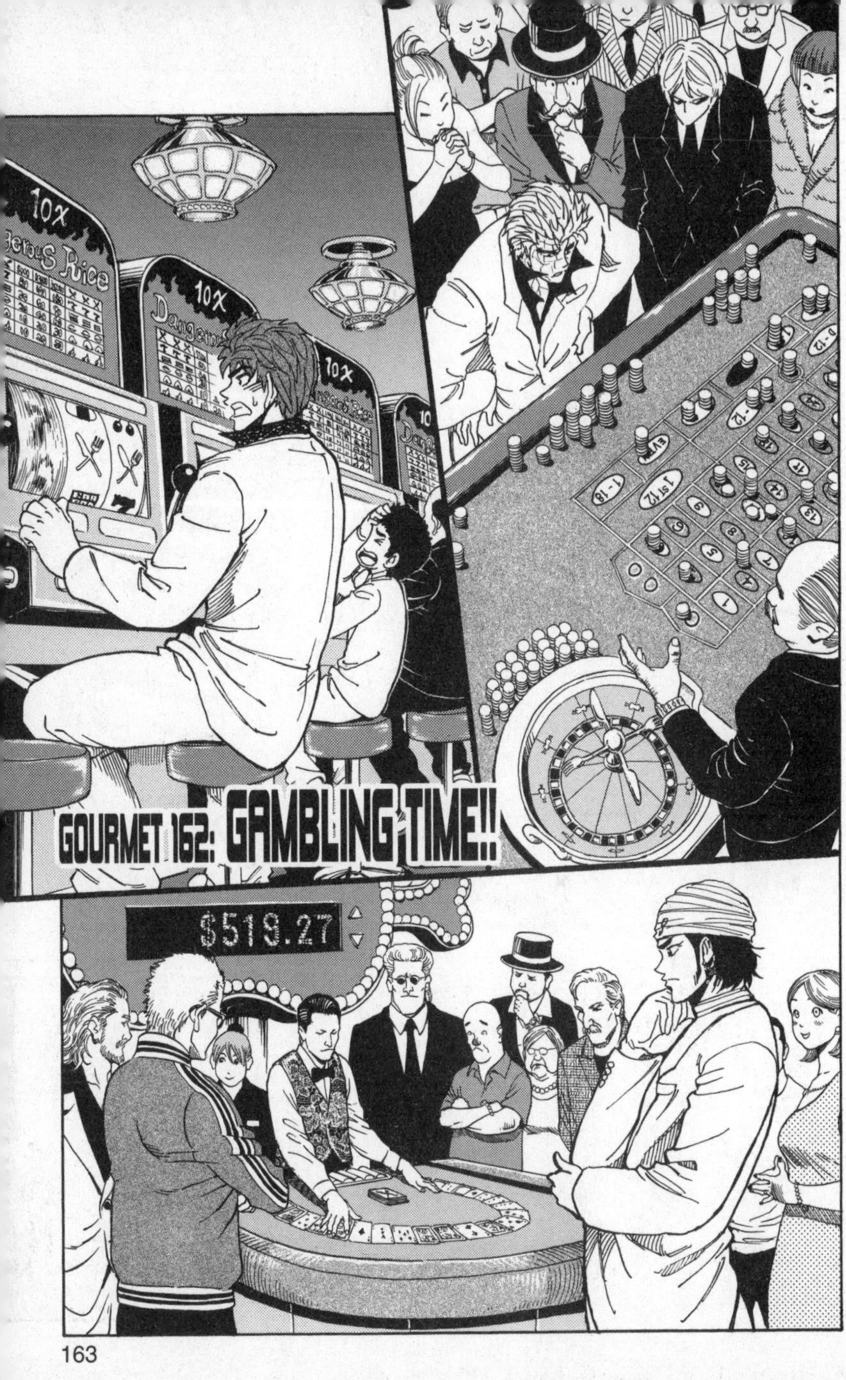
GOURMET 162: GAMBLING TIME!!
$519.27

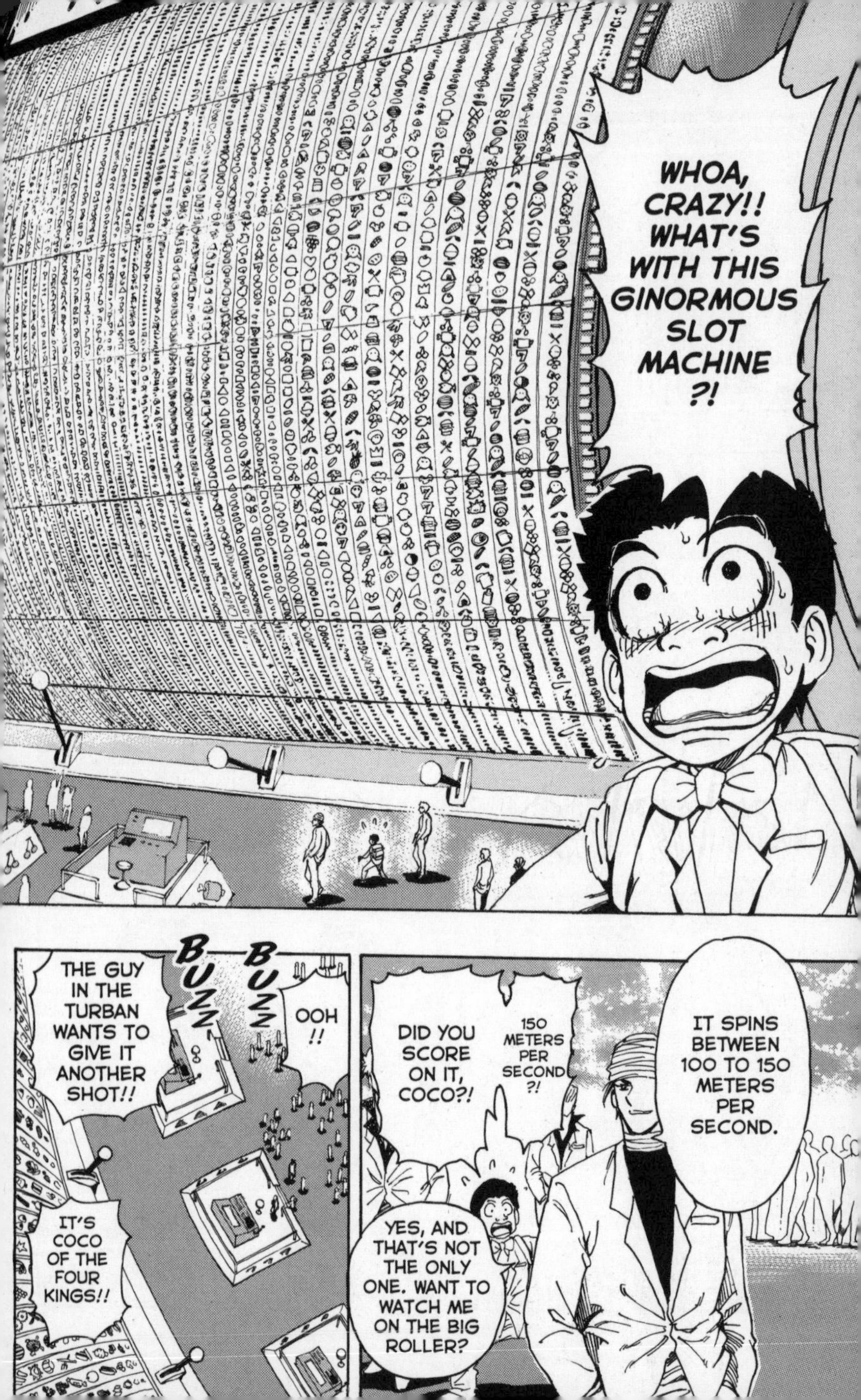
WHOA, CRAZY!! WHAT'S WITH THIS GINORMOUS SLOT MACHINE ?!
IT SPINS BETWEEN 100 TO 150 METERS PER SECOND.
150 METERS PER SECOND ?!
DID YOU SCORE ON IT, COCO?!
YES, AND THAT'S NOT THE ONLY ONE. WANT TO WATCH ME ON THE BIG ROLLER?
B-BUZZ
OOH!!
B-BUZZ
THE GUY IN THE TURBAN WANTS TO GIVE IT ANOTHER SHOT!!
IT'S COCO OF THE FOUR KINGS!!

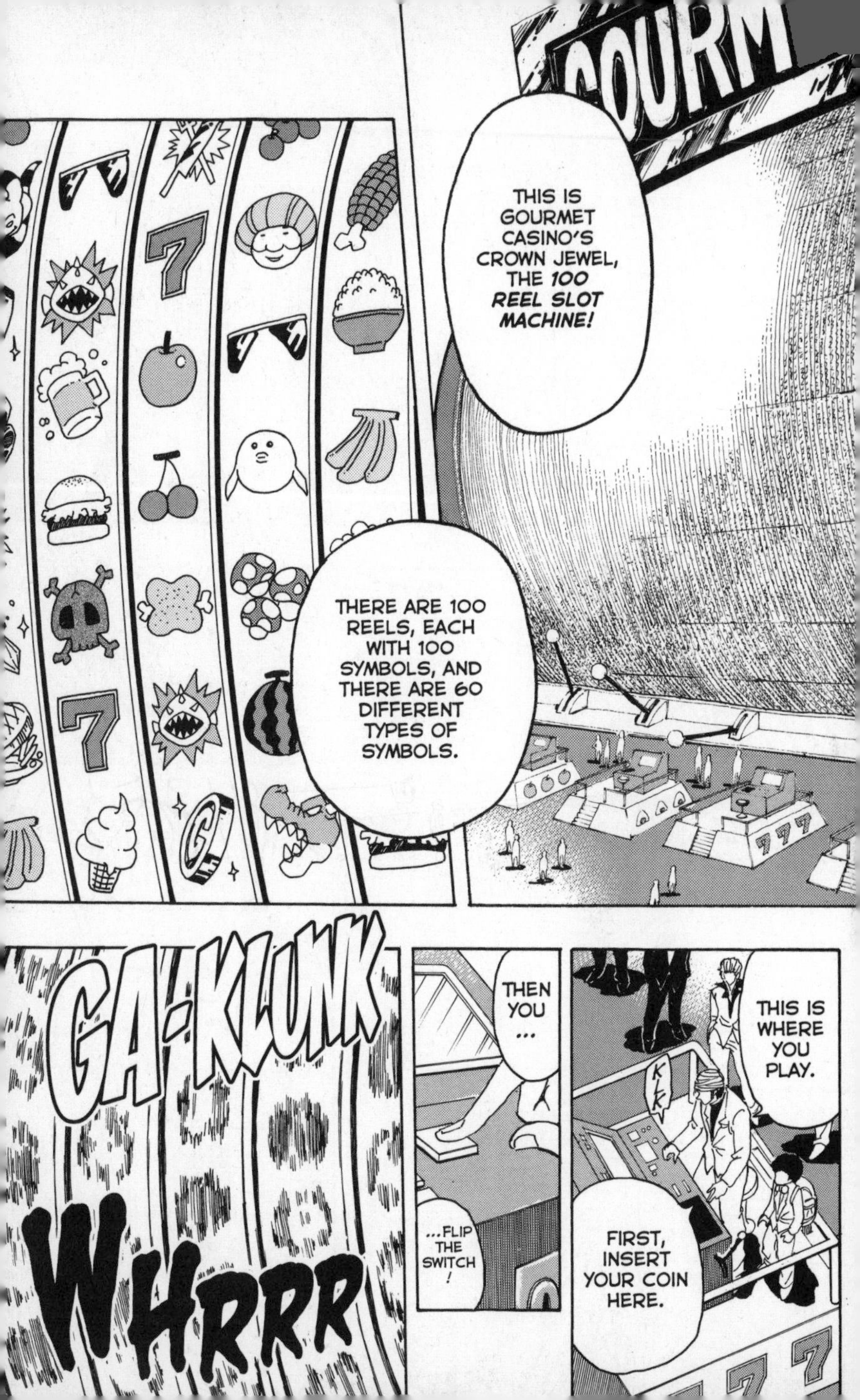
GOURM
THIS IS GOURMET CASINO'S CROWN JEWEL, THE *100 REEL SLOT MACHINE!*
THERE ARE 100 REELS, EACH WITH 100 SYMBOLS, AND THERE ARE 60 DIFFERENT TYPES OF SYMBOLS.
THIS IS WHERE YOU PLAY.
K-K
FIRST, INSERT YOUR COIN HERE.
THEN YOU ...
...FLIP THE SWITCH!
GA-KLUNK
WHRRR

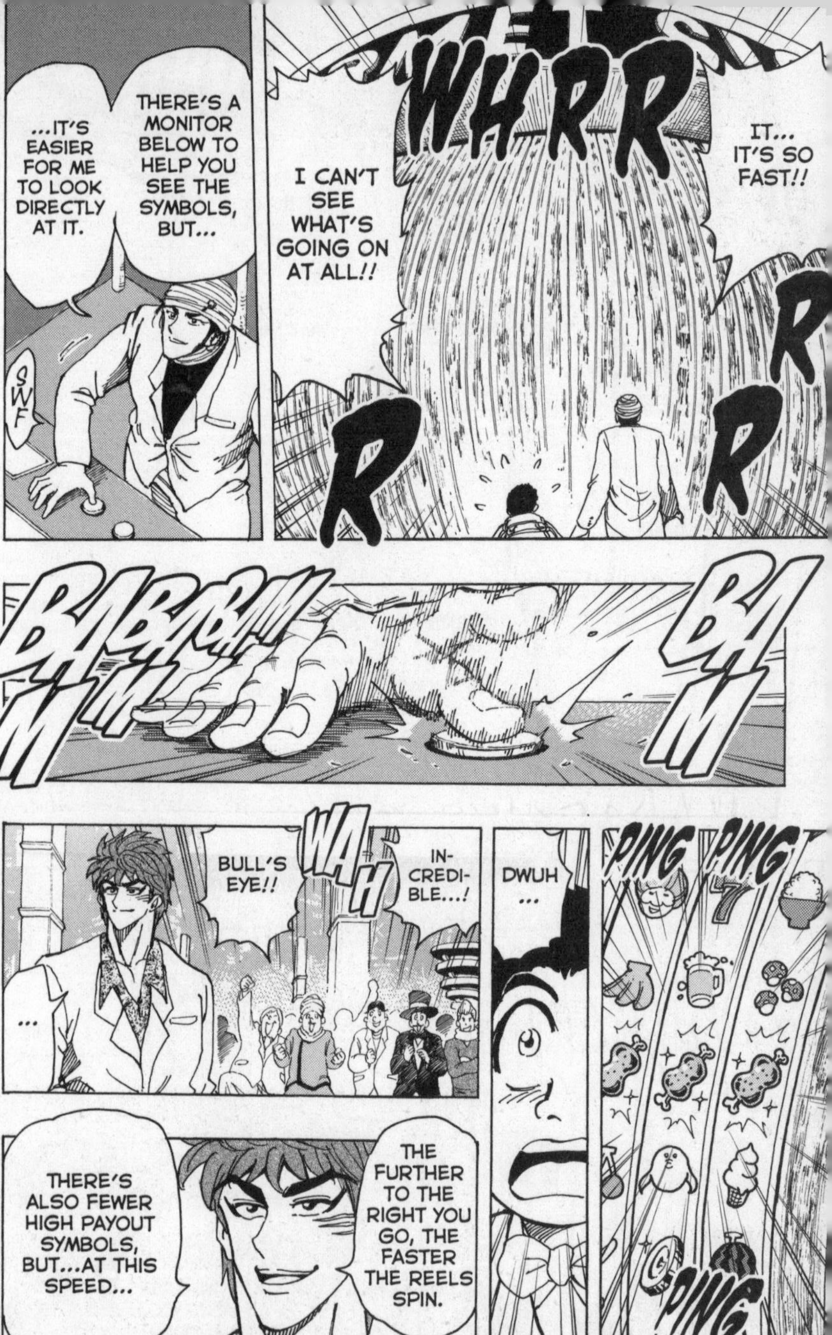
WHRR
IT... IT'S SO FAST!!
I CAN'T SEE WHAT'S GOING ON AT ALL!!
RRRR
THERE'S A MONITOR BELOW TO HELP YOU SEE THE SYMBOLS, BUT...
...IT'S EASIER FOR ME TO LOOK DIRECTLY AT IT.
SWF
BAM
BABABAMM
PING PING
PING
DWUH...
WAH
IN-CREDI-BLE...!
BULL'S EYE!!
...
THE FURTHER TO THE RIGHT YOU GO, THE FASTER THE REELS SPIN.
THERE'S ALSO FEWER HIGH PAYOUT SYMBOLS, BUT...AT THIS SPEED...

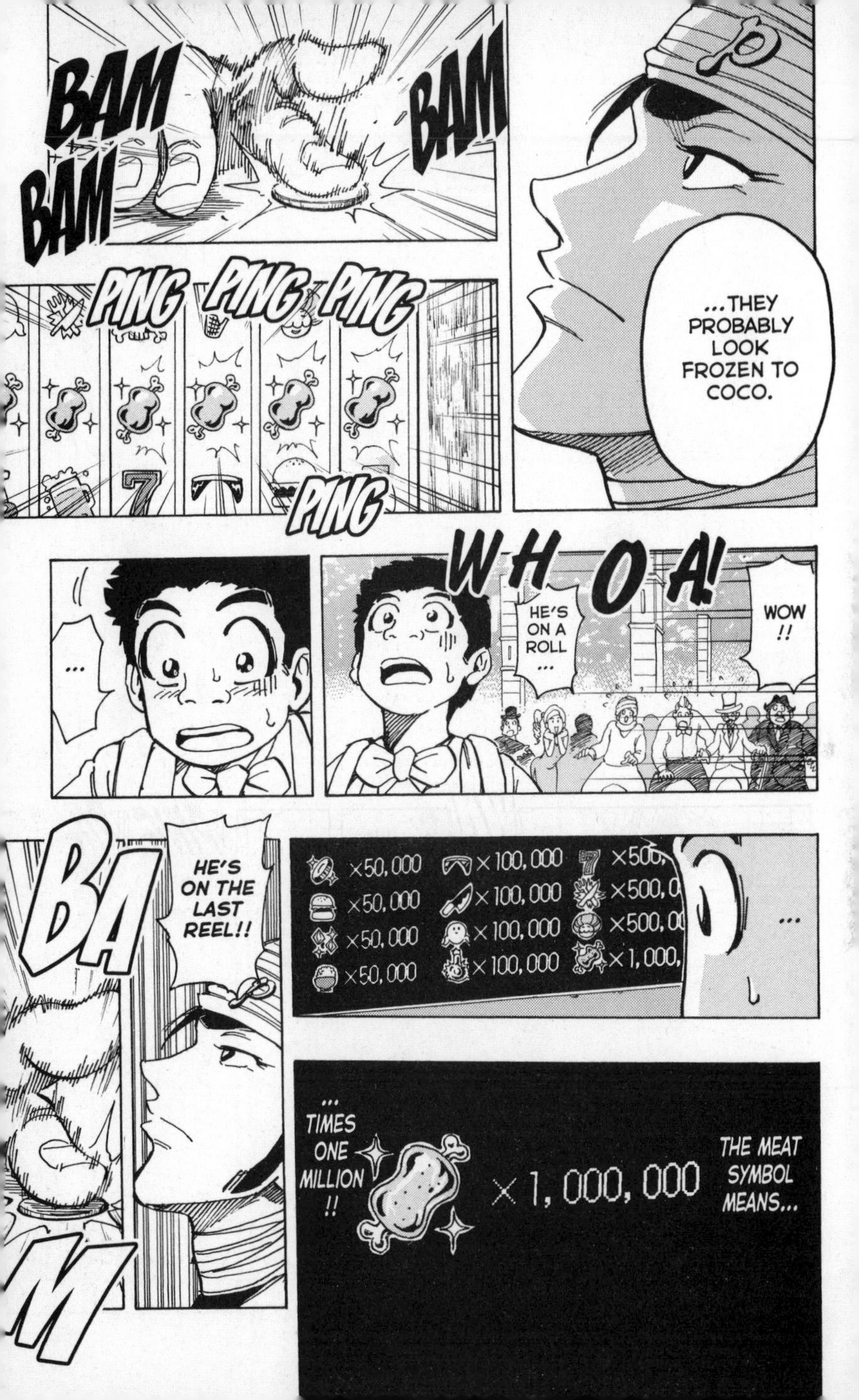
...THEY PROBABLY LOOK FROZEN TO COCO.
BAM
BAM
BAM
PING PING PING
PING
WHOA!
WOW!!
HE'S ON A ROLL...
...
×500,
×500,0
×500,0
×1,000,
×100,000
×100,000
×100,000
×100,000
×50,000
×50,000
×50,000
×50,000
...
THE MEAT SYMBOL MEANS...
×1,000,000
...TIMES ONE MILLION!!
BAM
HE'S ON THE LAST REEL!!

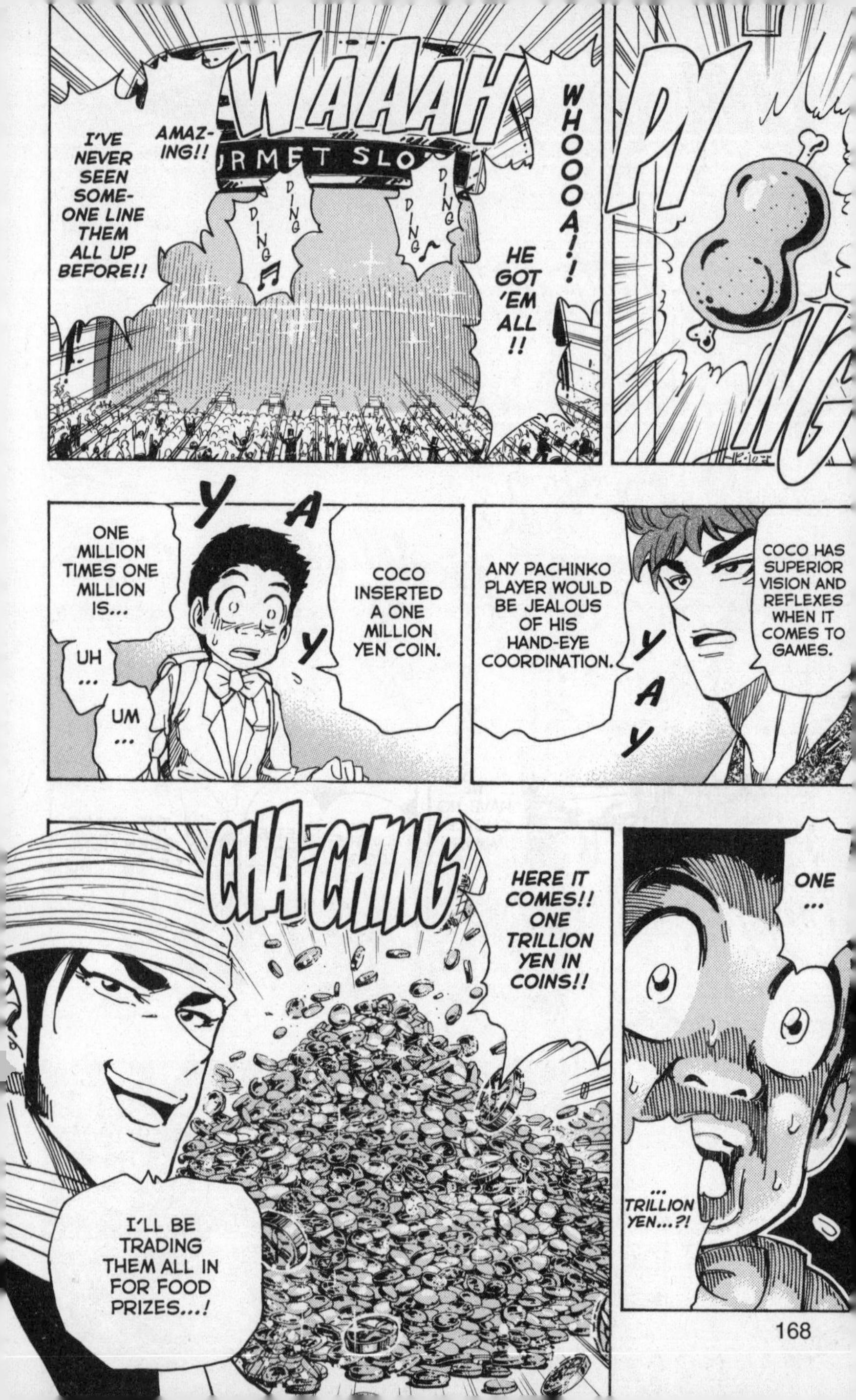
PI
NG
WAAAAH
WHOOOOA!!
HE GOT 'EM ALL!!
AMAZ-ING!!
I'VE NEVER SEEN SOME-ONE LINE THEM ALL UP BEFORE!!
RMET SLO
DING DING
DING DING
DING DING
DING DING
COCO HAS SUPERIOR VISION AND REFLEXES WHEN IT COMES TO GAMES.
YAY
ANY PACHINKO PLAYER WOULD BE JEALOUS OF HIS HAND-EYE COORDINATION.
YAY
COCO INSERTED A ONE MILLION YEN COIN.
ONE MILLION TIMES ONE MILLION IS...
UH...
UM...
ONE...
...TRILLION YEN...?!
CHA-CHING
HERE IT COMES!! ONE TRILLION YEN IN COINS!!
I'LL BE TRADING THEM ALL IN FOR FOOD PRIZES...!

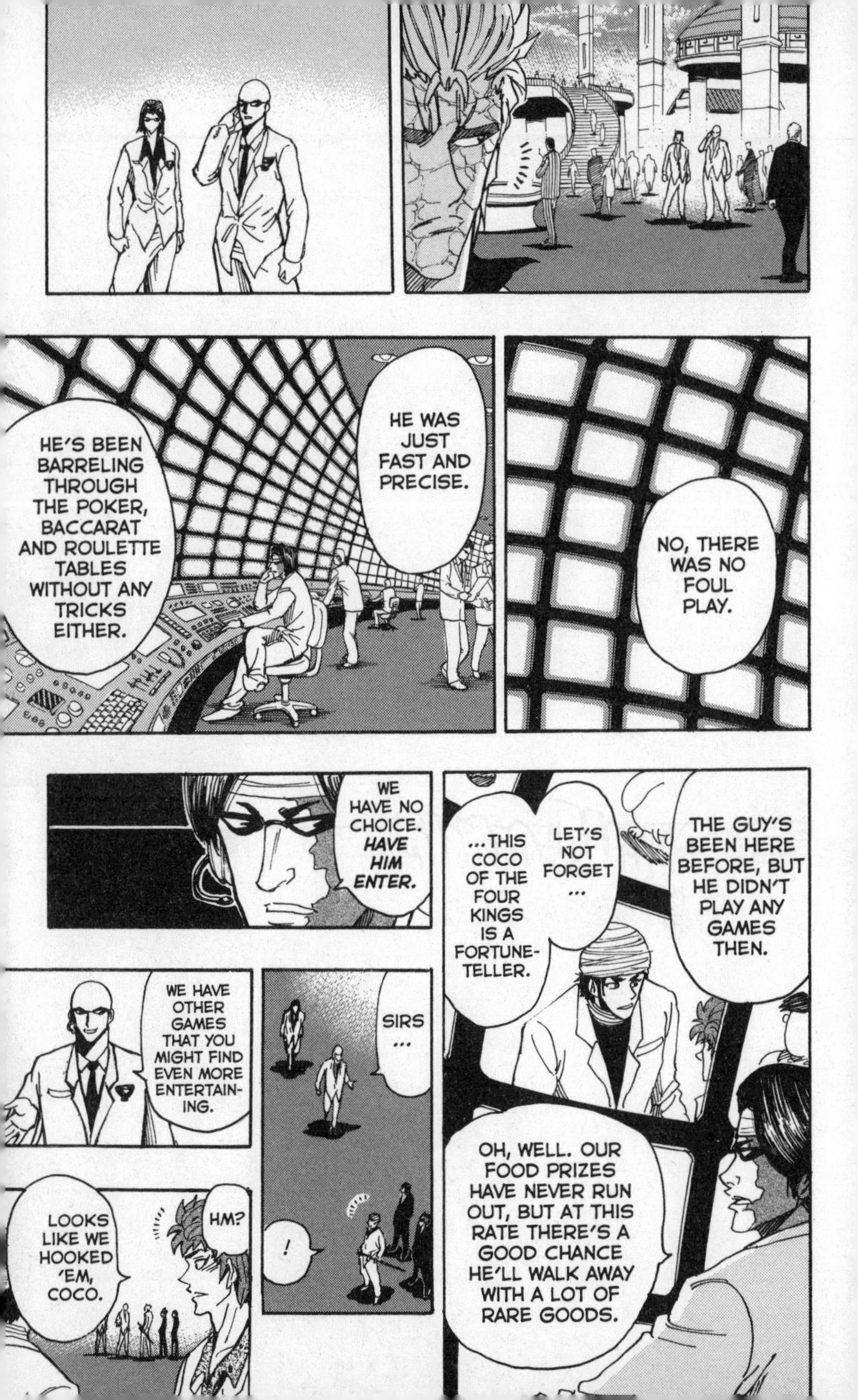
NO, THERE WAS NO FOUL PLAY.
HE WAS JUST FAST AND PRECISE.
HE'S BEEN BARRELING THROUGH THE POKER, BACCARAT AND ROULETTE TABLES WITHOUT ANY TRICKS EITHER.
THE GUY'S BEEN HERE BEFORE, BUT HE DIDN'T PLAY ANY GAMES THEN.
LET'S NOT FORGET ...
...THIS COCO OF THE FOUR KINGS IS A FORTUNE-TELLER.
OH, WELL. OUR FOOD PRIZES HAVE NEVER RUN OUT, BUT AT THIS RATE THERE'S A GOOD CHANCE HE'LL WALK AWAY WITH A LOT OF RARE GOODS.
WE HAVE NO CHOICE. *HAVE HIM ENTER.*
SIRS ...
!
WE HAVE OTHER GAMES THAT YOU MIGHT FIND EVEN MORE ENTERTAIN-ING.
HM?
LOOKS LIKE WE HOOKED 'EM, COCO.

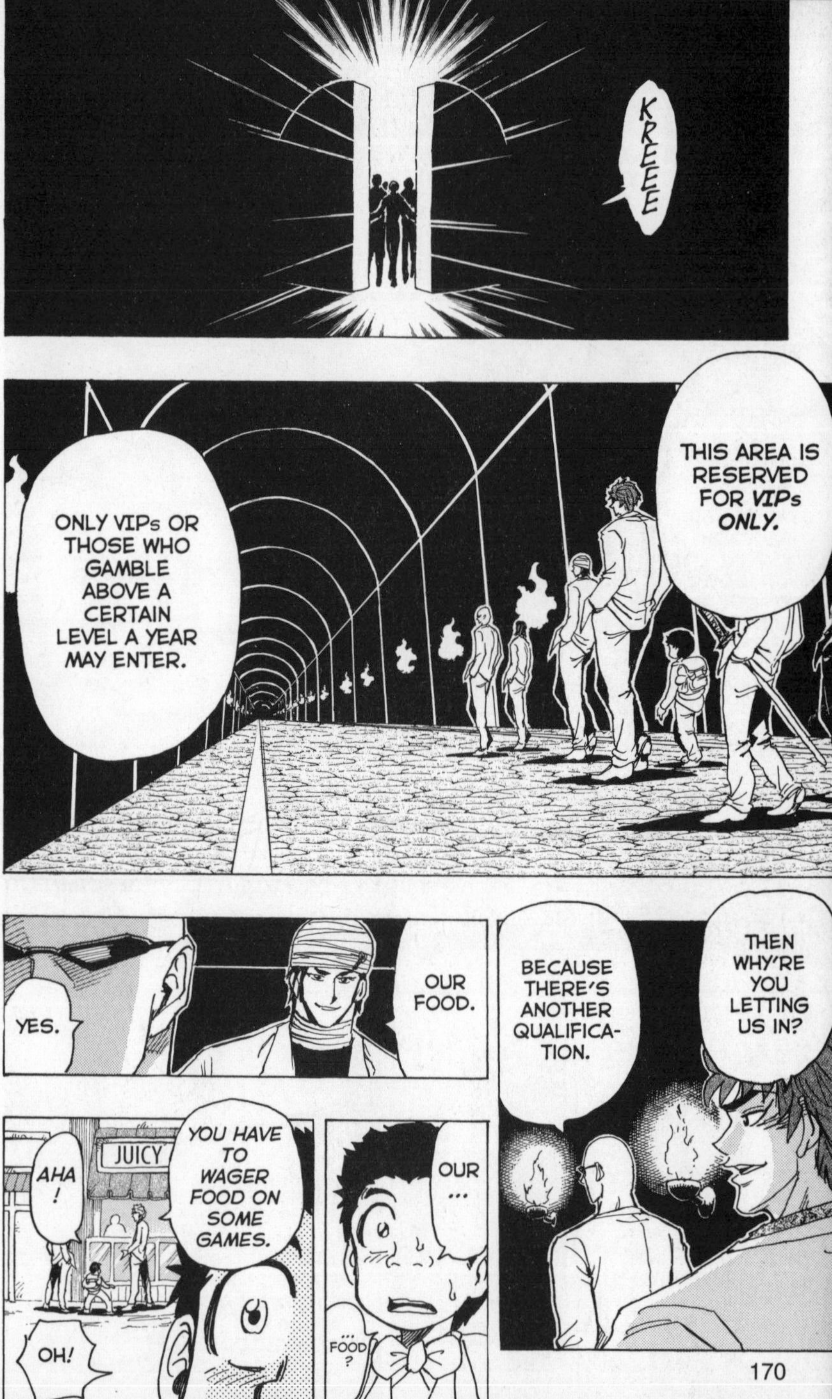
KREEEE
THIS AREA IS RESERVED FOR VIPs ONLY.
ONLY VIPs OR THOSE WHO GAMBLE ABOVE A CERTAIN LEVEL A YEAR MAY ENTER.
THEN WHY'RE YOU LETTING US IN?
BECAUSE THERE'S ANOTHER QUALIFICATION.
OUR FOOD.
YES.
OUR ...
... FOOD ?
YOU HAVE TO WAGER FOOD ON SOME GAMES.
JUICY
AHA !
OH!

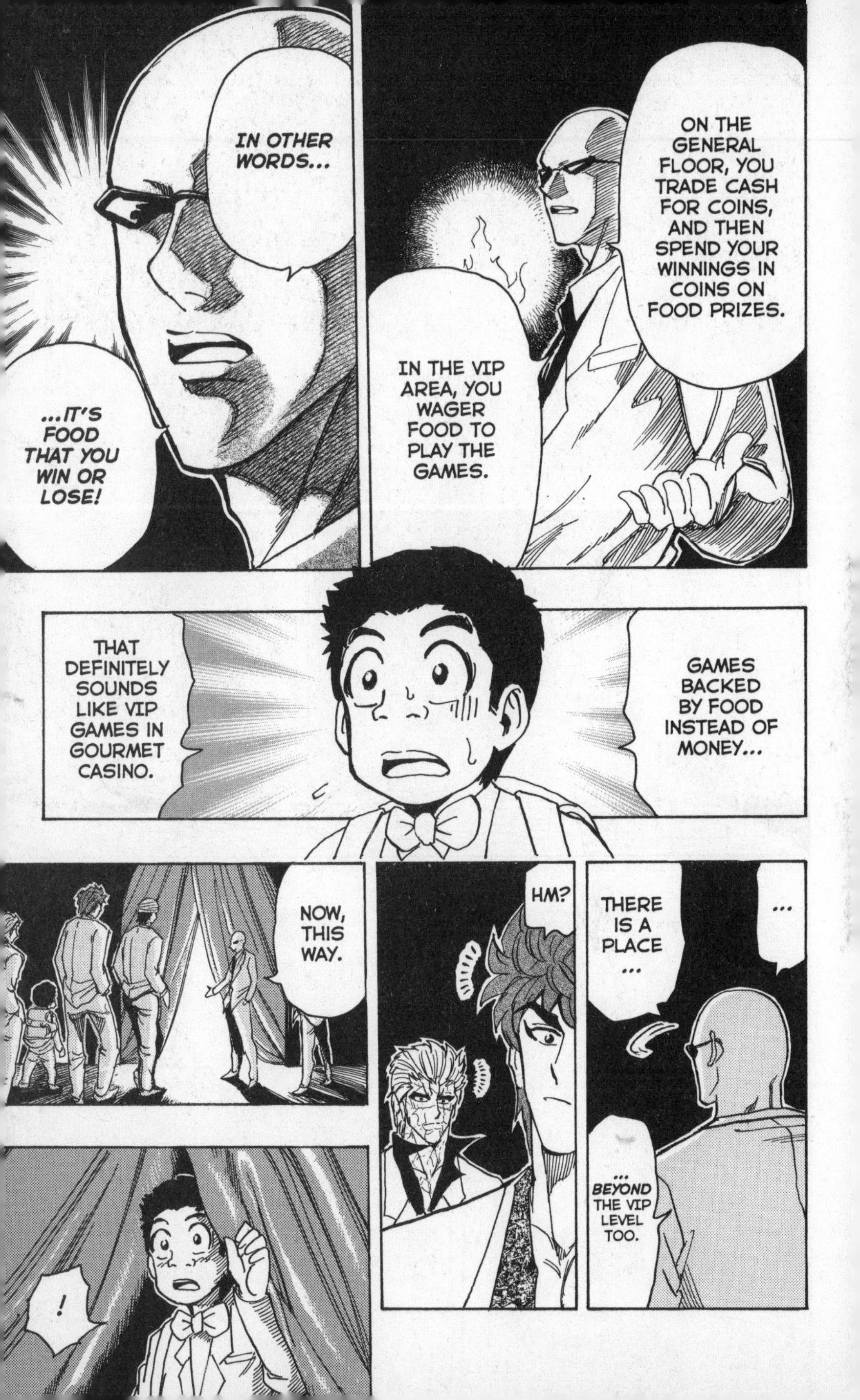
ON THE GENERAL FLOOR, YOU TRADE CASH FOR COINS, AND THEN SPEND YOUR WINNINGS IN COINS ON FOOD PRIZES.
IN THE VIP AREA, YOU WAGER FOOD TO PLAY THE GAMES.
IN OTHER WORDS...
...IT'S FOOD THAT YOU WIN OR LOSE!
GAMES BACKED BY FOOD INSTEAD OF MONEY...
THAT DEFINITELY SOUNDS LIKE VIP GAMES IN GOURMET CASINO.
...
THERE IS A PLACE ...
... BEYOND THE VIP LEVEL TOO.
HM?
NOW, THIS WAY.
!

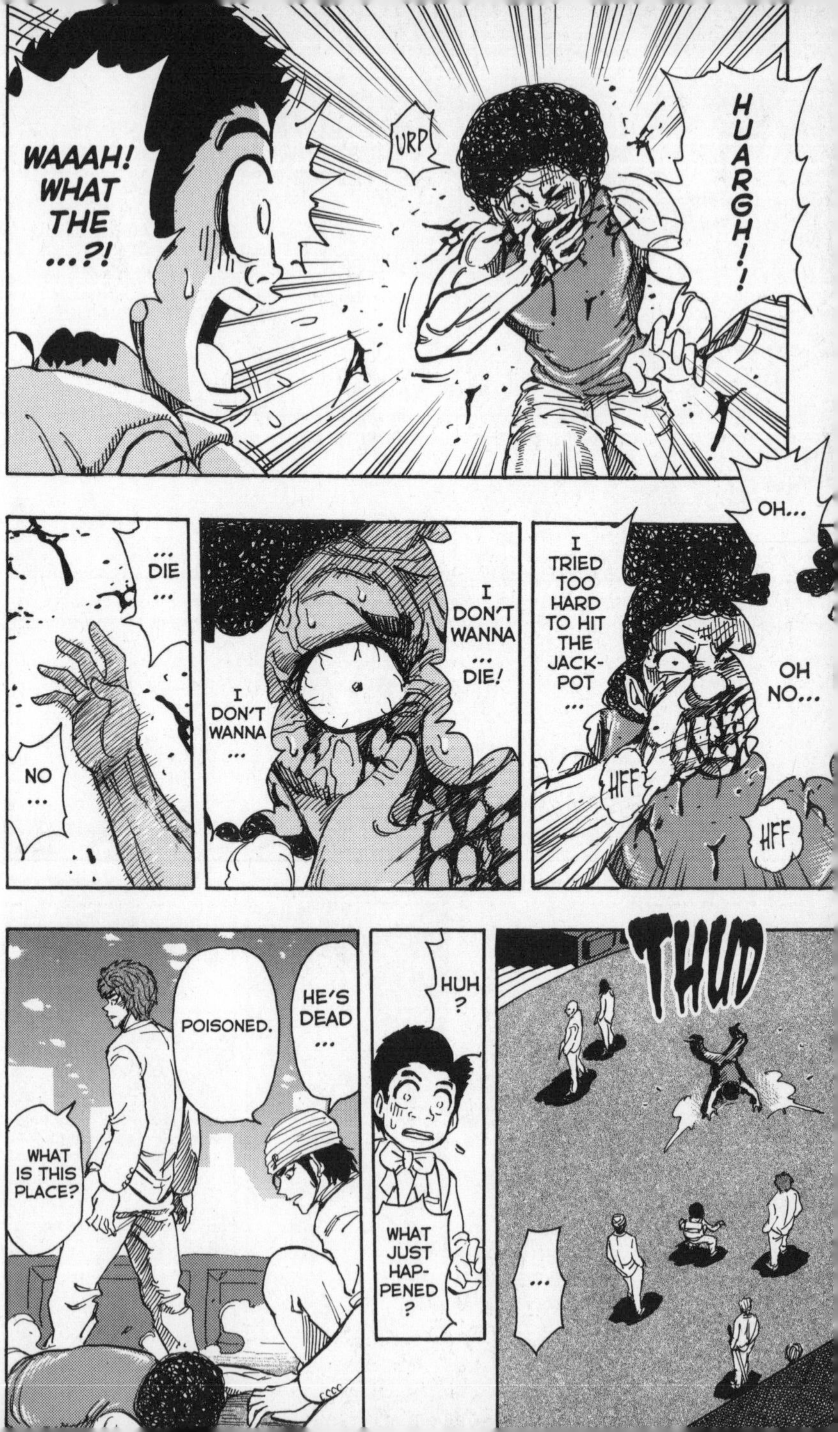
HUARGH!!
URP
WAAAH! WHAT THE ...?!
OH...
OH NO...
I TRIED TOO HARD TO HIT THE JACKPOT ...
HFF
HFF
I DON'T WANNA ... DIE!
I DON'T WANNA ...
... DIE ...
NO ...
THUD
...
HUH ?
WHAT JUST HAPPENED ?
HE'S DEAD ...
POISONED.
WHAT IS THIS PLACE?

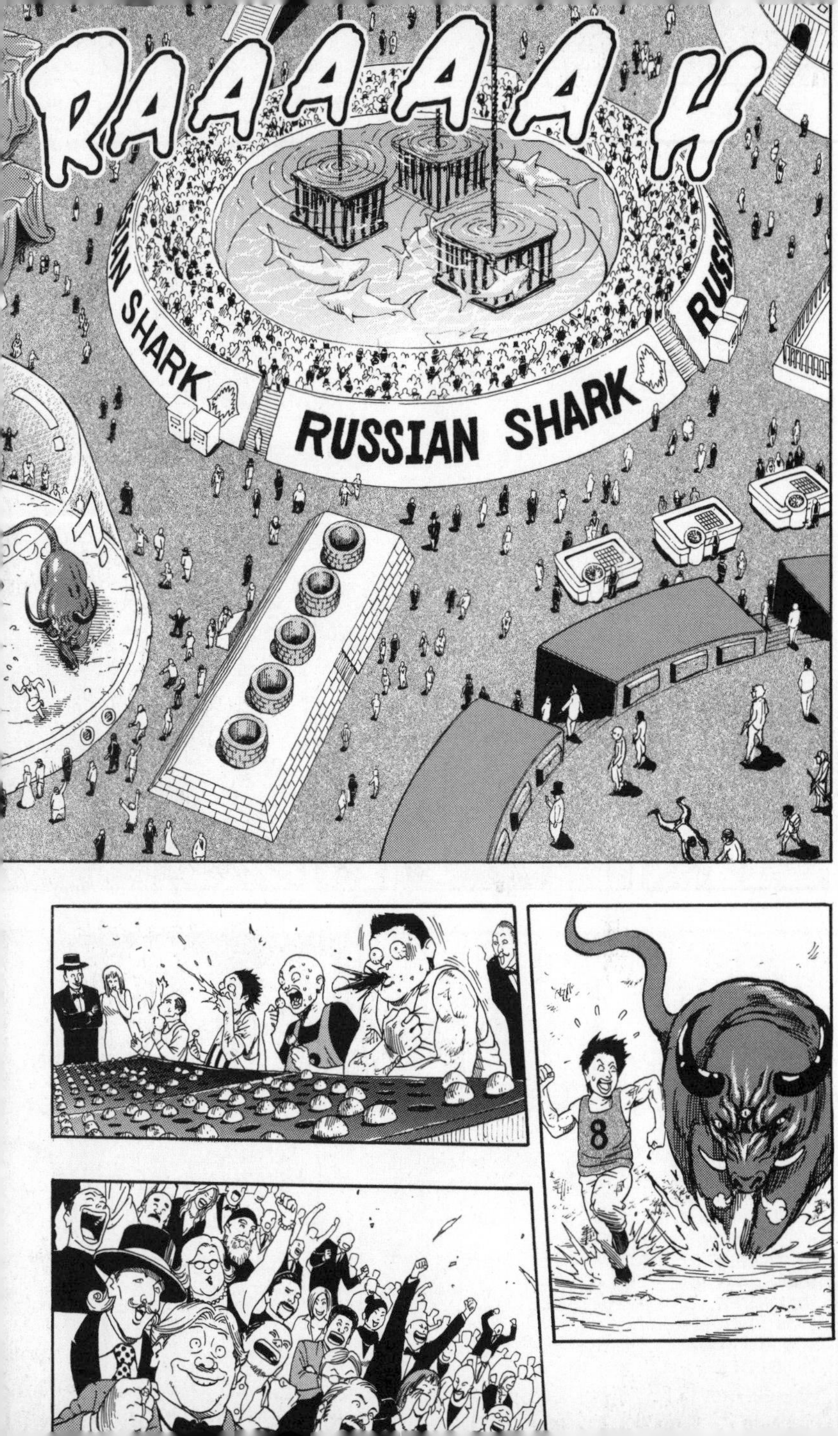
RAAAAAH
RUSSIAN SHARK
RUSSIAN SHARK
RUSS
8

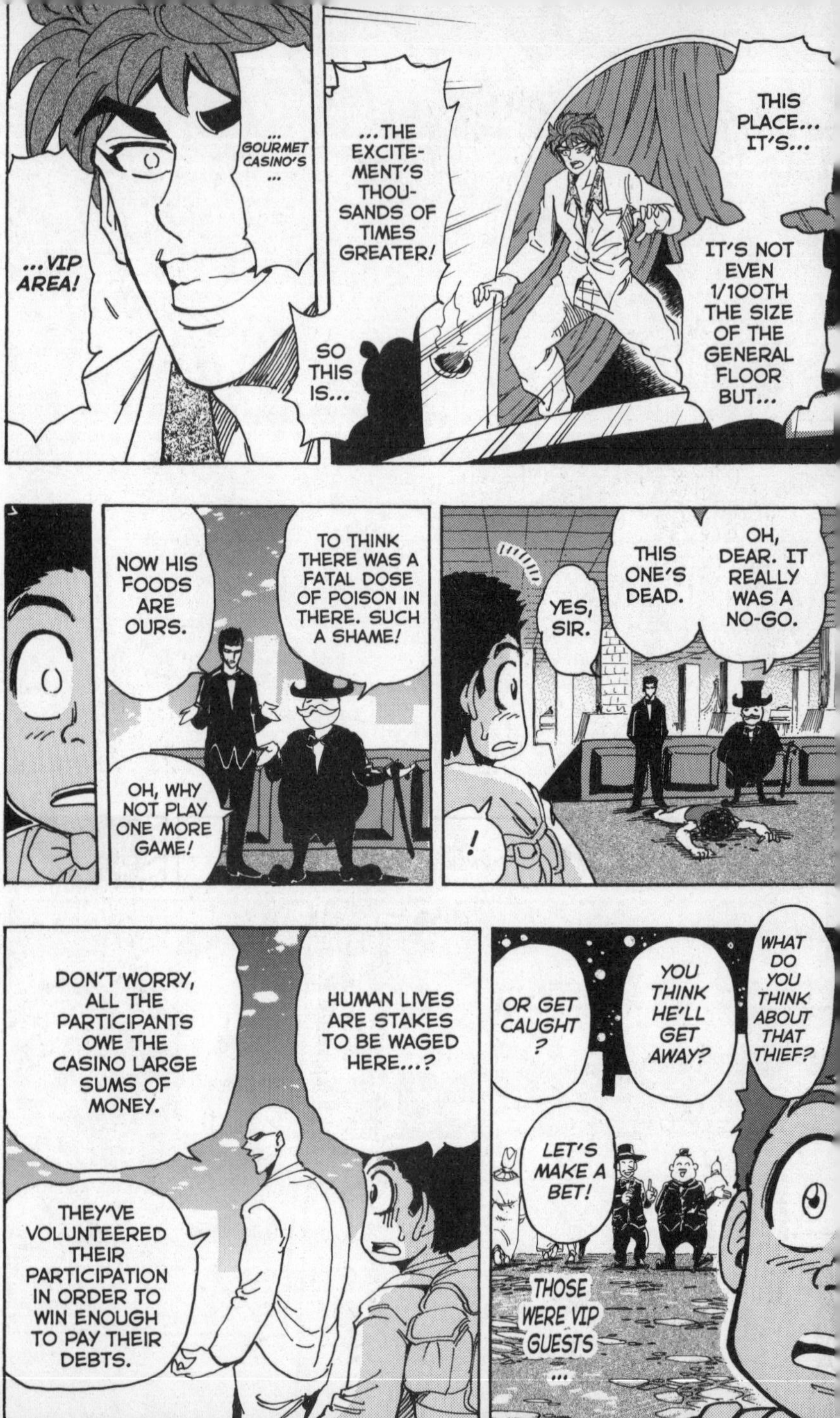
THIS PLACE... IT'S...
IT'S NOT EVEN 1/100TH THE SIZE OF THE GENERAL FLOOR BUT...
...THE EXCITEMENT'S THOUSANDS OF TIMES GREATER!
SO THIS IS...
...GOURMET CASINO'S ...
...VIP AREA!
OH, DEAR. IT REALLY WAS A NO-GO.
THIS ONE'S DEAD.
YES, SIR.
!
TO THINK THERE WAS A FATAL DOSE OF POISON IN THERE. SUCH A SHAME!
NOW HIS FOODS ARE OURS.
OH, WHY NOT PLAY ONE MORE GAME!
WHAT DO YOU THINK ABOUT THAT THIEF?
YOU THINK HE'LL GET AWAY?
OR GET CAUGHT?
LET'S MAKE A BET!
THOSE WERE VIP GUESTS ...
HUMAN LIVES ARE STAKES TO BE WAGED HERE...?
DON'T WORRY, ALL THE PARTICIPANTS OWE THE CASINO LARGE SUMS OF MONEY.
THEY'VE VOLUNTEERED THEIR PARTICIPATION IN ORDER TO WIN ENOUGH TO PAY THEIR DEBTS.

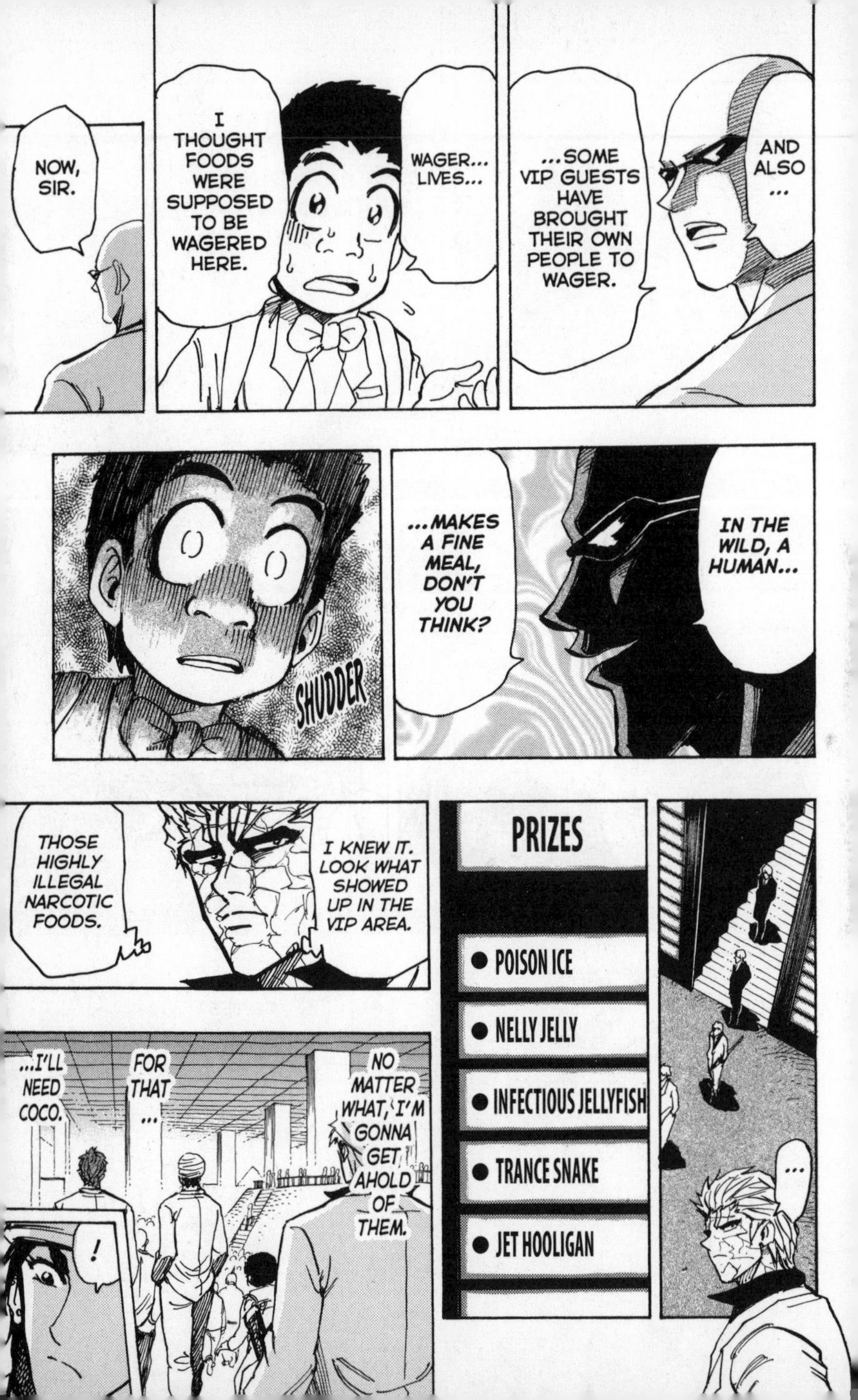
AND ALSO...
...SOME VIP GUESTS HAVE BROUGHT THEIR OWN PEOPLE TO WAGER.
WAGER... LIVES...
I THOUGHT FOODS WERE SUPPOSED TO BE WAGERED HERE.
NOW, SIR.
IN THE WILD, A HUMAN...
...MAKES A FINE MEAL, DON'T YOU THINK?
SHUDDER
...
PRIZES
● POISON ICE
● NELLY JELLY
● INFECTIOUS JELLYFISH
● TRANCE SNAKE
● JET HOOLIGAN
I KNEW IT. LOOK WHAT SHOWED UP IN THE VIP AREA.
THOSE HIGHLY ILLEGAL NARCOTIC FOODS.
NO MATTER WHAT, I'M GONNA GET AHOLD OF THEM.
FOR THAT...
...I'LL NEED COCO.
!

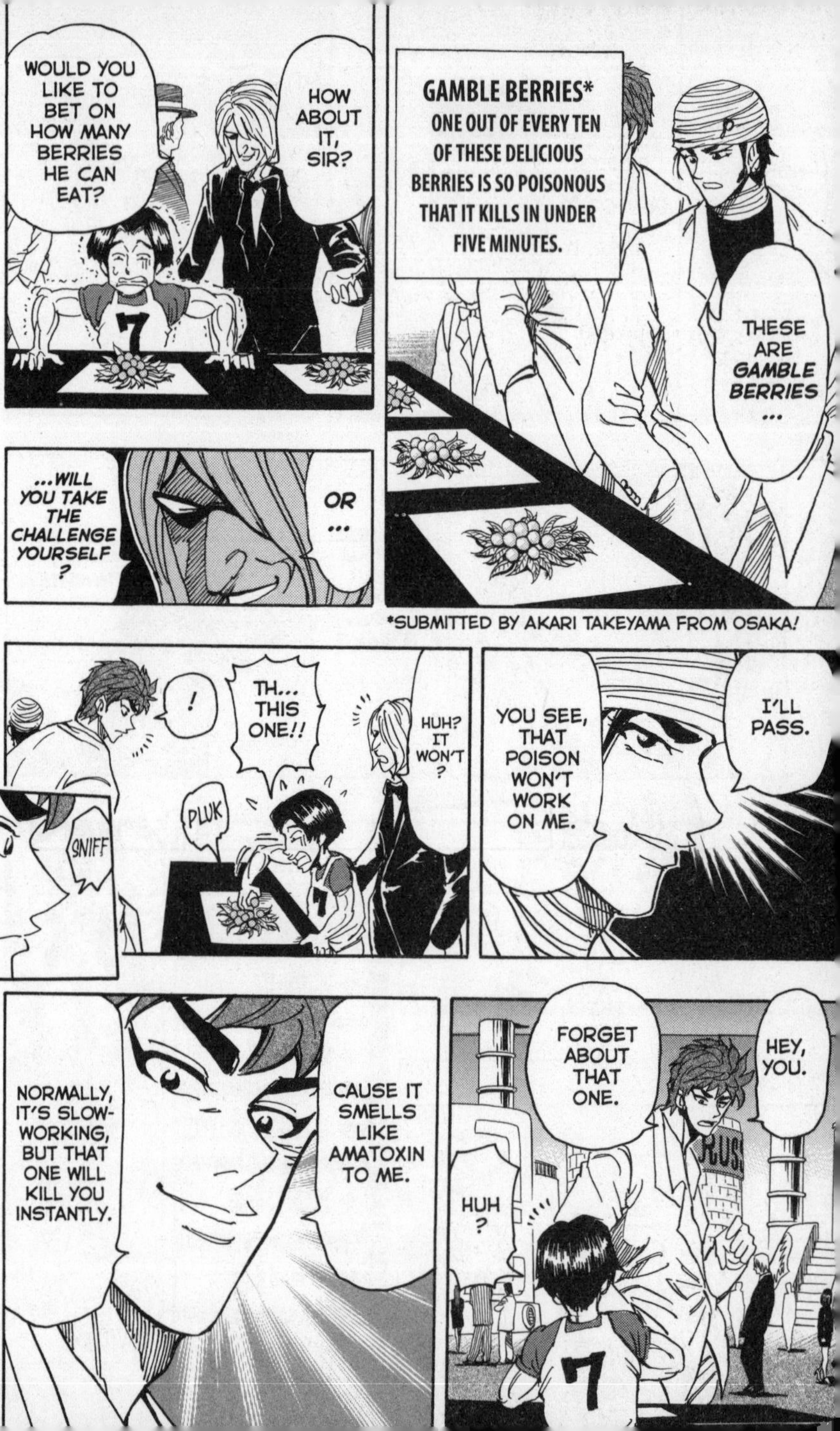
GAMBLE BERRIES* ONE OUT OF EVERY TEN OF THESE DELICIOUS BERRIES IS SO POISONOUS THAT IT KILLS IN UNDER FIVE MINUTES.
THESE ARE GAMBLE BERRIES...
HOW ABOUT IT, SIR?
WOULD YOU LIKE TO BET ON HOW MANY BERRIES HE CAN EAT?
OR...
...WILL YOU TAKE THE CHALLENGE YOURSELF?
*SUBMITTED BY AKARI TAKEYAMA FROM OSAKA!
I'LL PASS.
YOU SEE, THAT POISON WON'T WORK ON ME.
HUH? IT WON'T?
TH... THIS ONE!!
!
PLUK
SNIFF
HEY, YOU.
FORGET ABOUT THAT ONE.
HUH?
CAUSE IT SMELLS LIKE AMATOXIN TO ME.
NORMALLY, IT'S SLOW-WORKING, BUT THAT ONE WILL KILL YOU INSTANTLY.

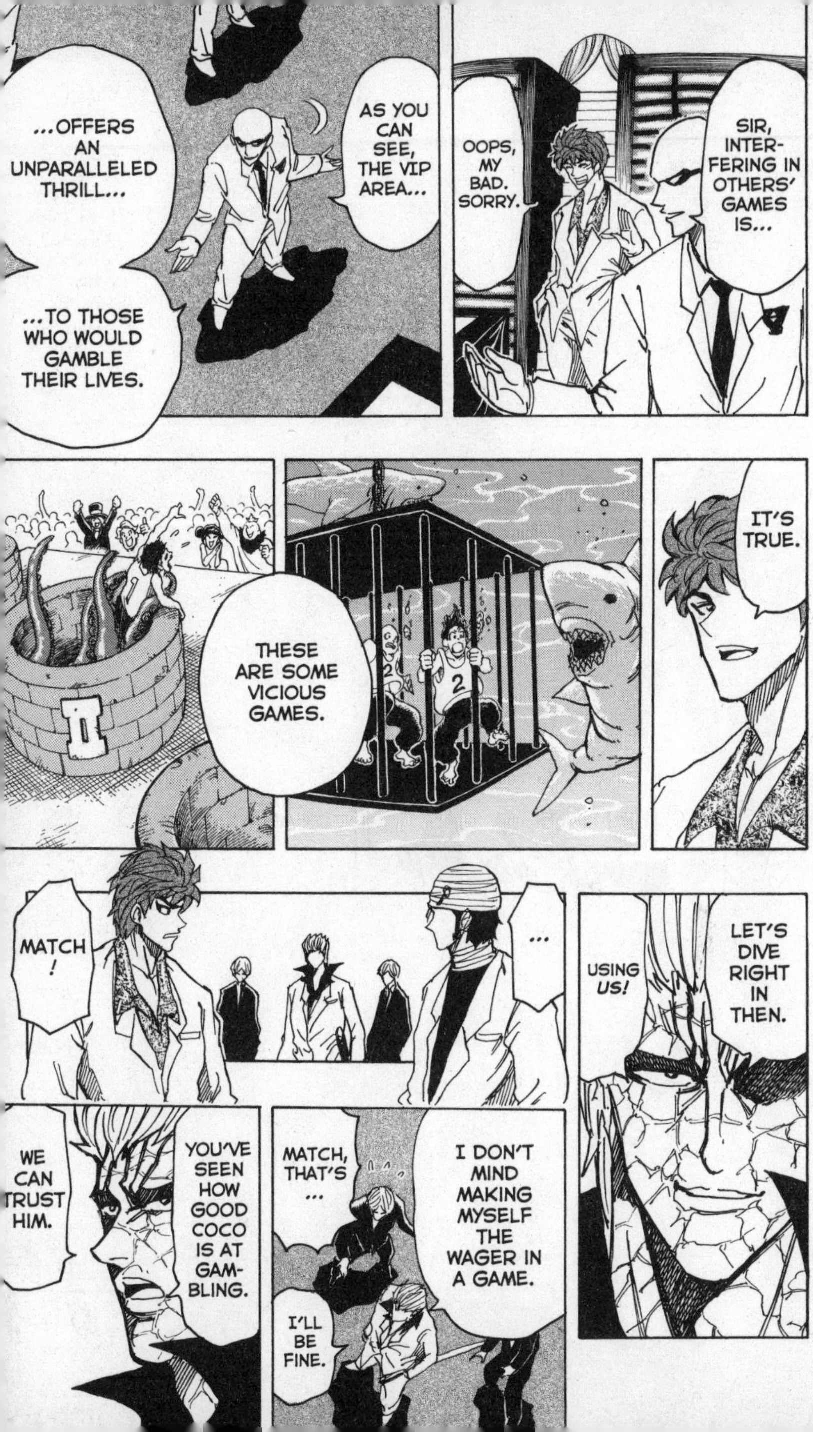
SIR, INTERFERING IN OTHERS' GAMES IS...
OOPS, MY BAD. SORRY.
AS YOU CAN SEE, THE VIP AREA...
...OFFERS AN UNPARALLELED THRILL...
...TO THOSE WHO WOULD GAMBLE THEIR LIVES.
IT'S TRUE.
THESE ARE SOME VICIOUS GAMES.
LET'S DIVE RIGHT IN THEN.
USING US!
...
MATCH!
I DON'T MIND MAKING MYSELF THE WAGER IN A GAME.
MATCH, THAT'S...
I'LL BE FINE.
YOU'VE SEEN HOW GOOD COCO IS AT GAMBLING.
WE CAN TRUST HIM.

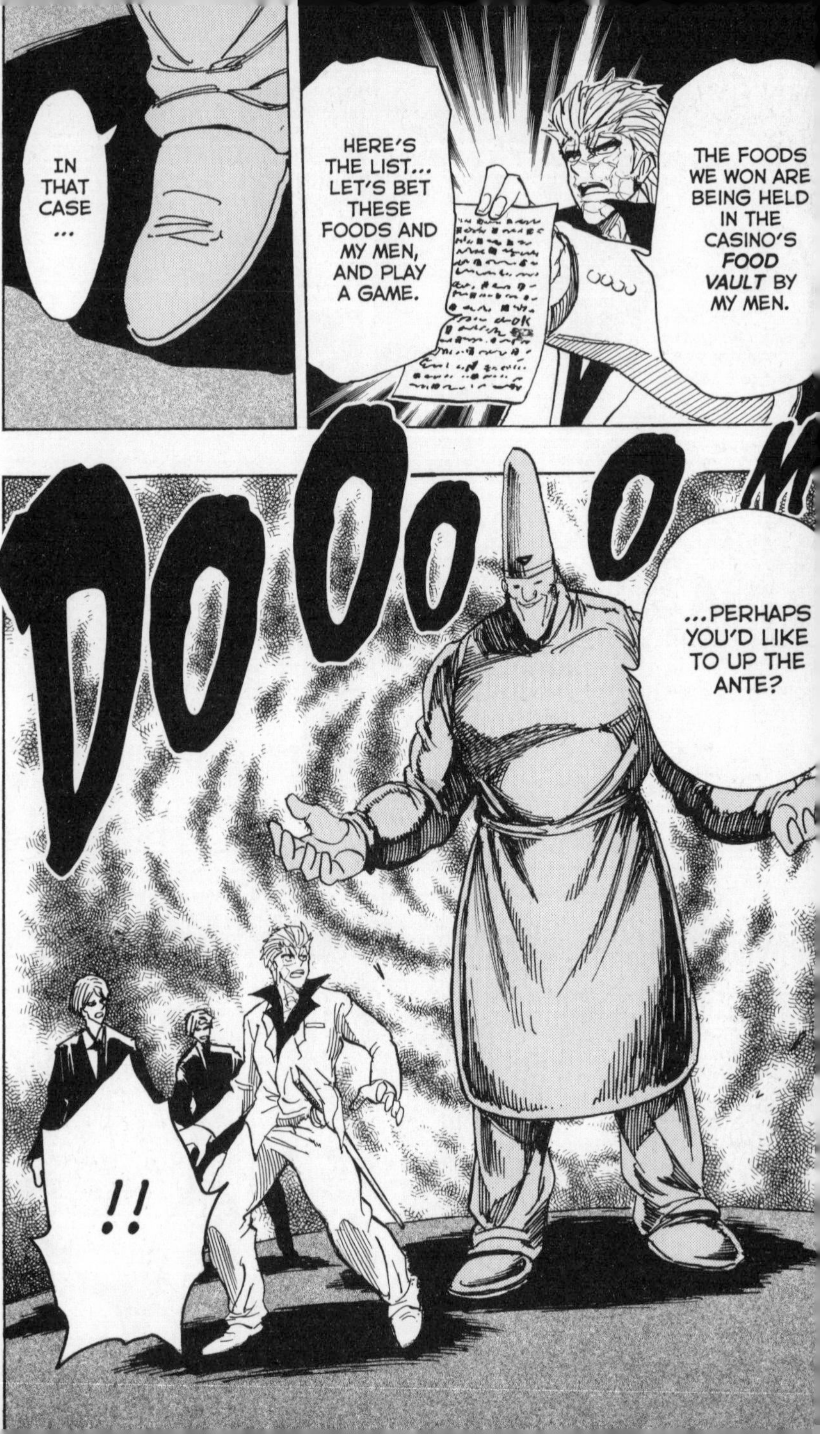
THE FOODS WE WON ARE BEING HELD IN THE CASINO'S *FOOD VAULT* BY MY MEN.
HERE'S THE LIST... LET'S BET THESE FOODS AND MY MEN, AND PLAY A GAME.
IN THAT CASE ...
DOOOOM
...PERHAPS YOU'D LIKE TO UP THE ANTE?
!!

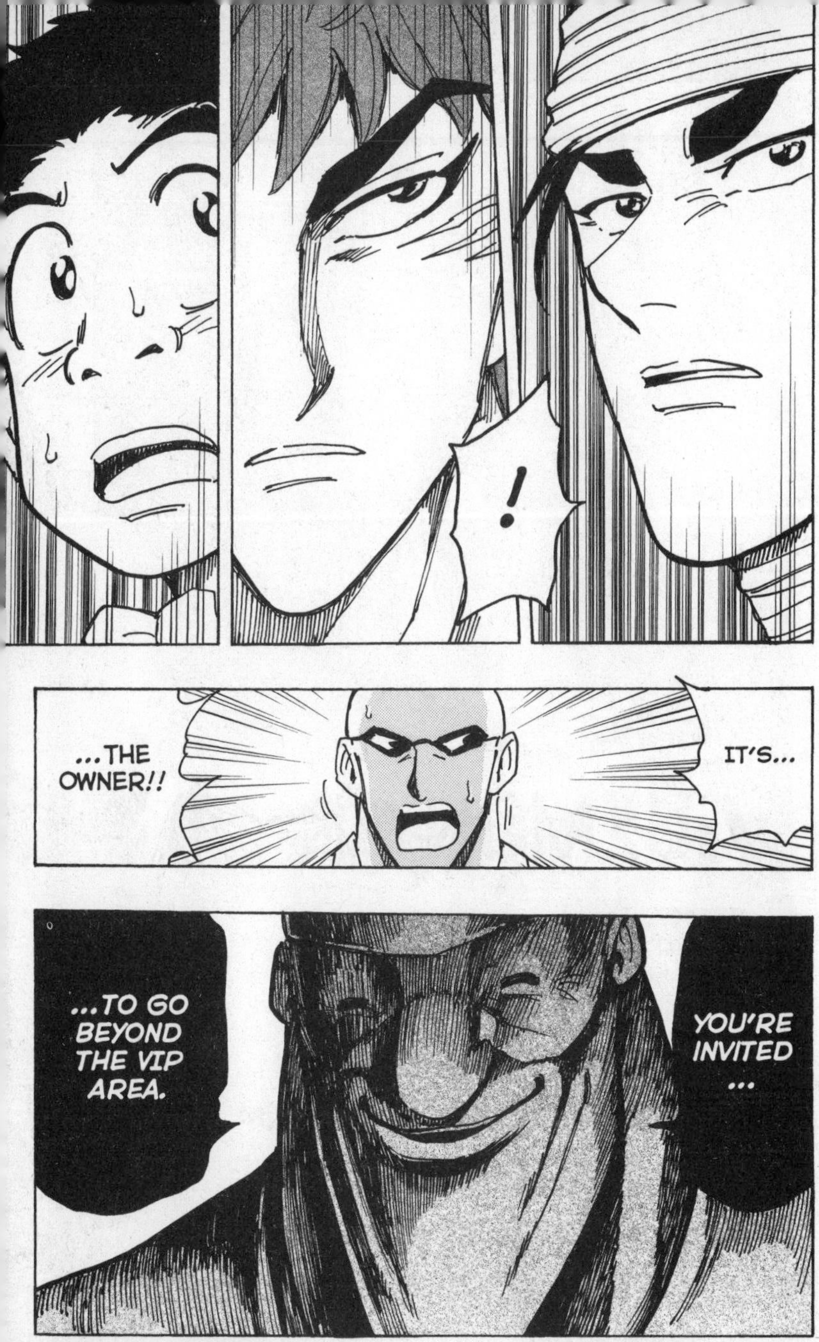
!
IT'S...
...THE OWNER!!
YOU'RE INVITED ...
...TO GO BEYOND THE VIP AREA.

TO BE CONTINUED!

CHARACTER PROFILE

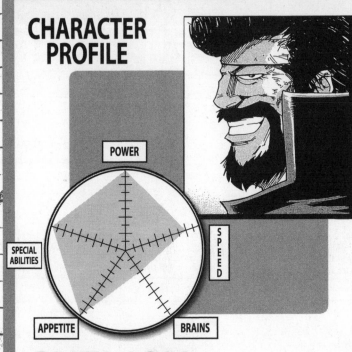

POWER

SPECIAL ABILITIES

SPEED

APPETITE

BRAINS

GUEMON

AGE: 48		**BIRTHDAY:** FEB 29	
BLOOD TYPE: B		**SIGN:** PISCES	
HEIGHT: 199 CM		**WEIGHT:** 200 KG	
EYESIGHT: 20/4		**SHOE SIZE:** 30 CM	

SPECIAL MOVES/ABILITIES: ● Gut Instinct

One of the members of the IGO's elite Biotope Zero. He carries the title of "Gourmet Gang Leader" and lives far away from civilization on the Wac Continent's Road of Three Hells, the only land route connecting the Human World and the Gourmet World. There, he singlehandedly prevents Gourmet World creatures from wandering into the Human World. He often seems to be zoning out, but since his days are filled with battle, he is actually a fighting specialist who relies on his almost god-like gut instinct.

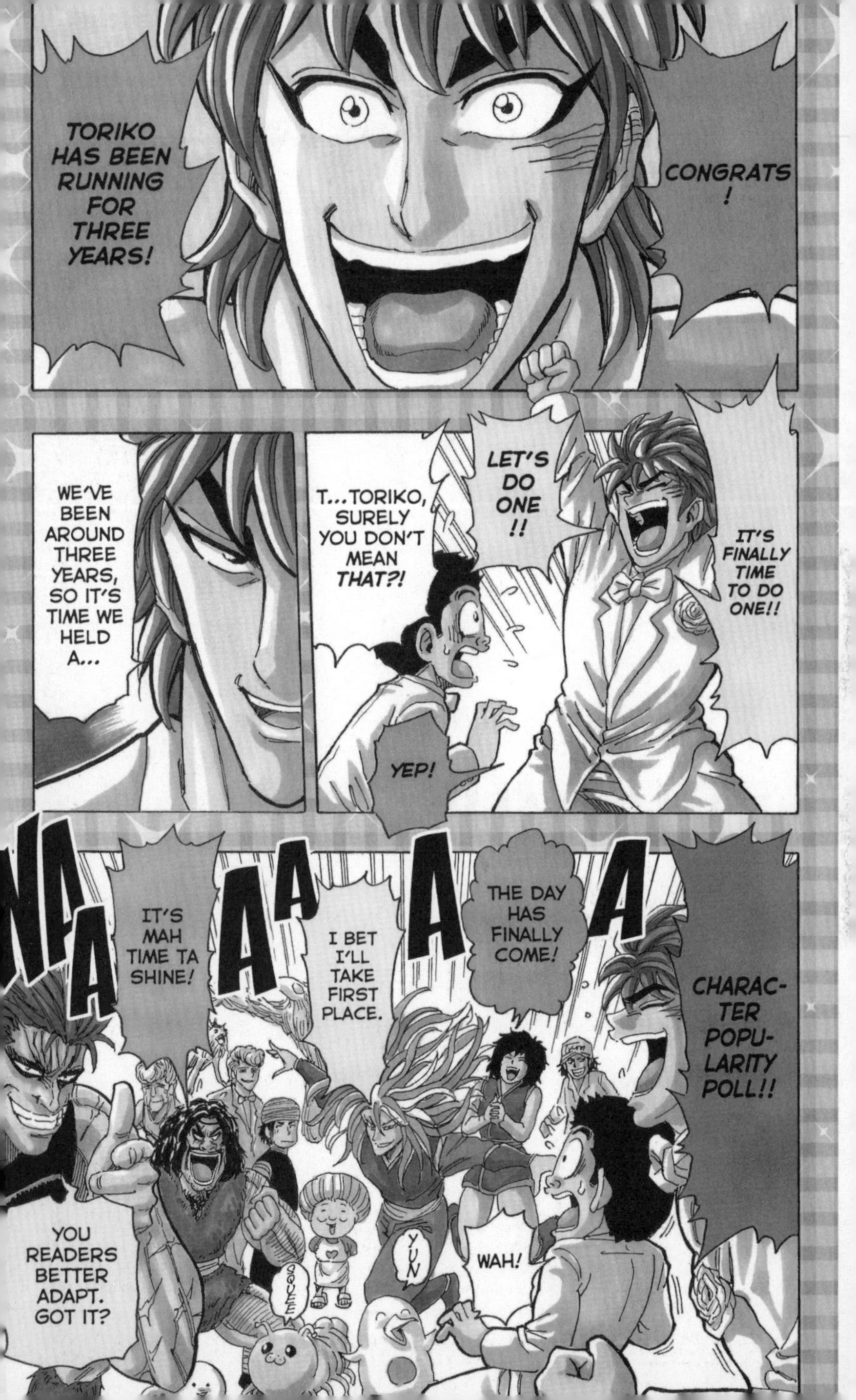
CONGRATS!
TORIKO HAS BEEN RUNNING FOR THREE YEARS!
IT'S FINALLY TIME TO DO ONE!!
LET'S DO ONE!!
T...TORIKO, SURELY YOU DON'T MEAN THAT?!
YEP!
WE'VE BEEN AROUND THREE YEARS, SO IT'S TIME WE HELD A...
CHARACTER POPULARITY POLL!!
NAAAAAA
THE DAY HAS FINALLY COME!
I BET I'LL TAKE FIRST PLACE.
IT'S MAH TIME TA SHINE!
WAH!
YUN
SQUEE
YOU READERS BETTER ADAPT. GOT IT?

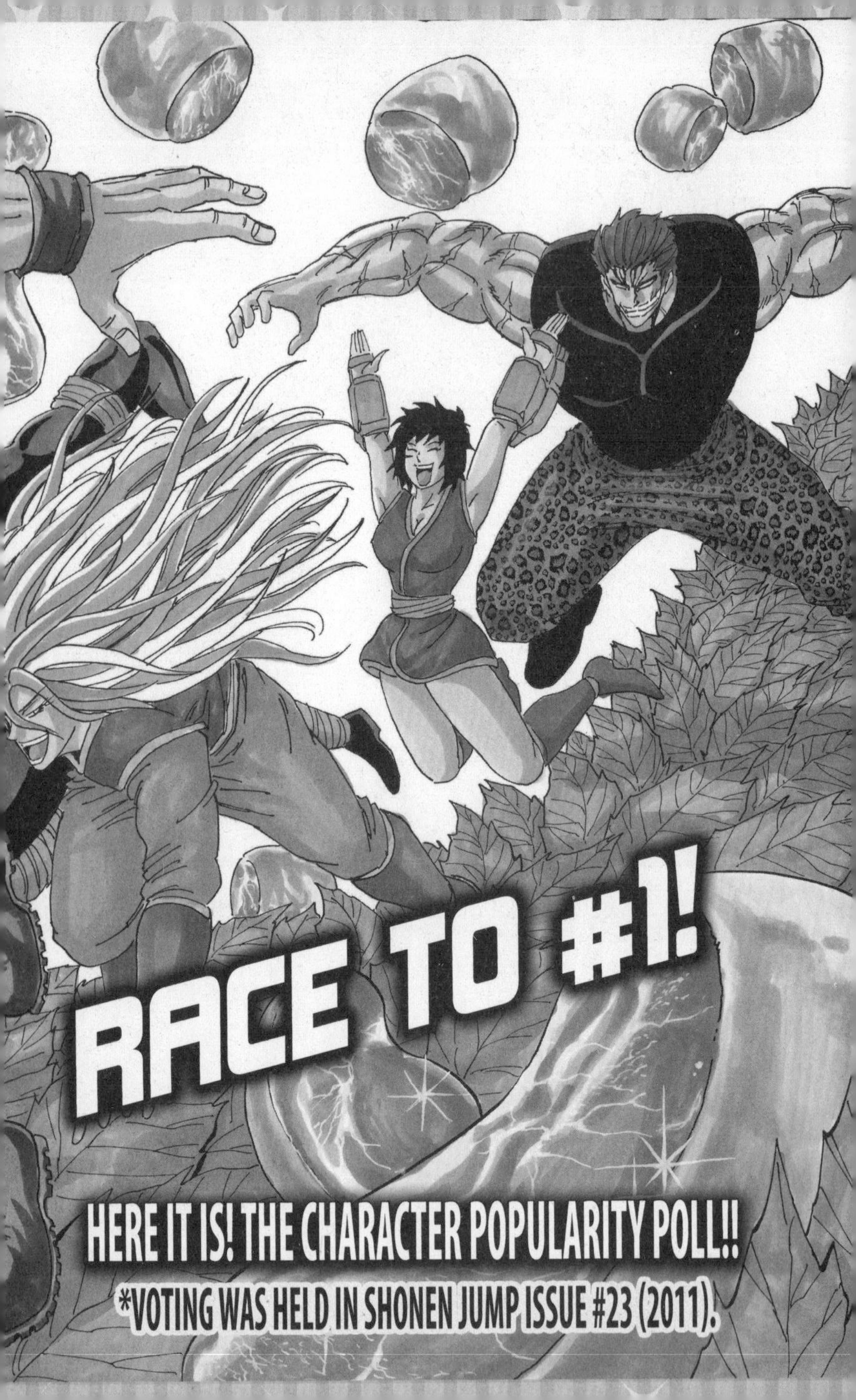
RACE TO #1!
HERE IT IS! THE CHARACTER POPULARITY POLL!!
*VOTING WAS HELD IN SHONEN JUMP ISSUE #23 (2011).

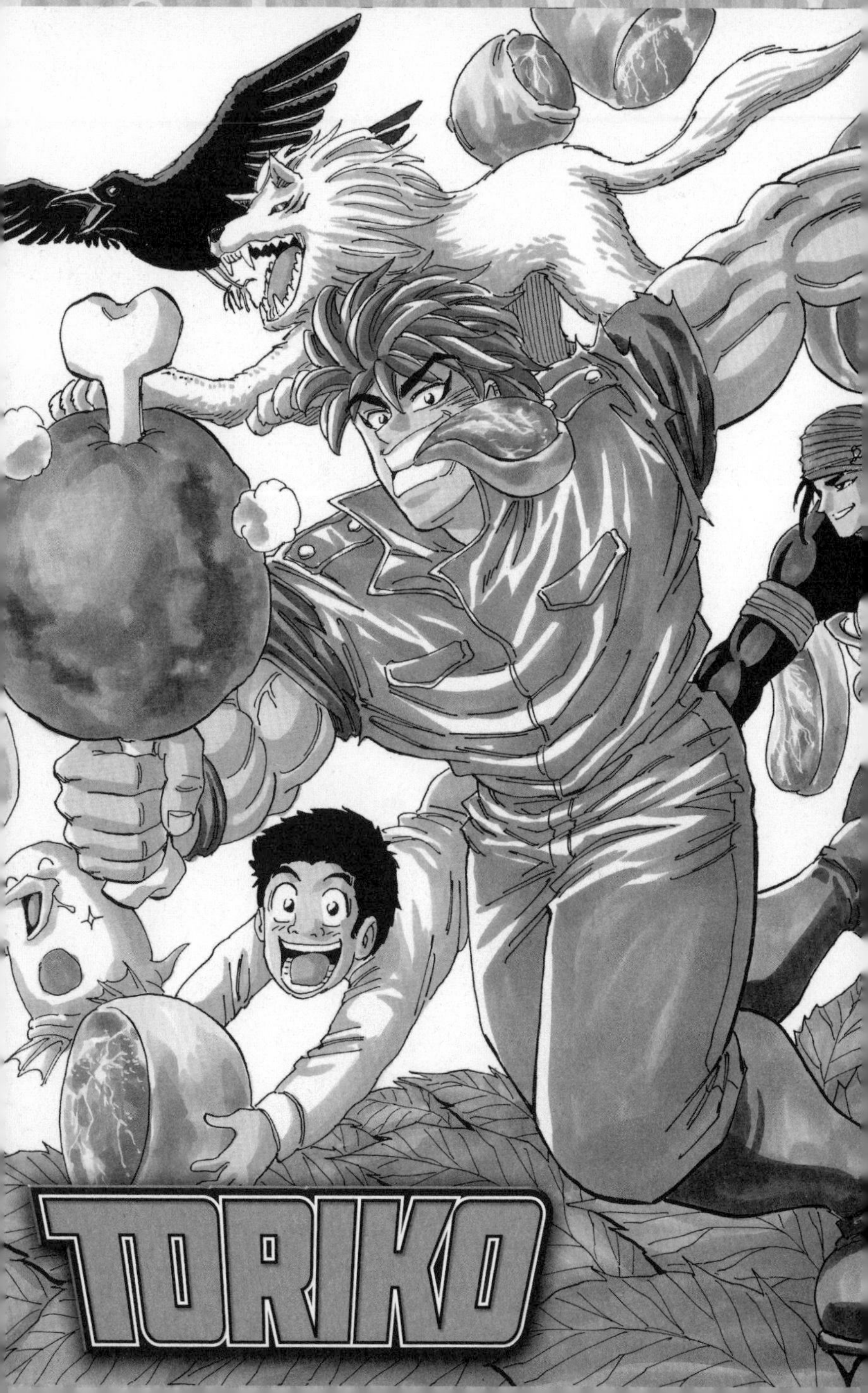
TORIKO

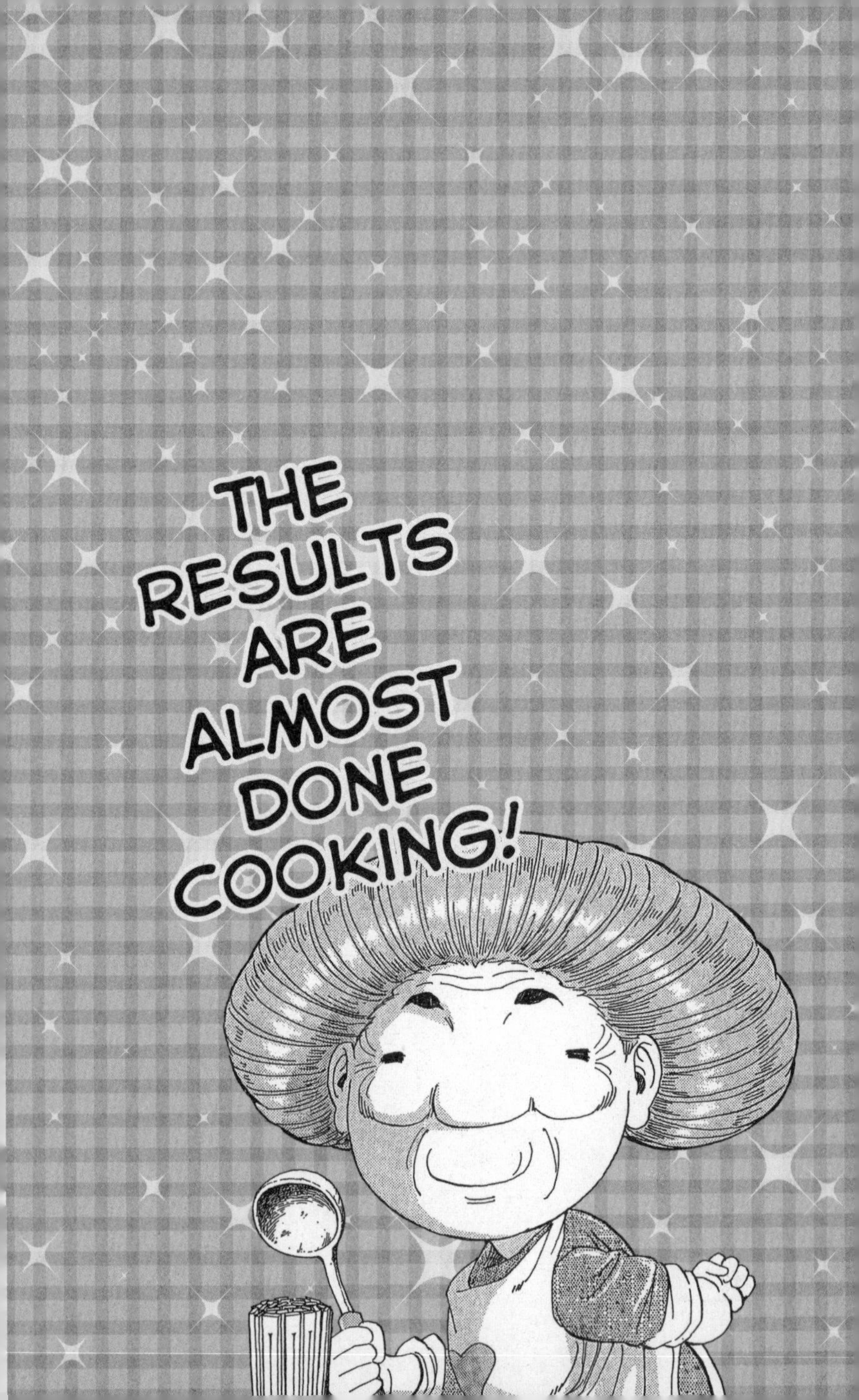
THE RESULTS ARE ALMOST DONE COOKING!

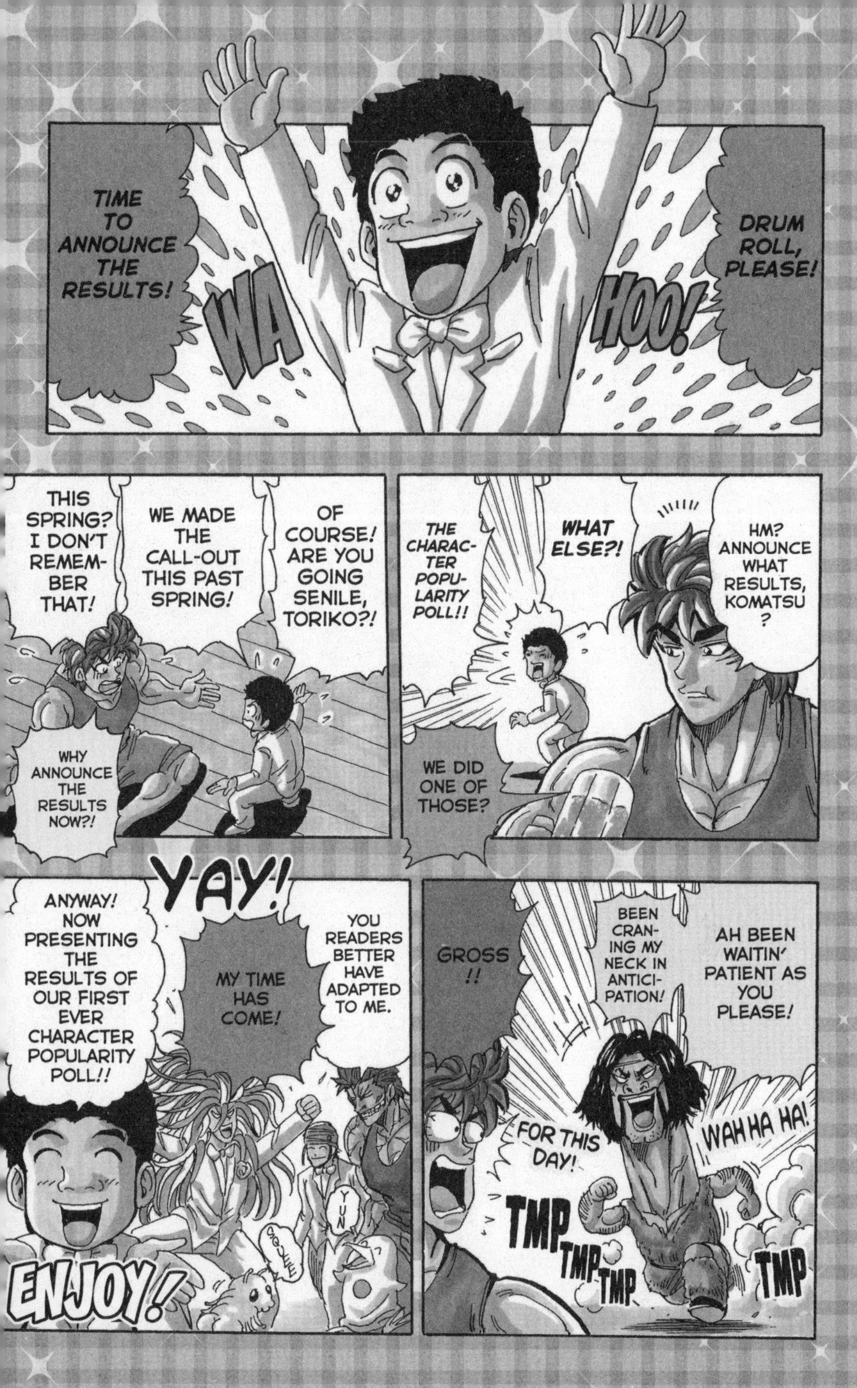
TIME TO ANNOUNCE THE RESULTS!
DRUM ROLL, PLEASE!
WA
HOO!
HM? ANNOUNCE WHAT RESULTS, KOMATSU?
WHAT ELSE?!
THE CHARACTER POPULARITY POLL!!
WE DID ONE OF THOSE?
OF COURSE! ARE YOU GOING SENILE, TORIKO?!
WE MADE THE CALL-OUT THIS PAST SPRING!
THIS SPRING? I DON'T REMEMBER THAT!
WHY ANNOUNCE THE RESULTS NOW?!
AH BEEN WAITIN' PATIENT AS YOU PLEASE!
BEEN CRANING MY NECK IN ANTICIPATION!
GROSS!!
WAH HA HA!
FOR THIS DAY!
TMP
TMP
TMP
TMP
TMP
YOU READERS BETTER HAVE ADAPTED TO ME.
MY TIME HAS COME!
YAY!
ANYWAY! NOW PRESENTING THE RESULTS OF OUR FIRST EVER CHARACTER POPULARITY POLL!!
YUN
SQUEE
ENJOY!

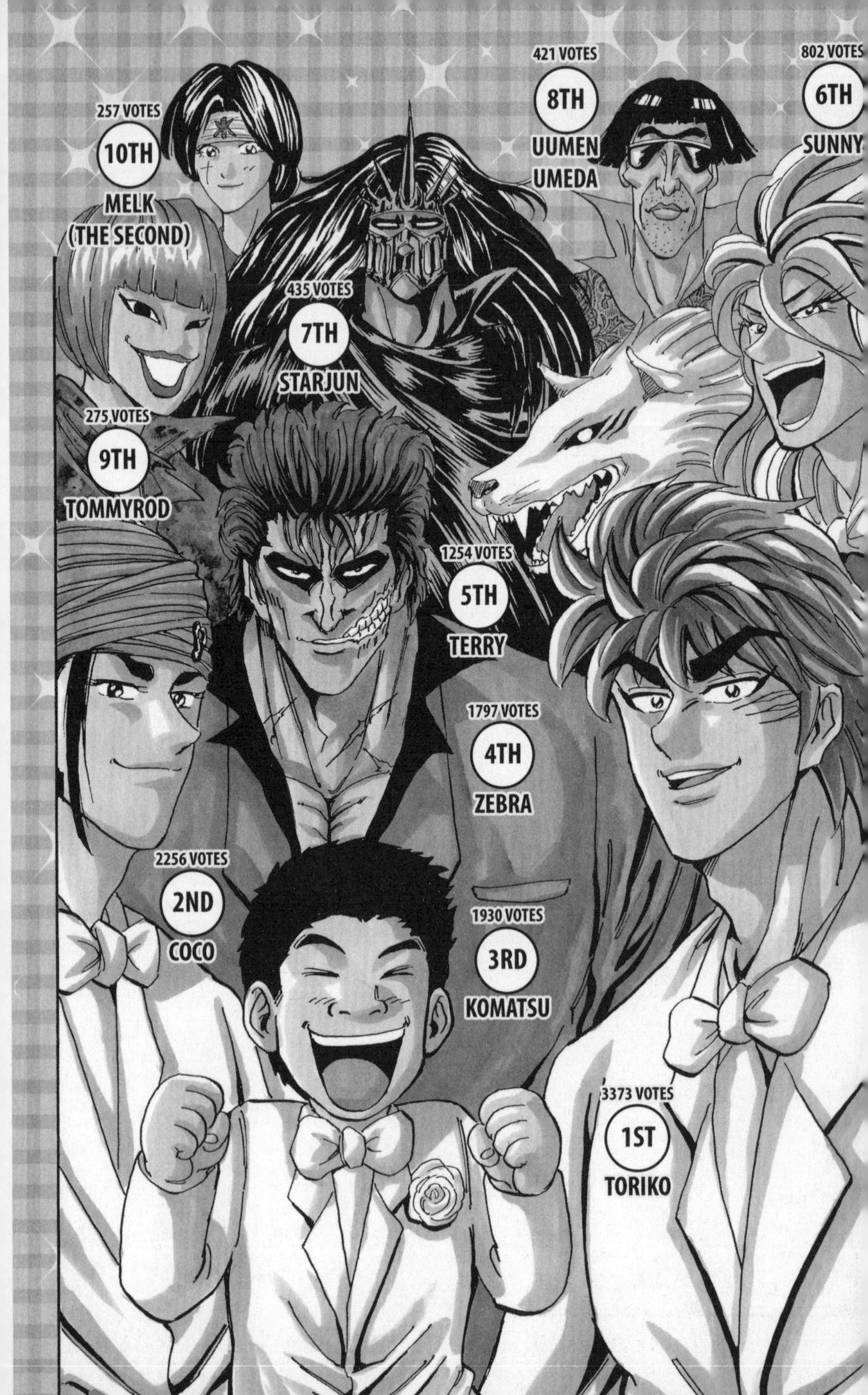
802 VOTES
6TH
SUNNY
421 VOTES
8TH
UUMEN UMEDA
257 VOTES
10TH
MELK (THE SECOND)
435 VOTES
7TH
STARJUN
275 VOTES
9TH
TOMMYROD
1254 VOTES
5TH
TERRY
1797 VOTES
4TH
ZEBRA
2256 VOTES
2ND
COCO
1930 VOTES
3RD
KOMATSU
3373 VOTES
1ST
TORIKO

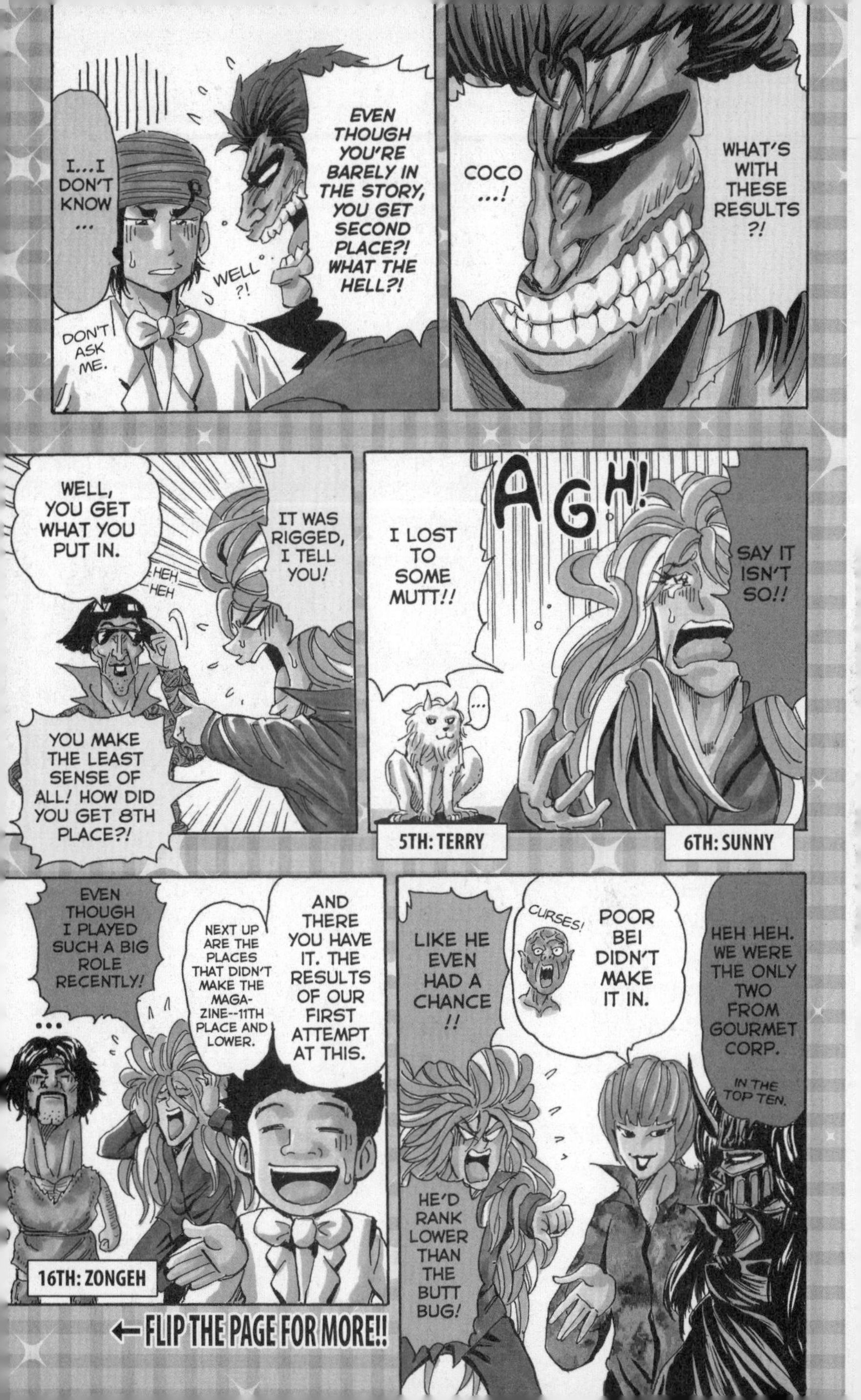
WHAT'S WITH THESE RESULTS?!
COCO...!
EVEN THOUGH YOU'RE BARELY IN THE STORY, YOU GET SECOND PLACE?! WHAT THE HELL?!
WELL?!
I...I DON'T KNOW...
DON'T ASK ME.
SAY IT ISN'T SO!!
AGH!
I LOST TO SOME MUTT!!
...
6TH: SUNNY
5TH: TERRY
IT WAS RIGGED, I TELL YOU!
WELL, YOU GET WHAT YOU PUT IN.
HEH HEH
YOU MAKE THE LEAST SENSE OF ALL! HOW DID YOU GET 8TH PLACE?!
HEH HEH. WE WERE THE ONLY TWO FROM GOURMET CORP.
IN THE TOP TEN.
POOR BEI DIDN'T MAKE IT IN.
CURSES!
LIKE HE EVEN HAD A CHANCE!!
HE'D RANK LOWER THAN THE BUTT BUG!
AND THERE YOU HAVE IT. THE RESULTS OF OUR FIRST ATTEMPT AT THIS.
NEXT UP ARE THE PLACES THAT DIDN'T MAKE THE MAGA-ZINE--11TH PLACE AND LOWER.
EVEN THOUGH I PLAYED SUCH A BIG ROLE RECENTLY!
...
16TH: ZONGEH
← FLIP THE PAGE FOR MORE!!

GRAPHIC NOVEL BONUS

PLACES 11TH THROUGH 30TH!!

11TH: RIN

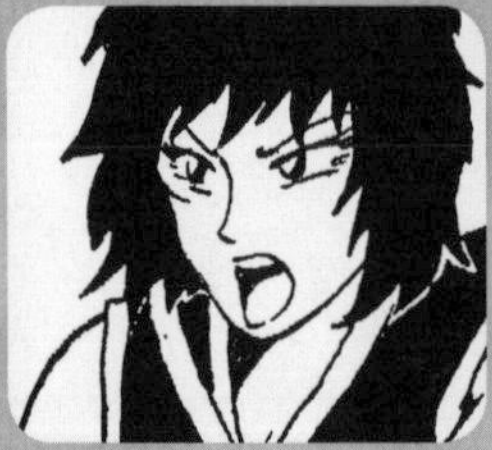

242 VOTES

12TH: WALL PENGUIN (CHICK)

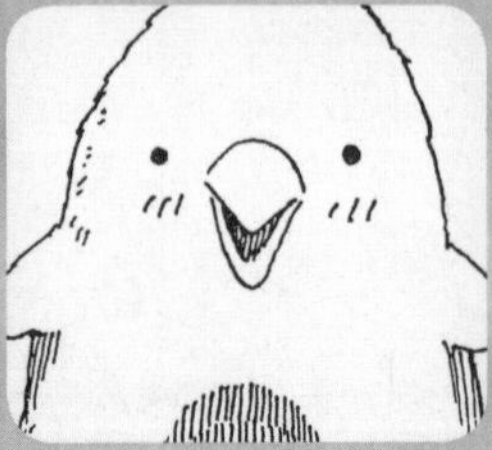

192 VOTES

13TH: TEPPEI

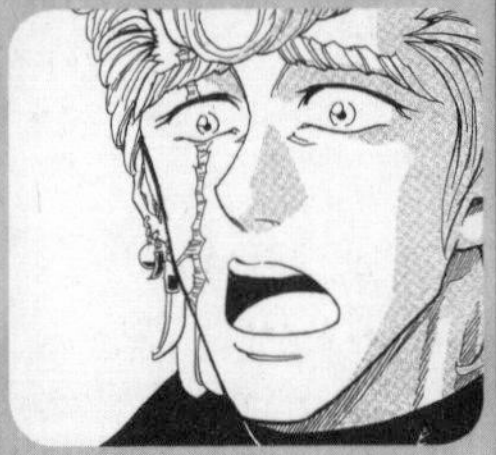

171 VOTES

14TH: PUFFER WHALE

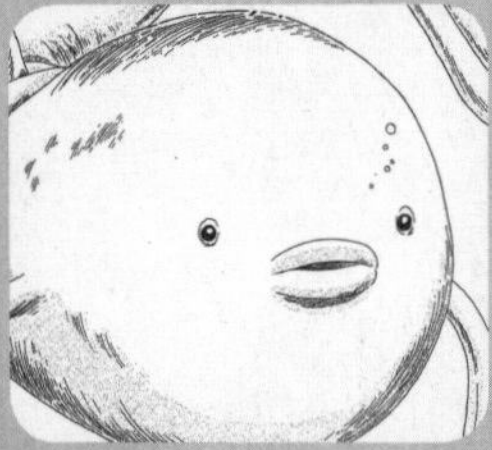

169 VOTES

15TH: BATTLE WOLF

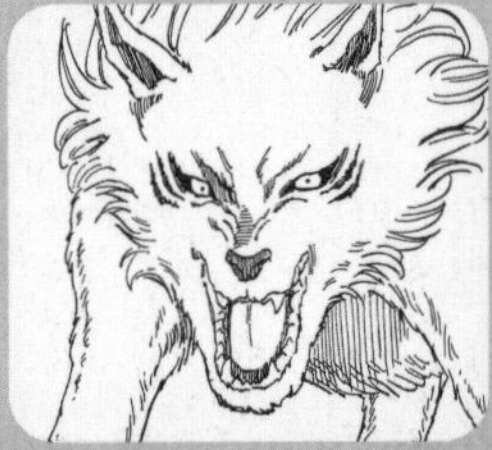

153 VOTES

16TH: ZONGEH

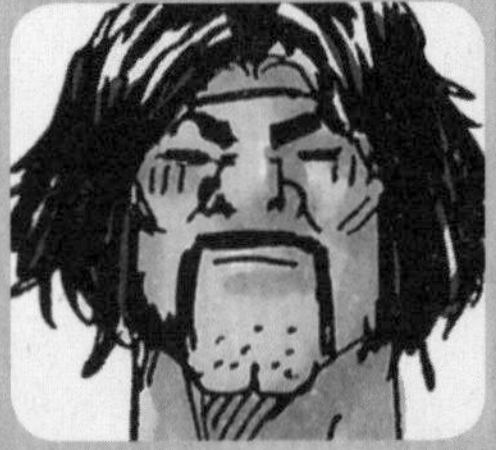

146 VOTES

17TH: JIRO	86 VOTES
18TH: KISS	65 VOTES
19TH: TOM	56 VOTES
20TH: MITSUTOSHI SHIMABUKURO	50 VOTES
21ST: SETSUNO	38 VOTES
22ND: WALL PENGUIN (ADULTS)	35 VOTES
23RD: MANSOM	33 VOTES
24TH: SALAMANDER SPHINX	29 VOTES
24TH: GT ROBOT	29 VOTES
24TH: ICHIRYU	29 VOTES
27TH: MATCH	28 VOTES
28TH: RAINBOW FRUIT	23 VOTES
28TH: GRINPATCH	23 VOTES
30TH: GARARA GATOR	22 VOTES

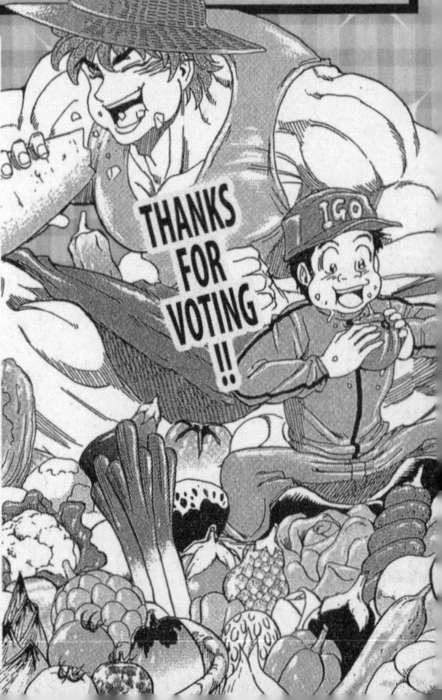

THANKS FOR VOTING!!
IGO

COMING NEXT VOLUME

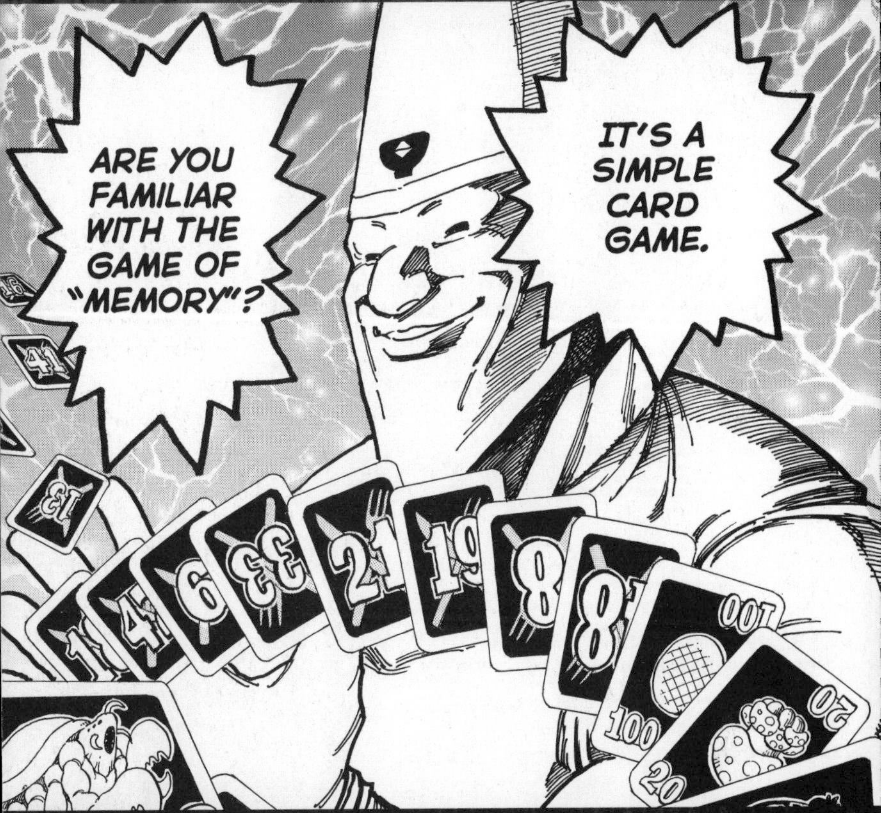

ARE YOU FAMILIAR WITH THE GAME OF "MEMORY"?
IT'S A SIMPLE CARD GAME.

GOURMET TASTING

Toriko and friends face off against the gruesome head chef of the Underground Cooking World, Livebearer, who wants nothing more than to eat their memories of food. In order to keep the contents of their brains from being scarfed down, Toriko will have to eat the grossest, squirmiest, biggest and most explosive foods ever to win a high-stakes game of "Gourmet Tasting"!

AVAILABLE DECEMBER 2013!